The NVA were taken totally by surprise by the speed and violence of our attack. I'm sure their only thought was to break contact. If they had attacked, they could have rolled the three of us easily, and it would have been a different story, especially with one of our weapons down. We secured the area. Standing there, panting and dripping sweat, coming down from the adrenaline rush, smelling the cordite and burned powder, nauseated by the sweet copper smell of blood, I happened to look at Jaybird's face. He had this expression like, "Wow! Two hours back in, less than forty-eight hours from leaving the States, and we're in the middle of it!" I had the same thoughts and feelings. Superspade looked at us and said, "Welcome back to the Nam!"

*Also in this series:*

SIX SILENT MEN: Book Two by Kenn Miller
SIX SILENT MEN: Book Three by Gary A. Linderer

*For Tony. Lots and lots of love.*

# THE STRONG FAMILY TREE

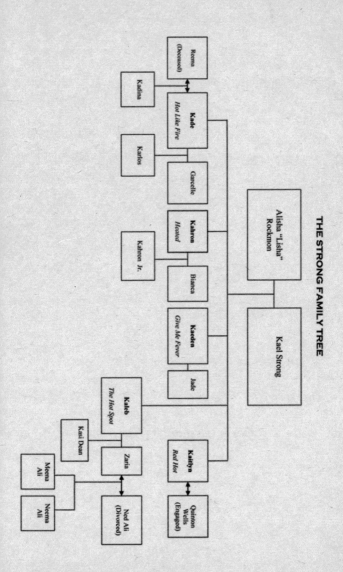

# SIX SILENT MEN

## 101st LRP/Rangers: Book One

## Reynel Martinez

BALLANTINE BOOKS • NEW YORK

A Presidio Press Book
Published by The Random House Publishing Group
Copyright © 1997 by Reynel Martinez

Published in the United States by Presidio Press, an imprint of The Random House Publishing Group, a division of Random House, Inc., New York, and simultaneously in Canada by Random House of Canada Limited, Toronto.

PRESIDIO PRESS and colophon are trademarks of Random House, Inc.

ISBN 978-0-8041-1566-7

Printed in the United States of America

www.presidiopress.com

First Edition: January 1997

# DEDICATION

**TO THE PAST ...**

I dedicate this book to the noblest and most courageous man I have ever had the pleasure of knowing. He was a leader of men and led through example and from the front.

**MASTER SERGEANT LLOYD "TOP" SMITH**

To Senon S. Chavez, who showed me the way, serving with Darby's Rangers, 1st and 3rd Ranger Battalions until Cisterna.

To the men who served, and the men who died with the Long Range Reconnaissance Patrol of the 1st Brigade, 101st Airborne Division, Republic of South Vietnam.

**TO THE FUTURE ...**

To my grandsons, Jake and Hunter Martinez, born on 2 December 1994. May your generation be the one to outlaw war.

# SIX SILENT MEN

Moving close to the ground
where the leeches live,
where the ants bite.
We are long taloned war birds,
our allies the Dragon ships . . . claymores.
Our stealth makes us invisible,
untouchable as the morning mist.
In the highlands the hills ascend forever.
Legs burning, shoulder straps cut deeply.
The ruck never gets lighter.
The rain never stops.
The sun never lets up.
Young feet look old, yellowed, wrinkled,
flesh turns to pus, jungle rot.
The RTO rides the airwaves humming a deathsong.
Phantoms and 105s scatter the Kalashnikovs.
Nightwalking on a carpet that glows softly.
They hunt us.
Lying motionless, we watch the black silhouettes
moving through the bush, our home.
Invisible . . . untouchable.
The Marauders.

BOSS WEISBERGER
30 December 1989

Carmel, California
25 June 1996

# INTRODUCTION

With the publication of this the first volume of the history of the 1st Brigade, 101st Airborne Division's Long Range Reconnaissance Patrol's experiences in Vietnam, I wish to pay tribute to their exploits and devotion to duty. They were distinguished in their willingness to take chances and risks. They were trailblazers for their successors, the Ranger units who succeeded them in the later days of the Vietnam conflict.

The recollections and personal experiences of these LRRPs characterize the boldness and unselfish devotion to each other. They were fitting successors to their forebears in the 101st Airborne Division.

S. H. MATHESON
Major General (U.S.A., Ret.)

# AUTHOR'S NOTE

This book is not intended to glorify war; there is no glory in war. War exposes how mean and vicious the human psyche is capable of being. It is the closest we get to legalized mass murder. Maybe one day we, as a human race, will elevate our consciousness enough to outlaw war and allow peace of mind to all humanity. God bless that day.

Originally, this book was intended to cover in one volume the history of the LRRP/LRP/RANGERS of the 101st Airborne Division in the Vietnam War and be co-written by Kenn Miller, Gary Linderer, and myself. But because of the length of the material, the publisher has decided to bring the works out in a series of three volumes, each of us covering the period with which he is most familiar.

My intent in *Six Silent Men* is to portray the men who served in a special operations unit, in a shooting war. They were special men in difficult times. This book represents six years of research and documenting, much of it devoted to taping recollections and patiently transcribing hundreds of hours of conversational interviews so as to retrieve the history accurately. With the passage of time, one cannot hope to capture conversations exactly as they occurred. This story is told by the men who served, and my job was basically that of a scribe for them. My objective was to be accurate and honest to the best of my ability. In *Six Silent Men*, I feel I have largely achieved both, and I apologize for any unintentional errors or omissions on my part. To all the fine and brave men who aren't mentioned by name in the pages that follow but who sweated and humped those Southeast Asian hills as Lurps with the 1/101st, my apologies and deepest respect.

First and foremost I wish to thank my family: my wife and friend, Sylvia; daughters Rene, Vanessa, and Hailey; and my only son, Marty. Thank you for supporting me on this lonely and difficult mission. My heartfelt thanks to Bob and Sue

Puckett for the initial editing of this book and to Kenn Miller for driving all the way to Idaho for the second editing of the book.

A special thank-you to Larry "Predator" Zajanc for the use of the transcribing machine that made this job easier and for his support.

A special thanks to Lloyd "Top" Smith, who, though dying painfully of cancer, helped me with his guidance, counsel, and recollections. My only regret was that he didn't get to read the book as he wished. Rest in peace, my special friend.

My thanks, too, to all the Lurps who took the time and effort to answer my letters and phone calls, contributing to the information being collected. It was your story and you wanted it told right.

A special thanks to those "Foul Dudes"—Boss Weisberger, Tom "Greek" Dokos, Dan McIsaac, Allen "Teddy Bear" Gaskell, and Vietnam veteran but non-Lurp Mike Heinz—for the special interest you took in the book. Also for the encouragement and moral support you gave me when I needed it the most. You made me cross those difficult mental bridges in order to continue the mission.

A thank-you to my former commanding general, Major General Salve H. Matheson (U.S. Army, Ret.), for reviewing the manuscript and writing the introduction.

Special acknowledgment to Randy Stamm for help with the Vietnam map.

A brother Lurp, Don Lynch, brought us all back together in June 1986, at Fort Campbell, Kentucky. It was a healing process. Since then we have floated white water in Idaho and met at reunions hosted by our parent organization, the 75th Ranger Regiment Association. For most of us, the emotional wounds left over from the Vietnam War have been healed and the bond we shared so long ago has been reawakened.

Stay a Lurp,
Stay alive.

*Reynel Martinez*

*Robin, Idaho*
*August 1996*

# CONTENTS

# Operations, 1st Brigade, 101st Airborne Division 1965–1968

1. Cam-ranh Bay (arrival, 29 July 1965)
2. Nha-trang (Operation BARRACUDA, 12–20 August 1965)
3. An Khe (Operation HIGHLAND, 26 August–1 October 1965)
4. Qui-nhon (LRRP Detachment formed, 15 October 1965; Operation SAYONARA, 1 October–11 November 1965)
5. Phan-rang (22 November–10 December 1965)
6. Bien-hoa
7. Ben Cat, Lai Khe (Operation CHECKER BOARD, 10–19 December 1965)
8. Song Mao (13–17 January 1966)
9. Tuy-hoa (Operation VAN BUREN, 15 January–21 February; Operation HARRISON, 22 February–15 April)
10. Phan-thiet (Operation FILLMORE, 16–23 April 1966)
11. Nhon Co (Operation AUSTIN VI, 25 April–19 May 1966)
12. Cheo Reo (brigade split, 20–26 May 1966)
13. Pleiku (brigade split, 20–29 May 1966)
14. Dak-to (Operation HAWTHORNE, 29 May–22 June 1966; Operation BEAUREGARD, 24 June–15 July)
15. Tuy-hoa (Operations JOHN PAUL JONES, SEWARD, and GERONIMO, 15 July–1 December 1966)
16. Kontum (Operation PICKETT, 2 December 1966–23 January 1967)
17. Phan-rang (Operation FARRAGUT, 24–29 January 1967)
18. Bao-loc (Operations GATALING I and II, 1–15 February 1967)
19. Phan-thiet (Operations GATALING I and II, 16 February–1 March 1967)
20. Di Linh (Operations GATALING I and II, 1–12 March 1967)
21. Song Mao (Operations GATALING I and II, 12–24 March 1967)
22. Tuy-hoa (brigade separated, 1–24 March 1967)
23. Phan-rang (brigade reorganized and refitted, 24–28 March 1967)
24. Khanh Duong (Operation SUMMERALL, 30 March–29 April 1967)
25. Duc Pho (Operation MALHEUR I, 30 April–7 June 1967; Operation MALHEUR II, 8 June–1 August 1967; Operation HOOD RIVER, 2–13 August 1967)
26. Chu Lai (Operation BENTON, 13–29 August 1967)
27. Duc Pho (Operation COOK, 1–10 September 1967)
28. Chu Lai (Operation WHEELER, 11 September–23 November 1967)
29. Phan-rang (reorganization and refitting, 26 November–3 December 1967)
30. Phan-thiet (Operation KLAMATH FALLS, 4–12 December 1967)
31. Bao-loc (Operation KLAMATH FALLS, 13 December 1967–13 January 1968)
32. Song Be (Operation SAN ANGELO, LRRP Detachment 1/101st disbanded, 14 January–5 February 1968)

NORTH VIETNAM

DMZ
Cai Thiet Quang Tri
Hue
Danang
Chu Lai 26 28
My Lai
Dak-to 14
Duc Pho 25 27
Kontum 16
An Khe 3
Pleiku 13
An Khe
Qui-nhon 4
IA DRANG VALLEY
Cheo Reo 12
My Phu
Tuy-hoa 9 15 22
Ban Me Thuot
Khanh Duong 24
Nhon Co 11
Nha-trang 2
Song Be 32
Cam-ranh Bay 1
Di Linh 20
Bao-loc 31 18
Phan-rang 5 17 23 29
SOUTH VIETNAM
Tay Ninh
Song Mao 8 21
Lai Khe
Bien-hoa 6
Phan-thiet 10 19 30
Saigon
Vung Tau
PLAIN OF REEDS
BINH TUONG
KIEN THO
MEKONG DELTA

SOUTH CHINA
SEA

VIETNAM

0 MILES 100
0 KM 100

# PROLOGUE

The real lineage of the Army Long Range Reconnaissance Patrol, Long Range Patrol, and Ranger units that fought in the Vietnam War goes back even further than the history of the United States of America—back at least as far as Roger's Rangers of the French and Indian War. In every American war, there has always been a need for special operations forces. These forces have traditionally been manned by volunteers recruited in the theater of operations, for the United States military has traditionally shied away from maintaining a peacetime special operations capability, until recently, and has usually had to start over from scratch whenever a war broke out.

The Vietnam War was different. The United States entered this war with a special operations capability already established and on the official military roles. Army Special Forces Groups, Navy UDT and SEAL Teams, Marine Corps Force Recon Companies, and Air Force Air Commando units were sending men to Vietnam years before the first major troop deployments in 1965—but when the war expanded with the introduction of conventional American (and North Vietnamese) troop units, it was quickly apparent that the established special operations capability simply wouldn't be enough. Once again, the American military fell back on perhaps its oldest tradition and put out the call for in-theater special operations volunteers.

This story is about the men who answered the call. These volunteers were young men, willing to take risks yet wanting to control their own destiny. Although they represented the melting pot of America, they were different from the average soldier; they were more independent, seeking adventure and testing themselves the way their predecessors had. As Lurps they were free to push themselves to the edge. They came together as strangers, with only the common Airborne background and the war as a shared experience. In the crucible of war they created a legend and, more important, a bond of brotherhood that would support and sustain them over many years and miles, and they forged new friendships that endure to this day.

The formation of the Long Range Reconnaissance Patrol, 1st Brigade, 101st Airborne Division began a history of seven long years of fighting against the enemy as the unit evolved to Long Range Patrol and eventually Ranger status as the war ground on.

# 1

## LONG RANGE RECON

### 1 101

# Fortuna favet fortibus
### (Fortune Favors the Bold)

In late May 1965, the Screaming Eagles of the 1st Brigade of the 101st Airborne Division were alert for deployment to the Republic of Vietnam. Two short months later, on 29 July 1965, the 1st Brigade, under the command of Col. James S. Timothy, arrived at Cam-ranh Bay. They arrived trained and honed to a fine-tempered edge, thanks to the efforts of a legendary warrior, Maj. David Hackworth, the brigade operations officer. The 1st Brigade had the finest NCOs and privates that ever laced up a pair of jump boots.

The Screaming Eagles were welcomed by Gen. William Westmoreland and Ambassador Maxwell D. Taylor, two men very familiar with the 101st Airborne Division. Ambassador Taylor had been the commanding general of the 101st Airborne from Normandy to the end of World War II. General Westmoreland had commanded the division from April 1958 to November 1960, and established its famous Recondo school.

When the 1st Brigade arrived in country, the battalion command groups knew that they would need intelligence-gathering units. The 1st Battalion, 327th Parachute Infantry established Tiger Force for their immediate needs in field intelligence. The 2nd Battalion, 502nd Airborne Infantry, under command of Lt. Col. Hank Emerson, formed what he called "hatchet teams" (later changed to Recondos), and the 2nd Battalion of the 327th named its unit the Hawks. Brigade staff, with prompting from General Westmoreland, knew that it would have to establish a reliable intelligence gathering and special operations force at the brigade level. In September 1965, the 1st Brigade issued a directive announcing the formation of a Provisional Long Range Reconnaissance Patrol detachment and asking for volunteers from within the brigade. The new LRRP detachment was to be commanded by 1st Lt. Joel Stevenson, a former noncommissioned officer who had served with Special Forces, then earned a commission at OCS. Lieutenant Stevenson was personally selected by the brigade commander to command the new LRRP detachment. It was a plum job that most officers would have given their eye teeth for. A very impressive man, according to the people who worked with him and knew him, Lieutenant Stevenson came up with the LRRP motto: *Fortuna Favet Fortibus*—"Fortune Favors The Bold"—to represent the LRRP detachment.

The detachment's first sergeant was M.Sgt. Phillip Chassion, a Korean War veteran who had been on the Advanced Airborne Committee at Fort Benning, Georgia. He had also served a stint with the British Army. Well respected by the enlisted men, he was a definite asset in the formation of the LRRP detachment for the brigade.

The infant LRRP detachment was formally established in Qui-nhon on 15 October 1965. With the formation of this elite unit a real challenge was directed to the men of the 1st Brigade, and a certain breed of men answered that call. Three hundred thirty-seven men volunteered and were interviewed, and thirty-two men were selected. Among those accepted was a man who came to be called the "Black Icicle."

## The Black Icicle

When the 1st Brigade arrived at Cam-ranh Bay, S.Sgt. Larry Forrest carried the battalion colors of the 1/327, and General Westmoreland, who remembered Forrest from his time as division commander, greeted him fondly by name and made a little joke about how they'd have to stop meeting like this. To men like Sergeant Forrest, war was the ultimate litmus test for a professional soldier. Arriving in Vietnam, he knew he was where he belonged. His whole life had been shaped for this moment. The legions of men who would come after him to Vietnam would not have the opportunity to arrive in country with a unit from a peacetime environment, having trained and soldiered as a group, building friendships and professionalism. Forrest was very proud of his unit and figured they were ready for anything, but in the coming months they would be finding out just how much they didn't know. When they arrived in country, they had not yet borne witness to the face of battle, had not yet seen the elephant come stomping among them. That would come soon. . . . And for S.Sgt. Larry Forrest, the most important part of his tour in Vietnam would not be with the battalion whose colors he carried ashore. It would be as a Lurp.

Larry Forrest was born Christmas Eve 1939 in Rockford, Illinois, to a proud black family of seven children. His mother was from Athens, Alabama, the oldest girl of a family of fourteen. His dad had grown up in a Louisiana orphanage. Larry himself had gone to fourteen schools in ten years, and was an A–B student. But as he grew older, he began to feel a little disillusioned with school because he saw that people who had degrees and were black usually didn't have jobs to match their degrees. School was very easy, but it wasn't a challenge anymore. His buddies were either being killed by the police or sent to prison. He didn't want that kind of fate but he was looking for a challenge, so he decided to become an infantry soldier. The catalyst for this was growing up in the subdued racism of the late forties and fifties. In those days, the Saturday matinees featured adventure serials starring Johnny Weissmuller, Frank Buck, and Clyde Beatty. These serials always portrayed the black man as an inferior, bumbling, cowardly person. As Tarzan, for instance, Johnny Weissmuller would swing through the trees, drop down in among 150 black African natives, and whup them all single-handedly. Then he'd swing up through the trees, kick two lions in the butt, all the while holding a couple of apes by the tail. Clyde Beatty and Frank Buck were African explorers, and whenever they ran into a lion, they would bravely shoot it while their black gun bearers would be so afraid that their eyes would go round like saucers, their hair would stand up on end, and they would tremble with fear. Larry Forrest just had to rebel against that nonsense. He was determined to prove his abilities by being a soldier. He'd grown up in the era of the Tuskegee pilots, the all-black 555th Parachute Infantry, and the all-black 2nd Ranger Company, so he felt he had a proud heritage to live up to. He wasn't consciously aware of all his motivation at the time, but Larry Forrest wanted to prove again that black men weren't stupid or illiterate—and that they weren't cowards. That, along with a yearn to change his environment, created a strong desire in him to become a professional soldier.

On 21 July 1955, as a sixteen-year-old tenth grader, Larry Forrest joined the Michigan National Guard's 26th Infantry Regiment, "Iron Fist" K Company, located in Grand Rapids, Michigan. They were still using old '03 Springfield rifles in the squad, for the Michigan National Guard was not exactly the cutting edge of the military art. At that time, the army came out with what was called RFA, or Reserve Forces Act, in which a National Guard soldier could serve six months active duty—most of it training. Forrest remembers going down to Fort Leonard Wood on a troop train for basic training. Their final stop was Cuba, Missouri, where they were to eat dinner in the train station before continuing on buses to the base. The restaurant manager at first announced that the black soldiers could not eat, then finally that they could eat but would have to do it outside, in the back. The sergeant in charge said, "Well, if they can't eat, nobody eats." So everybody stayed hungry all the way to Fort Leonard Wood. After basic, Forrest left Fort Leonard Wood by troop train and went to Fort Jackson for advanced infantry training. Advanced infantry training lasted eight weeks, and the remaining time of his six months was spent in what was called advanced-advanced infantry training. At the end of his six months, Larry Forrest decided to take a release from the National Guard and go active. The army sent him to tank school at Fort Knox. After tank school, he went to Germany and was assigned to a bridge outfit. While there, he went through ammunition supply organizational school, learning about ammunition and demolitions. In 1960, he left Germany and headed home. When he arrived back in the States, he reenlisted and went Airborne. He reported to Fort Campbell, Kentucky, and went through three weeks of pre-Airborne training, waiting for a slot at jump school, then graduated from Airborne school in September 1960. Larry Forrest was one of the top three men of his class, and General Westmoreland pinned his wings on the drop zone (DZ).

He went to his assigned unit, E Company 1/327, on a deuce-and-a-half truck and reported to the first sergeant, William Edward Wade.

"William Edward Wade . . . I never will forget that bastard," Forrest recalls. "When I reported into the company, he opened up his center desk drawer, pulled out a piece of paper, slid it across his desk, and said, 'Read that, boy.' "

Forrest read it. It was some kind of tricked-up honorable discharge from the Confederate Army.

"Now you understand where we stand?" asked the first sergeant.

"Yes, sir," said Larry Forrest. "I know exactly where we stand."

Forrest remembers this first sergeant well. "Whiskey Echo Whiskey—William Edward Wade—old time Airborne from World War II, Korea . . . Claims he used to ride a heavy drop out the tailgate. After the chutes deployed, hook up to the D ring, and jump again. . . . Claims he used to be first man out on a daisy chain: five or six guys hook up to each other, and the first man jumps, second man jumps—nobody's chute would open up until the last man jumped. His chute would open, and they would daisy chain open. They'd pop the chute, pull the risers down, and put them under their toes. Tree-top level, they'd let them slide out, the chute would deflate, fill up again, and stop them dead as a doornail, two–three feet off the ground. The army later outlawed the popping of chutes and throwing toilet paper out of the airplane, but that didn't stop old First Sergeant Wade from spinning the jump stories."

But First Sergeant Wade had already been told that Forrest had graduated among the top three of his jump school class. He put the discharge back in his drawer, looked at Forrest, and asked, "Boy, you want to go to Ranger-Commando school?"

Larry Forrest's eyes lit up, and he answered in the affirmative. A few minutes later, he was back on the deuce-and-a-half.

"No rest, no nothin'—down to Recondo school I went," Forrest recalls. "This was in November 1960, and Recondo school is where I got my first taste of intense patrolling."

The Recondo school concept was the same as Ranger school, minus the layover time and nonessential harassment. Recondo students averaged about five hours' sleep a week. They did everything in the Ranger school curriculum, and eliminated the sleep to cramp it down into five weeks. The Recondo school was General Westmoreland's idea, and Medal of Honor winner Lew Millett designed the program. Unlike the Fort Benning Ranger school, which the army considered a "leadership" course, Recondo school was a commando course for the enlisted paratrooper. Though the Recondo graduate's arrowhead patch was only authorized in the 101st Airborne Division, it was one of the most prestigious badges in the army—and one of the hardest to earn.

Larry Forrest was in class #8C 1960. They started the course with forty students; only about seventeen graduated. Three students are said to have drowned, and by the end of class #8C 1960, one instructor and a good number of students were in the hospital. It was winter, and they had to break the ice with poles for the water phase. The students had to get naked and make a poncho raft with two rifles and two steel pots, wrap up all their clothes on the raft, and swim it across. Forrest discovered that, after the initial shock, it was warmer in the water than it was out, so he volunteered to stay in and swim the small rope over for the rope bridges. The instructors soon caught on to why he was doing what he was doing, and they made him do fifty gorilla stomps as punishment. He had to jump up and down, beat himself in the chest, and go, "Ow, ow!" Gorilla stomps can kick your ass if you're already tired, but they do warm a man up.

The third jump in Recondo school was a class jump, and after landing, the students moved toward the objective on two or three azimuths, then met at a clandestine bivouac area. There they planned their attack on a village to rescue a "general." Forrest led the charge and in the brawl got kicked in the mouth. By the time he graduated, he had sprung his left hip, taken twenty-four stitches in his head, and had his arm in a sling. Once again, General Westmoreland did the honors, pinning the Recondo patch on Larry Forrest's fatigue jacket. Only five weeks earlier he'd pinned on Larry Forrest's wings.

When Forrest reported back to E Company from Recondo school, First Sergeant Wade told him to find another home, so he went down to A Company 1/327, where the "first shirt" welcomed him with open arms. Wade eventually got transferred overseas to Germany, and while he was there, he fell out of a jeep. His foot got caught in his web gear, and he was dragged to his death. The jeep driver said that he didn't know the first sergeant had fallen out of the jeep. The entire brigade had a party, a prop blast, to celebrate his demise.

Since the 1st Brigade had been designated the Desert Brigade, for the next four years Sergeant Forrest and the men of A Company 1/327 traveled to most of the major deserts of the world and trained extensively in desert warfare. Forrest made E-6 just when the name "Vietnam" was on everyone's lips. It was only a matter of time until a Stateside American fighting unit would be called for duty in that distant land, so it did not come as a huge surprise to the Screaming Eagle paratroopers of the 1st Brigade, 101st Airborne Division, when they were alerted for deployment in May 1965. Being an elite and strategically important unit, the 101st Airborne had an incredibly high concentration of excellent career NCOs and highly motivated enlisted paratroopers. (High caliber NCOs rotating from overseas duty or from other units tended to concentrate heavily in the 101st—more heavily there than in the rival 82nd Airborne Division.) When word of the deployment came down, the 1st Brigade then had the pick of the top NCOs and enlisted men (EM) from the other brigades.

Larry Forrest and his 1/327 comrades flew to Travis Air Force Base, and then bused to Oakland Army Terminal, where they boarded the USNS *Gen. LeRoy Eltinge*. On viewing the boat, one trooper remarked, "Hmm, I wonder what battle old LeRoy lost to have that tub named after him!" The *Eltinge* had come out of salvage—not dry dock, but salvage—and the railings were rusted at the bottom and falling off. Once underway, the ship would lean to the right for three days, and then to the left for three days. There was no air-conditioning, and even the ventilation went out as it passed Hawaii. Still, morale was high. The paratroopers had a ditty they sang repeatedly, "Vietcong, Vietcong! Here we come, here we come, Vietcong, Vietcong!" It was more a war chant than a song, but they sang it all the way over, and it carried far across the water. Forrest remembers their encountering a passenger ship one day, and everybody aboard it was out listening to the Screaming Eagles sing.

With A Company 1/327, S.Sgt. Larry Forrest was involved in several operations clearing the Cam-ranh Bay–Nha-trang area. The most memorable was Operation BARRACUDA, in which the objective was two hill masses west of Nha-trang. They drew their first blood in that area. On 24 August 1965, Forrest and company were trucked to Nha-trang, where they boarded LST boats to Qui-nhon. In Qui-nhon, they kicked off Operation HIGHLAND. The 1st Brigade's mission was to secure a base at An Khe for the 1st Cavalry Division (Airmobile). The operation had three phases, consisting of securing the Qui-nhon area; then Highway 19, connecting Qui-nhon and An Khe; and finally, securing An Khe, the location for the base camp. The initial landings at Qui-nhon were made by the 1/327. Next came a heliborne assault by 1/327 to secure the critical An Khe pass. This was the same pass where the French Mobile Group 100 had been virtually annihilated.

Sergeant Forrest lost his first man to combat up there on An Khe pass. It was also at the An Khe pass that he heard of the directive asking for volunteers for the LRRP detachment. This was a strange area. At night, the paratroopers in Forrest's platoon waited on top of grass hootches—a bamboo-framed hut roughly twelve feet square with a palm-thatched roof—watching with Starlight scopes as enemy soldiers tried to crawl up on them. Every now and then they'd pop one of the enemy, and the others would have to drag him back. It was just probing

action on the part of the enemy, just static defense on the part
of the Americans, and Larry Forrest must have found it slightly
boring, for he volunteered for the LRRP detachment.

To try out for the Lurps, Forrest had to get back to the
brigade rear, and to get to the brigade rear, he first had to get to
his company command post. This was not easy because his
platoon was deployed eight hundred meters away and was in
prime sniper country. The other men in his platoon were
unhappy about his volunteering for the new Long Range
Reconnaissance Patrol detachment. No one offered to accom-
pany Forrest back to the company command post. He made the
trip alone, hiding behind berms, crawling, dodging, ducking
sniper fire. The battalion commander, Lt. Col. James Wilson,
had choppered in to brief the A/1/327 company commander,
and when Forrest showed up, Lieutenant Colonel Wilson
asked the company commander who he was. "That's Sergeant
Forrest," came the reply. "He's volunteering for the Lurps."

The battalion commander picked up on things very quickly.
He noticed that Forrest had come that eight hundred meters
alone, and he knew why. The other men were pissed at him for
going to Lurps. This must have struck Lieutenant Colonel
Wilson as rather chickenshit, because he got mad. Of course, it
was controlled mad, and he didn't much let it show. He introduced himself to Forrest and offered him a lift back to brigade
headquarters in his helicopter.

When Staff Sergeant Forrest got back to brigade headquarters, he found a bunch of Lurp hopefuls hanging around a
shabby little old tent. It was a gloomy, rainy day, going on
evening. Word was that 337 men had volunteered. Lt. Joel
Stevenson and M.Sgt. Phillip Chassion were interviewing
people, and had already chosen the team leaders. But they had
apparently already heard quite a bit about him. Stevenson and
Chassion asked a lot of questions. They asked him what job he
was going after. He knew the team leader's slot was supposed
to be for grade E-7, and he was a junior E-6. Forrest said he
would like to try out for senior scout. Stevenson and Chassion
then asked him if he thought he'd be ready to be a team leader

if he were offered that job. Would he take it? Forrest said, "Sure." They thanked him and told him to wait outside.

"I went outside and sat up against a rock," Forrest remembers. "I don't know how long it was, but a little while later they came out and said they were going to read the names of the people who were chosen. The ones not chosen could go back to their units. So they started reading off the names: Team One, Team Two, Team Three, Team Four . . . They didn't call my name, so I thought I wasn't chosen. Then they said, 'We'll call off the four team leaders.' Team One was Pop Tomlinson. Team Two was Donovan Pruett. Team Three—I don't remember who that guy was because he didn't last long. And then they said that Team Four's team leader would be Staff Sergeant Forrest. My heart almost jumped out of my mouth. Something like this happens, instantly you're thinking, 'Am I up to it? Can I handle all this?' It looked like I'd have to be up to it, have to handle it. I had been chosen—not just as a Lurp, but also as a team leader."

It had already been explained briefly that the LRRP detachment would be a small Recondo type unit, and that it would use the Special Forces Project Delta as a basis for organization and operations. It was fully understood by everybody in the brigade that the Lurps would be a long range reconnaissance unit with a primary mission to collect intelligence information for brigade deployment.

Larry Forrest remembers that the scuttlebutt among the troops regarding the new detachment was that it was a suicide unit. Conventional wisdom was that there was no way in hell you could survive "out there" with six men. You couldn't live thirty minutes "out there" with only six men. Most of the old timers didn't want any part of it. They figured they were in deep enough shit.

Larry Forrest has a ready profile of the soldier who went to Lurps: "Another soldier on an ego trip, that's all it was—an ego trip, wanting to be the best. Wanting to know if you were as good a soldier as you thought you were. Time to check it out, and find out if you're capable of applying what you'd learned. One of my radio operators was a generator mechanic who finally convinced us to let him in. He worked out after awhile. A little shook up on the first mission, but then he settled down. Why did he volunteer? Just wanted to be a part of history, I think. Just wanted to be one of the best."

Looking back, Forrest figures that the interview might have been little more than a formality and that he had already been accepted when he went for it. But at the time he felt apprehensive, and he certainly didn't believe they'd make him a team leader. In 1965, blacks were just starting to get their just due. He had noticed that there weren't too many blacks up there around the tent where they were choosing the first Lurps. As things worked out, he ended up being the only black soldier in the original Lurp platoon.

The newly formed LRRP detachment got to pick the cream of the crop. With these volunteers came an experienced, battle-tested cadre of professional NCOs. Nowhere else in the brigade was such a wealth of talent congregated in such a small organization. This was the beginning, the birth of a special operations unit within a fighting Airborne infantry brigade in a shooting war. Everything was new, and the guidelines for establishing this intelligence asset came to roost on the concept established back at Recondo school at Fort Campbell. This knowledge was brought to the detachment by the men who volunteered. From platoon leader down to the most junior radio telephone operator (RTO), they were all volunteers, and most of them graduates of the Recondo school. To S.Sgt. Larry Forrest, being accepted into the Lurps and chosen to be a team leader presented the biggest challenge so far in his life.

The Lurps launched into a flurry of training. With the exception of what Special Forces Project Delta could pass down from its year of experience running long range recon patrols in Vietnam, everything was new. Communications was taught by the commo chief, S.Sgt. Ronald Bourne. Patrol tactics and hand-to-hand combat classes were taught by M.Sgt. Phillip Chassion. The headquarters section of the platoon was not included in the teams' training, but did its own training. Rarely did the field Lurps see any of the headquarters section—and then usually only the commo chief. All of the training was done by personnel within the Lurps. No one from any unit out-side the original Lurp platoon gave them training of any type. Operational training and scouting training was done by people within the platoon, primarily Lieutenant Stevenson, Master Sergeant Chassion, and the team leaders themselves. The medical training was done by the medics. The men were all cross trained in medical procedures. They knew how to give shots, how to aspirate, how to perform a cut down on the ankle if the blood vessels collapsed because of shock. The communi-cations training was done by the commo personnel and included basic training in Morse code. CW (continuous wave, i.e., Morse) radio operators were supposed to be O5-Charlie qualified, which at the time was the MOS (military occupa-tional specialty) number for Morse code operator. The platoon had men who could send and receive close to twenty to thirty groups a minute, the best in the brigade. The Lurps were doing it all themselves.

They established their own procedures. They created search concepts such as going into an area, traversing its circumfer-ence, and cutting the circle to see what was in it. They prac-ticed setting clandestine bivouac areas, breaking up into two-man groups, going out and coming back in a different direction, consolidating information, security, patrol security, and encoding and decoding messages—primarily encoding. They established a code system that even the Army Security Agency unit attached to the 1st Brigade couldn't break.

Because of his size, Forrest was normally matched up with Lieutenant Stevenson in hand-to-hand combat, and he remem-bers that Stevenson was a hard old dude. Individual team training took place, too. Teams created missions that they would plan from stem to stern, one-day patrols, walking through the jungle. Forrest remembers that he would walk out and leave his team members by themselves, then walk back through the jungle alone and tell them to get back the best they could. Each time he put somebody different in charge. Forrest learned that Staff Sergeant Fogt, who was his senior scout, was very capable of leading the team, perhaps more capable than he himself was. But Fogt just wasn't interested in being a team leader. He always said that he didn't think he was ready yet. Forrest knew that the unit Fogt came from had seen more death and destruction in combat, toe to toe, than any other unit in the brigade. The other scout, Sgt. Phillip Henry, came from the same unit and was also very strac (sharp).

The first Lurps trained in helicopter procedures so that once they hit the ground at the beginning of nautical twilight, they had the timing down and got to the bushes just as it turned dark. They'd sit silently for an hour, listening, then move to a secure place and sit the night out. The next day they would circle outward from their position and observe in detail—minute detail—every leaf, twig, tree, crevice, ravine, hill, knoll, path, creek, bird, animal—studying them in silence before moving. While the team was doing this, Forrest would normally check his map, resection, pinpoint the team's position, and see if his original plans, made in the rear, could be executed in the same way in the field, with the actual terrain underfoot; it never looked the same on the ground as it did from the air or on a map. But if a map recon was made to the point where the planner had all the major features in his head, he felt the features would announce themselves just like clockwork. The teams also trained to use local animal life to their advantage. If the men were quiet, motionless to the extent possible, in their own "lay dog" areas, the animals would go back to their normal routine. Then they could be depended on to give a warning if the enemy was coming. If the birds stopped chirping or flew or if the monkeys took off, something was afoot. The first Lurps also learned to understand each other, communicating, practicing hand and arm signals, trying to get to where they didn't have to worry about death, to where they could do things automatically and the team chain of command seemed like the natural order of things, with each man able to carry out any part in it. They understood the necessity of being able to depend 110 percent on each person.

Forrest doesn't recall how long the training cycle lasted. Because he was so busy, those were cloudy times for him. The team leaders took their teams out on practice missions, rehearsing all the intricacies of the SOPs that related to each team member's responsibility. Forrest can recall going out at Phan-rang, walking as far as the team could go, training and then walking back in. As far as training is concerned, the first Lurps did it all themselves.

One issue that the first, and subsequent, Lurps had to deal with was the handling of prisoners and detainees. When it came to military prisoners of war, the Lurps were under the same Geneva Convention legal restraints as all other American servicemen—but they could also find themselves in situations that very few other American servicemen ever found themselves. A five- or six-man Lurp team often can't spare men to guard prisoners, particularly when pressed by the enemy. Even in the beginning, before the Lurps had acquired much field experience, it was easy to envision situations in which a team might have to choose between killing prisoners or letting them go. The Geneva Convention and the personal moral feelings of individual Lurps might prohibit the killing of prisoners, but team survival in the field might depend on it. In such a case, it was generally held that a team should let any cumbersome prisoners go—for a second or two—and then kill them for escaping. But military prisoners of war were about the most valuable sources of intelligence information a Lurp team could bring back so they were not to be disposed of lightly.

Detainees—civilian detainees—were another problem. In Vietnam, "civilians" were not always really civilians, but even the truly innocent might compromise and bring disaster to a Lurp team. SOP (standard operating procedure) was to detain anyone who might have seen a team and be in a position to compromise it—and if detaining them was impractical, to kill them. In the field, the handling of prisoners and detainees was left, for all practical purposes, to the discretion of the team leaders. At least once, a soldier with homicidal tendencies tried to get into the detachment and was sent packing by Lieutenant Stevenson. And at least once, a team leader was forced by circumstances to dispose of some prisoners. It was understood that he'd done what had to be done, and no legal repercussions, no moral onus, was put on him. But the man did have to deal with his own conscience, and thirty years afterward he is still tormented by what he had to do.

Of course that was not the way things normally played out. Al Smith, another founding member of the detachment at that time, recalls a mission near the Cambodian border during which his team (he was not with it) had to detain some Montagnards who had stumbled upon them. The Lurps kept their detainees overnight, then released them on the extraction LZ (landing zone) the next day and waved a fond good-bye to them as they flew off. When Smith tells the story of his own team and the captive Montagnards, he is proud of its happy ending.

Even during initial Lurp training, the first Lurps knew that some of them would have to deal with this issue, and they understood that they'd have to deal with it on their own.

## The First LRRP Mission of the 1/101 Airborne Brigade

The 1st Brigade of the 101st Airborne had been introduced from the States primarily to operate as General Westmoreland's "Fire Brigade," and as such it had to be highly mobile, highly aggressive, and capable of operating anywhere General Westmoreland had the legal authority to send it. Because the 1st Brigade was expected to be able to operate anywhere in Vietnam on just a few hours' notice, it had to have a first-rate long-range reconnaissance capability of its own, in addition to the Lurp capabilities each of its subordinate battalions was developing to support its own operation. General Westmoreland had given the 1st Brigade the mission of developing its own LRRP concept and putting it into operation to prove that it would work. The 5th Special Forces Group's Project Delta had been performing long-range patrol work for a year by the time the 1st Brigade arrived, but while Special Forces recon teams were usually commanded by Americans, the majority of their team members were usually indigenous. Among ranking commanders in Vietnam during this period, there was a good deal of skepticism that recon teams manned entirely by American enlisted men could operate effectively in Vietnam.

Conventional wisdom said that a six-man team could not survive more than thirty minutes in the enemy's backyard, which was where Lurps would have to operate in order to be effective. General Westmoreland had a special affinity with the 101st Airborne, and he thought otherwise. Having introduced the Recondo concept into the U.S. Army, he had more than just a mild interest in the success of the 101st Lurps. When the time came for the first Lurps to pull real missions, those missions were to be a pivotal turning point for intelligence gathering at the brigade or division level and would be closely monitored by high-ranking officers. It was a test of a concept of operation, and General Westmoreland was personally interested.

The picturesque setting for the Lurps' first mission was twenty miles southeast of Phan-rang, in a quiet valley about three by five miles in size, running east to the ocean. A small mountain range, seven hundred to one thousand feet high, ran the length. From the ocean westward, the mountain range sloped gently for one-third of its distance, became very steep in the middle section, then descended to gentle slopes again for the remaining third of its length.

The mountain range was to be the area of operations for the three teams. On the left, to the north against the ocean, would be S.Sgt. Donovan Pruett, with Team Two, call sign Ancient Tracker 6. On the far right, to the south, at the mouth of the valley and the start of the mountains, would be Staff Sergeant Skau, with Team Three, call sign Ancient Tracker 7. S.Sgt. Larry Forrest's Team Four, Ancient Tracker 8, had the middle section of the mountain range, where the terrain was the steepest. Pop Tomlinson's Team One was in reserve.

Each team was to have an RZ (reconnaissance zone) about two thousand meters long and one thousand meters wide, running from the base of the range up to the ridge crests and peaks. The two teams at each end of the range planned to insert about two-thirds of the way up from the valley floor in their RZs, where they would work the top third of their AO (area of operation), then make their way down. Staff Sergeant Forrest couldn't use this plan because his RZ didn't have a flat spot or level terrain that was high enough for an insertion. Instead, he planned to insert at the foot of the mountains and work his way to the top. There was no intelligence available to the Lurps to negate this plan of operation.

The Lurps had been told that at least a company-sized Vietcong unit was carrying out harassing actions in the valley against a very busy Vietnamese lieutenant, whose platoon was actually hunting and finding the enemy, then fighting them and winning. In the eyes of the Vietcong, this could not be allowed because it might set an example for the other South Vietnamese units and cause them to do the same. The enemy was trying hard each day to pull this thorn from their side. The Lurps were sent in to help relieve the pressure on the lieutenant and his unit. They were to locate the enemy, and then regular infantry units would swoop in and kick their ass.

The enemy was a hit-and-run unit, and that led the Lurps to believe that the enemy was coming into the small valley, hitting the south Vietnamese unit, then leaving. However, they were to find out that this was not the case. After the mission, Forrest and his team were left to wonder whether the headquarters section was as naive as they seemed, or if the mission had been a test to see if a Lurp team really could survive a confrontation with a far superior enemy force in the enemy's backyard.

Maps, ammo, water, and food had been drawn by the team. Staff Sergeant Forrest's team SOP had set a minimum standard on ammo and equipment for a mission: a basic load of small-arms ammo was 120 rounds of M-16 (though most Lurps carried more) and at least six grenades, of which one had to be white phosphorus. Each man was required to carry a minimum of fifteen feet of detonation cord and a half block of C-4 explosive, one claymore mine, a map and compass, and the usual pace cord.* The first Lurps carried C rations for food. LRRP rations had only recently been introduced to Vietnam, but

---

* The man assigned to count the paces would tie a knot in the cord—e.g., every 100 paces—to keep track of the distance patrolled. This was especially useful in areas where dense vegetation made it difficult to navigate by taking bearings from known landmarks such as mountains.

seven days of the dehydrated LRRP rations would require approximately five gallons of water just to make them edible. The Lurps each carried two-quart canteens, plus a two- or three-quart flat bladder on the back of their packs. This water had to last seven days because they had a hard and fast rule never to visit a waterhole in enemy territory. The enemy had a habit of covering waterholes, one way or another, so for that reason, more than any other, the first Lurps didn't carry LRRP rations. In fact, the early Lurps had a big laugh when they were first introduced to them. Weight was a major problem for the first Lurps in figuring out the basic load for team members. Eventually they figured out a standard, by rationalizing that each day on a mission would deplete their load by the amount of water and food consumed. The radio operator always carried an extra-heavy load because the AN-PRC-25 radio weighed twenty-three pounds, so extra batteries were carried by scouts and team leaders. A radio operator's rucksack was the heaviest in a LRRP team.

Most of the first Lurps wore "tigers"—camouflage uniforms of tiger-striped cloth. Produced for Special Forces, these uniforms were acquired through bartering, or other means.

Watching his men working on their equipment, Staff Sergeant Forrest quietly appraised them. Staff Sergeant Fogt, the senior of the two scouts, was in his usual quiet mood. Fogt was a very reliable and combat-experienced NCO. He had arrived to take Staff Sergeant Skau's place as scout because Skau had been asked to take over Team Three. Fogt was senior to Skau, but he did not want the team. The junior scout, Sergeant Henry, was pensive and very methodical in whatever task was assigned to him. Fogt and Henry had come from a line company in the 2/502 Infantry Battalion, which was a plus because it made them very cautious in the bush and relentless in the use of correct jungle techniques. They had seen too many lives lost to be haphazard in functioning. Sgt. William Davis was the medic on the team. Always rigging his medical kit, he gave the team confidence in his ability to help them. Last was John Vaughn, Team Four's only radio operator on the mission. Vaughn had come to the detachment with a generator-mechanic MOS. Vaughn had begged long and hard to get into the Lurps, and then onto Forrest's team. He finally accepted him as his radio operator. John Vaughn had red-blond hair and very fair skin, so he had to keep himself covered with camouflage paint just to prevent serious sunburn. He had no LRRP training or even infantry training beyond basic. But he had heart. Lieutenant Stevenson must have had a lot of confidence in Larry Forrest and his team to allow the team to go on its first mission using a new guy as the senior radio operator. Team Four would be going out with only five men.

On mission day, the team slept in. Around 1100 hours, the men received their Operational Orders. Right after lunch, Staff Sergeant Forrest presented the Field Orders to everyone connected to the mission: the helicopter pilots, the brigade's Operation and Intelligence sections, Lieutenant Stevenson, the detachment commander, and Master Sergeant Chassion. Larry Forrest used the 101st's Field Order system, which remained in place throughout the Vietnam War: *Situation and Mission*; *Explanation* (all the detailed operational information); *Administration and Logistics*; *Command and Signal*.

These paragraphs, with subtitles, covered every aspect of a LRRP mission, including the procedures the team leader expected the pilots to follow in inserting the team. The pilots were always volunteers and could back out prior to the close of the Operational Order. If anyone involved in support of the mission had any heartburn over any part of the team Field Orders, it was to be hashed out at the briefing. Once the briefing was over, there was no backing out, and only the team leader could then make changes. At the close of the presentation the team leader asked, "Are there any questions?" If not, the briefing was over, and it was now too late to have any doubts. They were committed. As the first Lurps used to say, "The shit's on now!"

"Normally, we had no problems with the pilots going along with our plans," Larry Forrest recalls. "Once in a while, someone would have very pertinent questions or suggestions, which would lead to a change in the team leader's plan. However, on the whole, the pilots were impressed by the professional and confident air of the team leaders, and had no problem with the order. Anyway, it was an area they knew little about. It was hard for anyone other than the teams to comprehend the needs of a team out in the contested areas, alone for seven days. So support personnel did just that—they supported the teams."

Final inspection time was set two or three hours prior to lift-off. Staff Sergeant Forrest had time to go over the maps and routes planned with the team. He had to cover the SOIs (signal operation instructions booklets, which held all the codes, frequencies, and call signs for artillery, naval artillery, helicopter and helicopter gunship support, and jet fighter support, as well as an internal brigade brevity code, which changed daily). The SOIs, carried in the lower-left-leg pocket along with the map, were classified Top Secret. They were to be destroyed first if the situation got hairy—meaning imminent capture by the enemy—then maps, radios, and any written information a team might be carrying.

After reviewing all that, there was a little time to rest so Staff Sergeant Forrest just lay on his bunk imagining what was going to happen. An insertion flight is calculated to the minute: they would board the helicopters and take off with enough time to arrive over the LZ, land, and hit the bushes exactly at sunset. By the time they hit the bushes it would be dark, BNTT (beginning of nautical twilight time). This timing was absolutely necessary, Forrest felt, and would confuse the enemy each time it was used. They would not make a pass over the AO before setting down because that would alert the enemy that they were possibly going to land there. It could also give the enemy more time to get to a probable LZ and check it out before the team could clear the area. The team would sit off the LZ long enough to let the gunships fly over their position twenty seconds later. This was to simulate a Hawk Mission (using a helicopter for bait and gunships for ass kicking) if the Vietcong were around, throwing them off the fact that a LRRP team had just gone in. Then the helicopters would circle a few miles away at 2500 feet. After the team leader felt he was safely in, and had not been detected, he would release the aircraft to return to base.

The team would wait to be sure nothing strange was going on, then move to a better position to sit and listen, allowing their eyes to adjust to the dark, which took about forty-five minutes. At that time the team leader would decide whether to sit there and listen all night or to move again. The next day, at daybreak, they would start the recon of their AO.

Staff Sergeant Forrest recalls: "It was time! Time to mount up. Very little had been said by anyone on the team going out. Skau and Pruett had quiet teams, too. It seemed that no one had anything to say. When looked at closely, what was there to talk about? All plans were laid. We had gone over them many times. The chopper pilots were tuned in and set. What we needed now was movement toward our objective, not talk. Anyway, if we talked, we'd have to open our mouths. Then the butterflies would come out."

The seats had been taken out of the Hueys so no equipment worn by the men of the team could be caught or entangled as they exited the aircraft. As the team sat on the floor, Forrest had the men check their weapons. He was given a flight helmet by the starboard door gunner in order to communicate with the pilots during the flight. The pilot would check with him on final approach to the LZ to see if he'd decided to abort the mission. Just before exiting the aircraft, he would take the helmet off and toss it to the door gunner.

The familiar whine of the turbine engines began. The men had stopped fidgeting for a comfortable position and were settled down. Staff Sergeant Forrest glanced out the doorway and saw Lieutenant Stevenson with Master Sergeant Chassion watching them. Across the way was Skau's Huey, then Pruett's. Forrest heard the pilot's voice come over the helmet headset, asking for a radio check.

"Ancient Tracker Eight. This is Daddy Do-Right. Radio check, over."

"Daddy Do-Right, this is Ancient Tracker Eight. I hear you five by."

"Affirmative, Eight. We're lifting off!"

With that completed, the pilot pulled pitch. The chopper shuddered and slid to the left a little. The nose of the aircraft dropped down, and with the tail up it began pulling away from the ground. The blades above slapped the air hard, making the familiar popping sound, and the team was airborne. From the launch pad, Lieutenant Stevenson and Master Sergeant Chassion watched each team's slick liftoff into the darkening sky. All the hard work was riding on those three birds, and each of them privately wished they could be on one of those choppers.

The choppers flew together in formation for awhile, then split for a position favorable to their respective LZ approaches. Flying support for the teams was a "Hog" team of three gunships—three UHU1Bs rigged with two miniguns, rocket pods, and a maneuverable chin turret gun that fired 40mm grenades. They also had two door gunners. The UHU1Bs were deadly and quite effective, the predecessors of the Huey Cobra.

There was a sudden increase in radio traffic on Staff Sergeant Forrest's headset. The slicks were telling the gunships their relative positions to "dump time"—insertion. The pilot informed the gunships that he was ten seconds from dump, then called Forrest.

"Ancient Tracker Eight, we have negative enemy sighted on the LZ. I'm making final approach. Is it a go?"

Forrest answered, "Roger, Daddy Do-Right. It's a *go*."

The chopper laid over to the right and slid in toward the foot of the mountains. It was getting too dark to see any of the map reference points, just shadows. Larry Forrest would have to trust to the navigation of the pilots to put them into the right spot. The nose of the chopper went up, the tail dropped, and the aircraft flared for a stop. Forrest looked at the men and gave them a thumbs-up. They were going in! Forrest turned, took off his helmet, and handed it to the door gunner. The door gunner fumbled, trying to get it on his head quickly. He wanted to hear what the pilot was saying and get his hands back on the M-60 machine gun mounted in front of him.

When a chopper flares, it lifts its belly in the direction of travel in an effort to slow down. By the time it's over the dump point, it has slowed to a stop. Then, without touching or setting down, the ship rocks forward and begins picking up speed again in its effort to climb out of the area and leave. During the time the ship was stopped, hovering about three feet off the ground and rocking forward, the team jumped out and headed for the bushes. By the time they hit the tree line, the chopper was gone, its sounds covering the noise they had made dashing for the bushes. About twenty seconds later, the gunships flew over the LRRPs' position, looking for the enemy. However, the real mission of the gunships was to make the enemy think that a Hawk Mission was in progress, which made the enemy gunners shy and hesitate before firing on a helicopter. The helicopter is never allowed to set down. When a helicopter lands, the release on the pitch of the rotor blades creates a definite sound, a sound only made by a helicopter when it's sitting on the ground. The enemy was very aware of this and if within earshot would instantly know a helicopter had landed.

The team was in. The butterflies were gone, replaced by extreme caution. Adrenaline flowed furiously. All the senses became three to four times keener. At times like that, man is akin to the animals of the jungle—and just as dangerous because of his keyed-up state. He sees, smells, and feels better. He reacts more effectively than he ever imagined possible.

It was too dark to see all the men, so Staff Sergeant Forrest quietly called for a head count. All of them were present. He whispered to them that they were going to move toward the base of the mountain to seek better cover, thicker vegetation to hide in. At the LZ the soil was made up of fine white sand because that part of the valley had once been under the ocean. The light sand could silhouette the team for anyone looking down from the hills, and that could be a problem.

As they moved toward the hills, the Lurps thought they heard voices coming from the valley behind them. At first they rationalized that it was probably a couple of farmers coming in late from the rice fields, but there had been no farms indicated in the valley. Second, around there, men normally didn't work the rice fields, the women did. Third, the voices were getting closer to the team, not going away. Staff Sergeant Forrest knew then that they had a situation on their hands. By then, the choppers had reported the other dumps and were several miles west, at 2500 feet elevation, circling on an aerial platform, with twenty minutes of fuel time. If trouble developed, they would come back quickly, gunships and all, and extract any team needing assistance. Twenty minutes had passed. Team Four found better cover, but not much because the vegetation was still sparse. Staff Sergeant Fogt had found an old bomb crater. Between the hole, the darkness, and the sparse vegetation, Forrest decided they had enough concealment to wait out the people coming toward the team, and let them pass. The sounds kept getting closer.

Staff Sergeant Forrest recalls: "I sent Staff Sergeant Fogt forward fifty feet or so toward the hills as a lookout. That way, I'd have an early warning if we received company from that direction. I gathered the others into the bomb crater, explained the situation, and issued orders that no one was to fire unless I did first. I explained that we wanted the enemy to pass us by. We were on a recon mission and didn't want to make contact. I was certain now that they were Vietcong. No one else would be out there at that time of night. We assumed the normal circular defense posture: Sergeants Henry and Davis toward the hills, Vaughn and I toward the valley. The choppers had left their aerial platform, and were on approach to base. Furthermore, they were almost out of fuel."

The teams knew the importance and high profile of their mission. They knew that high-ranking officers would be monitoring their frequency. It flashed through Forrest's mind that they could really blow the detachment's future if they got into a fire fight with the enemy. Still, he didn't have time to worry about that; the mission always came first. He began to formulate a plan of action. He decided that if they made contact, he would fight back out into the valley through the oncoming enemy. There was no other good choice if extraction became their only option. But if all went well, they could swing either east or west in a loop, and penetrate back south into the hills at another point.

The Vietcong kept coming directly toward the team in the bomb crater. And they were beating the bushes to see if anyone had gotten off the chopper. Apparently, the enemy was not sure that had happened. If they had been, they certainly wouldn't be making so much noise, talking loud, and carrying on in a very nonchalant manner.

Questions nagged at Forrest's mind. Why were they coming at the team from open terrain? If the enemy element was an outpost, the main body would probably be facing them from the hills in defense. Then again, the VC could be a patrol returning to a camp in the hills. Or it could be the main body of Vietcong that they were supposed to find. Forrest hoped that was not the case. He decided that they needed to get Staff Sergeant Fogt back and prepare for a fight; the enemy was still headed in the team's direction. Forrest was about to send Sergeant Henry for Fogt when the team heard what sounded like an elephant coming down the hill, crashing through the bush. It was Fogt, and in a loud voice, he said, "They're coming, goddammit, they're coming!"

Forrest was about to ask how many and from what direction, but it didn't matter any longer. All hell broke loose. Still talking, Fogt jumped into the hole. A green tracer snapped over his head, missing him by a couple of inches. From the direction of the hills, a very heavy volley of fire followed the first tracer. Forrest's worst-case scenario had become a reality.

Larry Forrest also understood that soon his team would be in a trap, receiving fire from two different directions. He gave the order to open fire, and threw a grenade in the direction Fogt had come from. He wanted to stop any Vietcong that might have been following Fogt from charging the patrol's position. As the grenade flashed in explosion, he saw three bodies fly through the air. His grenade was immediately followed by another explosion in the same general area, and again bodies took flight. Sergeants Henry and Fogt were engaging the enemy with hand grenades. Taking the radio handset from Vaughn, Forrest keyed it and said, "Ancient Tracker One, this is Ancient Tracker Eight. We're under heavy fire from south and north, will advise, Wait. Out." In the radio procedure of the time, "Wait. Out" means for the other party to wait a few minutes. During the next few minutes, Forrest could hear communications coming over the radio, but he didn't intend to talk right then. He had asked them to "Wait. Out." Instead, he should have said, "Wait."

Vaughn and Davis were firing toward the valley when Staff Sergeant Forrest looked behind him. He heard a loud, high-pitched yelp from the direction in which they were firing. He hollered, "Hit hard! Don't let up!"

Staff Sergeant Fogt, or Sergeant Henry, yelled back, "What the hell you think we're doing?"

The team was getting low on grenades. All Staff Sergeant Forrest had left was his WP (white phosphorus) grenade. He decided to throw it in an effort to light up the area and be able to see better so he could choose a direction in which to break out. The WP grenade didn't help much, but it did create weak silhouettes at the foot of the hill. Forrest could make out the enemy running around, and it looked like Fogt and Henry were picking them off nicely. Whenever they fired, one of the silhouettes would drop or fall.

The team was running low on small-arms ammo, so Staff Sergeant Forrest knew they couldn't stay in their position any longer. He told the team that they were going to break out to their left front as they looked to the valley. Killing anything that even looked like enemy, they were to run about 150 yards then erect a defense perimeter. While waiting for the choppers, they would set up claymore mines, which by then would probably be the only ordinance left to help defend their position. If the enemy didn't try to overrun them, as last minute security they would detonate the claymores just before boarding the choppers. Forrest made sure everyone understood what was to happen. He made it clear that no one was to go until he gave the word. The talking, plus the short lag in firing by the team, encouraged the enemy to pick up his rate of fire. Forrest turned to Vaughn and said, "Call back, and tell them to get us out of here."

Vaughn lifted the handset to his mouth, keyed it, and shouted, "Get us out of here!"

My God, Forrest thought, he's out of it. He started to reach over Fogt to grab the handset, but Fogt beat him to it. Fogt keyed the radio handset, and said, "Daddy Do-Right, this is

Ancient Tracker Eight Alpha. 'Eight' requests immediate team extraction. Over."

The answer came back, "Wilco. On the way. Wait!"

Forrest had heard radio traffic and remembered Vaughn's answering in some fashion, so he was aware that headquarters knew they were in deep shit. Each time Vaughn keyed the handset, the loudspeakers back at base must have transmitted the noise of the battle they were in. It probably scared the shit out of them, especially with the team not answering right away. The fight had been going on for about twenty minutes.

Staff Sergeant Forrest took the handset from Vaughn, and asked him if he was okay. By the time of Vaughn's reply, Forrest knew that he really was okay. He keyed the handset and said, "Ancient Tracker One, this is Ancient Tracker Eight. Sit-Rep (situation report): negative WIAs, moving toward valley floor for extraction. Still receiving fire. Wait!"

With that said, Larry Forrest gave the order to break out. He was going to cover the team. Staff Sergeant Fogt had the same idea. Larry Forrest said nothing. He had wanted Fogt with the team, in case of further trouble, but when his Lurps broke out, Forrest was impressed. He had never seen men move so fast with all their gear on. There was no charge from the enemy. On the way out he and Fogt ripped off a magazine of ammo to dissuade would-be pursuers. It worked like a charm. All team members made it to a point about one hundred meters out into the valley. The claymores were almost ready. Four were set up, and four claymores should be able to stop a platoon. A slight surge of fear rushed through Larry Forrest when he realized that he could see everything very well against the white sand. If he could see, so could the enemy. But it was too late to change their plan. In fact, they had no other choice. To have gone left or right from the bomb crater would have meant paralleling the enemy's possible position. Forrest didn't feel that the enemy would follow the team into the open. The rate of fire slowed. He told the men to scoop out prone shelters while staying in the prone position, and not to return the enemy's fire unless they saw them coming. If the enemy didn't yet have a good fix on the Lurps' position, he didn't want to give them one.

The team heard the drone of the helicopters off in the distance. Then Daddy Do-Right called and informed them that he was five minutes out, and to be ready to mark their position in three minutes. Forrest reached for his white phosphorus grenade and found nothing; he had thrown it earlier. He asked for someone to pass him one. No one else had one. They had nothing with which to mark their position. Terror gripped him. Strobe lights and pen flares were not yet regularly issued to Lurps. Forrest knew he had made a tremendous blunder in not saving munitions to mark their position for night extraction. Then it dawned on him that he did have a way to mark their position. He said to the team, "Someone crawl out about twenty yards, and light a piece of C-4 as a marker."

Forrest recalls, "First, this was not the way to give an order. I should have named the individual that I wanted to execute the order. Second, this was clearly not the time to ask for a volunteer. I did neither, and got just what I should have—no response. So, in an angry voice I said, 'Fuck it, I'll go! Everybody stay here.' With that said, I crawled off quickly. I was angry at myself, and a little angry that no one had volunteered. When I reached a good distance, I stopped and pulled out a block of C-4. I had difficulty breaking the one-pound block in half, so I bit off the end of the plastic bag and decided to light the whole block. I didn't have time to screw around. Then it dawned on me: to light this shit, I'll have to strike a match out here in the open. A match in the open can be seen twenty miles on a clear night. The enemy wasn't but 250 yards away, at most, and when I struck the match I'd be a perfect target. I hesitated, thought, then scooped out a small hole about six inches deep and one foot in diameter. I placed the block of C-4 in this hole and struck a match. The first two didn't work, they just fizzled. Now I was really in a cold sweat. Bullets began to rain in toward my position, but the rounds were high. The enemy was having a terrible time estimating our distance."

The third match caught, and the C-4 began to glow with a brilliant blue-white light. However, one would have to see the light directly to get its full illuminating effect. The helicopter had this advantage, but the enemy probably couldn't see it because of the hole in which Forrest had placed it. Forrest crawled back as fast as he could. The radio crackled with a very happy voice. The pilot was elated that the Lurps had marked their position so well and said so. He said that he was coming straight in for the team, with no dry run or passes over the area prior to landing. Much of this was not procedure, but with little ammo and only hard choices, Staff Sergeant Forrest was past caring about procedure at that point. It was time to clear out!

The team heard noises from the direction of the enemy. There was no doubt that Charlie was coming, but the Lurps couldn't determine how many. The team waited until they could make out a few moving shadows. The shadows slowed, showing caution, so Forrest gave the order to fire the clay-mores. The blast wiped the view clean—no more enemy.

The helicopter was setting down by then, and the team dashed for it as a rain of bullets fell on the area. Everyone was on the chopper but Vaughn and Staff Sergeant Forrest when Vaughn sprang his surprise.

Forrest recalls, "Vaughn said, 'Sarge, I don't have the SOI; I left it in the hole!' I didn't have time to argue. I said that I would go back and cover for him while he went into the hole and retrieved the SOI. He took off, and I lingered to tell the pilot and Fogt what was up and not to wait more than two minutes for us. Then I followed Vaughn. I took up my position about five yards from the hole and began to wait. One must appreciate what our SOI consisted of at the time. It contained all the codes for our fire support, all the call signs and frequencies, including our own LRRP brevity codes. If the enemy got one of those, it would set the entire brigade's operation back until the entire SOI was changed and redistributed throughout the brigade. That's why we went back to get the SOI. It was also our first mission, and was supposed to be a showcase. We couldn't fail, not in that way. I waited what seemed like an eternity; then I saw two black shadows rushing in my general direction. I couldn't wait any longer. The jig was up. I fired a burst from my M-16, cutting down the two, maybe three, unsuspecting enemy. I then jumped up and ran in a crouch toward the chopper. I felt sick that I was going to have to leave a man and an SOI to the enemy on the first mission. When I got on the chopper and gave the thumbs-up signal to the pilot, guess who was sitting in the chopper? Good old Vaughn! He had gone to the hole and gotten the SOI, then returned to the chopper without me seeing him.

"The pilot turned around and began to count the team making sure we were all there. I vehemently signaled for him to lift the chopper out. But he continued until he had a complete count of the team—no one missing. Then in a controlled manner, he turned and pulled the chopper out. One should realize that during this entire episode, we were being fired on by the enemy. Normal pilots would never have come in with that amount of enemy fire, let alone sat there waiting for us to find an SOI, then count us before pulling pitch and lifting out! It was the same pilot who had put us in. When he heard our call for extraction and the fierce sounds of battle over the radio, he was already setting down at the rear, out of fuel. He tried to get one of the other pilots to come and pick us up, pilots who had full tanks of fuel. No one would budge. So, in a fit of rage, he and his copilot jumped in someone else's chopper, one that had fuel, and returned for us. The gunships arrived as we were leaving the area."

Team Four made it back, and the only thing that got wounded was the chopper. It had many holes, but no warning lights flashing anywhere on the dash. Flying back, no one said a word. Staff Sergeant Forrest was to find that this was normal for teams both going in and being extracted. Naturally, going in on an insertion would cause apprehension, and therefore quiet. Being extracted, one would think, should cause elation. But that was not usually the case. Forrest eventually concluded that men expect the chopper to fall from the sky, get shot down, or crash upon landing; not until they sat down at the helipad would they feel safe. Combat does that to people.

When they landed, the team didn't find the crowd that they thought might be waiting for them; just Lieutenant Stevenson and Master Sergeant Chassion were on hand. They were debriefed individually and as a group. They were also informed that they would be going back into that area the following night. Forrest was to choose another LZ farther up in the hills, and to inform Lieutenant Stevenson, who would tell the pilot.

Staff Sergeant Forrest doesn't remember anyone having trouble sleeping that night. They were drained. The following day, the team made corrections in equipment and ammunition. From the helicopter unit they obtained a strobe light that they would use to signal choppers at night. Strobes are very bright, pulsating lights with very narrow directional beams that make it difficult for anyone other than the approaching pilot to see. The team augmented it with a few flares. With a better under-standing of how much ammo might be needed to sustain them until help arrived, to a man, they added M-16 ammo to their basic load. The time that would pass before fire support would be available did not change—twenty minutes—but Forrest now understood that the team would not be able to stay long in one position during engagements. They had been lucky. For whatever reason, the enemy had not attacked their position in strength. They couldn't depend on that in the future, so they came up with "Red Dog."

"Red Dog was a system where we would take off running from the enemy," Staff Sergeant Forrest says. "Before begin-ning our run, we would call for help, give our position and the magnetic azimuth on which we would be Red-Dogging in, and obtain an ETA (estimated time of arrival). At that approximate time, we would start dropping red smoke as we ran. On arrival, the aircraft would level everything behind the last smoke grenade dropped. This was to help us many times in the future—it saved lives."

The team taped M-16 magazines together at the bottom, one up and two magazines down. With that system, all they had to do was flip the package over when a magazine was empty and slap in one taped alongside it. Three twenty-round magazines taped together gave them sixty rounds of quick firing. Unfortu-nately, loading twenty rounds into a twenty-round magazine caused a feeding malfunction, so it became standard to load just eighteen or nineteen rounds to a magazine.

Team Four was now ready to return to the AO. The next evening came quickly. The leaders were as happy as pigs in a corn cob factory. As far as they were concerned, everything had worked like clockwork the evening before. Now all that was necessary was for the team to get back in without big problems.

That evening, Staff Sergeant Forrest's team went back into their recon zone, higher up in the mountain range. The LZ was very steep so they had to claw themselves up to a spot level enough to spend the night. Expecting to be hit by the enemy from below, the team listened all night. But that didn't happen. They did hear noises from below, very distant noises. They were baffled about why the enemy didn't attack their position. With daylight, they saw that they were a good five hundred meters up and away from the lowest tree line, and two or three hundred meters east of where they had landed the previous night. The enemy acted as if they didn't know the team was up there.

Later that day an infantry unit was inserted in the west end of the valley. It deployed straight down the valley, sending a unit to sweep the side of the hills on their flank. Staff Sergeant Skau was coordinating with the infantry unit, telling them that the enemy was rolling up to the east, keeping ahead of their units. He was counting high numbers of enemy soldiers as they ran to the east, picking up troops as they went. The Vietcong would have to run out into the open valley, stop in the tree line and fight, or turn up the mountain and cross over. Forrest ordered his team to be ready to count, and prepared for a fight if the enemy swung up toward them.

Team Four counted as eighty-four Vietcong passed below their position. They did not turn toward the team, but kept going. So it was up to Staff Sergeant Pruett's team. The enemy would pass through his area, or stop and fight. Forrest doesn't remember Pruett's reports, other than the beginning of word that the enemy had turned and was escaping up through his AO.

When Team Four received orders to prepare for extraction, the choppers must have already been en route because only a few minutes passed before they arrived. That was the first time Staff Sergeant Forrest had to mount a chopper while it hovered with one strut touching the ground.

"We walked high for a while," Forrest recounts. "The LRRPs were now a factor in the intell mix, and requests for our services began to come in. Rumors of our exploits spread through the country like fire."

With this first mission came the nickname that was given to S.Sgt. Larry Forrest by his team—"Black Icicle." It was given to him because of his cool deportment while under heavy combat stress. Months after S.Sgt. Larry Forrest had left the LRRP detachment, new Lurps would still hear of the "Black Icicle," but most of them never had a face or name to attach to the legendary Lurp and warrior.

In late February 1967, the LRRP detachment pulled another mission in this same area, inserting by road on the west side of the mountain range.

## Alfred Smith and the start of LRRPs

When the 1/101st Airborne deployed for Vietnam, Pfc. Alfred Smith didn't leave with his unit. From the time he graduated Recondo school at Fort Campbell, in November 1964, he had been with Recon Platoon, 2/502 Battalion. Al Smith was part of the detachment that stayed behind and cleaned up the barracks. The detachment followed two weeks later on C-130s and arrived in Nha Trang before the USNS *LeRoy Eltinge* docked at Cam-ranh Bay. Al Smith then flew down to join the brigade. With Recon Platoon, 2/502 Battalion, he participated in Operation GIBRALTAR out of An Khe, in a place called Happy Valley, and Operation SAYONARA out of Qui-nhon.

In late September 1965 word filtered throughout the brigade that volunteers were needed to form a Long Range Recon detachment. Al Smith wanted to be in special operations because of the challenges that came with working in small teams. At Qui-nhon he volunteered with a group of guys from his platoon. He was interviewed by Lieutenant Stevenson, the LRRP detachment commander, and accepted into the organization. Alfred Smith's MOS was Airborne Infantry, Light Weapons.

On arriving in the LRRP detachment, Pfc. Al Smith was assigned as the junior RTO on Team One. The volunteers underwent a vigorous cross-training program. S.Sgt. Ronald Bourne, the LRRP detachment communications sergeant, was considered one of the top commo sergeants in the brigade. He put the would-be LRRPs through intensive commo training, covering radio procedures, SOIs, encryption techniques, field-expedient antennas, Morse code, and the care and trouble-shooting of the main field radio, the PRC-25. Sgt. Joseph C. Nash, senior RTO on Team One, and Sgt. Arthur L. Doame of Team Two, were two of the best RTOs when the detachment was formed. They also helped in the instruction. The AN-PRC-25 had 920 FM channels, weighed twenty-three pounds, had a range of about twenty-five kilometers, and kicked your ass when you humped it. The LRRP detachment put a heavy emphasis on communications, and the AN-PRC-25 was the primary link that kept the LRRP teams operational in the field.

Sfc. Guy "Pop" Tomlinson led Team One. "Pop was thirty-eight years old, balding, gray hair, although he didn't have an old face," Al Smith recalls. "He had blue eyes and was about five ten. He was stocky and very strong. Pop was from Charlotte, Michigan. He was married and pretty much true blue to the wife. Not much into going to town. Pop was a nice guy and very good under fire, very reliable. A good solid NCO. I have spent thirty years in the service, and when you become an NCO, you model yourself after somebody. I modeled myself after Pop Tomlinson."

Al Smith's accounts of initial Lurp training are almost identical to Larry Forrest's, except that, being a Pfc, Smith had more to learn. Because he was a rifleman cross-training as an RTO, he was given extra commo training to bring him up to the standards the new job demanded. In mid-January 1966, the Lurps moved north by LST to Tuy-hoa. When they arrived, they were utilized in an operational manner to support the maneuvering battalions of 2/502, 2/327, and later 1/327. This was called Operation VAN BUREN. Out of that operation came My Canh 2, on 7 February 1966, for which the Tiger Force Commander Jim Gardner was awarded the Medal of Honor posthumously.

Al Smith recalls that his team went out the night before the Tigers got hit. They were inserted twenty miles northwest of Tuy-hoa and landed on their primary LZ, a hilltop from which they could see a village below them. The team split up. Pop Tomlinson, Robert Doty, and Al Smith, carrying the radio, walked out to the southern end of the hill, a better location for eyeballing the village. When they arrived at the southern end of the hilltop with its heavy vegetation, they chose a large bush that opened out toward the village about a thousand meters away. Maybe they had not been as careful as they should have been. Or maybe the VC LZ watchers or trackers were particularly sharp that time.

Al Smith remembers that the three men had just taken positions overlooking the village. Pop Tomlinson was observing the village with his binoculars. Smith was sitting on the ground with his feet out in front of him and he had laid his rifle across his ankles so that he could slip out of his radio harness. The shoulder pads were off his shoulders and he was letting them slip down behind him. Doty, standing off to Smith's right, had laid his weapon against Smith's ankle. Pop was to the left, and Doty was looking around a big bush that was in front of them. All of a sudden Smith looked up, and Doty was waving his hand to be quiet, to be still. The Lurps froze. There was a hole big enough to see through in the green bush in front of Smith's face, and he peered through it. A head moved past. It was obviously a VC, and the VC stopped—and looked through the hole.

"The VC is looking straight through the hole right at me," Smith remembers. "I have camouflage all over my face, so he can't see me. But I can see him moving his head back and forth, trying to look past all the leaves to see what's on the other side of the bush, trying to focus. The VC can't see anything and moves a few steps more to my right. Doty is standing there. All Doty's got is the hand grenades on his load-bearing equipment (LBE). He had put his rifle down on my ankle. The VC moved away from the hole, and I started to get out of my harness to grab my rifle. As I start to move, a second head comes up, and again I freeze. Meanwhile, Pop Tomlinson is looking through the binoculars, and he doesn't know these two guys are there. Pop's not saying anything. He's not making any noise. He's just looking through the binoculars at something a mile away, with the enemy a meter or two from his position. The second Charlie comes up, and he's doing exactly the same thing as the first guy did. He's looking, moving his head back and forth, trying to see past this big leaf on the other side. Well, that big leaf is my face, and all I can really do is to stare at him. I squinted, so he couldn't see the whites of my eyes. I'm just looking, to see what he is going to do. If he puts his gun up, then I've got to move and grab my rifle. I'm looking at him, I saw his eyes refocus—I actually saw them. He is only a couple of feet away from me. When his eyes refocused, he realized what that leaf really was. His fucking eyes got as big as silver dollars. He realized it was me, ducked down, and made a grunting sound to the other guy. Doty grabbed his rifle, and I grabbed mine. But by then, these VC are already running away."

At first, the vegetation obscured the Lurps' view of the fleeing VC. Pop Tomlinson hadn't even seen them when they were peering at Al Smith. Before long, the Lurps see the VC on the trail, running into the village, going at a dead run. A few seconds later five or six black specks were running out the back of the village, running directly away from the team. Smith assumed the political cadre was bugging out. Another bunch came out of the village and started moving toward the Lurps. To the north, they saw another dozen or so slowly moving toward them. They linked back up with the rest of the team, but they had no place to go. Rice paddies and open areas were all around them, which was bad for movement but fine for LZs.

"We had to sit there as we watched these guys slowly work their way toward us," Smith recalls. "We called for helicopter

support, and there wasn't any. This was one of those deals. . . .
When we first formed up, we were supposed to have a gunship
and a slick on call at all times, sitting right there waiting for us,
ready to go. The more missions we got, the more reluctant they
were to leave two helicopters just sitting there doing nothing.
I'm not sure how long we sat on top of that hill, but we were
sitting there while these guys kept getting closer, and there was
no place to hide. There were some bushes for concealment, but
no cover."

When an extraction helicopter finally showed, the gunships
were already making passes as the VC came up the hill. The
extraction helicopter came flying in with the wind, and it was
tough for the pilot to maintain lift. As the Lurps got in the
chopper, they were firing back. They knew the VC were down
below them somewhere but couldn't see them. Al Smith was
on the port side of the chopper, and Doty was on the starboard
side. They emptied their weapons, and then away the chopper
went. The pilot had a tough time getting out of there, and the
gunship was right behind the ship, blazing away at whatever
the pilot could see coming up the hill.

When Team One returned to Tuy-hoa, the pilot of the gunship said, "Those last two guys that got in, as you guys turned
and ran, the VC were coming right up on top of the hill. They
were shooting at your feet just as you jumped in."

Al Smith had no idea the extraction was as dangerous as it
had been. He never heard a round, never heard a pop, never
saw any dirt flying. "We took off, landed, and lived happily
ever after," he said.

Team One was getting some hot chow back at Tuy-hoa
when the bodies began to arrive from My Canh 2. The dead
men were dressed in tiger fatigues, and later on, people from
Smith's old recon platoon assumed the dead Tiger Force
troopers were Lurps.

Al Smith recalls a mission out of Tuy-hoa where a new helicopter unit had been assigned to work with the Lurps. The
team was down on the airfield getting ready to board the helicopter, and the pilots of the slicks were talking to the Lurps
about how they had been working down in the delta. One of the

pilots said, "You know, we're looking forward to operating up here in the Central Highlands. It'll give us a chance to use our map reading. Down in the Delta, you get up there in the air at two thousand feet, and you follow a canal. There are no terrain features, no nothing. Here you've got mountains, so we're really looking forward to this. It's going to be a lot more interesting, to use our map reading."

As it turned out, the pilots really did need map reading practice. Team One was supposed to land on a particular LZ and then move north a couple of klicks (kilometers) to a mountaintop where they suspected the VC were setting up some defensive positions. From the air in the Central Highlands, there aren't many prominent terrain features, so at two thousand feet, it's hard to tell the hills apart. The insertion pilot got confused and put the team down on its objective instead of the infiltration LZ.

"As we were coming in," Smith says, "—and again, you're orbiting at two or three thousand feet a couple of miles away, and then you make your move—coming in, you lose altitude, drop down to treetop level, balls to the wall, and you come on the LZ. When you're traveling ninety knots at treetop level, you can't be heard coming, so we really did catch the VC by surprise. As we approached the LZ, all of a sudden I look out the door and I can see guys running. In some ways, I was a stupid kid; I didn't catch on too quick. It never occurred to me that the pilot would make a mistake like that. I'm saying to myself, What in the hell are the South Vietnamese doing here? I mean, shit, we're supposed to be the first ones here! And why are they running? Wait a second, they're *running*! The gunner on the other side starts blazing away. Sp5. Richard Clark, the medic, was sitting in the middle of the slick. I was sitting directly behind the pilot, Sgt. Bill White was next to me. Pop Tomlinson was sitting directly behind the copilot. S.Sgt. Robert Doty was next to Pop, and Sgt. Joe Nash was in the middle. Ron Bourne was in the helicopter as belly man. Clark swears that when the VC started shooting, he saw a tracer go in one door and out the other. There was a bullet hole in the side of the aircraft right next to Pop Tomlinson—and I mean *right* next to him. He's sitting at the leading edge of the door, so you know that strip of metal that's part of the door molding? Pop was leaning up against it, and there was a bullet hole there. The pilot had his web gear hanging over the back of his armored seat. He had a canteen on his web gear. As we flew away, the guys all breathed a sigh of relief. We were all kind of laughing, and Bourne taps me on the shoulder. When I turn around, he shows me the pilot's canteen that's right by my head. There is a bullet hole in it. He showed that to all the other guys first so they're all watching my reaction. I almost shit in my pants, and they all start to laugh. They know that I know where the canteen was. It's one of those things. Nobody is being mean, just all having a good laugh. Nobody got hurt. Doty said that when the VC started shooting, their machine gun was on his side of the aircraft. When the tracers started coming up, he almost fainted. As the door gunner started shooting back at them, one of the spent shell casings hit Doty in the chest—for a second he thought he had been hit. Doty was laughing about it later.

"We flew back to Tuy-hoa, regrouped, and went out again the next night."

## Donovan Pruett, KIA

The LRRP detachment had been living a charmed life until they got to Phan-thiet. They had been pulling successful missions and basically kicking ass on Mr. Charles, but things were about to change for the Lurps.

On 1 April 1966, the LRRP detachment was handed an operational warning order for a Lurp-team insertion into the northwest quadrant of the brigade AO. The recon team was to obtain intelligence information on the enemy forces working that area. Lieutenant Stevenson selected Team Two for the mission, commanded by S.Sgt. Donovan Jess Pruett from Deer Park, Washington. Don Pruett was twenty-nine years of age and very tall. He was thin, but big boned, and weighed around 170 pounds. He had high cheekbones, a nice-looking face, and, of course, he was heavily tanned. Don Pruett was considered one of the best team leaders in the LRRP detachment at the time. At senior scout on his team was S.Sgt. "Fang" Roedel. Junior scout was Sgt. Jackie L. Waymire from Huntington, West Virginia. Waymire was twenty-one and a big, stout guy. A former high-school football player, he was about 5'11", and weighed 210 pounds.* Senior RTO was Sgt. Arthur L. Doame from Clarksville, Tennessee. The regular junior RTO on the team, Sgt. Thomas Vernon, had been temporarily replaced by Sp4. Michael Flynn from Atlanta, Georgia. The medic on the team was Sp5. Joe Johnson from Alabama.

Al Smith spoke with Mike Flynn about what happened that day. Flynn said that Team Two had inserted without any problems, and for the next two days sneaked and peeked around its recon zone (RZ) on two occasions relaying information on VC sightings. Sometime during the morning of the third day, the VC became aware of the team's presence. Unknown to the team, it had become the prey and was being tracked. Trailing them to where they set up for a midmorning break around a tree, the VC silently low crawled close to the team's position and ambushed them. Donovan Pruett was hit by the initial burst of automatic-weapons fire. Shot through the chest and head, with a sucking chest wound, he was in very serious trouble. The team returned fire, taking the initiative away from the VC, then broke the contact. Grabbing their equipment and carrying their team leader, Team Two started the E&E (escape-and-evasion) run of their lives, but they were hampered by having to carry Don Pruett and by the determination of the VC to maintain contact. Team Two was in a running gun battle with the pursuing enemy.

When teams were in the field, the LRRP detachment used an L-19 aircraft as an airborne radio relay. The back-seater of the L-19 was usually a LRRP, who served as radio relay operator. On that particular day, Al Smith was on duty. After calling the rear base for an emergency extraction and to deliver a situation report on Team Two, the small aircraft continued to circle and monitor the team's progress, guiding them to a small LZ they had spotted from the air. As he talked with the team, Al Smith

*To learn more about Sergeant Waymire, and his death, see S. L. A. Marshall's *Ambush*, Jove Books, 1988.

could hear the chatter of automatic weapons in the background and the explosions of hand grenades. Team Two was running, carrying Don Pruett, and trying to shake the VC. Soon they started destroying their equipment to lighten their loads. Out of breath, and running on adrenaline, their anxiety about their team leader was being communicated over the radio to Al Smith. Being unable to help frustrated both the pilot of the L-19 and Smith. At one point, while waiting for the extraction helicopter and gunships to show up, the pilot told Smith he wanted to use the L-19's 2.75-inch white-phosphorus marking rockets against the VC. Al Smith relayed that back to Lieutenant Stevenson at rear base, who asked them to stay out of it because overhead cover prevented the L-19 from seeing the team as the men ran for their lives.

From the time the VC started shooting until the team got on the slick, over an hour had passed, but it seemed longer to Al Smith. Jack Waymire, the strongest man in the LRRP detachment, carried Don Pruett most of the way. He put all of his heart into the effort, but it wore him out. When Waymire wasn't carrying Pruett, he was falling back, exchanging gunfire and hand grenades with the enemy, and then catching back up with the fleeing team. Sp5. Joe Johnson, Team Two's medic, remarked later that Donovan Pruett kept saying he was in a lot of pain and asking for morphine. Johnson was reluctant to give him the morphine because Don had a head wound. Instead, he gave him a shot of saline water and told him it was morphine. And Pruett said, "Yeah, it feels a little better." There was nothing else Johnson could do for him.

S.Sgt. David Skau, Donovan Pruett's best friend, was bellyman on the extraction ship. Using the Red Dog procedure, the gunships laid effective suppressive fire on the pursuing enemy, giving the team some relief. When they finally arrived at the extraction LZ, the team popped smoke and directed the helicopter in. But the VC had infiltrated the surroundings of the LZ. As the extraction helicopter flared to land, the enemy opened fire with machine guns, causing it to crash. S.Sgt. David Skau helped evacuate the downed helicopter's crew and set its machine guns in a defensive posture. He also directed the gunships to place accurate fire on the enemy positions around the LZ. Dave Skau then took off and linked up with the exhausted men of Team Two.

After a second helicopter was called in, Team Two was extracted with David Skau. On the way back to base camp and medical help, S.Sgt. Donovan Jess Pruett died on the aircraft, surrounded by his friends. The fact that Pruett had come so close yet didn't make it back devastated the LRRP detachment. A remarkable display of personal endurance and valor had been shown by every member of Team Two, as well as the rest of the people involved. Al Smith remarks: "That was the first platoon member killed. You begin to think you lead a charmed life, you think you're good, and know you're good. The VC are a little afraid of you. You start thinking you can get away with anything. Donovan Pruett got killed on 3 April 1966, the day before my birthday. It was a terrible blow to the detachment."

## VC "Beware of Lurps" Classroom

The 1st Brigade moved south to Phan-thiet and began Operation AUSTIN. Phan-thiet was notoriously hot. During one of its patrols in August 1966, Pop Tomlinson's Team One, attempting to find a reported VC headquarters, stumbled into a situation of the kind that would eventually be reported and claimed by most of the other recon units in Vietnam.*

Phan-thiet wasn't the greatest terrain for recon work, but Al Smith thought it was going to be an easy mission. The enemy forces in this area were regional VC and were supposed to be a poor unit, not very well trained, not NVA (North Vietnamese Army). The Lurps had just come from Tuy-hoa, which was NVA, and they were supposed to be the "First Team." The area was flat, open, and extremely dry, so Team One didn't have the same kind of cover and concealment that it was used to at Tuy-hoa. On the second day of the mission, Team One was walking through the woods very slowly and carefully in the daytime. S.Sgt. Robert Doty was walking point.

*1/101st Airborne Division, Operation Report dated 13 August 1966.

"Doty went around this bush and just froze," Al Smith recalls. "You could see him hold up. He's got his rifle in one hand and the other hand free. The free hand is just waving us back to freeze. So everybody stops. There are only a couple of meters between each guy. We're pretty close together, even though it's daytime, but you want to stay close. Doty didn't turn around. He backed up. He'd found a class being taught. He was peering around the bush, backing up, and I couldn't hear anything from the other side of the bush. I don't know how close we were to the class. I never saw them. Nobody saw them, as far as I know, except Doty. He backed up, and I thought, 'Holy shit, how bad can it be for him to go backward?' There wasn't any talking, we just moved away, and when we got far enough away, Doty told us what he'd seen. We backed off and left the area that was the center of the base camp. I mean, if they're giving classes, you're *right* in it."

After moving about two hundred meters, the team bumped into a trail that led back into the base camp they had just left. There wasn't much cover and concealment, but they wanted to monitor the trail. A bamboo thicket next to the trail gave Team One the only concealment available. They set up within twenty to twenty-five yards of the trail. Al Smith remembers that it would have been easy to hit the trail with a hand grenade. Setting up in the bamboo thicket, the team prepared to watch and see what kind of traffic came along. They sent in a message to base about the classroom, and informed rear that they felt the trail led to where they had run into the classroom. It had to be a base camp. For a couple of hours, they monitored the trail.

Al Smith was tired enough to need a nap, so he let the others know he was going to rest and then dozed off. But not for long. "Something woke me up. I looked over to my right at Doty. Doty wasn't laying down. He was crouched over facing the trail, and his eyes were wide open. I mean his eyes looked like saucers. I thought, 'Oh, shit!' I'd been using my pack for a pillow, and I was behind a bush. I was well camouflaged. I very slowly rolled over to see what the hell Doty was looking at. . . ."

On the trail was a file of enemy soldiers that stretched out of view. Doty later told Al Smith that he had counted twenty-six and couldn't see the end. The point element had gone by the team, and it was now the main body that they were eyeballing. Smith very slowly rolled over on his stomach and behind his pack. He had a certain amount of cover, but not much. He could see that the line had stopped. It was the main body, and there were a couple of women in the group. One woman was pointing to the bamboo thicket. The guy behind her looked like he wasn't interested in what she had to say. The woman was carrying a Thompson, and she was pointing at the team. The guys around her weren't terribly interested, but she finally convinced the guy behind her that they ought to go check it out— "it" being the Lurps' position. Something in the thicket caught their eye. The VC were talking and the team was getting prepared. Smith readied his weapon, and all the other team members were doing the same. Nobody did anything. The team waited to see what the enemy was going to do. The minute the enemy took a couple of steps toward the team's position, the team opened up on full automatic.

"I figured their immediate action drill was to break contact," Al Smith said. "They just ran the other way. I know a couple of them went down. I know one went down anyway—the one in my sights. I was scared. When you're that close, it's a difficult thing to describe. We grabbed our shit and got out of there. Pop Tomlinson had sprained his ankle on the infiltration. We had landed in an open field that had been on fire. When we landed, it was still smoking, and the warm air over the field reduced some of the lift, so the helicopter didn't come down as low as we wanted, so we'd jumped out a little higher than we usually did. We couldn't really run that far or fast because Pop was limping. But we had to find an LZ quickly. Doty tossed a white phosphorus grenade, and we broke contact."

The team called for an extraction and took off in a direction parallel to the enemy base camp. The best they could find for an LZ was a small open field with some large trees in the middle. It wasn't big enough for a chopper to land in, so they used C-4 and hand grenades to knock the trees down. In the process of knocking the trees down, Joe Nash got a piece of shrapnel in the stomach. It was a small sliver and wasn't bleeding badly, so Doc Clark treated it.

The team waited around the LZ for the helicopters to come out and get them. Mike Flynn of the LRRP detachment was in the back seat of the L-19 flying radio relay that day. Every time the L-19 made a pass, the VC shot at it. The L-19 knew the LZ was hot. But when the extraction helicopter carrying Lurp Ron Bourne as belly man arrived, it wouldn't land; the pilot claimed they were taking fire. The helicopter flew around until it got low on fuel, then departed for Phan-thiet. When the chopper returned, Master Sergeant Chassion was aboard. Chassion later told the team that the pilot was reluctant to come in again. Chassion was an E-8 and the pilot was a captain, but Chassion leaned on him, saying, "You've got to go in, sir. You've got to get the guys out."

It was almost dark, and the team felt that if they stayed on the ground, they wouldn't make it through the night without an awful lot of help. They didn't know whether the help was available. The pilot kept circling around, complaining that there were still obstructions on the LZ. Finally, under Master Sergeant Chassion's firm insistence, the helicopter came in and extracted the team.

Al Smith adds: "We laughed about it later, but as we took off it seemed to me that we came awfully close to the trees. But then, we knew it was a small LZ. Clark was telling me that when the pilot pulled pitch, he was wearing gloves, and when he lifted up on the lever, the glove caught on his seat, and he couldn't lift it any higher. He couldn't let go of it, and he couldn't pull it any higher. He wasn't getting the lift that he wanted, and that's why we barely cleared the trees. That's as close as I've ever come to a tree in a helicopter, but we got out."

The next day a *Stars and Stripes* reporter was talking to Pop Tomlinson and the rest of the team. As Pop was telling him what happened, the reporter kept saying, "Well, is that all?" The tale clearly wasn't as dramatic as a John Wayne movie, and the reporter was obviously not terribly impressed, so he spiced things up, turning the story into an account of the Lurps' stumbling onto a VC class instructing on the subject of

"Beware of American Long Range Patrols." Since Doty didn't know Vietnamese, he wouldn't have even known if that really was the subject of the class. But the reporter's version made for good telling. The 101st Lurps got a kick out of the jealousy this mythical class disruption inspired in men who served in other recon units.

# 2

## LONG RANGE RECON
1 / 101
### Tuy-hoa

During mid-May 1966, the three maneuver battalions of the 1st Brigade were dispersed in three different locations. The 2/327 remained at Tuy-hoa, providing area security while on a stand down from major operations. The 1/327 and 2/502 were airlifted to Cheo Reo, the capital of Phu Bon Province, south of Pleiku. Their mission was to serve as reserve for I Field Force, operating in II Corps Tactical Zone.

### The Second Generation of Lurps

Around this time, the LRRP detachment started a recruiting drive because of rotation of personnel. The 1st Brigade, 101st Airborne had been in Vietnam almost a year, and the original members of the detachment were nearing the end of their tours. It was a whole new beginning, and Lieutenant Stevenson and Master Sergeant Chassion were charged with a complete reorganization of the detachment. Their job was easier because of their experience of the past six months. They just had to find that certain quality in a man that would enable him to operate as a Lurp. Among others, they found it in the person of a young sergeant by the name of John Dietrich.

John Dietrich was born, grew up, and graduated from high school in Baltimore, Maryland. He entered the army in July 1959 at Baltimore's induction center. He had grown up hearing

World War II and Korea paratroop stories from family friends, and even though he had never even flown in an airplane, he knew he wanted to be a paratrooper. After basic, AIT (advanced infantry training), and jump school, he was assigned to the 82nd Airborne Division, then later to the 505th Parachute Infantry Regiment in Mainz, Germany, where he served for eighteen months. In 1962 he was reassigned to the 501st Parachute Regiment, 82nd Airborne Division, at Fort Bragg, North Carolina. In 1962, under the ROAD doctrine, the battle group was reorganized into battalions. The proud, traditional regiments were redesignated as "brigades" numbered one, two, and three, and the battalions of each brigade came from different regiments. In 1964, as an acting sergeant, Dietrich went to Raider school at Fort Bragg, and then attended jumpmaster school. In 1965 he was deployed to the Dominican Republic with the 82nd. In the early part of 1966 he attended Ranger school. That was the final finishing school for Sgt. John Dietrich because already Vietnam loomed large in his future.

Dietrich arrived at the 101st Replacement Center at Phanrang in May 1966. While he was in Phan-rang, Lieutenant Stevenson, Master Sergeant Chassion, and Jack Waymire from the LRRP detachment were recruiting. John Dietrich remembered having seen Master Sergeant Chassion while training at the Advanced Airborne school, at Fort Benning, and he recalled that Chassion was the old head on the Advanced Airborne Committee. Well, they gave him their "Be all you can be" and "Sneak around for a year in the bush and recon" pitch, and John Dietrich was recruited right there. With him came a good friend named Paul "Country" Miller, a career NCO from southern Alabama. Having been with recon units in the 82nd Airborne, Miller also volunteered for Lurps, and so did another of their friends, Sgt. Tommy Alsop.

Master Sergeant Chassion made a big impression, but so did Lieutenant Stevenson. John Dietrich recalls Lieutenant Stevenson as a dark-complected man with very dark eyes who wore his Lurp hat in such a way that he always looked as if he had just stepped out of the bush. Dietrich remembers him as a really good commander. After Stevenson left Vietnam, he sent a letter back to the unit, thanking all the guys for buying him a Corvette. Lieutenant Stevenson was a quiet guy, and quite the shark. Between missions, Dietrich saw card games go two and three days at a time. And of course, being a card player himself, Lieutenant Stevenson often went up and played the officers, too. Whether at the card table or planning an operation, Lieutenant Stevenson was high-speed and knew all the drills. It always impressed Dietrich that Stevenson was so mature for a mere lieutenant. Of course, having been a Special Forces NCO before going through OCS and winning his commission, it was probably only natural that Stevenson was more mature and confident than the average lieutenant.

After a couple of weeks, the Lurps had most of their team leaders. Lieutenant Stevenson and Master Sergeant Chassion had asked some of the original members to stick around to help train and reorganize the detachment. Along with John Dietrich, the new replacements were the following: S.Sgt. Charles "Pappy" Webb; S.Sgt. Ronald Pitts; Sgt. Joseph E. Griffis; S.Sgt. Percy W. McClatchy; S.Sgt. Paul "Country" Miller; S.Sgt "Fish" Carpenter; Sergeant Stoddard, S.Sgt. Wilbur Sumpter; Sgt. Rudy Rodriguez; Sgt. Melvin Ruttan; S.Sgt. Tommy Russell; Sgt. Jerry Lavecchia; Sgt. William "Uncle Earl" Wheeler; Sgt. Jerry Roth; Sp4. David Coffee; Sp4. Timmions; and Sgt. Thomas Moore. Sgt. William T. Sopko, Sp4. James Jergenson, and Sp4. Franklin Lee also volunteered during this period. Unfortunately, Sgt. Tommy Alsop broke his leg, and was evacuated to Hawaii.

John Dietrich and the rest of the volunteers were flown north to Dak-to, the brigade's new AO (area of operation). For most of them, it was their first passage into war.

**In early June 1966, two battalions (the 1/327th and the 2/502nd) were airlifted to Dak-to in Kontum Province, in the heartland of the Central Highlands, for Operation HAWTHORNE, and the mission was to relieve an ARVN Regional Forces company besieged by a large NVA force at the Tou Morong outpost, twenty kilometers northeast of Dak-to. Some particularly vicious fighting occurred**

in this area against the 24th NVA Regiment. Operation
HAWTHORNE was concluded on June 20. A major enemy unit
had been rendered combat ineffective. The 24th NVA Regiment suffered 1200 KIAs (killed in action) in its encounter
with the Screaming Eagles. The 1st Brigade, 101st Airborne,
had suffered 48 KIAs and 239 wounded. For its efforts the 1st
Brigade was awarded the Presidential Unit Citation for
extraordinary heroism during Operation HAWTHORNE.

## Dak-to

On arriving at Dak-to, Lieutenant Stevenson and Master
Sergeant Chassion put the newly reorganized LRRP detachment through two weeks of extensive training, passing on the
knowledge that would keep a Lurp team alive in the bush and
enable it to accomplish their mission. A high percentage of the
recruits had previous training at the Fort Benning Ranger
school, the Fort Campbell Recondo school, the Special Forces
training group at Fort Bragg, or the 82nd Airborne's Raider
school, also at Fort Bragg. Even so, they had much to learn.

The teams were all new, and they had to hone their skills as
units. During short patrols out of the brigade area, they worked
on team integrity and immediate action drills, and went over
their team standard operating procedures.

The AN-PRC-74 UHF and single-side-band radio showed
up during this time, and the teams underwent training with the
beast. The brigade staff wanted Lurps to have long-range communications capability and pushed this particular radio on
them. At thirty-four pounds, the PRC-74 was a monster to
pack, both for its weight and for its bulk, which made it hard to
attach on a rucksack. The Lurp teams had trouble calibrating
the antennae and short-circuiting the radios. Staff Sergeant
Lambert, the detachment communications sergeant, worked
with the team RTOs to correct the problems, but the teams still
didn't like the PRC-74 because you had to be based up in order
to use it. It took time to string the antennae and calibrate the set.
The PRC-74 had a nickel-cadmium battery dry pack that held
seventy BA-30 batteries but wouldn't hold their charge. Even

so, the Lurp teams took the radios out in the field, tried them, and found them sorely lacking. The PRC-25 radio was proven as a very capable radio and the preference of the recon teams, but even so, months after the Lurps got fed up with the short-comings of the PRC-74, teams were still having to hump the damn things and trust them with their lives.

Country Miller and John Dietrich recall attending a survival class put on by two of the other men. The two trainers had chickens for a demonstration. One of them grabbed a chicken, cut its head off, peeling the skin back on the neck, and started sucking the blood out. People started falling out, gagging, and laughing and carrying on. Then the trainers turned the remaining chickens loose, and the other men had to chase them down. It was hilarious fun, but it was also a pretty good meal.

Sgt. John Dietrich was assigned as junior scout on S.Sgt. Percy "Mac" McClatchy's Team Three. McClatchy was a big bear of a man, around 240 pounds of solid muscle. He was hard-headed but fair, a man who always looked after the interests of the team. The other members of the team were S.Sgt. Donald Davis, senior scout (one of the original Lurps); and Sgts. Rudy Rodriguez, RTO; Thomas Moore, RTO; and Melvin Ruttan, medic. A stickler for schedules, Mac would come out of the premission briefs with a piece of paper detailing the schedule for team preparations right up to the moment the helicopters lifted off. Dietrich soon came to look on Mac as a mentor. John would later reverse some of McClatchy's leadership style, but he would adopt the way McClatchy operated.

S.Sgt. Paul "Country" Miller had initially wanted to be the operations sergeant for the LRRP detachment, but during his selection interview, Lieutenant Stevenson and Master Sergeant Chassion asked him if he would take a team-leader's position. Country accepted and was given Team Four. The other team members were Sgt. William Sopko, Sp4. James Jergenson, Sgt. Wilbur Sumpter, and Sp4. Franklin Lee as a medic. One man assigned to Team Four left shortly after training began, so it operated with five men throughout the time they were together.

McClatchy's and Country Miller's teams did a walk-out training mission from the brigade perimeter. The teams had to cross the Dak Pocko River, a major drainage for the area. They found two Montagnard canoes, paddled one across, set up a safety line, and used the safety line and canoes to ferry the team across. The river was pretty swift and had large boulders and holes. They had ferried one load across, and Country Miller and an RTO were next. Dietrich describes Country Miller as having that little-bear look: he was built stocky, square, like a wall locker with arms and legs. John Dietrich and Doc Ruttan made up the last load. As Country Miller's load was crossing, the RTO leaned back, and the ass end of the canoe started filling then flipped over, and all three men were in the water. Two of them paddled to shore, but Country Miller was being swept downstream. Running alongside him on shore, John Dietrich and Doc Ruttan managed to grab him by a patch of hair on his head. They dragged him up on the bank and froze the rest of the night. Funny thing: Miller had on all his gear, and never lost any of it. That set Dietrich to wondering if Country Miller hadn't been walking on the bottom.

Three teams, plus the headquarters element, were taken to an ASA (Army Security Agency) site called Tou Morong Outpost, on a steep, tall mountaintop. The ASA was using the site to eavesdrop on enemy radio communications with sophisticated hardware. The Lurps had to provide security because two ARVN (Army of the Republic of Vietnam) Ranger companies had recently been pulled off the outpost. It had been attacked two days prior to the Lurps' arrival.

The teams were on edge during the first night at the outpost, and the weather was very cold. Dietrich recalls that the next morning they were feeling more confident, perhaps even a little overconfident. Leaving his rifle at his position, Dietrich started canvassing the area, souvenir hunting, working his way down the hill, when he spotted a small bamboo hootch about thirty yards down the hillside. Dietrich walked down and looked inside. Sitting there, his legs crossed, rocking back and forth, and mumbling to himself, was an NVA soldier. Next to him was an AK-47 with load-bearing equipment that had Chinese communist grenades attached to it. With his heart in his mouth, Dietrich managed to say, "All right buddy, come on out of there!"

Dietrich was foolishly unarmed, and giving commands in a language the enemy soldier didn't understand, but he damn well meant it, and he must have had the sound of authority in his voice, for the enemy soldier crawled out, and Dietrich commenced to grab his equipment. He had the enemy soldier's AK-47 and grabbed that LBE with its Chi-com grenades. When Dietrich came trucking up the hill with his prisoner, people started diving for weapons. Then they realized what was happening and started laughing. Dietrich had captured an enemy soldier with the enemy's own weapon, which normally would be quite a feat. But he couldn't take any pride in it, since it had only happened because he had foolishly left his own weapon behind.

Dietrich's prisoner was wearing a gray uniform, floppy hat, and Ho Chi Minh sandals. He was suffering badly from malaria, which had probably saved Dietrich's life. Evidently, after the NVA had attacked the hill and pulled back, they'd left the soldier because of his condition.

Lieutenant Stevenson created a ruse to influence the prisoner into cooperating with his interrogation. He had S.Sgt. Larry "Black Icicle" Forrest, who was on his last days in country, impersonate an officer. The prisoner was being held in one of the bunkers on the hill and was being pushed around and intimidated by Lieutenant Stevenson and Master Sergeant Chassion and several other Lurps. Then Black Icicle walked into the bunker and jacked Stevenson and Chassion to attention, along with everyone else in the bunker. He berated them and ordered the prisoner untied and given some C ration peaches, pound cake, and hot chocolate. Lieutenant Stevenson's plan worked: After eating, the prisoner sang like a bird, giving the location of a division-size headquarters and some new weaponry. The following day, the Black Icicle left for the rear, ending his days as a Lurp.

Around June 1966, the LRRP detachment had a change of command. Lt. Joel Stevenson, who had commanded the LRRP detachment since its inception, was going home, and passing command to 1st Lt. Robert Deason. M.Sgt. Phillip Chassion, the detachment first sergeant, was also leaving. Lieutenant Stevenson and Master Sergeant Chassion had been the catalysts and the foundation of the original LRRPs. The two men had combined their professional knowledge and formed a new special operations unit in the midst of a war—and done it twice, which was a very distinguished accomplishment. Master Sergeant Chassion was replaced by Master Sergeant Harvey, who was with the Lurps for only about two weeks before being replaced himself by Sergeant First Class Acevedo.

Of all the different missions that John Dietrich went on, one stands out because it scared the hell out of him. This was the second or third mission out of Dak-to, and not a shot was fired on it. McClatchy's team had been inserted northeast of Dak-to. Jumping out of the helicopter on insertion, the Lurps literally ran over and knocked down a montagnard and his two kids. The team policed up the three terrified montagnards, took them farther into the bush, then went into a 360-degree security wheel, each Lurp covering his sector of the circular perimeter while nervously thinking about the very near future.* It was an ugly moment; the mission was compromised: They were supposed to dispose of whomever had seen them. As the montagnards just sat there, wondering what was going to happen to them, McClatchy turned around and quietly said to his teammates, "Let's go."

With a sigh of relief, the team took off and left the montagnards. It was almost dark. They based up in the thickest vegetation they could find. Knowing that Dietrich was partially night-blind, Rudy Rodriguez tightened up with him. During the night, the team heard the leaves rustling and occasional twigs breaking. The Lurps concluded that the montagnards they had turned loose had ratted them out to the enemy. They

---

*In the security wheel, the Lurps formed a small circle, each Lurp facing outward—his legs pointing toward the center—and having responsibility for the sector to his front.

lay there for thirty to forty-five minutes as the noise got closer and closer. Without warning, a horrendous, blood-curdling scream sounded. It was as if somebody was skinning a woman with a knife.

Rodriguez reached over, grabbed hold of Dietrich, and whispered in his ear, "If we haul ass out of here, you just hold on to my LBE. I got my knife in my left hand, and my weapon is on automatic. You just be shooting to the right, and I'll be shooting to the left. We're going to run through their asses!"

Just then about fifteen more screams rang out. The Lurps had just jumped up and were ready to run, when a flight of big, startled birds flew right through the team's position. Rodriguez fell on his back. Dietrich bounced off some bamboo and fell down. It took a second or two to realize what had happened and to recover from it. The Lurps had seen big, turkey-size birds before during daylight but had never heard them scream. They must have been feeding when the team's sudden move- ment startled them. Dietrich made up his mind, right then, never to get caught in that position again; getting spooked and damn near panicked by birds was hardly befitting an Airborne Ranger/Long Range Recon Patrol paratrooper.

Just before first light, the team left the night-halt position, moving out at triple time. They walked about four and a half miles, trying to put some distance between themselves and the bird scare site.

## Pitts Mission

On 20 June 1966, shortly after the bird scare, brigade staff decided to send three teams out in support of 1/327 and 2/502 operations then going on northeast of Dak-to. Operations and Intelligence wanted to confirm that a major ridgeline adjacent to the maneuvering battalions' operational areas was under enemy control. S.Sgt. Ronald Pitts's Team One, S.Sgt. Country Miller's Team Four, and S.Sgt. Tommy Russell's Team Two got the missions.

Team Four, led by S.Sgt. Country Miller, had Sergeant Sopko, Sp4. James Jergenson, Sgt. Wilbur Sumpter, and Sp4.

Franklin Lee. Their helicopter had overshot the primary LZ
and landed on Team One's LZ shortly before Team One got
there. And it was not a smooth insertion. Sp4. James Jergenson
jumped out of the helicopter and fell backward when he
landed, knocking himself out cold. Jergenson was carrying the
PRC-74 radio, and the damn thing's weight had pulled him off
balance. He came to quickly, with a bruised head and ego, and
Team Four moved up a small hillside to wait for Team One to
insert and move out.

Team One's insertion went smoothly, the team going into
the same LZ that Team Four had used a few minutes earlier
and then moving away from the LZ to set a security wheel just
inside the jungle. Here, the team leader, Staff Sergeant Pitts,
and another man noticed smoke about two hundred meters
away. Pitts radioed the insertion helicopter to make a pass over
the area. The helicopter started taking fire immediately, and a
few seconds later the team received fire from three sides. Pitts
called for gunship support, and the gunships knocked out several enemy positions, enabling the insertion helicopter to come
back to extract the team. Unfortunately, going in was easier
than getting out. The helicopter couldn't set down because of
all the dead trees and stumps littering the LZ, so the team
couldn't reach the helicopter to get in. That was before ladders
were routinely available to helicopter crews supporting Lurps,
and it might have been a very touchy situation if Sgt. Jerry
Lavecchia, flying belly man, hadn't reached down and pulled
every team member, one at a time, into the helicopter while
they were under fire. It was definitely time to get out of there.
Staff Sergeant Pitts hadn't been able to accurately count how
big the force was they had encountered, but it had been
sizeable.

With gunfire coming from all sides and the surrounding hilltops, both teams asked for extraction. After both teams had
marked their positions with panels, Pitts's team called in gunship fire on the ridges overlooking the LZ, and that improved
matters somewhat.

Overhead, in what had been Team Four's infiltration helicopter, Lieutenant Deason decided to get Team One out first

and then work on Team Four. He radioed down to ask Country Miller if he thought he could stay in on the hillside, and Miller's reply was, "Negative." When Team One got out, Team Four moved down in the direction of the LZ and came under fire right next to the LZ. As the team came running up to the helicopter, Country Miller was bringing up the rear, providing all the cover he could, his M-16 really barking. As had happened with the previous extraction, the helicopter couldn't land, so Lieutenant Deason leaned out and dragged everyone in. Again, the extraction was performed under fire without casualties, but when the extraction ship let the team off at Dakto after the mission, Franklin Lee got out of the helicopter, knelt down, and vomited. His teammates were grateful that he had refrained from vomiting on them in the helicopter.

Team Two, led by S.Sgt. Tommy Russell, had gone into another LZ, about one thousand meters away. The team got in safely, except for Sgt. Samson Seal, who suffered a broken nose when his radio handset bounced up and hit him after he jumped from the hovering helicopter. The team moved into the jungle and set up a security perimeter. A few minutes later, S.Sgt. Russell received a call from Lieutenant Deason stating the team would be extracted in a few minutes. But the extraction wasn't completed that night because Staff Sergeant Russell took a punji stake wound through his foot while moving to the LZ, which slowed him down some, and darkness set in before the team could be extracted. Early the next morning, an enemy soldier walked into the patrol's area. The Lurps tried to capture him but were forced to shoot him as he ran, giving away their position. Of course, if they'd let the enemy escape alive, he would have given it away, anyway. A couple of minutes after the Lurps had killed the soldier, two more Charlies came down to investigate, and Team Two killed both of them. Attracted by the team's fire, a whole mob then descended on the Lurps, and a fierce firefight quickly developed. Three World War II–era propellor-driven A1-E Skyraider fighter/bombers arrived to give a hand and Staff Sergeant Russell quickly put them to work. By mainstream aviation standards they were obsolete, but they found their continued reason for existence as ground-support aircraft in Vietnam. Skyraiders were slow enough to be accurate. They could linger over a target longer than jets, and the pilots tended to have very big balls and little fear of diving low against enemy gunfire. Russell later commented that they could have spit on the Skyraiders as they worked out against the enemy. With such help, the Lurps were able to break contact. When a helicopter did come in, for some reason it could only take out one man, and that man had to be Staff Sergeant Russell, the wounded team leader. Uncle Earl Wheeler took over the team until, with the help of the Skyraiders and gunships, the rest of the team was extracted.

Lieutenant Deason later commented that with all those NVA around them, the teams had been very lucky to have gotten out with only a punji stake wound. He felt the teams had done a great job. All three teams had been more or less shot out of their LZs, but they had still accomplished their mission. They had found the NVA force, estimated at two full platoons, covering the ridgeline and hillside.

While in the Dak-to area, the LRRP detachment pulled numerous missions in conjunction with the 1st Brigade's operation to relieve Tou Morong Outpost. The heavily jungled mountains in that vicinity made LZs rare, which enabled the enemy to better monitor helicopter insertions within their areas of operation. Contact was frequently made at, or close to, the insertion LZs, and fire on approach to LZs resulted in more than a few aborted Lurp missions. If you already knew the LZ was hot on the way in, you didn't send the Lurps in anyway—you backed off and called in the gunships or Skyraiders.

Country Miller recalls pulling several missions in support of the 2/502 Battalion, and he particularly recalls a mission close to the tri-border area, when a heavy fog enveloped the area, just after the team got off the helicopter. The Lurps could hardly see each other as they walked, and they had to secure positions in foxholes that the enemy had dug. They waited out the fog for three days, not knowing who was around them. During their stay, the team heard trucks, and what sounded like tanks, moving up and down a road, but because of the dense fog, they couldn't pinpoint the location of what they were hearing, and they couldn't get a visual sighting. Commo was terrible, but every now and then an airborne relay would come on station and check to see if the team was all right. On the third day, a helicopter pilot radioed the team and told them the fog might be lifting. Homing in on Country Miller's radio signal when the handset was being held on transmit, the pilot located the team and guided them to a clearing for extraction.

On checking his map after extraction, Country Miller discovered that his team had been across the national border of Vietnam.

**By mid-July, the 1st Brigade was back again in Tuy-hoa. For the first time since April, the entire brigade was united. With adequate time to rebuild and re-equip its line battalions, the Screaming Eagles prepared for Operation JOHN PAUL JONES. Their mission would be to secure Vung Ro Bay and the highway north out of Tuy-hoa, and to protect the important rice harvest in Phu-yen Province.**

### Teddy Bear

In an effort to keep the teams filled with the right sort of volunteer, the 1st Brigade LRRP detachment was almost constantly recruiting men. Not everyone was suited for Lurps. Some men volunteered out of line companies, trying to escape the danger, but then realized they had gotten more than they had bargained for. Others couldn't get a handle on the job during training or couldn't take the mission stress or just couldn't move quietly enough. On 20 July 1966, a young man who would eventually become one of the early record holders for seniority in the Lurps—two straight years—showed up at the LRRP detachment looking for a home. This was the great and infamous Allen "Teddy Bear" Gaskell.

Allen Gaskell was born in Brooklyn, New York, on 30 November 1946, and moved to Baldwin, Long Island, in 1949. He was raised in a blue-collar family, and his father was a construction contractor. He had two older brothers and was the youngest in the family. He went to Baldwin High School, where he was an average student, competed on the track team, and was elected student body president in his senior year, 1965. Apparently something of a straight-arrow and model youth, he was an Explorer Boy Scout, a member of the Order of the Arrow, an active member of the Methodist Youth Fellowship, and went to church even if his family didn't. We're talking 100 percent red, white, and blue here. Allen Gaskell was the sort who got goose bumps during the Pledge of Allegiance. His mother died during his senior year, and that's when he decided to join the army. Both of his brothers went on to college, one to Syracuse, and the other to Williams. In 1965, people were expected to go to work or go to college. The other alternative was to join the service. Gaskell decided to go into the Marines or the Airborne. The idea of jumping out of airplanes appealed to him. He had heard of Airborne all through high school, and Special Forces and the Green Beret were the big thing at the time. Earlier in his senior year he had asked about enlisting in the service, but the recruiter told him not to come back until he had graduated.

Gaskell entered the service on 16 August 1965. He went to Fort Dix, New Jersey, for basic training. His DI (drill instructor), was a huge, muscled black man, S.Sgt. Percy W. McClatchy. He would reappear in Allen Gaskell's life. Gaskell went to Advanced Infantry Training (AIT) as an RTO at Fort Dix, and then on to Fort Gordon, for training as a radio-teletype operator, where he learned Morse code. The MOS (military occupational specialty) for radio-teletype operator was O5C. He had a hard time getting to jump school because the army wanted to send him to Fort Hood, Texas. When Allen went to see the IG (inspector general) to complain that he'd enlisted to go Airborne, he was told he had no choice but to go to Fort Hood instead. Gaskell told the IG that he had called his congressman about jump school, which really got the IG's attention. He jacked Gaskell to attention and accused him of playing politics by going outside the service and his chain of command. He wouldn't be going anywhere in this man's army, by God! But that afternoon, his orders for Fort Hood were canceled, and he had orders for jump school. Teddy Bear had never actually talked with anyone at his congressman's office because it had been closed when he called, but he had left a message. By the spring of 1966, whole legions of young American men were taking desperate measures to avoid military service and the possibility of going to Vietnam, but Gaskell had taken desperate measures to go Airborne, which ensured that he would go to Vietnam. Sure enough, right out of jump school he was given orders to the 1st Brigade, 101st Airborne Division, Republic of Vietnam. He got some leave time and headed home, saw all his neighbors, and broke a lot of hearts. He was home for the Fourth of July, and the neighborhood where he grew up always had big block parties for the Fourth of July. That year, the block party served as his farewell. He met a girl on that leave—Mary Beth—and they had a passionate, long distance romance by mail.

I have to jump ahead here in my narrative in order to explain the nickname given to Allen Gaskell. Teddy Bear was named by yours truly, and by the general agreement of the rest of the Lurps. The nickname was given to him partially because of his demeanor but mostly because when he was wet he looked like a teddy bear. Teddy Bear was an outstanding Lurp, but maybe not the most typical one. One of his favorite sayings about Lurps was that he "loved the excitement and adventure of Lurping, but hated the violence."

Teddy Bear arrived in Saigon and went to Camp Alpha for less than twenty-four hours before being shipped out to Phanrang and the 101st. During his Primary training, Staff Sergeants Griffis and Pappy Webb came down to the area, and announced to the trainees that they needed certain MOSs for the Long Range Reconnaissance Patrol. They were looking for anybody who had Special Forces or Ranger training or was O5C trained. At that time the Lurps were getting ready to carry radios (PRC-74) that could use Morse code to effectively transmit longer distance. To Teddy Bear, those guys, with their boonie hats and their faded fatigues, were awesome. They looked real strac, and he really wanted into that unit. Teddy Bear and a friend of his named Allen Balcom had gone through

AIT together, and both volunteered for the Lurps. Along with them came David "Fireball" Dixon. They were taken out of P (proficiency or preparatory) training, and within a day were shipped up to Tuy-hoa. They joined the LRRP detachment on 20 July 1966.

Teddy Bear remembers that the training was really intensive and lasted three weeks. New guys underwent Ranger-type training all day long, starting at 0500 hours with lots of PT, wrestling, and hand-to-hand. They did rappeling, climbing, classes on E&E (escape and evasion), weapons recognition, demolitions, map reading, compass, and night movement. They had to cross-train for different positions on a team. All of the older guys were very helpful and fair, but they were tough. Some of the guys who volunteered for Lurps were washed out or quit. Finally, Teddy Bear went out on his first training mission.

## Training Mission

S.Sgt. Percy W. McClatchy was Teddy Bear's training team leader—the same McClatchy who had locked his heels at Fort Dix, the same one who had seen him as a loathsome civilian and had had the monumental task of turning him into a lean, mean, fighting machine.

Teddy Bear describes McClatchy as "a big guy, and quiet. About as black as you can get, real muscled; not a loud guy. He carried a Bible with him, and would read it often. He was real strac when he went out in the field, and he knew his stuff. Some guys accepted him, but there were some who didn't. It could have been racism, but I don't think it was that. You know, John Buford was black, and everyone liked him. I just think [it was because] McClatchy didn't take any bullshit from anyone. He went by the book, he knew what he was doing, and he would tell someone if something was off the wall. McClatchy was not a diplomat."

Teddy Bear's first training mission was in the mountains just south of Tuy-hoa. They got inserted in a hot area, and without knowing it, they had been put in an infantry battalion's area of operation. They landed at last light, in a swamp. As he jumped out, the medic made contact right away, letting off a couple of bursts, and then a couple of grenades came in. The team broke contact, and went into E&E. Finding a good location, they went to ground and laid dog. They were in a swamp, and Teddy Bear couldn't hear much because of the mosquitoes. The buzzing was like a siren, but the six silent men could hear Charlie looking for them, crashing through the brush, and splashing through the water.

When the sun came up nobody was around. The team was near a small stream that drained the swamp area. They walked up the stream a ways and then pulled away from it to firmer ground. A squad of VC walked by, laughing and talking, unaware of the team. The Lurps let them pass. They then found a couple of two-thousand-pound bombs that had failed to explode when they were dropped. They reported the bombs but didn't try to blow them. That afternoon, as they were getting ready to move out, H&I (harassment and interdiction) artillery rounds fired by a friendly unit came in on the team. They took some secondary shrapnel, and that's when they realized they were in someone else's area of operation. The team had a major problem: because a large mountain stood between them and base, it had no radio communication. They would have to wait until the bird dog* was up to relay radio messages the following morning. They also heard a firefight within a quarter mile of their location, and realized that one of our infantry units was operating near them. They were in the wrong place and had to endure the sporadic H&I firing during the night.

Staff Sergeant McClatchy made contact with the bird dog that evening. About the same time, Teddy Bear almost killed a bunch of monkeys. "We were right near the top of a wooded hill and close to the base of some large rocks," he recalls. "Victor Cisneros and I heard what sounded like people coming, and they sounded like they would be walking right into us. We were ready to blow them away. We could hear

*A Cessna L-19 which the army christened the O-1, in Vietnam the bird dog was used for reconnaissance, radio relay, and forward air (artillery) control.

*whoom! whoom!* and suddenly these monkeys looked over the top of the rocks. I remember McClatchy looking at me with the biggest smile on his face. He knew what they were, and he knew that I was just scared shitless!"

That evening, the Brigade S-2/S-3 realized that the team was in the wrong area when it took artillery H&I fire again. The following morning Staff Sergeant McClatchy's training team was extracted. Repercussions from this mission were felt by the LRRP detachment commander Lt. Robert Deason, who was relieved of command of the LRRP detachment. There was a controversy within the brigade as to who was at fault for inserting the Lurp team into the wrong area. All of the Lurps sided with Lieutenant Deason, feeling that he stood up for the men and was squared away. They also felt "officer politics" was coming into play, and Lieutenant Deason was the scapegoat. But for whatever reason, Brig. Gen. Willard Pearson relieved Lieutenant Deason of command. First Lt. Robert Friedrich was then placed in command of the LRRP detachment. He was a graduate of West Point and had been a training officer at the Recondo school in Fort Campbell, where some of the older NCOs in the detachment had known him. They told an amusing story about him unintentionally letting a raccoon out of a trash can during a classroom demonstration. The coon immediately ran up into a large tree. The lieutenant valiantly climbed up into the tree to capture the animal, whereupon the coon flew down the tree and attacked his ass, causing him to fall out of the tree.

Tuy-hoa was a very interesting place for the Lurps. John Dietrich remembers what he called a "wild ass mission," where a team was loaded on two Lambretta cyclos to insert. It was a crazy idea and lasted only long enough for everyone to see the foolishness of cyclo insertions. Some of the older, more experienced, Lurp NCOs had real questions about a few of Lieutenant Friedrich's ideas for running Lurp missions.

A Korean battalion was working in conjunction with the 1st Brigade in Tuy-hoa. When the VC command-detonated a 155mm howitzer shell, killing the whole staff of the battalion, including the battalion commander, the Koreans went in, cor-

doned and secured the whole place, and wouldn't let anyone
into the area. They killed every animal and human near the
small village where the event occurred. Not even a chicken
was alive when the Koreans got done.

## Percy W. McClatchy, KIA

In early August 1966, Staff Sergeant McClatchy's team was
assigned a recon mission south of Tuy-hoa. Team members
would be S.Sgt. Donald Davis, Sgt. Melvin "Doc" Ruttan, Sgt.
Rodolfo "Rudy" Rodriguez, and Sgt. Jerry Lavecchia. Lavecchia was the operations sergeant and was filling in for John
Dietrich, who had been dusted off because of his severe dysentery. The team went in and did a normal five-day terrain walk.
The mission had been uneventful, just a few sightings to be
reported, but on the morning of extraction, there was heavy
cloud cover and rain. Finally the cloud cover lifted, and the
extraction ship was coming in to take the team out. The team
held up on the periphery of the LZ in a 360-degree security
wheel. Staff Sergeant McClatchy stepped out to signal the
extraction ship with an orange panel, and one shot rang out.
Everyone immediately scratched dirt, looking for cover. They
called out a head count, and McClatchy didn't respond. Doc
Ruttan looked over at Staff Sergeant McClatchy, called again,
and received no response. Doc crawled over. Mac was sitting
on the ground facing outward, his rucksack on and his head
slumped to the side. He had been shot through the throat and
jugular vein, and his spinal cord was severed. He was dead. A
lone VC must have been watching the LZ and shot him.

McClatchy was a huge man; when the team's helicopter
landed, it took most of the team to lift the team leader's body
into the helicopter. It was a tremendous loss for the detachment
to have lost a man of his caliber—and especially to lose him by
such a fluke. S.Sgt. Percy W. McClatchy was killed in action
on 13 August 1966.

## Reynel Martinez
### Man Left on the Ground

S.Sgt. Donald Davis took over what had been Staff Sergeant McClatchy's team. The team then consisted of Sgt. John Dietrich, senior scout; Sgt. Rudy Rodriguez, junior scout; Sp4. "Doc" Ruttan, medic; and Sp4. Tom Moore, senior RTO. Sgt. Alfred "Fred" Hernandez, who was working as a junior RTO, had just been assigned to the team. Hernandez had recently come to Vietnam from, of all places, Alaska.

The detachment was working out of Tuy-hoa North and was given a standard recon mission. Several teams were to be inserted that evening, and Staff Sergeant Davis's team would be the last one in. Their insertion helicopter made several fake landings and then missed the primary LZ, inserting the team on its secondary LZ. As the helicopter flared to land, it took a B-40 rocket hit in the tail section. Luckily for everyone on the aircraft it was very close to the ground, so the hit just caused the chopper to slam down hard. At first, Sergeant Dietrich thought they had hit a tree coming in on the LZ. The team got thrown around by the aircraft's rough landing, then came tumbling out of the helicopter. They quickly formed a defensive perimeter around the aircraft. The door gunners dismounted their machine guns and filled in on the perimeter wheel the team had set up. They were in a small clearing, with a tree line not twenty-five meters away, and they were soon taken under fire by the enemy from several locations.

Sergeant Hernandez was carrying one of the radios for the team, and Sergeant Dietrich suddenly realized that in the heat of the action, Hernandez had unknowingly reverted to his native language and was giving the crucial information to the gunships in Spanish. Realizing what was happening, Doc Ruttan grabbed the handset and got Fred calmed down enough to start speaking English again. The gunships commenced their gun runs, and another slick came in, picking up the downed helicopter crew members and one member of the team. When the second bird came in, the rest of the team piled on and lifted off, but the pilot started hollering about a man still being on the ground. Suddenly the team realized that Fred Hernandez wasn't on the aircraft. Their helicopter banked around to return to the LZ to collect Hernandez, but another helicopter that had just finished inserting a team swung in and picked him up.

They ended up having to destroy the downed helicopter by having the gunships fire rockets into it, and the Lurps lost a radio and a couple of rucksacks that had been left in the aircraft. A half-moon-shaped piece of shrapnel from the B-40 blew through Tom Moore's rucksack, which stopped the piece just before it fully penetrated into his back. There was a moment of humor when Doc Ruttan placed a 4×4 dressing on Moore's back. The medic was trying to stop the bleeding, and was pressing firmly on the wound, when Moore got to hollering about him pressing so hard. Sergeant Dietrich told Moore that if Ruttan didn't press hard, he was going to bleed to death, which wasn't exactly true. But Moore quickly changed his tune and kept saying, "Press, press!"

### The Lurp Earring, a Family Tradition

Shortly after McClatchy was killed, a new tradition was formed in the Lurps. It would last until the 1st Brigade LRRPs were disbanded. Sgt. Rudy Rodriguez, now on John Dietrich's team, was from Calixico, California. One day in Tuy-hoa, during the rainy season, Sergeant Rodriguez told the team that they had to do something special for the group, something that would bring luck. Rodriguez brought out a box of gold earrings, which had recently been sent by his grandmother. She was one of the old folks who strongly believed in traditions, and she believed that if a man wore an earring in his left ear, no harm would come to him. Now they weren't just wire earrings; they were *thick* gold earrings, almost like a lead pencil at one end. This was John Dietrich's first encounter with earrings. Suddenly, all the guys were punching holes in their ears. They would get a shot of lidocaine in the ear then jam an eighteen-gauge needle through it. Well, the rest of the guys were doing it, so Dietrich did, too. But about two weeks later, Dietrich got half shit-faced, and as he was going through the tent opening in the operations tent, his earring caught on the tent zipper and just about jerked the side of his head off. That was the end of his earring days, but the rest of the team continued to wear them.

Meanwhile, Sp4. Allen "Teddy Bear" Gaskell was filling in on various teams. He served under a rich selection of team leaders, including S.Sgt. Joe Griffis, Sfc. Jim "Fish" Carpenter, S.Sgt. Charles "Pappy" Webb, and S.Sgt Ronald Pitts. Ages in the LRRP detachment varied from Teddy Bear, who was nineteen years old, to Pappy Webb, the oldest at thirty-six. Most of the senior NCOs were on their second tour and had at one time or another been in Special Forces. At Tuy-hoa, Teddy Bear shared a hootch with Sp5. Jim "Jimbo" Bethel, and Sp4. David "Fireball" Dixon. For a long time, most of the men in Lurps didn't know that Fireball was an orphan and had been raised at Boy's Town. They just wondered why Fireball never received any mail.

A Special Forces A-camp located northwest of Tuy-hoa was used as base camp for several Lurp missions. A major operation was in progress, and the Special Forces camp was a staging area. Teddy Bear recalls that they were sitting around between missions one day, when some AP reporters came by and asked them what the war was like. The Lurps commented that it was hell, but they were just kidding around. They were actually enjoying not being out in the field, and at that moment it wasn't hell, at least not for them. However, a couple of days later they were quoted in *Stars and Stripes* as saying how much hell the whole thing was.

As the operation wound down, the Lurps were going to do an insertion to monitor a couple of infantry AOs where they had already spent quite a bit of time. Staff Sergeant Pitts's team, with Teddy Bear assigned, had been doing a lot of these missions, and the men were tired. The team was inserted pretty close to the coast, and as soon as they landed, firing broke out. Teddy Bear was facing toward the rear and just firing away into the fields. He suspected the men of the team were faking a firefight to get extracted. But then some rounds went right over his head, so he turned around, and yelled at the rest of the team. "Watch it! I'm over here, you know!"

Some more bullets went over his head, so he turned around again, and he saw Staff Sergeant Pitts looking pretty pale. They were in a real firefight, but Teddy Bear hadn't realized it. They were only on the ground for about ten minutes when Pitts called in the choppers to get them out. Everybody thought it was pretty funny that Teddy Bear had gone through a firefight without knowing he was in one. Fake a firefight? The older Lurps laughed at Teddy Bear. Why, Lurps would never do anything like that.

About that time the Lurp missions began to change, the teams were being used by the line battalions as a form of bait— which struck Teddy Bear as being the job of battalion recon platoons, like the Tiger Force. On one occasion the battalion commander wanted Ron Pitts's team to go in, even though it was certain that the VC had the LZ covered. The Lurp teams were to initiate contact, and once they did, a reaction force would be in the air. Pitts was told that they could expect 100 percent casualties on the mission.

Even so, the team prepared to go. But that night around 0100 hours, the mission was aborted when General Pearson apparently found out about it. He didn't want his Lurps being used like that, so he chewed out the battalion commander for trying to waste them, and the team never went in. They woke the team up and informed the Lurps that the mission had been canceled by the general. At that point Teddy Bear mentioned to Sgt. Samson Seal that he might still make it to the ripe old age of twenty. Teddy Bear's surviving to his twentieth birthday became something of a standard joke within the team after that.

**In late October, the 1st Brigade turned over responsibility for the security of the area around Tuy-hoa to elements of the Republic of Korea 9th (White Horse) Division and the U.S. 4th Infantry (Ivy) Division, which had just arrived in Vietnam.**

**The brigade moved to a secured area on the coast south**

of Tuy-hoa, and spent several days resting and recuper-
ating from their nomadic role as the MACV (Military
Assistance Command, Vietnam) fire brigade. During this
lull in the action, the brigade was notified to ready itself
for Operation GERONIMO I. Intelligence reports indicated
the 95th NVA Regiment was operating in the mountains
in western Phu-yen Province, and its presence was a
threat to the rice-bowl area around Tuy-hoa. Once again,
the battalions of the 1st Brigade were given the task of
finding, fixing, and finishing the enemy.

## Boyhood Friends

Gene Sullivan was born 24 October 1944 in Camden, New
Jersey, and grew up in a typical middle-class suburban environment. He played football and other sports in high school
and worked hard academically. He went to Ryder College in
Trenton, New Jersey, for a year but ended up flunking out,
probably out of boredom. Gene joined the army on the buddy
plan, as Airborne Unassigned, with his longtime boyhood
friend, Bruce Redmer. They went through basic training at Fort
Dix, New Jersey, and advanced infantry training at Fort
Gordon, Georgia, then on to jump school at Fort Benning.
When they got out of jump school in August 1965, both of
them were assigned to Fairbanks, Alaska, as part of a group of
150 paratroopers who were going to be used in experimental
cold-weather warfare, the 171st Airborne Company. Of the
800 paratroopers who graduated with Gene, most of them went
to Vietnam. Alaska was cold weather country, where tempera-
tures would drop down to 60 below zero in the winter and
where there was no daylight over half the year. They did a lot
of garrison duty, with the normal peacetime-army soldiering.
Their squad leader, Sgt. Alfred "Fred" Hernandez, was good-
looking, smart, and crazier than a March hare. He was Cuban
and had a burning desire to liberate Cuba. Three years later,
Freddy would set a trend by hijacking an airliner to Cuba. A
friendship was struck among the three that would last a lifetime. Everyday, a five-mile cross-country ski run was part of

the company physical training, and Freddy sneaked a bottle of wine in skin gourds on the runs. They would take a short cut and drink the wine, until they were caught one day, which was the end of that.

Sullivan and Redmer both rose to the rank of sergeant (E-5), and Freddy was promoted to staff sergeant (E-6). It was an eighteen-month tour of duty, but after eleven months many of the men decided they wanted more adventure in their lives. In order to get out of Alaska, they had to either reenlist, or volunteer for Vietnam. Eight of them volunteered for service in Vietnam at the same time. They got what they wanted, but even though they were all friends, they went to different outfits.

Sullivan and Redmer arrived in Long Binh, South Vietnam, on 27 August 1966. During the first week in September, they were both assigned to a security unit in Saigon. They had lost track of S.Sgt. Freddy Hernandez at Long Binh. After spending four weeks in the "Pearl of the Orient," doing guard duty, they were reassigned to the 1st Brigade, 101st Airborne. When they arrived at Phan-rang for P training, they learned the Lurps were recruiting. Sixty people applied for three positions, and Sullivan and Redmer were two of the three candidates selected. But something happened with Redmer's orders, and even though he had been selected, he was shipped to an infantry line company.

Gene Sullivan recalls arriving in Tuy-hoa in late October and finding that Fred Hernandez was already there. He'd had no idea where Hernandez was until then. Seeing him in the Lurps was great. Sullivan was one of the youngest guys at that time, and it meant a lot to see a familiar face in Lurps. "The first thing I realized about a Lurp unit is that there are only six guys out there, and it's 'all for one, and one for all.' It's just like the Three Musketeers and that was not just rhetoric. They were dead serious about it. So my first day there, Freddy was telling me about wearing the earring for good luck. And the next thing I know, a couple of the guys came in with a bottle of Australian whiskey. They told me to take a couple of slugs, and I did. One of the guys, who was a medic, pierced my ear with a needle, then put a little string through it. He told me to just move it around a couple times a day, and I'd be fine."

It was a tradition that lived on long after Sullivan was gone. This was in 1966, and men piercing their ears was unheard of then, especially in the military.

At first, Sullivan was part of the headquarters contingent, not part of the recon teams that were going out from Dong Tre Special Forces Camp. There were tough nights—the guys going out by helicopter or sometimes just by foot. But he was there to monitor the radio and keep track of things. From that hilltop, Sullivan could see the Lurps' area of operation, and he developed a newfound respect for them. On his watch, a couple of them came back a little bloody; nobody got whacked real hard, just shrapnel incidents when the teams got into it with NVA units.

Sgt. Gene Sullivan was eventually assigned to S.Sgt. John Dietrich's recon team. His first mission was out of Tuy-hoa, with S.Sgt. Fred Hernandez, senior scout; S.Sgt Ron Sumpter, junior scout; and S.Sgt. Jerry Lavecchia, team medic. It was a standard six-man team, all experienced guys, with Sullivan, an E-5, the lowest-ranking member of the group.

Gene Sullivan recalls that it was his first time in the bush, and he was very green. "The first night on watch, around the middle of the night, I heard, 'Fuuck you, fuuuck you,' and I was so frightened that I remember waking up Fred, saying it was the NVA, telling us to go fuck ourselves. Fred had to point out that, no, that wasn't the case, it was a lizard. I look back on that now, and laugh."

One thing that the Lurps taught Gene Sullivan right away is that you don't fight the jungle; you learn to glide through so you're not breaking branches. He learned how to walk and how to listen. He learned how to quickly distinguish between the sounds made by a two-legged animal and those made by a four-legged animal. It reminded him a little of playing cowboys and Indians when he was a kid. When Sullivan first got to Lurps, they handed him a card of Rogers Rangers Standing Orders from the French and Indian War. It was back to basics, only this time it was for keeps. It wasn't any "Bang,

bang, you're dead," then getting up again a couple of minutes later. This stuff was for real. He tried to marshal up all the knowledge from his past, to remember the common sense lessons he was given, to listen to things they were telling him: Don't silhouette yourself against the sun. Don't go where the water is, you'll bring them with you. Listen, listen, listen. . . .

"I remember cursing myself," Sullivan recounts: "This never went away. Whenever we would get dropped into an LZ, you didn't know if it was hot or what was going to happen. The helicopter would flare onto the LZ, the team would be out in a second. You would make the run to the wood line, drop into a 360-degree security wheel, and listen. When the chopper pulled out, it would be real quiet. Your heart would be beating so loud that once the chopper pulled out, you're lying there trying to listen. Your heart is beating so fast that you're cursing the fact that your heartbeat is interfering with your hearing. I never did get over that."

## Dietrich's Hole in the Hat

Lt. Robert Friedrich, aka "Wild Man" Friedrich, went out on one of his first missions with S.Sgt. John Dietrich's team.

"To me, he was clumsy as a bull in a china closet," Dietrich said. "After we had gone through a Montagnard village, he ordered everything burned, and as a matter of fact somebody wrote a jingle, 'The captain don't ride well anymore, he kills pigs chickens and cows by the score'—something like that. They would walk around singing it. The montagnards were making punji stakes in the village, and we found some military gear. Friedrich told the men to burn the place down. That's when we were getting into our regular line company deal, a two-team deal. We captured a Yard, and he was different from the rest of them that I had seen in the mountains. These lowland Yards wrapped their heads in a kind of a turban. I had never seen this before. So we put this dude in a chopper, and flew him out of there. Right after that, we were getting tracked. I guess we stayed in the area for two days, and we could tell we were being tracked all the time. The last morning before we got extracted, everybody was up one hundred percent alert. Finally, it got full daylight, and some of the guys were eating with Friedrich, while I had already done a brief walk around our position and was walking back into it. Friedrich stood up, and suddenly about ten rounds on automatic came in high from the bush. Lieutenant Friedrich threw himself on the ground. He had one of those CAR-15s, and he just opened up on spray and shot a hole through my bush hat. He shot a damn hole through my damn bush hat! I was hot! That was a damn learning experience with Friedrich for me. Of course, that wasn't the first time he had shot something up. In Tuy-hoa, he shot up one of the choppers one time. We were flying over the ocean, test firing some weapons—and I believe he had the damn same CAR-15—and shot about eight holes, shooting on auto into the edge of the chopper from the inside."

## Twenty Years Old

On 26 November 1966, the LRRP detachment was given a Patrol Warning Order for a team to be inserted into an area of operation that was being vacated by one of the line battalions of the 1st Brigade. Their mission would be to monitor the area for enemy forces infiltrating back into the AO.

S.Sgt. Charles "Pappy" Webb's team was picked for this mission. The team members were S.Sgt. Joe Griffis, senior scout; Sgt. William "Uncle Earl" Wheeler, junior scout; Sgt. Samson Seal, senior RTO; Sp4. Allen "Teddy Bear" Gaskell, junior RTO, and Sp5. Jim "Jimbo" Bethel, medic. The team was staging out of the Special Forces A-camp northwest of Tuy-hoa, Dong Tre, in the monsoon season, which meant the availability of flying weather would be unpredictable.

The team was inserted at last light on 29 November. The LZ was located at the base of a hill mass, and as the insertion helicopter was coming into the LZ, it flew alongside the hill and onto the LZ. On the side of the hill, Teddy Bear saw a group of VC who wore expressions like "What? Are you people fucking stupid, or what?"

The team landed, secured a defensive position, and radioed

the sighting into base. They were told by Lieutenant Friedrich to go back up the side of the hill, and confirm that the enemy was there. Almost everyone on the hill side of the helicopter had seen the VC, but they were not believed. That was when Teddy Bear learned that, as a Lurp, sometimes you had to make your own decisions—especially if you valued your team's lives and your own. Irrational or stupid orders had to be danced around and made to fit the situation. This wasn't giving license to shirk responsibilities or act in a cowardly manner; it was just good, healthy common sense.

Pappy Webb radioed back and acknowledged, confirming the enemy's presence, and the team waited in its defensive position. After a decent amount of time had passed, Pappy radioed in and reported negative sighting on the enemy. Lieutenant Friedrich transmitted some coordinates and told the team to move to that position. The team looked at their maps and saw it was a god-awful long distance and the march would take most of the night. Pappy Webb rogered the transmission, and when darkness fell, he moved the team to a secure NDP (night defensive position). Pappy Webb decided right there that moving in the dark, especially on the valley floor, would be hazardous to the team's health. He also felt there was plenty of good hunting right where they were.

The next morning, 30 November 1966, about 0700 hours, S.Sgt. Joe Griffis crawled up to Teddy Bear. He had a beat-up old brownie in tin foil that his wife had sent him. Stuck in the stale brownie was a little bent candle that he lit. In a whisper, his mouth next to Teddy Bear's ear, he sang "Happy Birthday" to Teddy Bear, in honor of his twentieth birthday. It was raining heavily, a dreary morning as Joe Griffis divided Teddy Bear's birthday brownie into six equal parts.

The Lurps had just finished eating their meager portions of brownie when they heard movement below. Through the foliage they could see VC on the march. About seventy of the enemy passed close to the team's position on an obscure trail. The six silent men watched and noted the packs and rifles carried by the VC. They had a woman in front of the line and were beating her with their rifle butts, kicking her up the trail.

S.Sgt. Pappy Webb radioed what they had seen back to base in a SALUTE (size, activity, location, unit, time, equipment) report, and, of course, Lieutenant Friedrich wanted to know how they had gotten back to that location. The team leader lied and told him they had come back early that morning for a specific bullshit reason. Then Lieutenant Friedrich gave an incredible order: "Make contact with them. We have a reaction force in the air!" Pappy Webb pointed out that there were seventy VC.

"Yeah," the lieutenant replied. "Make contact, we'll have a reaction force in the air."

"I'm going to get killed on my birthday!" Teddy Bear thought.

Teddy Bear always carried a spare handset because Pappy Webb had a bad habit—but only when he talked to Lieutenant Friedrich: He would get pissed off and throw the handset. It was attached to a coiled cord that stretched, and it would go whipping and bouncing, and Teddy Bear would be ducking, bobbing, and weaving, trying to avoid getting hit by it. It usually struck something and broke, and then Teddy Bear would grab his spare and fix it.

The VC had walked on by, and Pappy Webb informed Lieutenant Friedrich that the enemy was out of contact range. The lieutenant told the team to follow them and make contact and once again said that the reaction force was in the air, but he was just relaying what he was being told to say by the battalion commander.

The team started following the enemy force early that morning and dogged them all that day. But the reaction force never showed. Every time it looked as if they might have a chance to engage the enemy, they would call the rear to check on the reaction force only to be told that there was some kind of hangup, but the reaction force would be right there. By late afternoon, the team had moved quite a way, they could see the enemy as the VC were topping a hill. They called the rear, and Lieutenant Friedrich informed them that the reaction force was actually on the way this time.

As the enemy was cresting the hill, they suddenly reversed

movement and started walking back toward the team. They must have discovered that they were being tailed. Pappy Webb's team started falling back and was informed that the reaction force should be close to their position. The team prepared an LZ only to watch the reaction force helicopters swoop in and land—about five kilometers away, down the valley.

The VC were getting really close to the team, so the men began running. As the men were moving, the gunships showed up. Because the gunships were seeing several different squads moving in the same direction, and only one of them could be the Lurps, Pappy Webb stopped his men and circled them into a defensive position then popped a smoke grenade. The gunships started kicking ass on the VC. Finally, a helicopter came in and extracted the team and flew them about five kilometers to join the reaction force, where they spent the night.

Reflecting on the mission and values of the Lurps, Teddy Bear adds, "You made your own decisions. We knew what we saw, but they weren't going to believe it. That's okay, but we're not about to go get ourselves killed just because they don't believe us. That's about when I think the Lurps started to get used as bait, and the missions began to change from recon to something else, and that's where I first found out that sometimes you have to distort what you radio in. If you say you see something, and they say, 'Okay, go out and check it,' you know it's just a pork chop, and you're going to wind up getting hurt. But with Pappy Webb and the guys I learned from, you radio back and say you went back up there, and they were gone. We were not about to get killed to satisfy someone's curiosity.

"I was taught early on to respect the VC as a very formidable enemy, and also to respect the Vietnamese people. Many of the older guys had been in Special Forces before, and they'd had a number of tours and had worked with the locals. That was the focus that they used. They just didn't shoot up people indiscriminately.

"Standing orders said that we were supposed to kill anybody we came across to prevent being compromised. Once I went on a mission with Ron Pitts as the team leader, out of Tuy-hoa.

There was a battalion of VC working in the area, and we were to move into their AO. We came across a trail, and an old man and three old women came walking down the trail as we were crossing it. We had to stop them because they had seen us and because they were going right into the VC AO. This was the first time that we would have to kill anyone other than armed enemy. I was really wondering if we were going to kill them. So I radioed in and told the rear we had been compromised, and that we had these four people. Friedrich told us to waste them. Pitts rogered that, then said to us, 'Okay, let's get out of here,' and sent the old man and three ladies on their way. I asked him if we were going to kill them, and he explained that, no, you didn't shoot unarmed civilians like that. You just radioed that you did. I think that was the way the older Lurps looked at things. Of course it happened that these people went down and told the VC. We could see them coming back up the hill. So it turned out that they were sympathetic to the VC. But you don't shoot unarmed people: you take them prisoner or you let them go. You don't just kill them, and I kind of appreciated that.

"I guess that was the biggest difference between the early and the later platoon."

# 3

## LONG RANGE RECON
1    101

# Kontum

On 4 December 1966, the 1st Brigade was pulled back to Tuy-hoa for a much-needed rest. Many of the 1st Brigade troopers were recovering from foot problems brought on by the continuous patrolling in the rain-soaked coastal plains. Three days later, orders from I Field Force were received to prepare the brigade to move out by airlift to Kontum in the heart of the Central Highlands for the start of Operation PICKETT. For the first time in the Vietnam War, an entire brigade was moved from one place to another in less than forty-eight hours. On 9 and 10 December, all three battalions deployed into landing zones in and around the Plei Trap and Dak Akoi valleys, twenty-four miles west of Kontum.

### Big John's Punji Stake Wound

S.Sgt. John Dietrich remembers that one of the teams was doing a map recon when a Montagnard Cong walked up on them. The Lurps had stopped for a break, and one of the RTOs, a young black guy who hadn't been with the Lurps for more than a month, had grounded his gear. He turned around and realized the Cong was staring at him from the side of the trail. The Lurp was just about three meters off the trail, and when he reached to get his M-16, a little tree was in the way, and he couldn't get his M-16 pointed in the Cong's direction. All he

could see was the man from the chest up. Then the young black
Lurp saw this old Mauser coming up. The VC fired on him, hitting where his collar bone attached, and blew his damn right
shoulder off. The whole top of his shoulder bone was pro-
truding from the exit hole, but he could still function; he
grabbed his gear and weapon and ran with the rest of the team
about a half mile to meet the aircraft at the LZ. He was evacuated to Hawaii.

The medic pulling drag that day was Robert "Big John"
Johnson, from Pittsburgh. Johnson had played pro ball for a
little while and used to talk about it a bit. For some reason, Big
John had washed out from the Special Forces medic course.
That doesn't mean he was a second-rate soldier, nor does it
mean he was a second-rate medic. The SF medic's course was
incredibly difficult, and maybe when he got to the "dog lab"
phase of the training, he just drew a dog that lacked the will to
live. The detachment was short of medics, so they tended to
shift from team to team.

The team was moving out at a good clip with the injured
RTO when suddenly they spotted VC paralleling them. Big
John dove to the side and landed on a punji stake that went
through his boot and up through his instep, coming out the
other side of his foot. It was a terrible wound, but Big John
managed to hobble the rest of the way to the LZ and board
the extraction helicopter under his own power. He was one
tough dude.

Big John was carrying a 9mm British Sten gun with an
attached silencer, a canvas-wrapped barrel, and a wire-butt
stock. When it fired, the only thing you heard was the bolt
clacking back and forth. The Sten guns were magazine fed
from the side, which some people found a little hard to get
used to.

The Lurps had obtained the Sten guns in a little horse
trading with CCC/SOG (Command & Control, Central/
Special Operations Group) in Kontum. A couple of Lurps had
floated over to their camp beforehand and knew the SOG
Green Berets needed a .50 caliber machine gun for a mission
that their Lieutenant Sisler was planning. Next thing the Lurps

knew, they had been sweet-talked into signing over "the damn fifty caliber from the mess hall." The brigade headquarters mess hall deuce-and-a-half truck had a "fifty" ring mount, so they were assigned a "fifty." Dietrich says, "We went down and signed for the gun with S-2, talked to the mess sergeant, and hand receipted it to SOG. In return for that, they asked us if we wanted to use their special gear for awhile. Each of the teams got a 9mm silenced Sten gun. We packed those Sten guns the whole time we were up in Kontum. Later the SOG team that Lieutenant Sisler led was hit severely by the enemy. Lieutenant Sisler played a heroic part in the fight and was awarded the Medal of Honor for his actions. The mess hall never got back its fifty but they didn't seem to miss it."

Bob "Big John" Johnson was evacuated to 8th field hospital for three weeks. Everyone was surprised when the hospital sent him back so quickly because they had performed surgery on his foot. Dietrich says that the hole in Big John's foot was still infected, so Johnson sat in the tent at night using a syringe without a needle on it to inject hydrogen peroxide into the wound. It eventually healed, but Johnson went to the field while it was still draining; there just weren't enough medics to go around.

Country Miller was inserted once on a mission supporting the 2/502 Battalion. Country and Dietrich were pretty good friends. Dietrich was handling the radios at base camp. About that time, Lieutenant Friedrich was supposed to be promoted to captain. So on his evening report-in calls, Country would ask Dietrich if the commander was a footpath (for a lieutenant's single-bar insignia) or a train track, meaning captain (whose insignia is two parallel bars). Dietrich reported that unfortunately it was a train track. On the third day, Country's team found several NVA and needed artillery support. Because of the proximity of the enemy, Country had to use the squelch code on the radio to walk the artillery in close to his team. With Dietrich prompting for the information, Country supplied the answers with squelch breaks. It took teamwork and a knowledge of how the other man thought. The drama was played out with by-then Captain Friedrich hovering in the background.

After the artillery had come in, the enemy beat feet. Dietrich suggested to Captain Friedrich that Country Miller's cool performance on the radio warranted an award of a Silver Star. The captain's reply was that if Country Miller got killed, he would put him in for the decoration.

Eventually, out of disagreements with Friedrich about how LRRP missions were supposed to be run, Country Miller left the LRRP detachment, and that was a loss for the Lurps. For Country there was something special about being a Lurp. He felt just bringing everyone back alive from a mission was an accomplishment.

About this time, when the brigade moved to Kontum, close to the Cambodian border, and the Lurps were looking for some new people, Sullivan and Hernandez found Bruce Redmer again. The Lurps were operating around Dak-to, which was heavy duty because there were tons of NVA there.

## Coffee Insertion

Gene Sullivan was a member of Dietrich's team when they were inserted into what was supposed to be a hot area west of Dak-to. The chopper flared onto the LZ, which was covered with elephant grass. Elephant grass usually grew about six feet high—what the team expected the height of it to be at this LZ. Coffee, the senior scout, jumped out first. Without hesitating, everybody was right behind him, boom, boom, boom. Gene, who was right after Coffee, waited to see him hit the ground, but he just disappeared. Sullivan thought, "Oh Christ!" but of course, he was already in the air at that point. The elephant grass turned out to be fourteen feet high. And the LZ was on a steep slope. So when he landed, Sullivan tumbled head over heels backward. When Coffee landed, his ankle was tucked under him, and he snapped it. The rest of the team hit hard, but nobody else was seriously hurt. Coffee had to be medevacked. The second night, Gene Sullivan started getting the chills, his first bout with malaria, and he had to be medevacked out. They were out for four days but found only a cold recon zone.

When Dietrich's team got back to Kontum, Sullivan's temperature was 105 degrees so the medics stripped him down, put him on a cot with a rubber sheet, and packed him in ice. Then he was out of there and on his way to Qui-nhon.

## Getting to Lurps

I, Reynel "Marty" Martinez was raised in San Patricio, New Mexico, a small community nestled on the Rio Ruidoso (Noisy River) drainage, which flows from the southeast ranges of Sierra Blanca. Land of Enchantment, Land of Chile. Spelled with an *e*, not an *i*. No kidney beans or tomatoes to spoil the taste. Our chile was roasted, peeled, and eaten with a generous amount of garlic and a trace of salt.

The members of our broad community, populated by families of mainly Mexican ancestry, were all involved in ranching and farming. Raising sheep and apples was the economic backbone of the little valley. This was Lincoln County, home of Billy the Kid, Sheriff William Brady, Pat Garrett, and the rest of the history of the *guvachos*. My ancestors had settled in the area from Mexico in the 1800s.

My younger sister and I were adopted into the family of Isidro and Paublita Chavez, who was my aunt. It was a big family, eighteen children. Our mother had died when I was four, and my father had no one to take care of us. He was married and had thirteen children of his own so we lived for a year in Juarez, Mexico, with my mother's relatives. But my father didn't like that, so he appealed to his sister to take us in.

We arrived in San Patricio when I was five, in 1951. Lost in a sea of emptiness, trying to find a father, I was enrolled in school and started learning English. I gravitated toward Senon Chavez, my adopted brother. If there was ever a hero in my youthful life, it was Senon. He was a wild one, this Senon. Full of energy and relishing any excitement or danger, thirty-five years old when I arrived in San Patricio, he was a person with a gleam in his eye. He was small in stature but stout of heart.

In 1955 we had a five-year-old stud horse that roamed the range and had bred mares, but he'd never had a rope on him.

He was a typical crazy stud horse, and it was spring. The horse was named Alacran (Scorpion), in honor of his disposition. One day Senon ran the horse into the corral with some mares, cut him out, and with the help of half the men in the valley got the stud hog-tied and saddled. It was a big social event, with lots of wine being drunk. Then they turned Senon loose into an open area in the orchard. It was a rodeo, and as soon as Alacran unloaded him, Senon got back on. This went on through the morning, interspersed with hits of La Copita, the wine the men favored. Senon was getting into it, and so was Alacran. I was nine years old, and I was impressed. Alacran, full of piss and vinegar, was snorting, bucking, farting, and shitting, all at the same time, and having a harder time unloading his tormenter as the day wore on. By sheer imposition of his will, Senon broke that stud from bucking and eventually made him into a good saddle horse. I never forgot that.

As I got older, Senon took me under his wing, and I rode the range on horseback, helping him take care of our sheep and cattle. He taught me how to hunt, stalk, read sign, and kill and dress game. The family had two hundred head of sheep, and a pack of wild dogs could quickly annihilate a flock. Our job was to eliminate the dogs. Senon was a crack shot. About this time I started to realize that there was something more to Senon, something that he missed. During quiet times, he would sometimes get a faraway look, and his features would take on such sadness. Sometimes he would hit the wine bottle for days. I knew better than to ask why.

When I was twelve, Senon came home late one night. He woke me up, saying, "Hey, Ranger, you're not supposed to be sleeping on guard duty." He started talking to me all in Spanish, and I knew this would be a different conversation from the kind we normally had. He even told me so.

I knew Senon had been in the service, but had never heard him say much about it. That night he gave me a glimpse of, and told me about, the Rangers. He was passing a legacy on to me. In our wildest dreams neither of us could have ever envisioned what a role it would end up playing in my life. Looking back, I can see this talk served as a release for Senon and prepared and set my personal "rendezvous with destiny." For the first time in my young life, I heard about honor and devotion to duty and to the brotherhood forged in war. I also sensed just what a burden Senon was carrying with him. I heard about a man named Darby and an outfit called Darby's Rangers. Senon told me, "I died at Anzio." At that age, I couldn't understand the statement, but it intrigued me with its finality.

Darby's Rangers were assigned some of the most dangerous missions in World War II. They spearheaded all the major amphibious landings in the invasions of North Africa, at Arzew, Algeria, Gela and Licata in Sicily, Salerno and Anzio in Italy. When they landed, the Rangers' missions were to seize and destroy the enemy coastal defenses and set up the initial beachhead defensive perimeters.

The raid at Sened Station in Tunisia was one of the most successful missions that the Rangers performed. Making a hazardous traverse across terrain the enemy thought impassable at night, they attacked and overran an enemy position situated on high ground. The Rangers killed seventy-five of the enemy with knives and bayonets, capturing eleven men and the position's weapons. They suffered twenty casualties, with one dead. All that took place in less than thirty minutes.

The 1st Ranger Battalion executed another night attack of strategic importance one month later at Djebel el Ank Pass with the same results.

The Rangers spearheaded the land attacks in the major battles of Dernia Pass, El Guettâr in Tunisia—for which they were awarded the Presidential Unit Citation for distinguished action—and Gela, Licata, Porto Empedocle, Butera, Messina in Sicily, and onto the mainland of Italy in Chiunzi Pass at Salerno, Venafaro, San Pietro, and ending at Cisterna. The 1st and 3rd Ranger Battalions also won the Presidential Unit Citation for their actions at Salerno. They always led the way against incredible odds, and Senon Chavez had been with them all the way.

At Anzio, at 0100 hours on 30 January, the 767 men of the 1st and 3rd Ranger Battalions entered the Pantano Ditch, in single file, and disappeared into the darkness. The Rangers

with Senon in B Company, 3rd Ranger Battalion were spear-
heading the attack off the beachhead and were ordered to take
Cisterna. There was a deathly silence on the battlefield as the
Rangers passed the point of no return. Of the 767 Rangers that
attacked Cisterna, six came back; according to the official history, the rest were either killed or captured.

Senon S. Chavez was among the captured and he spent the
remainder of the war in prisoner of war camps. It was a brutal
and harrowing experience. With the annihilation of the 1st and
3rd Ranger Battalions at Cisterna, and the 4th Ranger Battalion's taking over fifty percent casualties at Feminimorta,
trying to come to the aid of their brother Rangers, Darby's
Rangers ceased to exist. What remained of the 4th Battalion
was shipped to the United States and disbanded.

Senon told me these things with visible pride that night. It
wasn't a narration seeking sympathy, but the sharing of
momentous events that had occurred in his life. This was the
passing on of something held very special by Senon. Not many
people had been privileged to hear his tale. He told me that
when I grew up, if I wanted to be the best, I should keep company with the best. I never forgot that night, and I later took his
advice.

Arriving at the brigade forward area in Kontum on
Christmas Eve 1966 was a real eye-opener. As we flew into the
country around Kontum, it looked ominous. Big mountains
were covered with a deep, deep, green mantle of triple canopy
jungle. The clouds hovered low on the mountaintops like a
burial shroud. The war so far had been a distant shadow, but as
I got closer to the front, I could see signs of it all around. When
the C-130 landed at Kontum, the line companies were coming
in from the field for the Christmas truce. Helicopters were
flying in discharging line doggies, people who hadn't seen
clean clothes in a long time. There was a look and feel to those
men, as if they knew things and had had experiences that I
hadn't. And it made me feel nervous. In a place where people
were walking around with loaded weapons, grenades hanging
all over them, I stood out. Grenades, in my short military expe-

rience, had been accorded the status of a small nuclear bomb. The few times I had handled one, it had been in an atmosphere of constrained attention with instructors hovering over us like clucking hens. There was a feeling of contained violence here. I got stares ranging from contempt to sympathy. Concertina wire was everywhere, and claymores were emplaced close to the wire. This was it, no doubt about it.

A three-quarter-ton truck picked me up and drove me to the Lurp detachment area, where I was met by Master Sergeant Acevedo, the LRRP platoon sergeant, who showed me where to put up a hootch. Because it was Christmas Eve, all the Lurps were in, and they were drinking whiskey like crazy. They approached me, making comments like, "Who the fuck are you? What line company you come from? No, wait a minute, don't tell me, you're a fucking cherry in Nam. What the hell is the platoon coming to? Fucking cherries, I can't believe it. Here, fucking have a drink. I meant a fucking drink, chug on it, son." Every other word was a cuss word. But one guy started befriending me, Sgt. William N. "Uncle Earl" Wheeler. He was an older NCO, from the South, with a country accent. He was called "Uncle Earl" because he liked to say that General Earl Wheeler, the Chairman of the Joint Chiefs of Staff, was his uncle. With bright blue twinkly eyes, and reddish-blond hair, he was one of those medium-sized guys who could get downright dangerous when provoked.

Uncle Earl soon set about patiently showing me the proper method of drinking Tennessee whiskey.

"Now, a respectable man from the South always gets at least two chug sounds out of the bottle when asked to drink, son— not that you're mine, but that the sun is shining," Uncle Earl explained. "Now, let's try it again."

Getting hard liquor was damn near impossible for an infantry enlisted man, unless it was sent from the States. The rest of the evening was like a blur. Not being much of a hard-liquor drinker, I eventually passed out, coming to the next morning on the edge of an anthill with a pounding headache. I had puked and rolled in it and had ant bites all over my body.

I was one sorry-ass-cherry sight. I had never gotten the chance
to put up a hootch.

The next morning, Christmas Day, I organized myself
somewhat and set up a hootch. Captain Friedrich, the detachment commander, came over and introduced himself. With
him was Sfc. Ron "Ronnie" Pitts, who shook hands with me
and informed me that I was assigned to his team. Captain
Friedrich explained that after the holidays they would start
training classes for the new guys who had arrived with me or
would be coming into the unit during the coming week. Since
it was Christmas Day, he said, we would be getting a special
treat for chow: turkey with all the trimmings. With that, Captain Friedrich left me in the care of Sfc. Ron Pitts.

First, Sergeant First Class Pitts made it clear that my assignment on his team was just temporary until I was accepted by
him and the rest of the team. He took me straight to the Lurps'
little ammo dump, taking out four hundred rounds of M-16 ball
ammo, twenty magazines for the M-16, four M-26 fragmentation grenades, one WP (white phosphorous) grenade, two
smoke grenades, and one claymore mine. He then showed me
how he wanted me to carry this ammunition on my LBE (load-
bearing equipment). In the ammo pouches, magazines with
nineteen rounds each were placed with the primers closest to
the body, bullets facing out. Sergeant First Class Pitts explained that if you took a bullet or shrapnel hit, it might detonate a round, and if the primers were facing out, it would ruin
your day. He showed me how to tape a cleaning rod underneath the barrel of my rifle. While we were doing all that, he
was continuously pumping information out of me. His first
question was, "So you just got to Nam, huh?" He started
asking questions about my military background and trying to
find out what I did and didn't know, my knowledge of the use
and handling of radios, particularly the PRC-25. He told me
my position on the team would be junior RTO. He showed
me how to configure my rucksack, and what C and Lurp
rations he wanted me to carry. He explained that he wanted me
ready in case we had to go out in an emergency situation. He
also knew I had a million questions, and told me not to worry.

When we started training, they would all be answered. The next day, 26 December, we would be doing PLF (parachute landing fall) training for a jump scheduled for the 27th. He next introduced me to Sp4. Allen Gaskell, who was the senior RTO on the team. After making sure I had all my equipment ready, Sergeant First Class Pitts sent me to see Sergeant First Class Lambert, the communications NCO, who had recruited us at P training. Dave Stauffer and I got a briefing on the PRC-25 radio, radio procedures, and the SOI (signal operating instructions) in case we had an emergency and had to check radios out. Because our formal training wasn't to start for another week, they wanted us briefed and ready. This was my first insight into what the Lurps were all about: it was Christmas Day, a day off for the team leaders, yet they had taken the time to make sure we were ready. Of course, it was self-serving, but they were professionals. We spent Christmas Day eating a great meal.

On 26 December, we were issued steel pots (helmets) and spent the day practicing PLFs off the back of a deuce-and-a-half truck. The following morning we were trucked out to the airfield, where we drew T-10 parachutes and reserve chutes. We rigged up in our chutes, tied our weapons to our sides barrel up, and were inspected by the jumpmasters. We then boarded a C-130 Hercules aircraft. Since my arrival in Vietnam, I had not set foot outside a military encampment. Here was the first time for me, and I was going to be jumping into it.

Military parachute jumping is an exhilarating experience and can definitely crank up the adrenaline, no matter how many times you've jumped before. With the two side doors on the C-130 open, you really hear the four turboprop engines and the prop blast. If you're close to the door you can see the jumpmaster go through jump procedures. When he inspects the outside of the aircraft, the prop blast makes the skin on his face move like it's Jell-O vibrating on a hard surface.

I was on the inside stick of the starboard side of the aircraft, close to the door. I caught glimpses of the countryside and kept wondering where in the hell they were going to find enough open area in the jungle to jump. Then the jumpmaster stood us up, and we went through our jump commands. When the green light came on, we shuffled to the rear of the aircraft and jumped out. As I stepped to the doorway, I vigorously threw my static line to the rear of the aircraft, grasped both sides of the doorway, and hurled myself out the door, keeping a tight body position.

As the prop blast grabbed me, it felt as if a giant had grabbed my body and thrown me straight back violently. If your feet or legs are not together, when the second the prop blast hits, it will start opening your legs, and you'll start rolling and tumbling. If you don't exit the aircraft vigorously, when the prop blast hits you, you'll get slammed into the side of the doorway frame or skid down the outside of the fuselage. You don't want to screw up exiting a C-130 on a parachute jump.

As I came out of the aircraft, I felt we had screwed up. Right in front of my eyes, deceptively close, was the side of a mountain with thick jungle. We were so close, I could see individual trees. With a good exit from the aircraft, when the prop blast hits, you do a half turn that places your body parallel to the aircraft and facedown toward the ground. As I rolled into that position, I could see rice paddies with water in them. Our DZ (drop zone) was northeast of Kontum, a small valley bordered by mountain ridgelines, the valley floor consisting of rice paddies. A fourteen- to sixteen-knot wind was blowing down the valley, with gusts of up to twenty knots. That was marginal jumping weather. We jumped at an altitude of twelve hundred feet. I could tell from my descent that a good stiff breeze was blowing. I ran in place and got myself situated so that I was coming in sideways to land. As I landed, I was in about sixteen inches of water. My parachute partially collapsed, and I jumped up right away to finish the job, but it immediately refilled with air and jerked me off the ground. I landed facedown in the water, and the parachute started dragging me. I was traveling at a good clip, mostly under water, when I hit a paddy dike that flipped me in the air. I landed on my back. The whole time, I was trying to pull in the tension so that I could release one of my capewells but I wasn't doing any good, and it was getting to be a serious situation. Finally I pulled the butt of my rifle up and stuck the barrel in the ground. I plowed through the mud of the paddy until I reached the next dike, where the barrel dug into the dike and stuck fast. I thought my nuts were going to be squeezed through my throat. Quickly, I pulled the safety pin and popped the release on my chest. Wiping the mud out of my eyes, nose, and ears, I watched two guys get dragged past. I ended up chasing other guys who were being dragged, and collapsing their chutes.

Eventually we were picked up and delivered back to our area by trucks. I spent the rest of the day washing my clothes and equipment, cleaning my rifle, and getting the mud out of them.

## Sgt. Victor Cisneros Asskicks in a Kontum Bar

It was toward evening, and most of the guys had gone into town. All we had to do was walk out of the perimeter wire and down about a quarter mile to where the road ran into downtown Kontum. There were a couple of bars there, real close to our area. I had been working on my gear from the jump and just kind of sticking close to the Lurp area, when I noticed Sgt. Victor Cisneros, one of the seasoned Lurps, walking up to his hootch, which was close to mine. I noticed him right away because he had blood coming down the right side of his face from a cut on his right eyebrow. His right cheekbone had a big slash on it, and his upper lip had been split and was swelled way out. Someone had worked him over really good, and he was very pissed off. He reached into his tent, grabbed his LBE, and put it on. Grabbing his rifle, he jacked a round into it. I said something like, "What's wrong?"

He looked at me with murder in his eyes, and said, "What the fuck are you looking at, asshole?" That's the first time I saw anyone with "the look." It raised the hair on the back of my neck.

I stammered something like, "Nothing, nothing," and like a rabbit, popped right back into my hootch. Right then, I didn't care if he was going to kill the Pope. I heard him walking off, cursing up a storm. As his footsteps faded, I chanced a look out of my hootch. He was walking in the direction of the ville that was right outside of our perimeter. I was undecided about what to do. I tried to find my team leader, Sergeant First Class Pitts, but he wasn't in his hootch. None of the old guys were around. I walked over to the Lurp tactical operations center (TOC) tent, and found Sergeant First Class Lambert. I told him what had occurred, and that I was worried that Vic might be doing something crazy. As he was telling me not to worry about it and that Vic would cool off, we heard shooting in the village. I looked at Sergeant Lambert and shrugged, then walked back to my hootch. It set me to wondering what I had volunteered for.

Sergeant Cisneros came walking back a short time later, and I heard him in his hootch, but I wasn't about to come out of mine to talk to him. Before long, MPs showed up with M-16s, and took him away. Sp4. Jimmy McCormack told us the story:

Victor and Jimmy had gone down to the ville, and were drinking Ba Muoi Ba—Vietnamese "33" beer—in a little bar. As usual, the bargirls came over to get them to buy them "Saigon tea," a watered-down drink that was outrageously priced. Sergeant Cisneros was kind of a shy guy who didn't have much to say. He was quiet and soft-spoken and pretty much kept to himself. But one of the whores was sitting on his lap, trying to talk him into buying her a Saigon tea, when three drunk ARVNS came in. The ARVN lieutenant with them took offense to the bargirl's sitting on Victor's lap, jerked her away, and started slapping her around. Vic stood up and started to say something when the lieutenant pulled out a U.S. Army .45, cocked it, and held it to Vic's head while the other two soldiers took turns butt stroking Vic in the face with their U.S. M-1 carbines. The lieutenant finished off by smacking Vic in the face with his pistol, then sent the two Lurps packing from the bar. McCormack went looking into the nearby bars for some other Lurps, but Cisneros went back to the camp, got his ass-kicking gear, and walked to the bar.

When Cisneros entered the bar, the ARVNs were laughing it up, and they really started laughing when Vic walked in. The ARVN lieutenant made the really stupid mistake of going for his .45; Victor shot him through the forehead. The other

ARVNs were shot and killed as they went for their weapons. The only remorse that Vic felt was that in shooting one of the ARVNs, a round went right through the guy's skinny chest and hit one of the prostitutes who had hidden behind the bar, hitting her in the head and killing her instantly.

In general, the Lurps sympathized with Vic's feeling of guilt about the prostitute, but everyone felt that the ARVNs deserved what they got. While awaiting his court-martial, Sergeant Cisneros was returned to the LRRP detachment and placed under armed guard. Captain Friedrich drew up a guard roster, and whoever was on guard duty had to wear a holstered .45. After a while, the guys got tired of having to readjust the pistol belt every time the guard was changed, so they adjusted it to Cisneros's waist, and he wore the pistol belt and .45. Besides, Vic handled the duty-guard roster so in a way he became the sergeant of the guard. It was a very convenient arrangement, while it lasted. Sergeant Victor Cisneros was convicted of manslaughter only because the prostitute was killed, and he was sent to Fort Leavenworth for a while. I had been in the unit almost three whole days when this occurred and it got my attention!

We started LRRP training on New Year's Day 1967. It involved map and compass, communications, and coding, taught by the headquarters element of the detachment. Most of the training was done within the team itself. Sp4. Allen Gaskell, the senior RTO on our team, showed me how Sfc. Ron Pitts's team handled the PRC-25. We practiced team immediate-action drills. I was learning what my responsibilities were. Each of us had assigned duties when we were moving or stopped, in the security wheel at night. And we were responsible for being packed for the field. We followed the training format and SOP (standard operating procedures) that had been established when the detachment was formed. We went out to the CCC (command and control central) encampment outside of Kontum to use their range. While we were there, Fireball Dixon threw a Mark II pineapple grenade and it exploded in the air about twelve feet out. That was a major screwup because it was one of our booby-trapped grenades but there was no identification to that effect. It was a miracle none of us got hit by shrapnel.

After about two weeks with the unit, I made friends with a S.Sgt. Walter "Waldo" Bacheck, a Ranger with a fondness for eating glass objects, and insects if it would warrant a good payoff in the form of a wager. Waldo was of Polish descent, big and husky, and his muscular bulk looked deceptively like baby fat. He was fast, strong, and fearless. Years later, John Belushi's appearance, mannerisms, and wit reminded me of Waldo Bachek. Bachek had a barely discernible cleft upper lip. He used his eyebrows very expressively, and would arch them, animating his whole face. He was one hell of a character. One day we hitched a ride downtown, getting off close to the Shell gas station, then walked into a bar and had a couple of beers. Waldo was always on the prowl for something, but he never knew what until he saw it. Well, we were walking along, when suddenly he stopped me and said something like, "Lookee here, now. What do we have here?"

I couldn't really see what he was referring to because all I could see was about a hundred GI jungle utilities, freshly washed, pinned, and hanging on a lime-green cord. Bachek told me to keep an eye out for the mamma-san, then started whistling. Walking to the end of the lime-green cord, he pulled something out of the side pocket of his trousers and monkeyed around for awhile. I couldn't figure out what was so damn interesting to Waldo that he had to fuck around with a bunch of washed clothes. He finished up what he was doing, walked up to me, and steered me across the small street, where we stood for about thirty seconds while he whistled the same damn tune with an "I poked the pig" smile on his face. Suddenly there was an explosion where the clothes on the line were, and every damn uniform came down. I looked at Bachek and he proudly said, "Det cord. They won't use that against us!" Some industrious mamma-san had used what she must have thought was ordinary plastic-sheathed cord but was actually detonation cord. Waldo had put a blasting cap with a fuse on it, ignited it, and, presto, no more cord and about a hundred ruined jungle utilities with holes where they had been pinned or rested against the "det cord." He had the nerve to walk back to eye-ball his work, and you could see and hear the mamma-san raging and shrieking about the sudden doom visited upon her. She never realized that the perpetrator of the evil deed was standing there at the scene of the crime, congratulating himself on a job well done. Right then I knew Waldo was one smart, crazy son of a bitch. He took his Ranger tab seriously, and, with his innocent face, the sham was devastating. There wasn't anything Waldo wouldn't booby-trap or blow up. He was always experimenting. Months later, he would mangle his fingers a little when a blasting cap from a smoke grenade went off while he was attempting to crimp it onto a Mark II (pineapple grenade) screw-on spoon assembly. He eventually became my team leader.

I was assigned to Team One, led by Sfc. Ronald Pitts. Pappy Webb, Jim Bethel, Teddy Bear Gaskell, and Wilbur Sumpter rounded out the team. My first training mission was pulled northwest of Kontum. It was my first helicopter ride ever. From the air, the thick jungled mountains looked immense, clouds draping the hilltops like dark veils. What grabbed me was the thought that this was the enemy's home, and we were going hunting for them, all six of us.

We came into a small clearing to land, and the huge trees dwarfed the helicopter as it settled down into the green hole. We ran into the jungle and dropped into a circle, just the way we had trained. But now, it was deadly serious. About ten minutes later, the sounds of the jungle started up again; Pitts relaxed somewhat, and then Pappy Webb led us out. I was amazed at how quietly the team moved, and how slowly. All the old guys moved with a purpose, no actions wasted, and the intensity of their concentration underscored the seriousness of what we were doing. I was constantly shown little tricks of the trade and could see in myself how much of a liability a person with no experience could be. We humped mountains that were extremely demanding, in beautiful country that got downright cold at night. Being inside the jungle was a real eye opener. The thousands of varieties of plant life and insects were staggering. On the last day of the mission we were looking for an extraction LZ, and Pappy Webb said that if we walked down the steep mountain ridge we were on, we should be able to find an LZ in the drainage. So we slid down this steep side hill, seeming to walk on the treetops. But at the base, we could touch the other hill that rose just as steep on the opposite side. So much for an LZ. Nothing of any major consequence happened, other than I was faced with how much I didn't know.

On another mission out of Kontum, we flew contour down a narrow corridor of jungle that was enclosed by the steep mountainsides, heading for an LZ in a streambed filled with giant rocks. The helicopter perched a skid on a huge boulder that jutted out from the mountainside that was our LZ. We stepped onto the rock, and after the helicopter left we started down it but found out we couldn't get off the boulder. Because of the jungle growth, it had looked as if it was attached to the mountainside; in reality, it was a solitary column of rock that, surrounded by jungle growth, jutted straight up in the air. We were not carrying enough rope to rappel off it so we had to call the helicopter in to be extracted.

In the middle of January, the LRRP detachment received a new man by the name of Sgt. Derby Jones. Derby's father, Oliver F. Jones, was a colorful character in his youth, blazing a trail of bank robberies throughout the state of Idaho and breaking out of jail with a wooden gun in the city of Boise nine years before Dillinger's famous jail break. Born in Singer, California, Derby had seen prior service before enlisting into the army as Airborne Infantry in October 1965. He took the Special Forces test and passed and planned to go to Special Forces training after jump school. But at Fort Benning he was advised that due to his impressive record of juvenile delinquency in his civilian past, they wouldn't be able to secure him a security clearance for a while. He got impatient enough to go to the 82nd where he was assigned to B Company, 2/508. An exceptional soldier, Sergeant Jones made rank fast. As acting squad leader, he was moved into a room with a sergeant named Joe Hooper. They soon became good friends, and eventually went before a promotion board together. And they decided to 1049 (volunteer) for Vietnam. On receiving their promotions, they also received orders for reassignment: Joe Hooper to Panama; Derby to the 1/101 Airborne, in Vietnam. Nineteen months and a lifetime later, Derby and I ran into Joe Hooper in Bienhoa. He was headed to Washington, D.C. to receive the Medal of Honor from the President.

Derby Jones was assigned to Team One as junior scout. On his first mission he was loaded down and clumsy as an ox. "I was tripping over vines that I wouldn't have tripped over when I was growing up hunting. The first night, we slept on rocks, and it was miserable. I thought to myself that I had twelve months to go doing this. I didn't think I would survive the team because I was on a probationary period. Pappy Webb took a liking to me and started pointing out to me how to step, walk, and how to look around you at the same time. On the mission we monitored some trails that were close to a creek. We didn't see anything for five days, no animals other than the ones I was with. I was relieved that I didn't have to fire a shot because, trying to get through the jungle on my own two feet, I was lucky to be able to walk. After two or three missions, I felt more secure and at ease. I learned how to live in the jungle, what to look out for."

I got to know Derby as a team member and humped a lot of bush with him. We always worked together on the same teams, as they were shuffled around. On one mission Derby gave me what I felt was a real compliment. I was packing the PRC-74, and we had done some marathon humping, and everyone was beat. He told me he didn't know how I could hump such a heavy load and keep up. I told him I had no choice, but his comment made me feel good. Derby had lifer blood, but he was the kind of individual you would follow anywhere.

# 4

## LONG RANGE RECON
### Top Smith

With allied forces gaining offensive momentum, Head-quarters I Field Force ordered the 1st Brigade of the 101st Airborne Division to move four hundred miles south to its base camp at Phan-rang and to prepare for Operation FARRAGUT, with the mission of looking for secret base camps in Binh Thuan, Ninh Thuan, and Lam Dong Provinces. The brigade left Kontum on 21 January, by air and by land.

The 1/327 and the 2/502 battalions conducted coordinated search and destroy operations in Operation FARRAGUT with minimal enemy contact. The operation resulted in only 115 enemy killed. However the Chieu Hoi "Open Arms" program picked up speed with 475 enemy soldiers who gave up freely.

Operations GATLING I and II were next conducted in Lam Dong, Binh Tuy, and Binh Thuan Provinces during the first two weeks in February. Operation GATLING I was planned in response to intelligence reports indicating a suspected secret meeting place for a high-level enemy command conference in Lam Dong Province.

In late January 1967, a change of command occurred while the 1st Brigade was in Phan-rang. Brig. Gen. Salve H. Matheson took command of the 1st Brigade, 101st Airborne Division from Brig. Gen. Willard Pearson. Word in the brigade was that Matheson was the real thing, a fighting Airborne officer. The troops of the 1st Brigade came to know and respect Matheson as a ground pounder's general.

Born in Seattle in 1920, Salve H. Matheson was commissioned a second lieutenant in the Infantry Reserve upon graduation from UCLA. During World War II, he served with the 506th Parachute Infantry, 101st Airborne Division, participating in the Normandy Invasion, the liberation of Holland, the defense of Bastogne, and the seizure of the Berchtesgaden area. After World War II, he served in various commands within the 82nd Airborne Division. During the Korean War, General Matheson was the G-3 plans officer of the X Corps and participated in the Inchŏn and Wonsan landings, and through amphibious withdrawal from Hŭngnam. General Matheson was assigned to the 101st Airborne Division as deputy battle group commander in 1958, and in 1961 he was made commander of the 10th Special Forces in Europe. In March 1966 he returned to Fort Campbell as assistant division commander of the 101st Airborne Division, and in January 1968 he became our commander.

A bond of mutual respect developed between General Matheson and his Lurps, who eventually picked up the name of Matheson's Marauders. Jimmy McCormack painted that name on a piece of 4×8 plywood, and the LRRP detachment lugged it around on their numerous moves throughout South Vietnam. At that time none of the Lurps imagined that in two years Department of Army was going to give the Lurp units the colors and official lineage of the World War II Merrill's Marauders—in the 1st Brigade LRRP detachment, no one would have considered it a great promotion. Matheson's Marauders filled the bill just fine.

## Top Smith

In early February, a new first sergeant came to the LRRP detachment: M.Sgt. Lloyd L. Smith. A master blaster, he was slight of build, quiet and reserved, but not withdrawn. He exuded the calm confidence of a professional soldier.

Naturally, he created quite a stir with the old guys. Ron Pitts, Pappy Webb, and Uncle Earl Wheeler were all quizzed by the younger Lurps to find out if they had ever run into him. Pappy Webb and Pitts knew him from the Special Force's Special Warfare Center at Fort Bragg. The word from the old guys was that he was "strac," a stud—and this was a very good sign because first sergeants have a huge impact on a soldier's life. They protect you from the army you serve, they acquire the beans and bullets for you, and they bring the wrath of God on your young ass when you need it.

While 1st Sergeant Acevedo was still in charge, M.Sgt. Lloyd L. Smith quietly observed from the side. "Top" Smith, as he became known to all of us, introduced himself to me prior to flying to Bao-loc. He asked my name, where I was from, and who I was. Up to that point in my illustrious army career, answers to questions from first sergeants were always answered, "Yes, First Sergeant," or "No, First Sergeant," and I was always made to feel like a young turkey getting basted and readied for the proverbial oven. Not so from Top Smith. He made a guy relax and feel as if he cared for your morale and welfare. He wasn't God—but he seemed like God's First Sergeant. He was a man to be trusted.

For the previous five years, Top Smith had been involved with the Special Warfare Center, teaching counterinsurgency to allied and U.S. officers. He had also been the NCOIC (NCO in charge) of the logistics department for the center. On receiving orders to Vietnam, he got a special authorization to attend the six-week Special Forces Operations and Intelligence school for senior NCOs before coming to Vietnam. He tried to get his orders changed to come to Vietnam as a Special Forces team sergeant but was denied because his rank would knock a promotion slot out for someone for whom Special Forces might be grooming for promotion. When Top Smith arrived in Phan-rang with the 1st Brigade, they realized he would be an excellent candidate to take over the LRRP detachment. He was happily surprised that the position was open because that was what he had wanted to do. Top Smith later told me that his understanding of Lurps at the time was that they went out and looked for the enemy, and when they got ready to be extracted, they made contact. But after being with the Lurps for a while, he understood that that wouldn't work very well. Top Smith had a tremendously positive impact on all Lurps who served with him.

## The C-130

On 29 January, the Lurps were given a warning order to prepare for a mission scheduled for 1 February. As part of Operation GATLING I, the 1st Brigade was moving to a new area of operation in Lam Dong Province and would be doing a multibattalion infantry operation. Two teams were to be provided by the LRRP detachment for the purpose of monitoring the enemy's withdrawal, or reinforcement, into the area of operation. The 1st Brigade would shuttle in infantry battalions by C-130 airplanes into a remote airstrip outside Bao-loc. The airstrip had recently been extended and PSP (perforated steel platform) matted for this operation. The infantry companies would offload the aircraft, then board CH-47 Chinooks and Huey slicks to be ferried into their LZs. The first plane into the newly extended airstrip would contain the two LRRP teams; the detachment commander, Captain Friedrich; and the communications sergeant, Sergeant First Class Lambert. Also, aboard the C-130 was a skeleton crew from the S-2/S-3 (TOC)—under the command of Capt. William

Carpenter*—with their equipment in a deuce-and-a-half truck, and there was also a filled water trailer with a jeep and trailer. Upon landing, the Lurp teams would board slicks to be inserted. The two teams picked by Captain Friedrich were those of Sfc. Ron Pitts and S.Sgt. John Dietrich. I was junior RTO on Pitts's team.

As usual, the "hurry up and wait" regime was in full effect. We got to the Phan-rang airstrip around 0500 hours and waited around for the aircrew to arrive. Fully packed for a six-day mission and having gotten up very early, Pappy Webb, Danny Williams, Derby Jones, and I sat on the runway with our packs up against the tires of the C-130, trying to catch a few extra minutes of sleep. Just as the eastern horizon was starting to lighten, the aircrew arrived. The pilot, a lieutenant colonel, woke us up as he kicked the tires to check them during his pre-flight. Danny Williams asked the light bird if he had ever gotten a flat tire on a C-130, an interesting question asked half in jest. The pilot answered no.

---

*Captain Carpenter, our boss from S-2, had an interesting background. He was the famous Lonesome End when he was playing football for West Point. He made a name for himself in sports and also as an infantry company commander under Lt. Col. Hank "Gunfighter" Emerson's 2/502 Infantry Battalion, 1/101st Airborne.

During the Battle of Tou Morong, Charlie Company, 2/502, was inserted on the morning of 9 June 1966 to act as a blocking force ahead of the 1/327, which was sweeping in the direction of Charlie Company. As Charlie Company moved up a small rise, Carpenter's forward platoon leader radioed him and informed him that they could hear Vietnamese voices two hundred meters ahead of him, down in a small streambed. His platoon leader asked Carpenter if he wanted to set up the blocking force or go hunting Charlie. He replied, "Let's hunt Charlie!" Unknown to Carpenter, he was biting the tail of a terrible beast. They had bit into the 24th North Vietnamese Regiment. Charlie Company was swarmed and nearly overrun. At the height of the action, Carpenter made a very controversial decision to call napalm onto his own position. It broke the back of the North Vietnamese attack and bought time for Charlie Company to disengage from the enemy. It rang bells clear back into the U.S. In the army, it was much discussed and debated whether such an action was noble or foolish. For his actions, his battalion commander, Lt. Col. Hank Emerson, put Captain Carpenter in for the Medal of Honor, which was downgraded to a Distinguished Service Cross.

The crew chief lowered the rear ramp, and we boarded, looking for a place to sit. Because of the truck and gear in the aircraft, the pickings were slim. I found the jeep's driver's seat unoccupied, and I promptly claimed it. I fell asleep as we were taking off.

I awoke in midair as I was violently thrown out of the jeep then landed on my back. On my way out of the jeep, I hit the steering wheel with my thighs, bruising them. The interior of the aircraft was filled with red dust, and I could smell and see hydraulic fluid everywhere. I was starting to get on my knees when a figure stumbled out of the red dust cloud, completely covered with red dirt and hydraulic fluid, so that his eyes looked as huge as saucer cups. I thought, "My god, that's Derby, and he looks scared! We must be dead!"

I was getting up, but was flattened again as the aircraft bounced back down hard on the runway. I crawled to the side of the aircraft, pulled myself up, and looked through a small porthole to see that we were flying barely above trees, the props just chewing the shit out of their tops. I dropped down, trying to find a place to secure myself, because I thought we were crashing. It was a sickening feeling because I couldn't react in any way to help my situation.

"I thought we had taken a rocket through the plane," Derby Jones says. "I lurched my way toward the front of the plane, and saw Marty trying to get off the floor of the aircraft. We both looked out a window and saw that the plane was plowing through the tops of the trees with the props, just chewing through the trees. I figured our shit was *weak*!"

The aircraft eventually got airborne, and my fear turned instantly to elation as I knew I had survived another close call. Everyone was cheering, till someone said, "What the hell you guys cheering for? Take a look at this!"

Whoever had yelled was on the port side, and I was on the starboard side. I walked toward the rear of the aircraft and looked into the wheelwell. A monster tire had punched up through the metal, and was half inside the aircraft. Where the rear tire had been was a twisted wheel strut. Sergeant First Class Lambert was visibly shaken because he had been resting

against that wheelwell and had moved just prior to landing.
The crew chief climbed up into the cockpit, then came back.
He put on a safety leash, opened the doors of the aircraft, and
leaned out, checking the damage. There was a brief conference
in the cockpit and then another brief conference with Captain
Friedrich and Captain Carpenter. I was wondering how many
chutes the plane was carrying.

Mine weren't the only such thoughts. There was muttering
and an undercurrent of rebellion as we watched the two officers and the crew chief don air force parachutes; there were
only six parachutes in the aircraft. Realization of what the men
were thinking suddenly dawned on Captain Carpenter's face,
and when he smiled, it broke the tension. The crew chief said,
"Listen up, men! We got an aircraft with damaged wheels; the
port-side tires are gone or useless. On the starboard side, the
rear one is turned sideways, and we have one good one. We
have to throw everything out of the aircraft that might
explode—the extra diesel cans for the deuce-and-a-half truck
and the gas cans for the jeep. We have to chain the truck back
up because we broke the front chains when we hit the first time.
Anything that is loose has to be thrown out. We have to rig the
aircraft because we'll be flying south to Tan-son Nhut to do a
crash landing on a foamed runway. And no, *no one* is going to
be jumping out of this aircraft!"

That brought a few chuckles.

Everyone got to work securing equipment. We Lurps went
through our gear, and handed all the grenades and blasting caps
to Captain Friedrich and Captain Carpenter to throw out of the
aircraft. The major from S-3 had broken his leg because he had
been standing up when we slammed down the first time, and
the team medic, Sgt. Danny Williams, was working on him.
Meanwhile, one of the sergeants who had gotten on top of the
two-and-a-half-ton truck to throw equipment down, tossed a
rucksack or bundle that landed on the poor guy's leg, causing
him to scream.

CWO Gary Sauer, a helicopter pilot from the 101st aviation
section, had ferried his Huey slick in from Phan-rang the previous day and was on the ground waiting for us to land. His and

another aircraft were to insert the two Lurp teams when they landed. Sauer had once been an enlisted combat-ready crewman on an air force SAC B-52, in the days when you could still serve on B-52s as a noncommissioned officer. He decided to do some flying in helicopters and transferred into the Instant Army Aviator Program that the army offered in those days. He was discharged from the air force, had a little holy water sprinkled on himself, then was sworn into the army as a W-2. He went through training and went to Vietnam in December 1966.

He was sitting in his aircraft, reading a book and waiting for the first planeload to come in. "I heard it over the radio, or someone mentioned that an aircraft was inbound," he recalls. "Being a former crew member of a B-52 crew, I naturally looked up to see the aircraft on final approach. My aircraft was situated about one hundred yards off the runway, with a temporary radio communications tent set up about one hundred yards farther down the runway on my side. The runway had just been extended and blacktopped with PSP-matted overruns and built-up berms on each end. There was a depression in the runway about four hundred yards from the beginning. I watched the aircraft touch down, and a huge cloud of red dust flew out, with the rear tire flying back under the aircraft, going through the rear stabilizing aileron, ripping through it, flying in the air, and bouncing down the runway, chasing the C-130. The pilot had straddled the berm with his two sets of tires, and the aircraft's landing gear just couldn't take the shock. They started coming apart, buckling the aircraft as he was landing. I thought, 'I'm going to be a witness to a very nasty crash.' The aircraft bounced straight in the air, just clearing the depression in the runway, and while aloft the pilot pulled full power and started clawing his way back in the air. It was going to be close. My attention was divided between the plane and the tire that was rebounding down the runway, heading my way. I started getting worried that it was going to hit my aircraft, then realized it was going to miss me. It went right in front of my slick and headed toward the aircraft control center, going right through the tent, tearing it down. People poured out of it;

miraculously no one got hurt. The aircraft plowed through the trees at the end of the runway and finally got airborne. I couldn't believe the aircraft made it back up, but that was a testimony to the durability of the C-130 Hercules."

We squared the plane down as best as we could. The crew chief gave us the run-by on what would be happening on the landing. We popped all the escape hatches on the aircraft, two in the ceiling and both doorways, as we flew about one hundred miles south to Tan-son Nhut, and then stayed in the air to use up the fuel in the wing tanks. We spread four straps across the rear ramp of the aircraft and strapped all nineteen of us to the ramp. This was the part I didn't like at all. My feet were right where the ramp met the floor of the aircraft, and the two-and-a-half-ton truck bumper was at my chest level, about two feet away. I just knew we would be crushed by that truck.

We flew into the landing approach, and the pilot shut his engines down. When the doors on a C-130 are open, the engine sound and that of the wind coming in are extremely loud, but when the pilot killed his engines, all we could hear was the wind rushing in through the doors and top escape hatches. Just before the tires met the pavement, the pilot turned on some alarm bells that shot our nerves right up through the escape hatches. The left-front side tire of the aircraft touched down first, and when the weight of the aircraft settled down, it sheared off the rear tire, which was turned sideways. I believe that pilot did the best flying of his life that day because it seemed that he had to get rid of the left side tires in order to let the belly settle down on the runway. Otherwise, it would pitch him over to his right, and a wing would grab. The front wheel strut gave way, shoving the front tire right into the wheel well, allowing the whole belly of the airplane to make contact with the runway. An instantaneous sheet of flame, the kind you get when using a metal grinding wheel real heavily, instantly filled the whole doorway. We started plowing foam, and I began to appreciate its use in crashes. As we slid down the runway, the left wing started dipping, the aircraft yawed to the left, and the tail came to the right. We slewed off the left side of the runway, slipping off one runway onto another, by then sliding backward. Now our speed was being reduced dramatically, and I started to worry about the aircraft flipping over. We were supposed to stay strapped in until the aircraft was completely stopped, but we cut some of the straps, and I remember jumping out while the aircraft was still sliding. It hadn't completely stopped, but I didn't have any problem getting away from the aircraft, which was smoking and looking pretty much the worse for wear.

After the normal hanging around, amazed that the C-130 really survived the landing, we were trucked to a local hangar where we dropped our rucks and LBE. The hangar was packed with airtight aluminum coffins, the kind used for transporting the dead back to the States. We were then taken to an air force mess hall, which was a real treat. I hadn't seen such good chow in quite a while. They even had real milk, and I must have drunk a gallon. With our faded tiger fatigues, lack of rank insignia, and our high-speed look, we caused quite a stir with the flyboys. After lunch we went back to our rucksacks and watched one of the forklift drivers spill a pallet of four coffins on the hangar's cement floor. I don't believe they were occupied, but for some reason, the incident really disturbed all of us.

We got another C-130, a silver one with no cammo paint, and flew back to Bao-loc, where we had started just four hours earlier. We landed at Bao-loc full of anxiety, and taxied over to the unloading area. The crew chief dropped the ramp, and we were instantly blasted with red dust from a Chinook (CH-47) helicopter that was taking off. As we were walking to one side of the unloading area, the Chinook was about seventy feet in the air. It suddenly lost power, fell out of the sky, and rolled over. This runway was located on a plateau, and the drop off the side was not very far away. The helicopter rolled over a couple of times, down the side of the plateau, and came to a stop. We all ran over to help pull out the people, a load of line grunts going into the field, and they were not in very good shape. There were no deaths, but they were banged up pretty good.

The mission had been automatically scratched, and we were

put on perimeter guard. We had to dig in a bunker. I was
bunked up with Pat Kinser, and I did a dumb-ass thing.
Somehow, we had gotten some insect spray in a pressurized
can, and I sprayed some big huge black ants. Well, I couldn't
believe it—talk about stirring an ant nest. We spent the night
outside the bunker.

## Junk Insertion

During Operation GATLING, the LRRP detachment was
shifted from Bao-loc to the coastal town of Phan-thiet. This
area was very arid, and the water in Phan-thiet tasted horrible.
The LRRP detachment was assigned a mission by the S-2/S-3
shop. We would be going north about forty miles by Swift boat
and inserted during the night. The area of operations would be
a large coastal plain that jutted out into the South China Sea.
No roads crossed the region, and the terrain was desert, with
small rolling hills farther inland. Inhabited areas were notice-
ably absent on the maps due to the barrenness of the territory,
which was not conducive to agricultural activity. Enemy forces
in the area were being resupplied from the South China Sea,
and our mission was to obtain intelligence on where that was
occurring and to bring forces to bear in order to stop it. We
would be using air assets and a naval asset—an American
destroyer hugging the coastline—ready to support us. This was
an unusual mission in that none of the Lurps had ever been
inserted by naval transportation or used any naval gunfire for
support, at least not while I had been with Lurps.* Three teams
would be used for this mission. The team leaders were S.Sgt.
John Dietrich, S.Sgt. "Uncle Earl" Wheeler, and S.Sgt. Vincente Cruz, my team leader.

Our team consisted of S.Sgt. Walter Bachek, senior scout;
S.Sgt. Larry Christian, junior scout; Sp4. Elmer Kolarik, junior
RTO; Sp5. John Buford, medic, and me as senior RTO. S-2
was also assigning a scout dog and handler to Dietrich's team.

* *Special Men*, Dennis Foley, Ivy Books, page 133. A sea insertion was done
by 1/327 (Tiger Force) Recon Platoon in January 1966.

The dog's name was Satan. He was a black German shepherd with yellow eyes, and he was mean as his namesake. Most of the Lurps had been on missions using scout dogs, and we weren't all that thrilled to be working with them. They were good in their detection of the enemy, but were likely to whine or growl when the enemy was near. Also they tired easily, the heat and humidity sapping their energy. They needed a lot of water, and we didn't like sharing our water with them. We also had to deal with the dog's handler, who might be good in the field but was basically baby-sitting the dog. His attention would be on the dog, and he couldn't be relied on to be a part of the team. The dog and his handler probably operated quite well within an infantry company because of the larger numbers of men. But in Lurps, with our six-man team configuration, the employment of scout dogs was not realistic, and we considered them a liability.

Around 1800 hours, we were transported to the harbor in Phan-thiet and got to see our sea vessel, which had changed from a U.S. Navy Swift boat to two Vietnamese Navy junks. The South Vietnamese Coastal Group 28* was in charge of getting us inserted. We had serious doubts about the boats being seaworthy. Uncle Earl's team and our team were put on one junk and Dietrich's team on the other. Jungle Jim, from Uncle Earl's team, and I had put a couple of beers in a sock, and we were going to hang them over the side and drink them on our sea cruise; that idea was quickly dashed. For security reasons, they wanted all of us Lurps in the hold so no Vietnamese would see us leaving the harbor. Elmer Kolarik started puking the minute he set foot on the boat, and that set the tone for the rest of the trip. Below deck we were treated to the diesel fumes the junk was emitting, so we all turned green in a short time, and soon drinking a beer was the last thing we wanted to do. We took off, heading north, in the gathering darkness. These navy admirals didn't know a lick of English, but we were in their hands, and I could tell the mission was going

---

* 1st Brigade, 101st Airborne Division, After Action Report dated 6 March 1967.

to turn into a pork chop real fast. Our preops had been sketchy, and we'd had no overflight to check out the terrain. From our map studies, we could tell that blue lines—rivers and streams—were very few, so water would be a main concern. I personally was carrying five canteens.

After we left the harbor area, darkness settled in, and we went up on deck to escape the fumes and to breathe some fresh air. We traveled until around 0300 hours. Our admirals, with all their naval experience, then figured that we were where we were supposed to be, and with various hand gestures and smiles and nodding of heads, they informed us that we were at the end of the line. It was a moonless night, and all we had for light was the stars, but we could hear the surf breaking on shore, some distance from the junks. Top Smith picked Elmer Kolarik, who was six feet four inches tall, to be our depth dummy. Top stopped Elmer from sliding over the side with his rucksack; then he slid overboard wearing his LBE, a considerable weight belt. *Ploop*; Elmer disappeared from view, then came back up struggling to keep his head above water. As he clung to the junk, with some friendly persuasion from a couple of M-16s, we encouraged the junk drivers to edge in closer to shore. Once again Elmer tried out the depth of the water, and this time he could stand on the bottom with the water at shoulder level. That would put the water level right about my eyebrows. The mission was a go. We slid into the water and were handed our rucksacks once we were submerged. We were trying to maintain noise and light discipline, but we were very vulnerable at that point.

Over the side I went, and because I was considerably shorter than Elmer, the water was right at my chin. That was a little better than I'd expected. I started working toward the shore on the sandy bottom. Wave action on sandy beaches scours out pockets of sand, which makes it deeper in spots. I was completely under water in just a couple of steps. All I could do was grab the end of the antenna on the PRC-25 in my rucksack, push myself off the bottom, get a breath of air, then go under and scuttle like a crab, dragging my rucksack toward the shore. I kept bobbing and scuttling like that until I could stand up with my head out of the water. I had a few moments of panic, and thought I wouldn't be able to make it to shore with my equipment. Try swimming while holding a ninety-pound rucksack in one hand, a slingless rifle in the other, and wearing thirty pounds of ass-kicking hardware on your person. It isn't easy. Thank God Mr. Charles didn't have a reception committee waiting for us on shore.

Meanwhile, on S.Sgt. John Dietrich's junk they were having their own problems. Dietrich still wonders what in the world Friedrich had in mind for that mission. His mindset was that we were going to be high speed, and when we pulled into the harbor area, it was really a letdown. He recalls jumping over the side and seriously wondering if we were going to make it or not. Everybody was doing water survival, bouncing off the bottom and then getting a gulp of air, until we finally got about nose high. Dietrich remembers it being a serious struggle for a few minutes. Freddy Hernandez lost his rucksack in what turned out to be a swimming exercise. It was a wonder that we all didn't drown. Dietrich remembers the black scout dog, Satan, and the handler with his team, because everybody was weighted down with gear for them. The Lurps were carrying the handler's and the dog's water, and all the handler was carrying was the dog food. Dietrich struggled up to the beach and checked to make sure everyone was accounted for. John Dietrich carried a little field notebook with him, and he jotted down at the time: "Small boats, and what's wrong with aviation support? Craft could not make designated landing point. Navy knew this before we started; two men very ill from ride, not combat capable; we got landed seventy-five meters from the beach. One man almost drowned. Wyche said waves were from four to eight feet in his swim. God help us if we had gotten hit on insertion."

The first guys on the beach set up security while the remainder came ashore. Once all three teams got together, we went inland about 150 meters and set up a security wheel between some heavy brush and a grass-covered sand dune. Lloyd Smith took command of all three teams, and decided we would wait for daylight to get a bearing on exactly where we were on the map. He sent out a three-man team and they made a 360-degree recon around our immediate area. We were assigned guard duty and waited for daylight. . . .

Right before dawn, we went on 100 percent alert, per SOP. When it was light enough to see, I went to exchange my chambered night round in case it had sweated, which can cause a jam. I noticed that the brass on my ammo had oxidized. Brass and salt water don't mix at all. All my magazines were in similar shape, and it was the same for anybody whose ammo had gotten wet—and everyone's ammo was wet. We had to break into shifts to clean all our ammo. My radio came next. Because all of the radios had gotten wet and the salt water was affecting them, we had to field-strip them. Handsets were the major problem with the radios. I always carried a spare and had wrapped it in two plastic battery bags. After taking the battery out of the radio and replacing it, I carefully wiped the points where the handset plugged into the radio, then did the same with the antenna connection. After I put my radio set back together, I was the only one who could effectively transmit and receive without a lot of static. However, I could not contact the bird dog that was supposed to be orbiting as our radio relay, and neither could the other RTOs.

While that was going on, Top Smith had been trying to determine exactly where we were. He sent a couple of team leaders in opposite directions. The terrain around us was level, with sand flats extending inland up to a mile in places and no district terrain features to refer to. The sand was a pure white, and the glare off it was fierce. The sand flats broke onto scrub brush with a lot of cacti. It seemed everything had thorns. It reminded me of the vegetation in southern Arizona.

After the team leaders came back and counsel was taken, it was determined that the terrain didn't match up with our maps. In fact, we realized we weren't even on the map sheet we had. It was hard to determine whether we had been inserted north or south of the RZ. Those navy jugheads had to be totally incompetent to leave us that far off—either that, or they had done it on purpose. One thing for sure, it was only early morning, and already it was getting unbelievably hot. It was going to be a scorcher, and water would be a critical factor soon.

Top figured we had landed north of the RZ, so he decided to take two teams and move south, with Uncle Earl's team reconning farther north, looking for water or a familiar landmark but keeping within radio range.

Jungle Jim Cody remembers: "I went over the side opposite Marty [Martinez]. I never was in such deep water. I remember for the most part keeping my ammo dry. It was having to hold your whole pack over your head that got to me. The teams split up the next morning and went in opposite directions. That afternoon after we split up, I was on point, and we had moved inland somewhat. We were paralleling this trail, and I kept hearing movement on the other side of a big dense thicket. We kept stopping and listening, waiting for something to happen. We didn't actually make physical contact, but they somehow got onto us. Chuck started searching, and we started to back-track and started hauling ass. We knew we were compromised, and we started running. They were always behind us, and it wasn't like they were pressing that hard. They weren't coming up fast on us; they just kept tracking us. We dropped everything except for water and ammo, and we kept setting booby traps as we went. We could hear them detonate in the distance. It confirmed our fears, and it slowed the enemy down. It was scary because all of the teams were completely severed from any contact with U.S. forces. I always thought that if they had really pushed, as tired as we were and low on water, they could have easily caught us. But fortunately they stayed back, thanks to the booby traps slowing them down. At that point, our only thoughts were trying to link up with the other teams, and, obviously, the safety in numbers."

Dietrich and Cruz's team took off, heading south, and by noon it was unbelievably hot. It must have been 115 degrees. We were trying to conserve our water. We were paralleling the beach, about three hundred meters in, because we wanted to be able to signal any boat that might come by. At one point, one of the guys from our team passed out from heat exhaustion, and eight guys just walked right by him. Even Doc Buford walked right by him, and then realized he was the last guy in line. He called out to us to stop, and we dragged him into the shadow of a tall sand dune with a steep backside. We took our empty canteens and filled them with sea water, wetting him down thoroughly. Top realized we were all getting danger-ously close to suffering from heat exhaustion—and, more deadly, heat stroke. We were in no position to deal with that kind of casualty. We moved farther inland and found good shade under some scrub trees. We decided we would wait until evening, then travel during the cool of the night. That after-noon we got word from Uncle Earl's team that they were being chased, which changed our decision. We would have to wait in place and see what developed; the only help for the other team was us.

Rudy Lopez, who was on Dietrich's team, recalls: "This was supposed to be a secret insertion, but when we were getting onto the junks, it was still daylight, and there were a lot of Viet-namese people around, a lot of locals, looking at us. A lot of us got sick on the junk ride. It was the diesel fumes in the holds that got us sick. Man, I was sick, and it wasn't because of the ocean! We inserted about 0300 hours, and I remember these Vietnamese navy guys were a bunch of chickenshits. They didn't want to come in close to shore. Our team was the only one on our junk. When the junk stopped moving, the first guy into the water, I believe, was Ralph Church, senior RTO on our team. We were holding his ruck, and he went over the side and was holding on to the side of the junk; then he let go, and he just disappeared. He went down and then came back up. It was pretty deep, but he said we could do it. We all took off our bush hats and stuck them in our shirts, and one by one we went over the side, and then we were handed our rucksacks. I held on to mine. I didn't have it on. I would go down, hit the bottom, jump up, get some air, go down, jump up, get some air. That's what we all did until we got on shore. Once on shore we had to clean all our ammo and radios. I remember Marty had some steel wool that we used to clean the connectors on the handsets. I never got my radio to work. The only radios that were working were Dave Stauffer's, on Uncle Earl's team, and

Marty's radio. We thought we were where we were supposed to be until it got light. We took off, heading south, and it was hotter than hell. We had to stop because one of the guys passed out from the heat. We were running out of water fast, and it was pissing everyone off because we had to share our water with the scout dog. The handler hadn't humped enough water for himself and the dog. Walter Bacheck spoke up and said according to the Ranger manual, we should be able to dig a hole there and hit water. I used to do anything Bacheck asked, so I started digging with my canteen cup. Other guys helped. We dug a hole, and it felt like we moved two tons of sand, but we never hit water. It was a good try. That afternoon, a B-52 strike hit pretty close to us, causing the ground to shake. So ended our first day."

The other two teams hadn't linked up with Uncle Earl's team, but they felt that Uncle Earl had shaken the people who were tracking him. They were farther inland, looking for water, and traveling south also. The next morning, while it was still dark, we again edged in closer to the shoreline and started moving south. It was a scorcher of a day, and we hadn't found any water. It was starting to get critical, because almost everyone was out of water.

Around 1300 hours, we heard a boat coming north heading up the coast, right off the coastline. It was an American Swift boat, and you could tell he was looking for something. The guys started laying their signal mirrors on him, and I was dialing through my PRC-25, trying to raise him. He caught the flashes of our mirrors, and swung back around. Every weapon on him was covering us as he lay idling about 100 meters off the beach. Dietrich's two men, Bruce Redmer and Bill Post, stripped and swam out to the boat. It seemed that they were on the boat forever. Bacheck had his binos fixed on the boat, and everyone was asking him, What are they doing? What are they doing? Walt smiled his sly smile as he answered, "It looks like they're eating something, and drinking a cold beer!"

Everyone wanted to strip and swim out to the Swift boat. Never mind how Waldo knew the beer was cold. . . . Meanwhile, Redmer and Post told the boat crew our frequency, and they contacted us on the PRC-25. Top got on the horn with them. He informed them who we were and asked them to contact 1/101st and let them know we needed a resupply of water, radios, batteries for the radios, and handsets. The Swift boat in turn contacted their higher command. It came back to us that a full search was going on for us, but that it was concentrated almost twenty miles south of our present location. We had walked about ten miles south from where we were inserted, so our junk admirals had inserted us almost thirty miles north of where we were supposed to have been! They had reported that they had put us in on our insertion point but we were in a free-fire zone, and the B-52 strike from the day before was a testimony to that. Wow! The Swift boat had been part of the search, but it was on their own initiative that they had traveled so far north. Lucky us! We were informed that our destroyer support was steaming north and would soon be in position to support us. Meantime Redmer and Post swam back into shore, bringing a couple of canteens with them, which we promptly drank. We gathered empty canteens and tied them up with a rope, and they swam back out to the Swift boat. Redmer and Post returned to shore with the canteens full and a special treat of ten cans of Coke and some fried chicken. The chicken was wet and salty, but it was delicious! And yes, they had drunk an ice-cold beer apiece. Damn Walt! Only Rangers knew that kind of shit! I only wished those Swift boat drivers had inserted us. Things would have been a lot different.

Top Smith had contacted Uncle Earl's team and told them to head toward the coast to link up with us so we could be resupplied. Because of Uncle Earl's encounter with the Charlies, Operations and Intelligence wanted us to stay in the field and recon the area farther inland.

Jungle Jim Cody recalls, "We kept working our way back to the coast, but we ran out of water before we ever reached there. It seems like someone had made contact and a destroyer was coming off the coast. He was our relay, and I remember then I always felt good because we had fire support. I remember coming back into a little deserted village along the coast. We found a well and dropped a bucket on a rope down into it. We were so thirsty, and it was such a desert terrain, but when we pulled the bucket back up, there was a dead bird in it with the water. Still, we just drank around the dead bird and didn't care. It was the sweetest tasting water. We eventually linked up with two other teams. At one point I was lying back on my rucksack and someone broke out a Coke. I wondered where in hell it came from, because obviously that's something you're not going to hump. I was sitting, drinking the Coke, and it was hotter than hell. But the sugar, you know—you're so drained, but that sugar felt so good."

Captain Friedrich wanted to keep the mission going. He had earlier sent a radio message to have the men march until they dropped. When the resupply finally came, he opted not to set the chopper down, but to fly by and drop the water bivets and supplies. The water bivets were dropped first, but they kept bursting when they hit the ground. It was then decided to go ahead and set the helicopter down. Cody was wearing black PJs and hiding behind some bushes. He had heard me radio that we had some friendlies wearing black PJs and not to fire on them. And he remembers that the team came out and went to the chopper. Cody thought they had gotten the word to them about black PJs, and he stood up. At that point, he was looking at the door gunner and saw him grabbing his machine gun and bringing it to bear on him. Cody was just shitting bricks as the other Lurps yelled, "Hold your fire! Hold your fire!" It was close.

Satan and the dog handler were extracted, but another dog team came in their place. It was put with Cruz's team. We made sure the dog handler had sufficient water for himself and his dog, but before the day was over, they were both dragging ass. After getting resupplied, the three teams split off in separate directions. We based up for the night, which was uneventful. The following day we checked out a couple of small deserted hootch complexes, with no results. The new recon zone was starting to look like a dry hole. We found a trail, paralleled it most of the afternoon, and worked our way inland about six or seven miles. The recon zone was fairly flat, with desert terrain and a lot of short, thick, scrub bushes six to eight feet high.

Early evening, we came across two small hills, actually humps about 100 meters apart. The trail ran between them, and then gradually meandered to the left. We walked about three hundred meters past the little hills, then decided to find a place to base up for the night. Larry Christian found a good site in thick brush about forty meters off the trail. There was enough of an opening inside the thicket to accommodate us. We couldn't see the trail, but would be able to hear anything moving on it. It was still really hot, so we got in a security wheel and sat down, just trying to recover some energy.

As I was sitting there, I happened to look at the dog. He had been in a very relaxed mode, but now he put his nose in the air and started moving his head back and forth, seeming to become very alert. The handler was lying back against his rucksack, eyes closed, very much into being miserable, so I nudged him with my rifle. I motioned with my eyes toward the dog. The handler's eyes narrowed, and then he looked at me, and I knew already the dog was doing his job. We alerted everyone out of the heat-induced stupor, and pretty soon we heard Vietnamese voices. They were coming down the trail we had been paralleling, toward us and the small hills. There were lots of them. These folks were not into noise discipline. They got abreast of us on the trail and we could clearly hear what was apparently an NCO giving orders, and we could hear rifles and packs being unslung. This was bad. They were breaking for camp, right there on the trail. There had to be at least forty or fifty of them. They were totally relaxed, talking to each other like they were glad to stop humping. About then, I was wishing I could understand the language. Soon they were breaking into the bushes to urinate. Through the underbrush we could see feet and legs. After they took care of their bodily functions, they started gathering firewood for the evening meal.

Of all places to pick, they chose the area right next to us. Meanwhile the scout dog was making a low growl in his throat. We were all lying flat on the ground on our stomachs. The team leader (TL) warned the dog handler through sign language that the dog had to shut up, or he was going to kill him with his knife. Of course, that attempt would have made more noise than the dog was making. Actually, the dog was doing well. The handler would admonish the dog, and the dog, lying on his stomach, would lay his head on his front paws; then, still looking in the direction of the gooks, he would emit a kind of quiet whine. He would pick up his head and cock his ears when a gook walked our way. Pretty soon, we could smell the aroma of cooking food. It made me hungry, but we weren't going to eat that evening; we couldn't afford to break into our rucksacks and take the chance of making noise. The vegetation around us was so dry and noisy that we didn't dare try to slip away. We were going to wait them out.

Eventually, we could tell they were settling in for chow and talking up a storm. So we took the opportunity to call in and report. Using a series of prompts and responses through squelch-breaks on the radio, the TL was able to inform the relay about our situation. They would be keeping two gunships on standby through the night, along with a reaction force. The navy destroyer was on station and ready to assist us. We knew the Vietnamese would be moving out in the morning, and we planned our move on them then. We settled in for a long, sleepless night.

It was a long night. The enemy laughed and talked late into the evening, obviously feeling secure because of their numbers and the desolation of the area. They didn't know that forty meters away lay seven men and a dog, planning their destruction. It was a good lesson for all of us Lurps, lying there.

First light came and went, and we discovered that those boys weren't early risers. We had contacted our relay and arranged to have the gunships lift off when we gave them the word. There would be two slicks with the gunships, and the slicks would extract us. The Charlies finally started stirring, and soon we could smell a couple of fires going. The previous evening they had all been coming out to piss, but now they were having their morning constitutional, and, man, did it start stinking. One modest fellow came so close to us that, for a second, we thought he was going to actually walk right into us. Luckily, we always chose the thickest bush to lay dog in. This fellow came right up to the thicket we were in, turned around facing his fellow soldiers, dropped his PJs, laid his rifle on the ground next to him, and started grunting. He couldn't have been more than five meters away from where I was lying on my stomach. Too damn close!

When I saw those guys coming out, I had turned the volume down on my radio to nothing. Now we could hear them getting ready to take off. I turned the volume back up on the radio and gave the word to the gunships to lift off. We had already arranged to have the destroyer fire a volley onto the trail where it passed through the small hills. When we heard the VC leave, we started walking away from them in the direction they had come from. The TL called in the fire mission. We could hear the rounds impacting; then the gunships arrived on station and took over for us. They directed us to an opening about 100 meters away. Meanwhile the gunships were making runs. The slicks came in, and I boarded with the TL, Christian, the dog handler, and the dog. Captain Friedrich, our dearly beloved detachment commander, was on the helicopter. The rest of our team was picked up by the second helicopter. I caught snatches of conversation between the gunships, and it sounded like Charlie wasn't having a very good day. Captain Friedrich informed us that an infantry platoon was being inserted to check the bodies. We took off, to the south, joined by the other slick, and flew back to Phan-thiet.

## Rock Mountain Mission Outside Phan-rang

The LRRP detachment left Phan-thiet in a convoy with elements of one of the brigade's line battalions and drove back to Phan-rang. Twenty miles south of Phan-rang and a few miles south of the little village of Ngoc Tinh, the convoy halted during the late afternoon. Every truck in the convoy stopped, and everyone got out of the vehicles. To a casual observer, it looked like a pit stop, but it had all been planned. The infantry and the rest of the personnel in the convoy remounted their vehicles and drove away, but the four teams from the LRRP detachment had gone into the vegetation on the side of the road.

It was a stay-behind mission, and after dark we walked a

couple of miles to our objective, a small mountain range that dominated the coastline south of Phan-rang. On the east side of the high terrain, two separate large ridges ran northeast and southeast, and then they headed due east into the coastal plains to form a wide, open valley facing the China Sea. The hill mass, made out of big boulders, was the strangest terrain feature the Lurps had ever walked in. It stood out in the middle of the rice paddies and was the beginning of foothills where VC were active. Arriving at the base of this solitary "boulder mountain," the teams split up and continued their individual missions. The very first reconnaissance missions pulled by the 1/101st LRRP detachment, in January 1966, had been in that same mountain range and valley, but we didn't know it at the time. Doc "Wolfman" Kraft had joined the platoon in Phan-thiet, and this mission was to be the last part of his training.

Teddy Bear Gaskell and Doc "Jimbo" Bethel were thinking about getting lost on this mission so that they'd be listed missing in action for a while. They had heard that recovered MIAs got thirty-day leaves, and that sounded good to them. Teddy Bear and Bethel were on Uncle Earl Wheeler's team, with Wheeler, Kolarik, and Sid Tolson. They had been given twenty-four hours to get to the top of the mountain. Instead, it took them three days to get to the top. Going up the boulders was like going up steps with twenty-foot risers, and nasty shrub brush was growing among the boulders. They spent the night on top and were told the next morning to look for an LZ so they could be extracted. It took them forty-five minutes to get down to the bottom on the other side of boulder mountain. But when they got to the bottom of the mountain and were waiting for the choppers, TOC aborted their extraction. Instead, the team was resupplied with water and food, after which they went up the hillside a ways. On the northeast side, near the base of the mountain, was a small pagoda that they observed two VC walking toward, one of them carrying a rifle. The team called in artillery on them but didn't see if they were hit. The team split, with two men staying behind and three going down and across to see if they could find anything. With Uncle Earl walking point and Teddy Bear pulling his slack, the

three Lurps came up on a small clearing with some boulders
and a lot of shrubbery at the far end. After they crossed the
clearing, Uncle Earl circled one of the big boulders only to find
a VC right on the other side, ready to blow his head off. Uncle
Earl hit the rock, but dropped his weapon, then jumped and fell
back over Teddy Bear—who was trying to fire a round over
him but couldn't because the boulder was in the way. The
Lurps, who had decent lines of fire now, suffered jams, so they
started throwing hand grenades over the big rock. There was a
lot of sound, a lot of fury, but the Lurps weren't too sure how
much their hand grenades were actually accomplishing. Uncle
Earl's weapon was still up on the rock, so Teddy Bear went up
to get it. They finally broke contact, but instead of going back
down the trail, they slid down the boulders. At that point gunship support came in, and when they fired, the hot shell casings
fell down the back of the Lurps' shirts.

After the gunships departed, the team made its way back
down to the bottom and linked up with an infantry company.
The grunts wanted to go back up, so the Lurps were put on
point for the line company. Teddy Bear, on point, got to a small
clearing close to where the engagement had taken place and
pointed it out to the company commander. Teddy Bear was
told to move out, that they would be right behind him, so he
took off with Uncle Earl in trail. They crossed the clearing and
had gotten to just about the very same place again, scared to
death. When they turned around, of course, nobody was behind
them; the infantry had stopped at the other side. Pretty soon an
infantry NCO appeared and told them to pull back because an
airstrike had been called. The airstrike blew the hell out of the
place—or at least seemed to. But when they went in after the
airstrike, there were mines everywhere, and the area was
heavily booby trapped. Teddy Bear found Bouncing Bettys*
that had been booby trapped with trip wires. They also discov-

* Antipersonnel mines that hurl a "fragmentation projectile" into the air. The
projectile bursts three to six feet above the ground, hurling fragments in all
directions.

ered big caches in natural caves under the boulders, and of course, the infantry shouldered the Lurps aside to get to them.

My own team leader on this boulder mountain mission was Waldo Bacheck. Top Smith was along as scout. David Coffee was also a scout. Ralph Church, RTO; David "Fireball" Dixon, medic, and I was an RTO. Arriving at the base of the mountain, our team started climbing what looked like a huge pile of room-sized boulders. One of the best ways to move was to duck and slide under and between the boulders. On the second day, we had been moving steadily up and around, and when we got to the east side of the mountain, we could see a flat plain that extended to the coast, a very dry region with ten-foot-tall scrub brush.

We took a break in the opening between two house-sized boulders. It was the hottest part of the day, and we were all lulled by the heat and noise of the insects. We had been sitting for about ten minutes when suddenly I sensed that something was wrong. I was fourth in the line of march, and I detected some slight movement at the rear of the team, near Fireball. I glanced at Fireball and saw that he had turned white, and his eyes were bulging out. At first I thought Charlie might be approaching us from our rear, but Fireball's attention wasn't toward the rear—it was right in front of him. Because of the shrubbery between us, I couldn't see what was there. Fireball wasn't moving at all. Earlier, I had heard a sound like some-body blowing out, only much more high pitched, like an expelled hiss. I slowly leaned back on my rucksack and saw movement. My eyes focused on the motion, and I froze. Standing directly over Fireball, about three feet high, weaving back and forth, was a cobra! I recalled seeing a cobra at P training. The instructors had spoken about finding cobras close to Phan-rang. This one was a dusky, dark color, and its hood wasn't very wide. But from where I was sitting, it was very intimidating, very aggressive in its posture. It was standing over Fireball, crowding him, and when it hissed, its hood flared, which was meant to intimidate. By this time, everyone was aware of what was going on, but nobody was getting up or moving around. We were unsure of what to do. Next to Fireball, Ralph Church brought his rifle barrel up slowly. He said later that he'd thought about shooting the snake, but he'd concluded that even if he didn't miss, the bullet would go right through the snake and ricochet all over in the confined space between the boulders. We had all been sweating heavily while humping, but Fireball was now drenched. This scene probably lasted about two minutes, and then the snake suddenly disappeared from my view. Slowly, the color returned to Fireball's face. Crazy Fireball later gave us his deep-throated braying laugh and told us that he had stared the cobra down, and it ran away. All of us were snake paranoid for awhile.

We spent the following day glassing the open plain that ran out to the coast. In the afternoon, we spotted some Charlies walking inland from the coast. We fired them up with artillery. The next day, we started working our way to the top. The actual "hilltop" was more a ridge. About one hundred yards wide, composed of boulders lying on top of each other, it ran north-south for about a quarter mile. Near the top, we found a large chamber formed by three huge, towering boulders. At the base of the largest boulder, a big rock had been chiseled flat, like an altar, on which was a two-foot-high statue of Buddha. Fresh fruit surrounded the Buddha on the rock altar, and someone had left a glass of water. This was up near the top of the boulder mountain, and it was hot as hell. It had the feel of a special place, a place of peace and prayer, and we weren't exactly dressed for Sunday service. We felt like we had no business being there—all of us except Fireball. As we started to leave, crazyass Fireball went to the altar, picked up a banana, peeled it, ate it in two bites, then threw the peel back onto the stone altar.

Working our way down the west side of the mountain to get ready for extraction, we were ribbing Fireball for eating the banana and bringing the wrath of Buddha on our young asses. Of course Fireball thought that if Buddha hadn't wanted him to eat that banana, he wouldn't have put it there. It was hard to argue with that kind of thinking. While waiting for the extraction bird, Coffee thought he spotted someone in the rocks. He started shooting, and pretty soon everyone else was shooting. He was shooting an M-79, and somehow he got a sliver of metal from one of the rounds in his leg, but it was nothing serious. I never saw anyone and thought we were basically shooting at shadows.

We spent about four days enjoying the comforts of Phanrang, and that first night we all partied like crazy. Teddy Bear and I had bunks right next to each other at one end of the barracks. Jimbo Bethel came around that night and wanted Teddy Bear to get up and party some more. But Teddy Bear–John Wayne Gaskell had a low tolerance for booze, and he had passed out on us. Not really meaning to do any harm to Teddy Bear, Bethel grabbed his cot and flipped it upside down. Teddy Bear hit the cement floor with a loud whack, but it never woke him up. I got up and pulled the cot off him to see if he was all right, but Jimbo Bethel took offense at that and started punching me around. I really didn't want to fight until he got me on the barracks floor and his flailing started to hurt. I maneuvered myself on top of Bethel, and was about to give him a good punch, but he moved his head and I smacked the metal leg of the cot that was next to it. We crawled outside, both of us, and had a good cry together. I had a badly swollen right hand for the next few days.

About the third day back, Teddy Bear and I were on our bunks, and the conversation led us to our disagreeing about something, so we walked down to the other end of the barracks, to let another Lurp determine who was right or wrong. As we were walking, a helicopter flew over the barracks, and suddenly we heard a huge bang. We turned around and walked back to our bunks. Lying on the concrete floor beneath Teddy Bear's bunk was an M-60 machine-gun barrel. When the helicopter had taken off, the door gunner must not have locked his barrel down, and when he leaned the M-60 down, the barrel had come off. It had plunged through the hootch's tin roof, through the poncho liner on Teddy Bear's cot, through the mattress on the cot, tore the hell out of the springs of the cot, then chipped the concrete under TB's bed. If Teddy Bear had been on his cot, his day definitely would have been ruined. Just another example of how fickle fate was.

## Change of Command, LRRP Detachment

While in Phan-rang in mid-March, the Long Range Reconnaissance Patrol detachment commander, Captain "Wildman" Friedrich, was replaced by 2nd Lt. Daniel Francis McIsaac, a master blaster. Daniel "Mac" McIsaac was born with a twin sister on 25 July 1943 in Boston. He had a learning disability, and left school in the ninth grade. He joined the Army on 11 September 1961 when he was seventeen years old. He went through basic, AIT, and jump school, and was assigned to B Company, 506th Infantry Battle Group. But it was in the 101st Airborne Division that professional attention was finally paid to his dyslexia. The results were miraculous. He'd always assumed his reading difficulty came from the fact he was just stupid. But once he was treated for dyslexia, it was like scales falling off his eyes. He became an avid reader and first-rate soldier. Before long, he was one of the youngest NCOs around. He graduated from Recondo and Jumpmaster schools, then reenlisted, applying for OCS (officer candidate school). He went to infantry officers candidate school at Fort Benning and graduated with honors. After graduation, he served at Fort Rucker, Alabama, as the executive officer of the Pathfinders. From there he was ordered to Vietnam and sent to the 1st Brigade, 101st Airborne Division, assigned to command the Long Range Reconnaissance Patrol detachment. It was his first solo command, and commanding a special operations unit during a shooting war was the highest test any officer could undertake. The Lurps were a unique group of individuals, and he had his hands full. Fortunately, Mac had Top Smith to provide the guidance that only a senior NCO can give.

One day during our down time in Phan-rang, I was coming back to camp from somewhere with Teddy Bear. As we approached the Lurp barracks, a bunch of Lurps ran out, cussing and laughing, saying "Damn you, Fireball! You're going to get us all killed!" We could hear Fireball's crazy braying laugh from inside. Fireball had been inside, working on his booby traps, trying to get a smoke grenade fuse to fit on an M-26 fragmentation grenade. It was a tricky task: you couldn't just interchange the heads; you had to take the blasting caps off and recrimp them back on. Of all the Lurps, Fireball and Waldo Bacheck were the ones who really liked to experiment with explosives and booby traps. Lieutenant McIsaac recalls that Fireball always wore a claymore mine in a "homemade" holster on his chest. He had shortened the wire from the claymore's blasting cap to the clacker. He said that if he was about to be captured, he would detonate the mine, killing himself and whoever else was around. Waldo Bacheck always argued with him about it because Waldo didn't want him wearing that mine armed while he was pulling drag for us, which was where the medic usually walked. They must have come to some kind of understanding because Fireball kept on wearing a claymore.

## Malaria Takes Joe Griffis

In December, several Lurps had been stricken with malaria, most of them infected while in the Tuy-hoa area. Later they all ended up in the hospital at Cam-ranh for six weeks. Freddy Hernandez, Joe Griffis, Pappy Webb, and Pat Kinser were all there, and Rudy Lopez joined them in February. Gene Sullivan had spent New Year's Eve 1966 in a cold shower because he had a relapse, and his fever had spiked. The medics made him stand under a cold shower until his temperature dropped, while he cursed them for trying to kill him. On 25 February 1967 an incident occurred that was forever imprinted on his mind. Gene Sullivan recalls that a woman doctor, a major, came into the ward. "We were all in those blue hospital pajamas, and we had to snap to attention. She took one look at my ear and saw my gold earring. She wondered out loud just what the hell was this. I had to explain to her about 101st LRRP, how everyone has one, and our commanding general had given approval. We got the okay, and that was fine, and she let it be. We were drinking Kool-Aid there, the four of us, and laughing about what had happened with the major. Suddenly Griffis, who had only six weeks to go on his tour, told us, 'I'm not feeling so well, guys. I'm going to head back and lie down.' We said all right, fine. We finished our Kool-Aid. It wasn't more than thirty or forty minutes, and when we went back, S.Sgt. Joe Griffis was dead. His temperature had shot up, and his spleen had ruptured. It was terrible because he was such a great guy, and it had been so sudden. He was one of the finest team leaders in Lurps at that time. It really devastated all of us. I eventually recovered and went back to the outfit. It was at Khanh Duong."

# 5

## LONG RANGE RECON

1 / 101

## Khanh Duong

Headquarters, I Field Force ordered the 1st Brigade to move to Khanh Duong in Khanh-hoa Province, and to prepare for Operation SUMMERALL, which would be conducted in Phu-yen, Khanh-hoa, and Dar Lac Provinces. The LRRP detachment was part of a large convoy of 248 vehicles that departed from Phan-rang. Not a single enemy action was encountered on the way to Khanh Duong. On 30 March 1967, Operation SUMMERALL was kicked off by the 2/327 Battalion. Operation SUMMERALL was concluded on 29 April without a single major enemy contact. Half of the 1st Brigade's enemy body count of twenty-nine was killed by the provisional Long Range Reconnaissance Patrol detachment.

### Puke Palk and Jungle Jim Asskick, or How
### We Caught Them Sitting on Their Hands!

In early April, the 1/101 was on an operation called Operation SUMMERALL in central Vietnam, in Khanh-hoa Province. The Lurps were working out of Khanh Duong when S.Sgt. "Pappy" Lynch's team received a mission order. Intelligence reports indicated there were confirmed sightings of VC main force troops in the recon zone. The Lurps' mission was to confirm those sightings and identify the unit.

Pappy Lynch was an old noncom from World War II, a wild

bastard and good in the field. In his forties, he was a serious old fart to be humping the bush. Pappy reminded me of what the Marlboro man would, or should, look like. He was tall, wiry, and balding, with eyes that twinkled in merriment or mischief. The ladies would consider him handsome. He was a free spirit, and the few stripes on his sleeves were a confirmation of that. He was perfect for the Lurps. Jungle Jim Cody remembers Pappy breaking his ankle on an insertion. Pappy couldn't go out with the team, but upon the team's return, he took them down to the bars. Pappy proceeded to pound down the beers and ended up dancing on the tabletop, collapsing the table and breaking the cast on his ankle. I remember him scrounging some potatoes and onions from the general's mess and sitting around peeling them, then frying them up while he, Ron Pitts, Pappy Webb, Uncle Earl Wheeler, and a score of us lesser folk would play mumblety peg. He was a good man.

The senior scout on Pappy Lynch's team was Jimmie Lee "Jungle Jim" Cody. Cody was born and raised in Cocoa, Florida, a small ranching town about midway down the length of Florida, off in the swamp. He went to high school at Cocoa High School, and was raised with all his cousins and brothers, in a family environment with a small-town southern heritage. He played football, was in the band, and grew up hunting and fishing in swamp terrain. His youthful swamp crawling made him more comfortable with his surroundings in Vietnam than most people with city backgrounds. During his last year of high school, a Special Forces training maneuver took place near Cody's home. He was intrigued by it and went out to watch with a friend, with whom he later ended up joining the army on the buddy system. He and his friend drove the Special Forces soldiers around, picking up beer for them and running errands. They were intrigued with Recondo-type personalities.

Cody had three brothers, all of whom were in the army—one of them a grunt in Korea, one with the 82nd Airborne, and the other with a leg artillery unit. Cody graduated high school in 1965, and it came time to do his stint in the army. Naturally, with a brother in the Airborne, that was what Cody wanted to do, but deep down Vietnam was also calling. He enlisted

22 June 1965 and did basic, Airborne AIT, and leadership schools at Fort Gordon, Georgia, then went on to jump school at Fort Benning, Georgia. Half the class went to Nam, and the other half went to Fort Bragg. Cody was in the latter group. When he got to Fort Bragg, he started putting in Form 1049s to volunteer for Nam, but six months passed before he got orders. In July 1966, he was going through in-country training when the army found out he could type. He did three weeks of typing before they let him go, and he was offered a job in the rear, in administration, but he declined.

Cody was sent to the forward area, up in Tuy-hoa, and then found out that he had been listed as AWOL the whole time he was typing. He was assigned to A Company 2/327. When he arrived at the company area, he was issued a pack and a rifle and was put on the first supply chopper headed out to the field. He saw a lot of action, staying with his line company until he came to the Lurps in December 1966.

"Looking back, I always looked at myself as a grunt," Cody recalls. "Your first experience in country has the most bearing on what your attitude and self-concept is. The line company was a lot of strange people, just plain guys from a multitude of different places, all thrown together. You were placed in strange and crazy situations, which bonded all the men and was unique. I got my cherry busted with the line company. Almost the whole time I was with them, I walked point, and whenever our platoon was on point, I walked it. I carried an M-16 most of the time and carried an M-79 grenade launcher for a month and a half. But thank God, I never had to be an RTO. I looked at the Lurps, and they had a good record, they weren't always getting their asses shot off, and they seemed to have a mystique about them. They obviously had a good record for keeping their people alive."

The eliteness of the Lurps appealed to Cody, and so he volunteered. He was surprised to be accepted. He didn't think that just anybody coming off the line with a grunt background would be a candidate. Looking back, he thinks line infantry experience was a big plus. He didn't have the sophisticated training that guys in the Ranger outfits received later on, but he had training that you wouldn't get at a Ranger school: he was trained by Chuck, who he thinks taught a better school.

Cody got his orders for the Lurps in Kontum about the first part of January, as his company was getting ready to go back into the field. Less than a week later, Jungle Jim went out on his first mission with Lurps.

The junior scout on Pappy Lynch's team, and Jungle Jim's "slack man" was Sp5. Virgil "Puke" Palk from Waverly, Tennessee. Puke was a Special-Forces-trained medic who would rather shoot them than do the bandaging. I never saw him work as a medic while in Lurps. Senior RTO was Sp4. Dave Stauffer from San Francisco who liked to smoke Lucky Strikes. Dave and I had come into the Lurps together. The medic was "Jimbo" Bethel. Pfc. Sid Tolson would be the junior RTO, and at seventeen he was the youngest man in the Lurps—in fact, too young to be in Vietnam legally. It was "Killer" Tolson's first mission. He would be carrying the PRC-74, the big, heavy radio. Sid was working as a radioman but knew absolutely nothing about it at the time. He didn't seem particularly nervous about the coming mission. But since it was his first mission, what did he know?

"I had a funny feeling about the mission the morning we left," Jungle Jim said. "Just a nagging. We were inserted early in the morning, and everything went well. We came upon a trail right off the LZ, and followed it, staying off the trail, contouring it out about forty meters. Around lunchtime, we crossed the trail, taking care in doing so. We moved off the trail about forty meters, into some thicket for concealment, but we were still able to monitor movement on the trail. We sat in our security wheel, covering our sectors. We would eat lunch in pairs and watch the trail for awhile. . . ."

Cody was leaning back on his rucksack, looking back down the trail from where the team had come. He was just kind of mesmerized by the horizon, watching but not really seeing. He'd been humping all morning and was hot and tired. All of a sudden, forty or fifty yards away, he saw a Chuck with a pack and rifle turn the trail as he walked up it. At first Cody couldn't believe what he had just seen. He started to reach behind to tap

Puke Palk, but someone behind him had knelt to get into his pack or something, and the movement caught the Charlie's eye. Cody was ready to raise his rifle to his shoulder but was watching to see if anyone else was with the guy, which was what Cody was expecting. He assumed he was eyeballing the point man. The Charlie stopped as soon as he saw movement, then turned around and started hauling ass back down the trail.

"We jumped up, our packs still on the ground, and Puke and I took off after him," Cody said. "Obviously at that point we were compromised, and we had to take him out. We took off without a whole lot of direction, other than that the team knew what we were doing and that we would be right back."

Cody and Puke followed the Charlie off the trail for a ways, then decided speed was more important, so they jumped on the trail. After moving down the trail a bit, they then decided to get off it. When they didn't see the soldier, they stopped. Then they heard something. They moved at a controlled pace in the direction of the noise, expecting to make some contact. Cody and Puke couldn't quite be sure of what they were hearing, but as they got closer, the noise became more pronounced.

"You're moving, and it's hot, and your heart is pumping, so you're really breaking a sweat but you're trying to keep your breathing down so you can hear better. It's hard to keep all that in control as you're moving. The foliage we were going through was so thick that we had to move slowly to get through it without making noise."

The two Lurps had been moving fifteen or twenty minutes, when they broke into an unanticipated clearing and found themselves on the edge of a bunker complex, with hootches hidden in the vegetation. The clearing was invisible from the sky or the trail. Cody and Puke had luckily hit it at an angle. As they walked up through the vegetation into the clearing, a Charlie walked out of a hootch in front of one of the bunkers, stopped, and looked back at them. Apparently the guy they had been chasing belonged with these folks. They had been alerted and were up and moving. The two Lurps and the enemy soldier stood there, ten or fifteen yards between them, each side watching, waiting for the other to make the move. Suddenly, the Chuck raised his rifle and spit off a couple of rounds, firing prematurely. He blew it. The rounds kicked dirt a couple of feet in front of the two Lurps. It was a situation where there was no thinking it through, no time for making decisions; they just reacted. Cody took off running straight at the Charlie, firing on semiauto, dropping the man. He ran over the top of a bunker right into the edge of the village. Now things went chaotic, and Cody was firing on full automatic.

"A tribute to Virgil 'Puke' Palk," Cody said. "I never stopped to think, Is he going to back me up? It's just one of those things where you've been out in a number of situations where the other guy has been tested. You don't have any doubt that he will be there for you. And sure enough, as I got there, there was a hootch to my left flank, and a lane of fire all the way around me. The VC are running. It was like jumping into the middle of a chicken coop—they're just running everywhere. I started opening up, and Palk ran up. He was behind me the whole time I was moving, and he stopped, off to my right rear shoulder. We had not exchanged a word since breaking into the clearing. He was standing facing the other direction. We were really going through magazines; it was a target-rich environment. We kept spraying, and they would run into it. We had caught them 'sitting on their hands'."*

Cody doesn't remember whether, after the initial burst, they received any return fire or not. The enemy was busy running, and the two Lurps were busy shooting. They didn't have time to aim. Picking targets would be too slow. They fired from the hip, kept firing, and changed magazines. It was just like jumping in the middle of a beehive, or an ant hill. Cody and Puke were just trying to take down as many enemy as they could, shooting people at rifle length. They had the element of surprise totally on their side.

"At one point as some Charlie was trying to get away, he ran into Palk. He bounced off Palk and Virgil bumped my right shoulder. I looked back, and the gook just ran past and took off again. We fired through hootches and threw grenades over

*1st Brigade, 101st Airborne Division Afteraction Report, 17 Apr 1967.

hootches and into some bunkers. I could tell we had them down, and they were taking the hit. But the surprise wasn't going to last forever, and we had to get out of the complex fast. We grabbed as many packs from the bodies lying around us, and from inside the nearest hootch, as we could carry, then backed out of there and started hauling ass. I don't have any idea how much time was involved while this had been going on. You have no concept of time at such moments. It was all in slow motion.

"I remember breaking through the bush, just running with abandon, with the man on my ass. And you just forget noise discipline, you're running for the gold; you're tired, you're sucking massive air, and your adrenaline is just absolutely coming through your ears. We hit the trail and took it, trying to make the fastest time possible. We came to a fork in the trail and stopped to get our bearings. We heard movement in the vegetation bordering the trail and got into position, ready to fire at whatever came. We were both ready to open up on the noise but kept holding our fire, holding our fire, waiting for them to show. I just had this feeling not to shoot—you know, the kind of sixth sense that you go by and you don't question. After a few tense seconds, finally a bunch of little kids broke through onto the trail. They spotted us, and they just took off again in the opposite direction. They had been in the village, and when they scattered, they just ended up coming our way. We almost opened up on them and I am glad we held our fire. I wouldn't want to have that on my conscience."

By that time Cody's sphincter was the size of a pinhole. Both of them just kept thinking, kept hoping, they were heading in the direction where they thought the rest of the team was. The two Lurps had entered the village/bunker complex through the jungle, and it was very easy to get disoriented.

Meanwhile, the team had heard the firefight break out and had dropped back to a more defendable position, but Cody and Puke didn't even know where they were in reference to where they had left the team. The rest of Pappy Lynch's team had found a little cove of trees and set up a defensive perimeter. They heard all of the firing and explosions going on, so they called in and asked for a reaction force. During the movement to the new perimeter, the rest of the team had captured a woman prisoner.

Cody and Puke eventually linked up with the rest of the team, and Pappy Lynch was seriously pleased to see them. He asked about the tactical side of the situation, and they told him the enemy was behind them and heading their way, or so they thought. Cody and Puke filled in on the 360-degree security wheel and waited. They figured that the enemy was on the way, and they would be in contact again soon.

"Pappy Lynch radioed in and told the rear they had a woman prisoner. Before confirmation had been received on whether a reaction force was on the way, Pappy was trying to decide whether we were going to saddle up and put the fast shuffle on, or stay put. If we were going to take off, we would have to off the prisoner. Somehow this got back to S-2, and they were really insistent on getting the prisoner out."

Confirmation came that the reaction force was being inserted a short distance away, and the Lurps moved out to make the linkup. Working toward the unit, the team hit a clearing. Brigade wanted the prisoner, and they wanted her right now. They weren't thinking of taking the team out, just the prisoner. Brigade sent out a chopper, and when it came in to land, in the clearing, Cody ran out with the prisoner and jumped into the chopper with her. Before he could get off, the chopper took off with him in it. It was the brigade executive officer's chopper.

"We flew to the small clearing where the reaction force had been inserted. As we were coming in to land in the middle of the clearing to drop me and my prisoner, I looked down and was surprised to see my old line company, my old platoon. It was just coincidence. Immediately I recognized seven or eight guys whom I had known when I spent time on the line. When I got off the chopper, we had a reunion right there. I remember the exhilaration of this whole thing, having made it through the contact, then to see all my old comrades. It was just a superb moment, one that will never be equalled."

Cody's team eventually linked up with his old line platoon,

and the Lurps were extracted to the rear area in Khanh Duong.
That night, Intelligence decided that they wanted the team to
go back in the next morning, and find out what it was that they
had gotten into, to try to get some depth to details on the enemy
unit. The next day Pappy Lynch's team took a whole line company into the enemy camp. Cody was surprised that they were
able to find the place because it was so well concealed, an
excellent example of the enemy's expert use of terrain and
vegetation.

"The enemy had abandoned the camp and taken the bodies.
At the rear of the camp I could see how we had entered the village. We found where the bodies had gone down and could see
the blood trails and drag marks where they had been hauled
away. The strange thing was finding where we had made our
stand. Empty magazines were scattered where we had been
reaching and slamming them in, emptying one and reaching
for another and slamming it in and emptying it—just letting the
rounds fly. At the time I didn't know what Palk was doing. It
was like a bowling alley: I had that lane and this one, and you
took down anything and everything in those lanes. He stood by
me and never hesitated. I could see evidence of his handiwork
all around. There were some underground bunkers into which
we had tossed grenades. We could see damage in there but
couldn't get a count because there were tunnels going out of
the bunkers. I think the prisoner that the team had taken had
said there were nine confirmed killed. Who's going to keep a
count like that? It had to have been more. The afteraction
report stated that there were forty-something in that village.
That's an easy number, because in such a confined area and the
way it was camouflaged, we couldn't see what was on the other
side of the hootches. When we were firing through the
hootches, we were hitting and picking up the ones on the other
side. I just remember hitting a hell of a lot of people," Cody
told me.

The intelligence gathered from the captured materials
and the interrogation of the prisoner indicated that Cody and
Puke Palk had hit a Regional Province Headquarters of the
Vietcong. It was defended by two platoons of a main force

Vietcong company. The afteraction report indicated nine confirmed killed—probably confirmed only by the prisoner—but
no estimate of wounded. The prisoner revealed that they
thought they were being attacked by a superior force. The
enemy's only concern was breaking off contact and escaping.

Pappy Lynch's team had resupplied when coming out the
previous day. The line company had all of the information it
needed, so the team split off from the line company and continued the mission. They were supposed to link up with one of
the other Lurp teams. Cody says: "We crossed a ridge and cut
a trail right at the top. We were working our way down the trail
trying to get off it. It was around 1400 hours, and all of a
sudden shit opened up. I could tell just immediately it was a
30-caliber machine gun. We all dived for cover, and I went
backward over a rock, lunging for cover, and as I was lying on
my back on top of my rucksack behind the rock, I looked over
and there was Pappy Lynch sitting there laughing at me. He
was just sitting there laughing, and I remember telling him,
'This shit is getting old.' We came out of our packs and
crawled up to take a look at what was happening. When we
were coming over the ridge to link up with the other team, they
got hit. Whoever was hitting them had come over the ridge and
was firing down at this lower ridge, where the other team was.
I can't remember who they were. Our team started flanking the
machine gun, and we opened up on Chuck. They were surprised to find us on the ridge. They broke contact and took off.
That was two back-to-back days with hot activity. It was a hot
little area."

Gene Sullivan returned from his bout with malaria and was
happy to see his good friends Bruce Redmer and Freddy Hernandez in the Lurps. He went into the tent where his cot was set
up, and Freddy Hernandez was there. Gene had bought one of
those stupid pillows with the ornate leaf design. It was the only
pillow he had. His happiness was short-lived, ending about the
time he draped his gear on his cot; a bamboo viper was sticking
out from underneath the pillow.

"I jumped back and pointed at the thing, and started yelling,

'*Viper!* Viper!' Gene recalls. "My yelling brought a couple of guys into the tent. I said, 'Fred, look, a viper!' He started to reach for it and I said, 'No, Fred! No, no!' All of a sudden he reaches under the pillow and, quick, snatches the snake. He started wiggling it around his hand real fast, and I yelled, 'Fred, what the hell are you doing!' All of a sudden it slipped out of his hand, and the damn thing fell right on my chest. I screamed and just threw it off my chest and went running out of the tent. I was holding my head and checking myself to see if I'd been bitten. Then the snake was suddenly slung at me, right across my shoulder. I screamed again and ran another hundred yards. Then I heard all this laughter behind me, and I realized that son of a bitch Fred Hernandez was behind it all. He had found that damn viper earlier that day and had cut its head off and was just laying for me. It gave me quite a scare. Those guys had a real good laugh on my part."

Sullivan remembers John Dietrich going on R&R in late January or early February. He went to Hawaii and met his wife, who had come over from the States. She told him he stank and should take a shower. John told her he had just taken one. She told him to take another.

Sullivan recalls, "We just carried the smell around on us from Vietnam. I remember when I first got in country, and the whole place smelled like a wet dog. That was the best description I could come up with over all these years. Vietnam smelled like a wet dog."

### Hernandez on Point

In one of the first missions pulled out of Khanh Duong by the LRRP detachment, S.Sgt. John Dietrich's recon team was picked to insert west of a 1st Brigade infantry battalion area of operation. On the team was S.Sgt. Fred Hernandez, Sgt. Bruce Redmer, Sgt. Gene Sullivan, Sgt. Bill Post, and a medic.

The team knew VC were in the area. Fred Hernandez was on point, wearing black pajamas and a bandanna tied around his head. He was leading the team just a few meters off a trail, and they decided to cross. Freddy stepped out on the trail, and suddenly a VC, who was just a few meters down the trail, started waving at him, and inviting him to join the others down on the trail. Freddy stopped, with the rest of the team still in the bush. Somebody on the team had picked up on what was going down, because they threw up the "enemy in sight" signal. Freddy didn't lose his cool. He made an arm wave at the dude and stepped back in the bush.

They all ducked down right away. It was a "What the fuck do we do now?" situation. Off to the side of the trail were punji stakes. Sullivan didn't know how old they were, but he wasn't too happy to be lying next to punji stakes with the enemy out on the trail calling to one of his teammates.

The enemy called out to Fred again. Because he didn't answer the first time, Fred figured he had better do something at this point. He tried to mumble something, but it didn't work. They knew right away that he wasn't one of them, and the VC started firing and missed. Sullivan's face was so deep in the dirt, he thought he was going to get an abrasion from it. The team broke contact and ran like crazy for a good half mile, parallel to the trail.

Finally they got into some brush about thirty yards off the trail. Gene Sullivan moved up to monitor the trail, taking only the magazine in his weapon. He took a position next to a big anthill ten or twelve feet high. After a while, he realized the other guys had eaten, and were laagering up. Nobody had come out to relieve him. Standing his rifle against a tree, he tried to hand signal, but no one noticed. Suddenly, a twig broke behind him. He slowly turned. Walking no more than seven or eight feet from him was a VC in a long-sleeve khaki shirt, with shirttail out and black pajama shorts. He was carrying an old German Mauser rifle. The VC looked up suddenly, and Sullivan realized the VC had that Mauser at his hip, pointed his way. Sullivan didn't dare move. He didn't blink. He didn't do anything. He was just praying for someone on the team to see what was going on. Then he looked at the VC's eyes, and realized that the man didn't really see him. The man was alert, but Sullivan blended in well with the vegetation. Even so, the VC kept moving in the direction of the team's position. When the

VC was far enough past not to see Sullivan's movement with his peripheral vision, Sullivan reached for his rifle, pointed it at the VC's back, and pulled the trigger. Nothing. He had the safety on. Laying the rifle in his lap, Sullivan *very* slowly, afraid of the sound of the selector switch, started to switch it to full auto. Suddenly, one of Sullivan's teammates coughed. The VC spun around and looked right at Sullivan. Sullivan looked right back at him and fired a burst—and missed! The VC took off.

"All of a sudden I hear another VC right behind this guy, coming up on the other side of the anthill with a carbine," Sullivan remembers. "This dude turned, and ran, too. I fired another burst and again didn't hit anyone. I come racing in, the team asks what's going on, and I said, 'Two VC! Two VC!' In a matter of seconds we're fired on, and it's coming all around us. We grabbed everything we could, broke contact, and ran until it was almost dark. That was my first experience in a firefight."

## Dog Story

When the LRRP detachment was in Khanh Duong, I was out with Bacheck's team, on a mission with a dog team. The dog was a solid black German shepherd with yellow/gold eyes, a real son of a bitch. Satan had been awarded a Silver Star and Purple Heart, or so we had heard. Satan liked to bite and didn't much care if you were Vietcong or American. In the rear area, he had bitten about everyone in the detachment. There'd be no warning, no growl—just a nice, mean bite. Well, I'm walking, taking care of my sector, nice and easy, and in no big hurry. Satan is following me in patrol order. We had all been reassured by the handler that Satan only bit in the rear. That was fine by me, because I had more important things to worry about. Suddenly, there's an intense pain on the right side of my rear end, where the cheek meets the back of the leg. It took me by surprise, and I let out a suppressed yelp. I turned around, and I swear that damn Satan was smiling at me. The dog's handler came up to me, and whispered, "The dog is bored." He didn't just nip me—he left some nice holes.

Soon after we came out of the field, Satan bit Top Smith on the arm. Right after that, while we were awaiting our next mission, the dog handler came to our area, carrying on about how somebody fragged Satan and killed him. I don't know who did him in, but I was a suspect—as was Top. Rumor in the detachment said it was Fireball. In a way it was too bad. The dogs didn't have a DEROS (date of estimated return from overseas) date. I would rather have seen Satan charge a machine-gun bunker and win the Medal of Honor. Even so, I always thought it was a bad idea to integrate Lurps and scout dogs.

## Point Contact

We had just inserted into our primary LZ northwest of Khanh Duong when we ran into what must have been a couple of LZ watchers. A few rounds were exchanged, gunships were called in, and the team was picked up in two separate choppers, three to a slick. We never gained altitude, but contour-flew all the way to the secondary LZ. When S.Sgt. Walter "Waldo" Bacheck, Sgt. Derby Jones, and I were inserted into our secondary LZ, we jumped out of the chopper and headed for the woodline. I had taken about ten steps when I ran across a high-speed trail that cut right down the middle of the LZ. It looked well used. Jumping across it, I joined Waldo and Derby in the tree line and received a radio transmission from the second helicopter carrying Pat Kinser, Franklin Lee, and Paul Martin. I didn't believe what I heard and asked them to repeat it. Bacheck, keeping a sharp eye on where the high-speed trail meandered from, briefly looked at me and whispered, "What did they say?"

I told him, "They're short of fuel and are going back to refuel."

Ol' Walt went kind of bug-eyed and said, "Shit."

He nodded to Derby Jones; he didn't need to explain. Derby got us into some deep vegetation and found a good defensive perimeter. We had to lay dog and wait for the rest of the team.

A three-man team sure seemed small, especially with that overused trail so close by. I motioned silently to Bacheck to see if he wanted me to put the long antenna up, but he shook his head no. I was glad. If we had to shoot and scoot, I wouldn't have the time to take it down. We laid there, in the defensive wheel, listening as the jungle sounds came back and watching our area of responsibility. It was quiet, just the way we wanted it. About forty minutes later, the squelch broke on my handset. The rest of the team was five minutes out and approaching from the opposite direction that we had taken. I relayed back that the team should unass (leave) the starboard side of the slick and take a two o'clock heading (the nose of the helicopter being twelve o'clock). I said that we would be at the tree line waiting and pointed out that Derby was wearing black PJs, so the door gunners should carefully identify their targets before shooting.

The first gunship zoomed by, and then the slick was flaring, and the rest of the team was heading our way. We linked up, went back into the woodline about seventy-five meters, and laid dog. I cleared the choppers, and a few minutes later Pat Kinser led in the direction Walt pointed out. The LZ was situated in a flat area where two drainages from a large mountain mass joined. There was an expanse of double-canopy jungle, and a rolling ridge separated the two drainages. We proceeded up the right-side drainage, halfway up the ridge, paralleling the top. Our recon zone was in the left drainage, which was bigger and part of a hill mass; the trail from the LZ ran down the gut of it. We went about two hundred meters, then crossed over into the other drainage and bumped the trail. Backtracking, we recrossed the ridge and followed it for another two hundred meters. We were gaining too much elevation, so Walt decided to try going over the ridge again. If we bumped into the trail again, we would have to cross it. We went back over the top, and about one hundred meters on the other side we came across the trail again, where it bent a little to the right and then doglegged to the left. We posted security and were crossing when Pat Kinser heard a noise. The movement was on the trail, toward where we had inserted. I had just crossed the trail, and

Paul Martin was right on it, when Pat and Derby opened up. They were firing on a VC squad that was probably coming to check on what the helicopters had been doing in their area. Pat and Derby killed the first two and with Bacheck's help put the hurt on a couple more. One moment the three of them were standing up or crouching, doing their thing, then suddenly all of them were running in front of me and to my left. Spouts of dirt were following them, and it dawned on me that the line of little spouts was heading my way. The rounds went right around me, chewing up the foliage as I emptied my weapon toward their source. As I was changing magazines, I could hear Paul Martin, Waldo, and Derby shooting, and Pat cussing up a storm because his weapon was down. What we estimated to be an enemy squad broke contact and ran. We also were breaking contact, with Franklin Lee now on point.

Paul Martin remembers that as we were beating feet getting away from the contact area, suddenly his feet were moving, but he wasn't going anywhere; his rucksack frame was stuck between two thick bamboo stalks. I was behind Martin and remember hearing Bacheck growling at me to get him loose. I put my shoulder down and popped him out. It was funny at the time.

We got about seventy yards away from the contact site and went into a security wheel. I motioned to Paul Martin to put up his long antenna. He looked at me like I was nuts, but he did it. Even so, he couldn't make contact, so he took it down. After a brief time, Walt motioned Derby and me to go with him to secure the enemy weapons and check the bodies. Working our way back slowly, we came upon two bodies lying where they had been shot. A couple of good blood trails led away back up the trail, in the direction Charlie had come from. One of the dead had a pack, and both had weapons. I learned that Pat Kinser's weapon was down. The first NVA, carrying an SKS, had been seven meters from Pat when Pat put him down. But the second NVA, right behind the first, started shooting at Pat. A bullet struck the barrel of Pat's M-16, right behind the sight post, knocking it out of his hands. Derby Jones, acting as Pat's "slack man," and doing his job really well, killed the second

NVA. By that time, Waldo had added to the shooting. It had been a perfect coordination of firepower, using the immediate-action drill to a point-contact. One of the dead Charlies was wearing a tan canvas belt, and the buckle had a star in the middle of it: we were dealing with NVA. Derby cut off the belt and Pat Kinser got the SKS from the NVA point man. He eventually took it home as a war souvenir.

We rejoined the team in the security wheel. We still had not made contact on the radio. We worked our way back up the ridge to gain some altitude and finally found a spot where we could establish radio contact with the TOC for the 2/502, for whom we were working. We figured we were compromised, and they would probably extract us and reinsert us. After a brief interlude, we were told we would be resupplied with ammo and a new M-16, and then were to continue our mission.

We found a semiopen area that was big enough to take a chopper. They dropped off the ammo and M-16 rifle and took the enemy weapons and pack. After the resupply, we put some distance between ourselves and the resupply LZ, taking a long, circuitous route back into the recon zone. We spent the next four days finding sign of the enemy but never actually seeing any. We were extracted on the morning of the fifth day and flown back to the 2/502 Battalion TOC to be resupplied and reinserted on a new mission.

We landed on the firebase that was serving as battalion headquarters for the 2/502. Finding a small copse of trees within the hilltop firebase perimeter, we started repacking our rucksacks and refilling our empty magazines. We were to be reinserted that evening at last light. Configuring your rucksack for a Lurp mission took some attention. You couldn't just throw things in and then begin emptying your rucksack looking for a certain item when you needed it in the field. The biggest bulk of the load was food. We had experimented with one meal per day but found that that usually wouldn't sustain a man in the field. And we had to take enough to provide for the possibility of the mission's being extended. Five days' rations consisted of three days' C-ration cans packed in socks, each sock containing one day's ration of two complete meals, and two days' LRRP dry rations, two complete meals per day. Those items were packed in reverse order from how they would be eaten or used. The other luxury items packed into a rucksack were a wool sweater, poncho liner, claymore, extra battery for the PRC-25, and maybe a two-quart water bladder, if you were lucky enough to have one. For Lurps, spare radio batteries and claymores weren't luxury items, they were necessities. Attached to and carried outside the rucksack were two canteens of water, with water purification tablets taped to the cap links, two WP (water phosphorus) grenades, a half-pound block of C-4 in a canteen pouch, ten feet of detonating cord, two time-fuse igniters, and a small, taped-over bottle of Tabasco sauce, which was the preferred ration condiment for most of the Lurps. The RTOs usually configured the radio at the top of the framepack, the rucksack below. If we had to shoot and scoot, they could drop the rucksack and still have the radio, a recon team's most important item. Sometimes it was carried inside the rucksack. The monster PRC-74, at thirty-four pounds, was a nightmare to pack, not only for its weight but also its awkwardness for packing. Every team member's pack was configured in the same manner so that each man knew where his teammate carried everything.

As we were busy packing in the shade of the small trees, we were joined by a tall, lanky man in his midforties. He wasn't wearing insignia, but he carried himself with the calm presence of a man born to command. He sat at the base of one of the small trees we were gathered around and started rolling a cigarette. He had brought over a two-quart water bladder and offered us a drink. As we were discussing our sightings of the enemy, he opened up his map, and we pinpointed the locations involved. He asked where we thought enemy movement might be flowing to, where basecamps might be located. He had a long discussion with Bacheck and the rest of us about where we might look and what to look for on the coming mission. I remember his tobacco-stained fingers and eyes that had seen it all. He hung around us the good part of the afternoon, and then got up and wished us luck. As the man left, I asked Derby Jones who he was. He looked at me incredulously, said a few choice words about my ignorance, then told me that it was Lt. Col. Frank Dietrich, "Gunslinger," commander of the 2/502. He had also been Sgt. Dietrich, the main character in *Those Devils in Baggy Pants*, the famous Ross Carter book from World War II on the 504th Parachute Infantry. He was also a veteran of the Korean War.

Six months earlier, while serving with the 2/509 Airborne in Mainz, Germany, I had read three books in the post library while awaiting my reassignment to Vietnam, the afore-mentioned Ross Carter's *Those Devils in Baggy Pants* and James Alteri's *The Spearheaders* and *Darby's Rangers*. I was searching for information or an insight that might help me when I got to Vietnam. I had learned more about the Rangers and Senon, and what he had told me so many years before as a young kid. I also remembered Lieutenant Colonel Dietrich as one of the legendary figures out of the ranks of the Airborne during World War II. He'd been an enlisted man then and was an enlisted man's officer, the kind that rarely make general officer's rank. He was the best of the best. Encountering him was better than meeting the President.

Around mid-April, S.Sgt. Walt "Waldo" Bacheck's team was given a patrol warning order for a mission twenty-five miles northwest of the 1st Brigade forward base camp at Khanh Duong. The team consisted of Sgt. Pat Kinser, scout; Derby Jones, scout; Sp4. George "Rommel" Murphy, RTO; Sgt. Danny Williams, medic, and me, RTO. We were under operational control of the 2/502, commanded by Lt. Col. Frank Dietrich. We inserted at last light, as was normal. The area of operation was an expanse of plateau. The terrain was triple-canopy jungle on rolling hills, with small open areas of ele-phant grass. In the jungle areas, the highest canopy was around 120 feet, the second canopy at around fifty to sixty feet. There were huge soaring trees and a jungle floor thick with vines, fronds, liacanias—every plant struggling with its neighbor for survival. There were also a lot of birds and every imaginable sort of insect, like monster centipedes. It was a beautiful, yet

harsh, primitive environment. The drama of war made us that
much more aware of our surroundings.

The next morning we started gridding our RZ, searching for
signs of Charlie. Toward afternoon, we came upon a trail and
actually walked it a ways, with Danny Williams covering our
tracks. Eventually we came to a junction of five trails. Bacheck
decided we would monitor traffic so we moved west off them
about twenty-five meters onto a thickly jungled low rise. We
found a dense bamboo thicket and based there for the night.
Derby and Bacheck went back out and grenade booby-trapped
two of the most used trails that led into the junction. The two
trails skirted the rise we were on, and ran down into a wide,
leech-infested creek bed. We radioed in our location and
settled in for the night with the fuck-you lizards. The next
morning, after Derby and Kinser had made a 360-degree recon
around our position, some of us started eating our morning
breakfast in shifts.

Suddenly we heard Charlies walking down the trail, talking
and laughing, without a care in the world. Abruptly, one of the
booby traps went off, shattering the morning stillness. We
heard screaming and moaning, fading as it went away down
one of the trails. After a while we went out and examined our
handiwork. A dead Charlie, wearing all black pajamas, with a
rucksack and an SKS, was lying just off the trail. He had been
mangled pretty good by the grenade, and a good blood trail ran
down into the creek bed. Derby, Bacheck, and I slowly paralleled the trail on the rise and spotted the silhouettes of six or
seven hootches about 150 meters from our NDP (night defensive position). We rejoined the others, then Bacheck and Derby
went back to the dead VC and booby-trapped his body, figuring someone would be back to get him.

Meanwhile, I had gotten in communication with the bird
dog, which had just arrived on station for the morning call in.
Bacheck returned and requested an airstrike on the hootch
complex. We worked our way back down the small rise to
where we could observe and adjust the airstrike. Pat Kinser and
Derby Jones climbed a tree and displayed an orange panel so
the bird dog could see our position, then an air force F-104

came on station and dropped his bomb load on the target. At about 100 meters' distance, we were close to the target but well protected by the undulating terrain. Even so, we could really feel the concussion of the bombs, and debris crashed down on us. On his last pass, the jet jockey used his 20mm cannon. Kinser and Derby almost fell out of the tree when the 20mm casings rained down on them because the pilot made his gun run directly over us. The casings hitting the trees and shrubbery around us made it sound as if we were under fire. Of course, it was only funny *after* we found out what had happened.

After the bomb strike, we went down the rise and into the hootch complex. We felt pretty cocky and thought we had buried whoever might have been down there. But the bombs had landed to the right of the hootch complex, missing it completely. The VC had been using the hootches as a way-station and small base camp. We found evidence of recent use of the place, and a blood trail that went on through the complex. We also uncovered a cache of rice, cooking utensils, packs, weapons and grenades, as well as bunkers with tunnels that ran deeper into the ground. We radioed in our find and were advised by the 2/502 TOC that they would be coming in to pick up the equipment, so we located a small well of an opening in the jungle for an LZ, and Lieutenant Colonel Dietrich's helicopter flew in. We were all surprised and thought it was pretty cool that he had personally come in to pick up the stuff. As the helicopter lifted, he gave us a thumbs-up, and we returned it.

After the helicopter left, we went back into the hootch complex and followed the blood trail for quite a distance, but eventually it disappeared. We meandered around for the next three days, and though we saw sign of the enemy, we never made anymore contact. On the evening of the third day, the 2/502 TOC called us and told us that an infantry company would be closing in on the area we were in and that we would be extracted the following evening.

We had come almost full circle and were close to where we had booby-trapped the dead Charlie. Waldo Bacheck wanted the booby trap disarmed because he didn't want one of

Dietrich's ground pounders to set it off, so Derby Jones and I were elected to do the job. Of course, during the last three hot days, the corpse had ballooned out to the bursting point, and the stench was so terrible it made us gag. Derby thought we could shoot an M-79 round into the body and detonate the booby trap, so we fired a couple of rounds, but the thickness of the undergrowth made it impossible to get enough distance from the body for the M-79 rounds to arm themselves, and they failed to explode. Then Derby and I decided we would get close enough to the body to lob two grenades on it and run. Of course, as we were running, both of our grenades *and* the booby-trapped grenade went off, exploding the body and showering us with bits of body parts. The stench was so over-powering that as I was running, I threw up. Growing up on a ranch, I had been around a lot of dead animals, but nothing compares to an overripe human corpse. Walt Bacheck thought it was really funny. His genuine concern for line doggies wasn't the only motivating factor. Waldo's twisted sense of humor was probably the reason he sent Derby and me to do the job. Derby Jones claims he didn't vomit, but to this day I don't believe him.

On another mission out of Khanh Duong, I went out as secu-rity for Bacheck when he was retrieving a booby trap. Bacheck liked to use a claymore that takes an electrical blasting cap and uses two battery cells from a radio battery. He would tie a loop in the wire that ran to the blasting cap, and skin a portion of wire in the loop, cutting the excess wire that ran to the battery cells. Using that length, he would tie another loop, leaving a tail piece about eight inches in length with the last two inches bare. He would wrap the bared wire around the unstripped por-tion of the loop going to the blasting cap, then tie his trip wire to the loop going to the battery cells. When the trip wire was hit, it would slide the bare wire lead down to the bare wire in the loop, making contact, and *kaboom*, you had just ruined somebody's day. Normally, when retrieving that type of booby trap, you went right to the claymore and unscrewed the blasting cap. Then you could take down the booby trap, and if something went wrong, the only thing blown up would be the blasting cap. Well, either Bacheck was testing me or he was just plain crazy, but he went right for the loops and started unwrapping the bare wire from the loop. I told him I would prefer just to be a witness to his madness than to be a part of him when he turned to a red mist. He just gave me that "I poked the pig" smile of his. Crazyass Bacheck!

Anyway, the 2/502 TOC informed us the morning of our scheduled extraction that instead of extracting us, they wanted us to hump out and link up with two other Lurp teams at a specific location by a specific time that evening. Bacheck pulled out his map, looked at the coordinates, and discovered that we were a little over eleven kilometers from the rendezvous. You didn't question Lt. Col. Dietrich's orders but said, "Yes, sir, " and got to humping.

On a compass bearing, we started humping in the morning. As the day progressed, we broke out of the triple canopy and into flatter country where there were more open areas of elephant grass mixed with shrubbery four to eight feet tall, and copses of tall jungle intermingled throughout the area. On the way we discovered tiger pits—about four feet wide by six feet long, and about six feet deep—dug into a trail we chanced across. The VC lined the bottom of such pits with three-foot-high punji stakes of fire-hardened bamboo, sharpened to a point and smeared with human excrement, camouflaging the pit with a grid work of thin bamboo strips overlaid with grass and dirt. Tiger pits were primitive and simple but ingeniously deadly works of art. Used for ages against the big cats that roamed Southeast Asia, they worked even better against men. Derby and Kinser noticed the pits because they were old and rain had revealed the edges of the pit.

We arrived dog-assed tired at the rendezvous point, the crossing of a stream that wound through an open area. The crossing was an old ox trail that split on one side of the stream and went east and west. Signs of old human habitations were visible around the area. An infantry company about 300 meters downstream from us was also awaiting extraction.

We met the other three teams there, and it was like a Lurp reunion out in the bush. Ralph Church, Larry Christian,

Vincente Cruz, Elmer Kolarik, Fireball Dixon, Ron Gartner, Teddy Bear Gaskell, Pappy Lynch, Dave Stauffer, Sid Tolson, Puke Palk, and Jungle Jim Cody were all there. We passed the afternoon fishing with "Du Pont lures" (M-26 hand grenades). Overlooking the stream crossing, about 150 meters out, was a small knoll. We had received word that we would be spending the night there, so we decided to base the three teams up against the bottom of the hill. Because we were out of rations, the TOC told us the line company would supply us with C rations to last until the next day. Jungle Jim Cody, Puke Palk, and several others, with me carrying the radio, went to get the resupply. Cody remembers that we had radioed the line company, and they confirmed that all their troops knew we were coming into their perimeter, but when, walking point, he popped up into the infantry's perimeter, the line doggies gave him their "Where in the hell did you come from?" look.

We secured some rations, returned to our position in the tree line overlooking the crossing, and someone actually built a small fire. It was kick-back time, and we were bullshitting, relaxing. Three teams and a line company close by probably made us feel a little more secure than we should have. Bacheck told me to pull guard, watching the stream crossing and an open area upstream from it. It was getting into late evening, and I was sitting outside of the tree line when suddenly, about seventy meters upstream from the crossing, out popped a Chuck, in black PJs, with a rifle. Six more Charlies emerged from the river's edge growth. All were dressed in black, except one in khaki. They were about 125 meters away, and all were carrying weapons. I was trying to signal the guys inside the tree line about what was happening. The Charlies stopped about sixty-five meters away, midway into the open area, and the khaki squad leader started arm-signaling his other men. I couldn't believe they were not alerted to us. I had him in my sights and should have pulled the trigger, but I was torn between shooting and alerting the rest of the Lurps. I thought if I fired, the enemy would center on our position, and if they opened fire, one of the Lurps might get hit. I left my position, and low crawled a short way to attract the Lurps' attention.

Finally, someone saw me frantically signaling. They came pouring out, and it was kind of comical. They were searching but were looking downslope, clear to the creek's edge, but the squad of VC was right below us, heading to the river crossing. Derby Jones and Bacheck finally spotted them. Puke Palk and Jungle Jim took off to our right to buttonhook their movement. The rest of us, basically on line, walked down a ways and opened up on them. By the time we opened up, they had almost crossed the stream. Both sides threw lead at each other for a while, then broke contact. Neither side was willing to cross the stream, and it was near dark. It was a squandered opportunity, and on my part I wish I had just taken a shot. It opened everyone's eyes to the safety and security in numbers.

One of the first missions that Lieutenant "Mac" McIsaac went out on was west of Khanh Duong. The other team members were Staff Sergeant Gilmore, a Ranger who was a little hard of hearing; Pfc. Sid Tolson, Sp4. Patrick "Mother" Henshaw, S.Sgt. Larry Beauchamp, and Sp4. David "Fireball" Dixon, as a medic. The team was inserted at last light, and the insertion went well. The next morning, they started gridding their recon zone, looking for sign of Mr. Charles. The terrain was triple-canopy jungle with occasional small open areas of elephant grass. They found some sign of enemy activity, and around the third day of their mission they found some hootches with cement cisterns full of rice, packs, and other equipment. They had just discovered the hootches and were checking the area adjoining when suddenly Sergeant Gilmore froze, then said, "There they are." Mac, who was pulling slack for Gilmore, saw nothing but trees and shrubbery. Once again, and with a sense of urgency, Gilmore said, "There they are!" Gilmore raised his rifle to shoot, and Mac suddenly saw three or four VC. Gilmore, Mac, and the next person in line, Beauchamp, all opened up at the same time, and several of the VC went down hard. The team waited a period of time before approaching the kill zone. They didn't find the bodies but did discover several blood trails.

"A blood trail was a strange thing to follow," McIsaac

reflects. "At the end of it, you might find somebody with just enough strength to pull the trigger and kill you. We followed one blood trail, and the blood was in big bunches and clumps. When a man or animal bleeds profusely and quickly, the blood starts to coagulate, and it starts looking like clumps of raw liver. This was the first time I had shot anyone—actually had someone in my sights and fired. We located the first VC, and he was alive. He had been hit about three times, one of the rounds opening his stomach terribly. His intestines had spilled out and, because of the peristaltic action, were flipping and moving around like earthworms. It was a nauseating sight. Fireball Dixon wrapped some triangular bandages around his stomach to contain his guts and moistened the bandages. The VC was carrying an American .45 Colt side arm and had some documents, a little blue shaving mirror, and some pictures of his wife and children in a small rucksack. It really brought it home that he was a person with a life other than this war. It turned out later he was a Vietcong lieutenant colonel of a local group. We called in a medevac and extraction as we secured the area. We found other blood trails, but couldn't find any other bodies around the immediate area. We did a hasty retreat from the area, carrying this wounded VC officer, and we were fortunate to find an LZ quickly because there were other VC in the area and we needed to get out of there. The medevac came in, and it was a Huey 'Echo' model, with doors attached and no door gunners. In our haste we threw the guy into the left side of the helicopter. The door of the helicopter had some latches that, when closed, attach and keep the door closed. When we heaved the guy into the helicopter, part of the bandage and intestines caught on the latch and pulled some of the intestines out, eliciting a loud moan from the man. It had been unintentional on our part. We piled onto the aircraft and headed back to Khanh Duong. He was interrogated and subsequently died of his wounds. After the mission, the brigade intelligence officer, Major Morton, gave me the .45 pistol and the little blue mirror. I used the little blue mirror to shave during the rest of my tour in Vietnam."

## Meeting Jaybird

When we had first arrived in Khanh Duong, there was nothing around the area where the brigade encamped. It was just a bare field, dominated by a solitary ridge that nosed down to the valley where the brigade area was located. What few houses or small villages there were, were quite a distance from us. Then the teams left on their missions. Our team (Bacheck's team) went out on a five-day mission, pulled out, resupplied on a firebase, and was sent back out again into a different RZ under operational control of Lieutenant Colonel Dietrich, call sign: "Gunslinger." Returning a few weeks later, we flew into the area. To the east of the brigade forward base camp was the road we had originally driven in on, but now buildings stood on both sides of the road. A "strip" seemed to have sprung up overnight. After squaring away our individual equipment and showering, we went to check the strip out.

The Vietnamese had hastily built a little strip of dirt-floor bars and whorehouses, just for us. The signs painted on the bar fronts were really unique. I recall a photograph of Derby Jones standing beneath a sign that read LOVE FOR YOU HERE BAR and in smaller letters, like an important Madison Avenue advertisement feature: STEAM AND CREAM. Derby still has that picture. The flimsy beer gardens were framed with whatever wood the proprietors could scrounge and covered with large sheets of the thin metal that beer cans are stamped from. The thousands of Carling and Falstaff labels covering the sheets gave the places a certain atmosphere. Surrounded by these designer walls, a bunch of us pounded back semicold beer—and in Vietnam anything semicold was a real treat. We wiped the rice husks off the Ba Muoi Ba beer bottles and, more important, the rust the bottle caps left on the bottle rim. For fifty piasters extra, they would spin the beer bottle on ice and get it really cold. An important trick I learned in Vietnam was to place a bottle on its side on a block of ice and spin it with the palm of your hand vigorously back and forth in the same place on the ice. Try it.

It was getting toward evening, and the brigade had an evening curfew policy, but we were in the bar that had what we considered to be the best-looking women. Because of a shift in operational mission, one of the line battalions was on stand-down and refitting to go back out, so a lot of line doggies and Lurps were in the bar. We were getting into drinking and carrying on and didn't want to leave. Everyone was excited and happy and having a good time. A couple of MPs had already wandered through the bar yelling that it was close to curfew, but no one paid them much mind. Finally an MP staff sergeant walked in with a young redheaded Pfc. The sergeant was looking pretty strac for Nam. With his shined jungle boots and a tailored, pressed uniform, he looked out of place among the rest of us, even though some of us had on clean clothes. Placing his hands on his hips, he bellowed out an impressive, "At ease!" The din in the bar receded somewhat, but that was just a knee-jerk reaction to the army command. This was something of a challenge, and it got more than a few peoples' attention. But that MP sergeant really screwed up when he yelled in a swaggering, John Wayne booming voice, "All right, hit the trail, or go to jail!" A sullen quiet fell over the bar patrons. People were not quite sure what they'd heard. Then, everyone spotted it as "Bullshit!" at the same time. It was like a mental jelling, precipitated when some line doggie yelled out, "Fuck you!" A sudden explosion of beer cans, Ba Muoi Ba bottles, and other assorted articles rained down on the two MPs, who hauled ass out of the joint, ushered out by jeers, laughter, and shots fired through the roof by people who were packing pistols, of which there were quite a few. The red-headed MP dude didn't look like a happy camper. He was only performing his duty, and he clearly didn't have his heart in it. I think he could understand the situation better than the strac sergeant. I gave him credit because he was the last one out of the bar—of course, his sergeant was leading the exit. That's the first time I ever set eyes on Jay "Jaybird" Magill. And, along with the rest of those in the bar, I threw beer in their general direction. I remember the occasion as one of drunken exhilaration—horse-laughing the cops right out of the bar. The Vietnamese were scrambling and really happy that everyone wanted to order another beer, and the barmaids and whores were cackling and laughing and giving the MPs their favorite "big finger," the right arm cocked in the air, the palm of the left hand slapping the underside of the forearm and sliding down to the elbow and grasping it. The big finger!

Eventually a jeep-mounted megaphone pleaded with us to come out. We finally did come out of the bar, and there were no repercussions for any of us. MP Jaybird Magill came over to Lurps in June of 1967.

## The VC Nurse

While we were in Khanh Duong, our operations sergeant, Sp5. Len Abate from Camden, New Jersey, went out on a visual reconnaissance mission in an observation helicopter and helped capture a VC nurse. The helicopter and pilot were the ones who gave me my try-out ride when I applied for helicopter flight school. CWO Gary Sauer, who flew for the 101st Aviation Company and knew the pilot well, related the events to me. "When they captured that VC nurse, they were looking around with Russell Maxson, flying a three-seat Hillier. They got into one valley that was loaded with high grass and landed the helicopter to check on something. They both got out of their ship, left it running, and were checking it out, when suddenly about fifteen enemy soldiers popped out of the grass and started running. Russ Maxson and Len Abate shot a couple of them with their M-16s. They got back in their helicopter, which was still running, and took off. One guy got up and started running, so they ran him down with the bubble of the helicopter, knocking him off his feet. They found out then that it was a female, and later learned that she was a VC nurse. They landed and fought with her, trying to get her into the chopper. As soon as they lifted off, she stopped fighting. They took her back to our base camp at Khanh Duong and put her in a detention center ringed with concertina wire."

While operating out of Khanh Duong, with Sgt. Franklin Lee as a medic, we had a chance encounter with a lone VC soldier who had abruptly walked into our team's security wheel.

Thinking the soldier would realize his situation and submit, Sergeant Lee leveled his rifle on the man. The Charlie went for his weapon, which was slung on his shoulder. Franklin Lee had no choice but to shoot and kill him. The weapon turned out to be a World War II–era German Schmeisser machine pistol. When the team got back to Khanh Duong, General Matheson, hearing that we had captured a Schmeisser, came down to the LRRP detachment area to take a look at it. General Matheson was very familiar with the weapon, having jumped in with the 506th Parachute Infantry, 101st Airborne Division, into Normandy on D-Day. Throughout the war with the 101st, he had fought in Holland and at Bastogne, up against the Germans all the way.

In late April 1967, the 1st Brigade was alerted for movement to Quang-ngai Province in I Corps. The 1st Brigade was being placed under operational control of Task Force OREGON. Just prior to leaving Khanh Duong, Gene Sullivan was sitting around, talking with Bruce Redmer about the move. The line battalion across from the LRRP detachment area had a big campfire going, and the line doggies were relaxing, glad to be out of the field. Bruce Redmer said, "You know, these poor bastards, they don't know what we're getting into, but I guarantee we're going to run into a lot of trouble."

The LRRP detachment left Khanh Duong by convoy early the morning of 1 May 1967. We traveled first in a convoy to Nha-trang. It was a beautiful drive, and when we broke through hills on the outskirts of Nha-trang, there, set against the emerald-green jungle for a background, was a giant pure-white carved statue of Buddha in the lotus position. Over fifty feet high, it dominated the landscape. We then boarded a navy LST that took us north up the coast to a place called Duc Pho.

# 6

**LONG RANGE RECON**

1

101

## Duc Pho

### Task Force OREGON

Task Force OREGON had been created in response to the general military situation existing in South Vietnam in the early part of 1967. While the 1st Brigade had been busily engaged in operations along the coast in II Corps, the major MACV (military assistance command, Vietnam) effort had been directed at relieving pressure against Saigon in III Corps. Operations CEDAR FALLS and JUNCTION CITY had proven very successful and had given MACV the offensive momentum in III Corps it had been seeking. To make up for its losses in III Corps, the enemy began to exert increasing pressure on U.S. and ARVN forces in I Corps. Unable to spare a division from operations then going on in II and III Corps, MACV created Task Force OREGON in an attempt to consolidate its momentum without losing its gains around Saigon. Creating a provisional HQ out of I Field Force assets, borrowing support units from various U.S. Army commands, and consolidating three separate and independent brigades—the 196th Light Infantry Brigade, the 3rd Brigade of the 25th Infantry (Tropical Lightning) Division, and the

1st Brigade of the 101st Airborne Division—under a single command, commanded by Maj. Gen. William B. Rosson.

The arrival of Task Force OREGON in southern I Corps in May 1967, gave the hard-pressed marines working the AO a little breathing room, and allowed them to move units that had been tied up in Quang-ngai Province north to reinforce the DMZ. This also allowed the 1st Cavalry Division to extend its operation north along the coastal plain, opening up Highway 1 all the way to Da-nang.

## Duc Pho

Duc Pho was in the southernmost district of Quang-ngai Province. The government of South Vietnam and its military forces had never had much influence in that area. The province was a bastion of Vietcong political power, and most hamlets were under the control of the enemy. The population backed the insurgents, which made it a dangerous place.

Duc Pho had a different feel to it. You could sense Charles around you, and he was better trained and motivated there than in most places. The remote ranges of mountains and valleys to the west of Duc Pho were home to main force Vietcong units and the noted 2nd VC Regiment, and the soldiers who made up the Vietcong units had lived in or had been working around that area for some time. Well organized, they would sector and grid their respective areas of operations. They were tenacious, and frequently they brought the fight to you. They had developed the art of the booby trap to a vicious and deadly level. Every unit that had ever operated in that AO had had its nose bloodied—1st Cavalry, 173rd, 25th Infantry, 101st, and the 1st Marine Division.

The marines had been involved in heavy fighting in this area. Four months earlier, from the top of Nui Dang hill, Carlos Hathcock, the famous marine sniper, set the record for the longest kill (2500 meters) using a .50-caliber machine-gun with a reworked butterfly trigger and a twenty-four power Urtel scope mounted on it.

The terrain in areas like the Song Ve Valley and other valleys to the southwest, such as the Crow's Foot, was very difficult to operate in as a Lurp because we were easy to see and track. The open rolling hills were covered with elephant grass; heavy vegetation was found only on the blue lines.

## Operation MALHEUR I

Phase One of Operation MALHEUR I began on May 11, with air assaults by the 1/327 and the 2/502 into the mountains west of Duc Pho. Their mission was to locate and destroy VC/NVA forces and neutralize their base camps. Their sister battalion, the 2/327, combat-assaulted into the same area the next day to cut off escaping enemy units.

### Cruz Mission

On 10 May 1967, the Lurps received a Patrol Warning Order for a three-team mission that was to be inserted into an area of operation bordering the eastern edge of the Song Ve Valley; about eighteen klicks northwest of Duc Pho. Two teams would be inserted at last light on 13 May. The third team would be inserted at first light on 14 May. Lt. Daniel "Mac" McIsaac was alerted to the mission by the brigade S-2 (intelligence) officer, Major Morton. The LRRP detachment worked directly with the brigade S-2. The three teams' primary mission would be a thorough ground reconnaissance of each team's recon zone, searching for NVA base camps, trails, and supplies, and also watching for infiltrating/exfiltrating enemy forces that were reacting to an operation mounted by 1/327 Battalion, 2/327 Battalion, and 2/502 Battalion. In addition, the team's secondary mission was to be particularly alert for any sign of American prisoners or bodies. A five-man Lurp team from the 3/25 Infantry Brigade LRRP had just recently been lost.* Unless compromised, the three teams would be in the field for six days.

---

*"Radio contact was lost at 2030 hours, soon after insertion. The next day search teams found where the Lurps had made their last stand. Two bodies were found. Three team members were missing. Blood trails and thrashed vegetation indicated they were probably wounded or dying and dragged off by the enemy." 4th Infantry Division Board Proceedings dated 28 June 1967, 135th MI Group DA Form 339 dated 19 July 1967, and DA MIA Reports dated 11 March 1971.

After the warning-order briefing, Lieutenant McIsaac met with M.Sgt. Top Smith and discussed the type of operation and the teams already deployed. They selected S.Sgt. Pappy Lynch's and S.Sgt. Larry Beauchamp's teams to insert on 13 May. S.Sgt. Vincente Cruz's recon team would be inserted at first light on 14 May. Members of that team consisted of S.Sgt. Larry Christian, senior scout; Sgt. Derby Jones, junior scout; Pfc. Sid "Killer" Tolson, junior RTO; Sp4. Elmer Kolarik, senior RTO, and Sp4. David "Fireball" Dixon, medic. There had been some last-minute changes on this team because I was the assigned senior RTO on S.Sgt. Cruz's team but was leaving for the rear that day to take my warrant officer flight test at Cam-ranh Bay. I tried to get out of going, but Top Smith told me that since it had already been set up, he wanted me to go take the test. I had been waiting since early February for an opening to take the written test. Even so, I had a feeling about this mission, and did not want to miss out on it. I didn't know then just how much it would affect my life. I took off for the rear while my team got ready for it.

Sid "Killer" Tolson was assigned to Cruz's team for the mission. Sidney Styron Tolson was born on 3 November 1949 in Norfolk, Virginia. An orphan, he was adopted while still a baby. He went to Portlock Elementary and on to Oscar Smith High School, where he was on the wrestling team. At fifteen he quit high school and got married. The family had one child, and Sid decided to join the army. They eventually had three children and were married for seventeen years.

At that time, with a signed parental consent form, a young person could join at the age of seventeen. Sid's aunt was an office manager for a local shipyard in Norfolk. She was also a notary-public, and Sid had seen her notarize car titles and other papers. So he went down one day with the form that he had gotten from the recruiter, forged his mother's handwriting—which he could do very well—then snuck into his aunt's desk when she left the office, got her notary, clamped it to the form, and forged her name and expiration date. He was gone a couple of months before anybody knew where he was, and when he finally told his wife and mother, they weren't too happy about it. Sid Tolson entered the army in August 1966, at the ripe old age of sixteen. He went to basic training at Fort Bragg, North Carolina, and went to Fort Gordon, Georgia, for advanced infantry training. Then he went on to jump school at Fort Benning, Georgia. After jump school he was assigned to Vietnam, to the 1st Brigade of the 101st Airborne Division, the "Puking Buzzards."

Sid went through P (proficiency or preparatory) training at Phan-rang in February 1967. During his week of training, the Lurps came down to recruit volunteers for the LRRP detachment. Sid had talked to Captain Friedrich and gone down to the Lurp barracks there at Phan-rang. The whole 1st Brigade was back at rear base at the time, and he was supposed to move down the next day, but orders had already been cut for him to go to the 1/327, so they actually made him load his gear and go to the 1/327, which was just down the road. But during the early evening, he was called to the commanding officer's office, where an angry captain gave him a rash of trash because he was going to the Lurps. Then Captain Friedrich came for him. Sid spent one night in the rear area, then moved out with the Lurps the next day.

Lt. Dan McIsaac and Top Smith notified the three teams and briefed them on the insertions and reviewed the available landing zones. After the lieutenant and Top Smith made their recommendations, they turned the rest of the planning over to the team leaders and assistant team leaders. Then Lieutenant McIsaac and Top Smith reviewed S.Sgt. Walter Bacheck's mission, which was already in the field. On 13 May, S.Sgt. Vincente Cruz, Sgt. Derby Jones, and S.Sgt. Larry Christian went out on the overflight to check out their primary and secondary LZs. After picking them, they returned to Duc Pho. No special equipment would be carried; it was a basic sneak-and-peek mission. Derby Jones didn't see anything special about the mission; he was a seasoned Lurp. On the other hand, the missing LRRP team made him think pretty hard about how things could stack up rapidly against a team.

The Minute Men were the slicks (UH1D, Delta model), of the 176th Aviation Company, assigned to the LRRP detachment for insertion and extraction of the teams. The Muskets, utilizing "Frogs" and "Hogs," were the gunships of the 176th Aviation Company that provided fire support to the Lurps. Frogs and Hogs were terms used to describe two different varieties of gunships. The Frog was a UH1B (Bravo model) gunship that had a pod of seven rockets on each side, miniguns, and a traversing 40mm grenade launcher mounted on the nose of the helicopter. The Hog was a UH1C (Charlie model) that had a forty-eight-unit rocket pod on each side and two manned M-60 machine-guns.

On the evening of 13 May 1967, S.Sgt. Larry Beauchamp's team was inserted into its recon zone. The team consisted of S.Sgt. Fred Hernandez, senior scout; Sgt. Bruce Redmer, junior scout; Sgt. Gene Sullivan, senior RTO; Sp4. Rudy Lopez, junior RTO; and Sp4. Brian "Wolfman" Kraft, medic. Sergeant Sullivan remembers that as soon as the team was inserted, the Lurps heard a lot of voices around them. They didn't know where the enemy was, but Sullivan felt the team was already compromised and could be in real trouble. Then Hernandez and Sullivan spotted two NVA across a small stream from the team's position. They could also hear voices on the team's side of the stream. Staff Sergeant Beauchamp informed Sullivan to radio in that they were compromised and needed to be extracted.

As the chopper was coming in to pick them up, the team fired up the two NVA. Sgt. Fred Hernandez used a magazine of tracers to mark the target across the stream for the gunships. Sullivan recalls that Hernandez's tracers went right into one NVA, who was dressed in black. One of the gunships coming down the river fired a couple of his rockets a split second later, and the rockets impacted where the tracers had gone. The target smoked for about thirty seconds. There was nothing left of the two NVA.

Then the team jumped on the chopper, and they were up and out of there. When Sergeant Sullivan heard the TOC say it wanted to reinsert them a mile away, he turned to his team and told the Lurps to start firing out the door. When they did, he got on the radio to advise them that the Lurps were low on ammo. Of course, the team didn't want to be reinserted because the area was just too hot. They felt the enemy was well aware of their mission and that the element of surprise had already been lost. Control decided to send the team back to base camp. By the time Staff Sergeant Beauchamp's team was resupplied with ammo, it was too late to go back out, so it was decided they would be reinserted in the morning.

S.Sgt. Pappy Lynch's team was inserted at last light on 13 May. The team consisted of Sgt. Jimmie Cody, senior scout; Sp5. Virgil "Puke" Palk, junior scout; Sp4. Dave Stauffer, senior RTO; Sgt. Ralph Church, junior RTO; and Sgt. Jim "Jimbo" Bethel, medic. The insertion was successful, and the team lay dog for the night about four hundred meters from the insertion LZ. Doing a map study, Pappy Lynch and his two scouts agreed that a clearing at the base of a small hill shown on the map looked like a perfect site for a village or base camp. The next day they made their way slowly over a couple of ridges, and by evening they were in position, overlooking a small hootch complex.

On 14 May, S.Sgt. Vincente Cruz's team was up before first light. They made C-rat coffee and put on their camouflage in the communications tent, where there was generator light available. As usual there wasn't much talking. Loading their rucksacks onto Rommel's war wagon, they drove down to the helicopter pad as the eastern sky was starting to get light. They met the chopper crew, and the last-minute details were rehashed. They then locked and loaded their M-16s, checked their safeties, and climbed into the helicopter. When the pilot hit the trigger on his collective to engage the starter, it produced a high-pitched whine, and as the pilot introduced fuel to the igniters, the jet engine wound up to a start. To the Lurps the sounds struck a chord of loneliness and made them aware of the danger that was coming. With the helicopters on fast idle, warming up, the team secured Lurp hats inside tiger shirts, and each man went into his own headspace. The flight in was an introspective time in a Lurp's life and many Lurps will remember the feelings that special moment brought on, each man deep in his own reflections.

At 2500 feet, it was downright chilly. The sun could barely

be seen on the eastern horizon as the slick and two gunships flew toward the dark west. The copilot gave the five-minute-to-touchdown signal, and the last mile was down on the deck, contour flying. Kolarik and Cruz were in the middle of the chopper, Jones and Tolson on the port side, Dixon and Christian on the starboard. The LZ rushed up at them; then they were off the chopper and running for the tree line about thirty yards away. The chopper was out, the gunships made a pass over the LZ, and quiet slowly returned to the jungle.

It didn't last long. Soon there were voices, lots of voices, yelling in Vietnamese, and then *pow, pow, pow*—signal shots. Kolarik radioed in that the area was loaded with people. Staff Sergeant Cruz moved the team a little farther away from the LZ and into a better defensive position. Derby Jones and Larry Christian did a fast 360-degree recon around the position and found some well-used high-speed trails. The pair also found a communications cable one and a half to two inches in diameter and spotted people working on bunkers. Feeling they were compromised and that they needed to beat feet quickly out of the immediate area, they quickly returned to the team.

Having inserted onto the valley floor, the team would have to go to the high ground in order to get away from all the people. Sgt. Derby Jones led them off, humping hard, climbing straight up a huge mountain mass. The climb was a leg-burner but it rapidly gained the Lurps some elevation. The Lurps felt they were being trailed because every once in a while rifle shots were fired and answered. They humped hard for two hours straight, moving through heavy jungle growth, their heavily loaded packs severely testing their endurance.

Staff Sergeant Cruz received a radio transmission from the LRRP communications chief, Staff Sergeant Tauffer, at rear base. With a sense of urgency, he told the team that they were in the wrong area, and to look for an LZ. They needed to be extracted as soon as possible. Their former insertion LZ was suggested, but Cruz declined; it was definitely being monitored. Most likely every LZ on that valley floor was covered. The team continued its lung-burning climb. . . .

What the team did not know was that an Arc Light (B-52 air

strike) was laid on for that area within four hours. Somehow the team had been inserted into the wrong area. Diverting the airstrike was out of the question.

Lieutenant McIsaac, above in a helicopter, informed the team that there appeared to be an LZ, a bomb crater, on a knoll nearby. The Lurps humped their asses off and got to the knoll, but a lone tree occupied the middle of the crater. To allow a slick in, Fireball Dixon blew the tree down using C-4, but the crater was situated on such a steep part of the hill that getting a chopper to land would still be impossible. The team members would have to be rope-slinged out. By this time another helicopter had arrived on station, and it was carrying a rope with harness sling attached. Both helicopters would be used to extract the men.

When Lieutenant McIsaac learned that the team needed to be extracted, he had gone to the helicopter pad. Before leaving he intuitively grabbed a hunk of half-inch hemp rope out of another helicopter and took it with him.

"We had a special bond going with the pilots," Lt. Dan McIsaac says. "We had established within the LRRPs that at any time during an operation, if a ship went down, we would immediately change our mission to rescue that pilot and crew. These gentlemen went out of their way to help us when we were caught. When you were behind enemy lines with six men in a firefight, you really appreciated knowing these people would go the extra mile to help you. In this instance, repeated attempts were made to get into the LZ. At one point the pilot was actually cutting down the treetops with the rotor blades on the helicopter. This may sound dramatic—and when you're sitting in the chopper and watching the green fly all over the place, it *is* very dramatic. Having been the executive officer of the Pathfinders, and having worked with helicopters for quite some time, I understood that the rotors themselves were hollow, with a honeycombed filler. The first three inches of the blade are made out of brass and at any second they could disintegrate from the tremendous beating they were taking. Our only option at that time was to utilize the rope that I had brought aboard the chopper. I tied it off to a D ring in the floor of the helicopter, leaving enough of a tail end to tie around my waist. The gunner in the helicopter held me by my belt and the rope around my waist, and I lowered the rope. By this manner, one at a time, we were able to extract these people from the area of the upcoming B-52 strike."

Fireball Dixon was the first man roped out with the harness sling. The next helicopter was for Sid Tolson, who thought the pilot had some big nuts busting tree limbs with his blades to get the rope to him. Larry Christian was laughing when he helped Sid Tolson with the rope. He ran it under Sid's rucksack and tied it in front with a square knot and a half hitch for a safety. Sid wasn't too impressed with the half-inch hemp rope. When he got up in the air, he had his rifle slung on his shoulder, and his rucksack was still heavy since it was just day one of the mission. So, there was Sid Tolson, hanging on to the rope, the eighty pounds of rucksack trying to pull him over backward, thinking, "Please set this bastard down!" His hands were starting to knot and cramp up from holding on, but if he let go, he would have fallen to the ground. Lieutenant McIsaac, flying belly man, could see that Sid was going to be in big trouble soon. After ten or fifteen minutes' flight, they set him down on the LZ where S.Sgt. Larry Beauchamp's team had been inserted, twenty minutes earlier. Sid Tolson then linked up with Beauchamp's team. His hands and arms were so knotted up from cramps that one of Beauchamp's men had to untie the rope. After going back two more times, the two helicopters had extracted the entire team. Beauchamp's team was pissed because they felt every NVA for miles around knew what was happening. Cruz's team regrouped on the ground, and the Lurps were astonished to find that new maps and two orange water bladders were waiting for them. They were to insert with the water bladders, fill their canteens, then bury the bladders. A helicopter came in and picked up Staff Sergeant Cruz's team for reinsertion, and Staff Sergeant Beauchamp's team beat feet, putting some distance between themselves and the overused LZ.

"And herein is the rub," Lieutenant McIsaac says. "That team should have been extracted and pulled back, refitted, reoriented for a new mission. As it was, the orders came down from brigade that this team should be extracted only to a temporary position, then reinserted again in the same area, but outside of the B-52 strike. In my opinion, this was not appropriate. I said that, but there was only so much weight a lieutenant holds when dealing with staff officers. It was already known that it was an area of heavy NVA and local VC activity. Both teams were already compromised, and we were asking for trouble."

Staff Sergeant Cruz's helicopter lifted off the regrouping LZ, gained some altitude, banked to the left, and headed for the new insertion LZ, which was less than a mile away and on the same mountain ridge line. The helicopter landed in an open field on the side of a hill. It was probably not the pilot's fault because of the impromptu planning of the mission and the short duration of flight, but the team felt they had corkscrewed into the LZ and could be easily pinpointed. They were coming in for insertion and things were happening fast. This was a pork chop! They should not have left the slick, but someone went in so everybody followed.

The Lurps found themselves on a little knoll in an open field, with four- to six-foot elephant grass, the only concealment being a dry creek bed two or three hundred meters distant. The creek bed meandered down a little valley that contained the only real foliage around. The vegetation in the creek bed was only fifteen or twenty yards wide. The ridges paralleling the valley were covered with open fields of elephant grass and small patches of vegetation. The little valley led into a bigger valley, and at that junction was a village. Anybody standing anywhere on the ridges or in the valley could have seen the team.

It was getting into late afternoon when they inserted. The men were tired and thirsty, and their canteens needed refilling. Carrying the water bladders, they hoofed it into the dry creek bed and made radio contact. Staff Sergeant Cruz informed Control that the RZ was a bad place for a Lurp team. Cruz had now studied his map thoroughly, something he hadn't had the luxury of doing prior to being inserted. He hadn't picked the

LZ, and other people's decisions, in a snowballing effect, were steadily endangering his team. He was informed that the team should base up for the night, and that it would be pulled the following morning. The men refilled their canteens, buried the bladders, and moved down the creek bed a couple of hundred meters toward the village. Then they based up.

There was nowhere the team could go. There was no cover, and the only concealment the team could use was in the dry creek bed and there the vegetation wasn't very wide. The team found the thickest vegetation, which was on the steep embankment that formed the side of the creek bed, and based up in it, placing the radios next to a good-sized tree. They were in a very dangerous place, and the danger was compounded by the fact that they didn't move again after dark.

Rain fell around 2200 hours and it continued until just before daybreak. Guard went well all night, and everybody was awake for first light. The team stood to in the morning and exchanged the night round out of their weapons to prevent a jam—in case the round had sweated during the night. When it got light enough to see, David "Fireball" Dixon walked out to the team's left, with weapon and LBE, to make a 360-degree recon and a nature call.

The Lurps were relieved that they were being pulled out that morning. Sid Tolson was sitting, with Elmer Kolarik seated in front of and slightly below him. Cruz was to Sid's right and back, and three or four meters off to the right of Cruz was Christian, and then Derby. They were more on the level with Kolarik and Fireball, closer to the creek bed. The team was based with their backs to the elephant grass that grew onto the banks of the creek bed.

Derby Jones recalls they had spread out in case they got hit, one of those basic instincts that goes with the job. Nothing unusual had been heard during the night. Derby had just finished heating some water with C-4 to make coffee. It had just stopped raining, and it was deathly still and dreary. Suddenly they all heard the dreaded sound of a bolt being racked back and then moving forward. Everyone froze, then Derby remembers, "I yelled, 'Hit it!' and rolled to my left. At the same time that I yelled, and as I was rolling, they opened up. It was a tremendous amount of firepower, with every one of the enemy on full automatic. I rolled underneath a shrub with some rocks close to its base, and it saved my life because the guy following me with his fire peppered the shit out of it. Deep in my soul, I knew everyone was targeted. We were had, and the only reason we were getting a half-ass chance is someone on their side had screwed up. In the first two seconds Kolarik, Cruz, Tolson, and Fireball were all hit—and so was one of the radios."

Sid Tolson recounts that he heard the bolt go forward, and time stood still. "It was a lifetime of stark terror in a split second, because you *know*. . . . The foliage was falling, being cut to shreds by the bullets. They opened up on us big time! I was leaning to the right, reaching for the grip on my weapon, when *thwwaack*, the first bullet hit me in the face. It hit right beneath my right eye, came through the roof of my mouth, the hard palate, through my tongue, then hit the left side of my jaw and blew it out. Getting hit on a hard bone, especially the face, is a tremendous blow. It's like Mickey Mantle trying to make a home run with your face. When I came to, I couldn't see, and my ears were ringing terribly. I regained consciousness in time to have a grenade explode next to me, peppering me with shrapnel and sending a piece right into the cornea of my right eye. With the tremendous amount of hydrostatic pressure caused by the bullet, my throat, mouth, and face instantly swelled. All I could do was gurgle and try to keep my airway open to breathe. I could see after a bit with my left eye, so I crawled toward the elephant grass twelve feet away."

As Sid Tolson was hit, Staff Sergeant Cruz was rolling and bringing his rifle up, but he took a round through the right side of his chest. It went through his right lung and exited the right side of his back, blowing out a huge hole. The force of the round slammed him into the ground, and in the process he lost the grip on his rifle. Cruz took two more rounds in the back as he desperately crawled into the elephant grass, trying to escape the kill zone. In the hail of bullets, Elmer Kolarik managed to pull the pin on a hand grenade and throw it. In the process of throwing the grenade and twisting and turning to get back down to ground level, he took a round through the back of the right shoulder, going through the socket bone and out his arm, gouging a huge hole and numbing his whole right shoulder and arm. He, too, crawled into the grass, in an attempt to escape the withering fire. Moments earlier, Fireball had walked out upstream to the team's left, facing into the creek bed, reaching the edge of the vegetation no more than thirty feet from the others. He must have seen the enemy, and he was turning around to try to warn the others when two rounds slammed into his head, killing him instantly. The enemy was in an L-shaped ambush formation in the creek bed, and wrapping on the team's right. Christian had not been hit, but all he could do was lie flat and let the bullets swarm by him, waiting for the enemy's first magazines to be exhausted.

Pure numbing terror reigned for the first five seconds. Since the Lurps had all initiated ambushes, there was no doubt in anyone's mind that this time they were on the receiving end of a well-laid one.

With the lull in the firing that came as the enemy finished their first magazines, Derby rolled to his right and started laying down fire as fast as he could. Christian was doing the same, and they kept at it, going through at least ten magazines, alternating fire and throwing frags after every magazine. Sid, Cruz, and Kolarik had all crawled into the elephant grass and were in various stages of agony. But Cruz weakly shouted at Kolarik, "Get the radio! The radio . . ." Kolarik went back out of the grass and into the foliage area where the radios were based. It was a distance of only ten feet, but it was where all the rounds were hitting. The incoming fire was becoming heavier. . . . He grabbed his radio and crawled back into the elephant grass. When he tried to transmit, Kolarik discovered that the handset had a bullet hole in it. He crawled back, grabbed Sid Tolson's radio, and crawled back into the elephant grass once more. Sid's radio was useless but the handset was still good. On his hands and knees, drooling, trying to keep breathing, Sid vaguely saw Kolarik change the handset one handed and try to contact the rear.

While crawling into the grass, Cruz had taken two more rounds through the back and later took two more rounds in his legs as the fight raged. He was moaning horribly, mostly because he could barely breathe. And his moaning was attracting fire. Sid also took two more rounds in the back, about ten minutes later. Kolarik's right shoulder had been savaged terribly, and he had been shot in his other arm, so he could use only one arm—and that one only weakly. Still, he helped save the day with the radio.

Trying to gain an edge, Derby and Christian expended a tremendous amount of ammo. But the NVA regrouped and then attacked from two different directions, coming in a U-shape, trying to envelop the team and push them downhill. Derby and Christian were on the team's right flank (down-stream) and had a firing angle into the creek bed and the base of the enemy's L, where the majority of them were concen-trated in the attack. They started ass-kicking again, and then Derby saw a grenade come sailing into his area. He rolled to his left and tightened his body as much as possible. *Whaamm!* The concussion slammed him and he felt a hot stinging in his crotch and legs, but all he could think was, "Man, I can't get hurt! That will only leave Christian!" He got a willie pete grenade and popped the handle off, counted a couple seconds, and threw it where the last grenade had come from. It exploded, and he could hear screaming and moaning coming from the area. "That's a lick on you," he thought . . .

Derby and Christian kept firing and moving, trying to make the NVA think there were more than two Lurps actually able to fire. It worked, but only because of the ferocity of their counterattack. Derby was lobbing grenades and firing his sawed-off M-79, trying to get air bursts on the trees. Ten min-utes into the fight, as the incoming fire started tapering off, Derby heard someone screaming for Doc Fireball, and he real-ized that Fireball must be down and not doing his job. Derby could see that the three wounded needed first aid immediately if they were to live. He speed crawled down to the medic bag and equipment and what had once been their position. The enemy had not worked their way up the embankment, but they were not more than twenty-five feet past the equipment in the creek bed.

Derby grabbed the medic bag and crawled back into the elephant grass. He started working on Staff Sergeant Cruz, who couldn't breathe because his right lung had collapsed. Cruz had taken two other rounds through the left lower back, but they had not penetrated into his chest cavity. Plowing up his back, the rounds had ripped it open something terrible, but Derby couldn't do anything about that. Cruz had also taken two rounds above the knees. Derby tore open a compress bandage, split the plastic in half, and placed them on the entry and exit holes, then bandaged them tightly with the compress bandage. He started a serum albumin on Cruz because he was bleeding so badly. Derby couldn't do anything for Sid Tolson's jaw because Sid wouldn't be able to breathe if it was bandaged. A round to Sid's back left shoulder blade had gouged out a chunk of meat bigger than Derby's hand. He didn't try to bandage that, either; Derby didn't have time to do anything except keep Tolson alive. About five minutes later, Sid took another round, a little lower on the left shoulder blade. This one went under the scapula. Derby then tended to Elmer Kolarik. Kolarik's right shoulder was ripped wide open from the shoulder to the elbow. Derby could only place Kolarik's arm in a cravat (triangular bandage). The whole time Derby was administering first aid, sparse but steady fire was coming in, as if there were fewer of the enemy and they were shooting at sounds. Derby went upstream, toward the enemy, found Fireball's body, dragged it back, then wrapped it around the remaining good radio. The team was lucky Derby did this because Fireball's body absorbed several more rounds after that, and they could have killed the radio. Then Derby collected ammo and grenades from the wounded and flung them to Christian, who had been firing steadily the whole time.

Elmer Kolarik was on the radio for what seemed a lifetime, trying to get help, but at last he got it. When the gunships finally showed up on station, the team marked its position with a panel. A small element of the enemy was still firing into the

(*above*) Gen. Willard Pearson talking to original LRRP detachment at Tuy Hoa, March 1966. (Larry Forrest collection)

(*left*) Lloyd "Top" Smith, 16 May 1967. (Top Smith collection)

(*left*) S. Sgt. Larry Forrest (Black Icicle), team leader, Team No. 4 (profiled in Chapter 1). (Larry Forrest collection)

(*right*) Static display of weapons and equipment. Left: PRC-74 with earphones, antennas. Center top to bottom: Car-15; M-16 with XM-148 grenade-launcher under; sawed-off M-79 with homemade leather holster; Randall knife; machetes. Right: PRC-25 with antennas and handset. (Author's collection)

(*left*) Team No. 2 (L-R): Donovan Pruitt (MA), Roedel, Doame, Johnson, Jack Waymire (KIA), Thomas (in front). (Alfred Smith collection)

(*left*) Ronald Gartner at Phan Rang, RVN, January 1967. (R. Gartner collection)

(*right*) Team No. 1. Standing (L-R): Alfred Smith, Joe Nash, Dick Clark. Kneeling (L-R): Bill White, Doty, and Pop Tomlinson. (Alfred Smith collection)

(*left*) Eve of junk insertion (Chapter 4). Standing (L-R): Elmer Kolarik, Jungle Jim Cody, unidentified, Ralph Church, Larry Christian, "Uncle Earl" Wheeler. Kneeling (L-R): John Buford, Rey Martinez, Jimmy McCormack, Dave Stauffer. Note some of the Lurps are wearing black PJs. (Author's collection) (*right*) Just prior to raid out of Khanh Duong, RVN, April 1967. (L-R): Jungle Jim Cody, Rey Martinez. (Author's collection)

(*below*) Top Smith briefing the Lurps prior to a raid, Len Abate looking on. Khanh Duong, RVN, April 1967. (Author's collection)

(*below*) Prior to raid out of Khanh Duong, April 1967. Standing (L-R): Gilmore, Dan McIssac, Top Smith, Puke Palk, Larry Beauchamp. Kneeling (L-R): Larry Christian, Waldo Bacheck, Freddy Hernandez, Rudy Lopez, Ronald "Brother" Weems. (Top Smith collection)

(*left*) S. Sgt. Vincente Cruz took seven rounds during fight at Duc Pho. (Author's collection)

(*right*) Allen "Teddy Bear" Gaskell, Chu Lai, October–November 1967. (Allen Gaskell collection)

(*left*) Sgt. Derby Jones, Duc Pho, RVN, 14 May 1967. This picture was taken the evening before Cruz's team was hit. (Derby Jones collection)

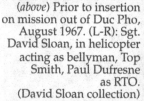

(*above*) Prior to insertion on mission out of Duc Pho, August 1967. (L-R): Sgt. David Sloan, in helicopter acting as bellyman, Top Smith, Paul Dufresne as RTO. (David Sloan collection)

(*above*) S. Sgt. Lester "Superspade" Hite, Chu Lai, October 1967. (Tom Dokos collection)

(*left*) Allen "Lurch" Cornett, Chu Lai, October 1967. (Boss Weisberger collection)

(*left*) S. Sgt. Ronald "Brother" Weems, Bao Loc, RVN, December 1967. (Tom Dokos collection)

(*below*) Craig Vega's team, west of Tam Ky, September–October 1967. Call sign Firebug-348. Standing (L-R): Gary "Fannie" Fandel, Craig Vega, Jack Kenny. Kneeling (L-R): Bill Scanlon, Mike Worrell, Marty Dostal. (Bill Scanlon collection)

(*above*) Christmas Day 1967 after being hit by NVA on hill Bao Loc, RVN. Standing (L-R): Tom "Greek" Dokos, Harvey Bieber, Peppy Wenglarz, Doc Jones, Brother Weems. Kneeling (L-R): Eddie Cecena, Moroch, Clay Wentworth, Jerry Prouty, Woods. (Tom Dokos collection)

(*left*) The Randall knife that was given to Top Smith by Lt. McIssac on behalf of the LRRP detachment (Chapter 10). The inscription reads "To Lloyd 'Straight' Smith, from Long Range Recon, 101st Abn, Vietnam, *Fortuna Favet Fortibus* [Fortune Favors the Bold]." (Top Smith collection)

area, but once the gunships started working out, the enemy began leaving the area. The enemy had hit the team hard but had failed to follow through and mop up. The surviving Lurps had been lucky. Help was on the way, and the wounded just had to hang on. Sid Tolson and Vincente Cruz had lost a lot of blood, and Elmer Kolarik was pretty badly off, too.

S.Sgt. Larry Beauchamp's team had moved off their LZ and based up just off the ridgeline. They were on the same ridgeline as Cruz's team, but higher and over a half mile away. As dawn came, they heard the roar of gunfire, and they knew right away it was Cruz's team. Quickly they started monitoring the radio and getting ready to go to their aid. They made several attempts to communicate with the team but were greeted with silence. Finally they heard Kolarik, calm and collected but very weak, saying they had dead and wounded and needed help. He was speaking very slowly, as if he was fading out. They heard a lot of firing in the background as Kolarik spoke. Beauchamp's team thought that Cruz's team had been overrun. They called in and requested to abort their mission so they could go to the aid of Cruz's team, but they were told to maintain their position as reinforcements were on the way for Cruz's team.

That morning, Lieutenant McIsaac was notified by Top Smith that Cruz's team was in heavy contact and had casualties. McIsaac asked Top to keep him abreast and called the brigade tactical operations center. He asked for support in the form of gunships, reaction force, and extraction. Lieutenant McIsaac was given a helicopter number at the pad and told that gunships and slicks were being scrambled. The reaction force was an element from Charlie Company, 2/327. Mac strapped on his LBE and two claymore bags with ten magazines apiece. Over that, he draped a seven-magazine cloth bandolier, then took off for the helipad. Arriving there, he jumped into a slick, and the chopper took off immediately. The beautiful clear-blue morning made a horrible contrast to the voices coming over the radio. McIsaac will always remember Kolarik's calm presence under fire and his description of the killed and wounded. McIsaac finally asked him, "Can we consider you as one of the wounded?" Kolarik said yes, and McIsaac's heart went out to him.

Lieutenant McIsaac landed and joined the reaction force on the ridgeline northeast from where the team was located. As he landed and spoke with the commanding officer of Charlie Company, Mac bumped into an old friend, Sgt. Jerry A. Norris. They had been privates, corporals, and sergeants together at Fort Campbell. Lieutenant McIsaac fell in with Sergeant Norris's squad, and they became the lead element of the reaction force. "As we came to the area where the fight had taken place, it was kind of a circular clearing," McIsaac says. "And to get through it you had to stoop through some bushes. As I looked through it, I could see the team members scattered around. There was blood everywhere. And there was Kolarik on the radio. His arm was in a sling; his shoulder and arm were just torn apart. He was calmly speaking on the handset of his PRC-25. I can best describe his wounds as his flesh hanging off. It looked similar to a leg of pork that had been fileted open. His bicep muscle underneath was visible. Yellow sinews were visible, and there was plenty of blood around, yet he was still calmly talking on the radio."

Jerry Norris was putting his team out. Then the commanding officer of C Company came in, and the rescue was in danger of turning into a clusterfuck; everybody was hanging around looking at what was going on. Mac looked back over his shoulder at the next trooper to come through the bush. The man was stooped over as Mac looked at him, pointed at his face and said "You—I want you to start a perimeter right out there at twelve o'clock!" The trooper lifted his head, and Mac saw that it was Lieutenant Colonel Abud, the battalion commander of the 2/327, call sign Black Panther. The colonel looked at Mac and smiled; then he turned around to the captain and said, "You—I want you to start a perimeter at twelve o'clock right there, right now, get going!" Lieutenant Colonel Abud was very supportive.

Sid Tolson can recall seeing a black guy with a helmet walk into their little blood-splattered perimeter. The shooting was over, Sid's adrenaline level had come down, and he was just feeling very weak. "The black guy was trying to bandage my face, and I wouldn't let him because I couldn't see. He was putting the bandage over my good eye, and I kept pulling it off. I had lost a lot of blood and was going in and out of consciousness. My blood pressure was so low, they had to do a cut down on my right arm at the evacuation hospital. I remember being so cold on the chopper ride out of there, like I was flying on the outside of the helicopter. I was passing in and out of consciousness on the ride back."

Sid Tolson was seventeen years old.

Lt. Dan McIsaac received a radio message from Major Morton and Brig. Gen. Salve Matheson, the "Iron Duke," that they were flying overhead and would help extract the dead and wounded. "I have to give them their due," McIsaac says. "General Matheson really cared about the Lurps and cared about the people who were in it. He cared about our welfare and well being, and I don't think he ever tried to put us on missions to squander us. I can say the same thing for Major Morton. Jerry Norris and I, along with several line doggies, carried Fireball up to where he would be picked up. The chopper was flown by WO Carlos Melendez, who exhibited exceptional flying skills, making a difficult hover over a wind-buffeted hilltop. I remember when we passed Fireball into the chopper, it was hovering about five feet off the ground. Thick, black blood was dripping out of the hole in Fireball's head. He did not have an exit wound in the back of his head, which I would have expected. He was also without his individual weapon, though he was still wearing that claymore mine in a shoulder holster." Fireball never had a chance to use his claymore that day.

Everyone on Cruz's team was flown back to the brigade aid station. George "Rommel" Murphy helped unload Cruz off General Matheson's helicopter. He was lying on his belly on the stretcher, and Rommel saw where a round had blown out of his back. There was a great big gash just under Cruz's left shoulder. He was conscious when they unloaded him, cussing and raising havoc. Next, Fireball Dixon was unloaded off the same chopper. Marty Dostal, who transferred to the LRRPs after this incident, was working as a medic at the aid station that day. He knew Fireball Dixon from Fireball's visits to the aid station to refill his medical bag. They had partied and were friends, and Marty had broached the subject of joining the Lurps to Fireball. Marty Dostal was shocked when he grabbed Fireball's dead arms and, with the help of someone else, set him aside for Graves and Registration. He had handled plenty of dead men, but Fireball was the first person he had known personally who had been killed. A few minutes later, George Murphy was asked by G&R to identify Sp4. David Allen Dixon. Rommel Murphy identified the body of our friend and brother Lurp, Fireball.

Lieutenant McIsaac flew out some of the gear from Cruz's team. When they were going through it at Duc Pho, Rommel Murphy held up Fireball Dixon's web gear. On the web gear were Fireball's ammo pouches and canteens. There were also fragmentation grenades, and in the firefight an AK round had pierced the spoon of one of the grenades. The pin that held the handle onto the grenade and kept it from detonating had been shot away to just a hair's width of sheet metal. If that piece of metal had snapped, a live grenade would have dropped in their midst. Several of the rucksacks had received multiple hits, and there were holes in the magnesium frames from the AK-47 rounds. Rommel Murphy says that the worst thing about unloading the team's equipment from the helicopter was the stench. He picked up two rucksacks, and both were covered with blood.

Meanwhile, S.Sgt. Pappy Lynch's team had monitored the contact over the radio. They understood that Cruz's team was in a bad way. To Jim Cody it sounded as if the team was getting wiped out. But they couldn't get confirmation. Every time they tried to call in to find out what was happening, they were told to keep the airwaves clear. Cody remembers getting frustrated and pissed. The team was really upset. They were looking down on these hootches, and had suddenly seen activity. Five to seven guys were moving around with packs down there. The Lurps called artillery, and Jim Cody gave them the coordinates and azimuth to the target. Cody asked for

HE (high explosives) on the first round, but that was refused because it was policy to come in with a smoke round first. Cody was damned pleased the smoke round was dead on; it was just too bad it wasn't HE. The team immediately called for fire for effect, but by the time the rounds came in, the enemy had already scattered. This added to the team's frustration because all they ended up doing was tearing up the hootches.

Everyone concerned with the Lurps during this action had differing estimates of the reaction time from opening rounds until Staff Sergeant Cruz's team got help. It ranged from forty-five minutes to two hours—but all estimates agreed that it was too long. Beauchamp's team was the closest to Cruz and listened to the whole ordeal. Charlie wasn't finished yet. When time finally came to extract Beauchamp's team, the pilot asked for smoke. Gene Sullivan tossed out a red smoke grenade. The pilot called back that he had red and purple smokes visible. Sullivan called back that his smoke was red. The enemy had tried to lure the extraction ship into an ambush.

When Cruz's team got hit, it was a total shock to the Lurps. We didn't feel that we were invincible, but we had done so damn well. Now our unit had been touched—and touched bad. Losing a team like that was a hard blow to the LRRP detachment.

It would have been a fitting epilogue for this sad story that at least Lieutenant McIsaac had seen his old friend Jerry Norris again. They made plans to get together when the 327th rotated to the rear area in the next few days. A few days later, when Norris's outfit did rotate in, Mac went down to see him. But Jerry Norris had been killed the same day he helped load Fireball onto the chopper. Coming on the heels of what happened to Cruz's team, and indirectly related to it, that was really devastating news to McIsaac. It was the first time Lieutenant McIsaac had lost men under his command.

For his actions in the defense of his team members, Sgt. Derby Jones was nominated for the Distinguished Service Cross but was awarded the Silver Star. S.Sgt. Larry Christian was also awarded the Silver Star.

## Lurch

On 10 May, Lloyd "Top" Smith and I had caught the afternoon flight headed for Phan-rang, our rear base. Top Smith had business with Finance and Records concerning several members of the detachment—business like promotions and pay, that only a first sergeant can do if he really wants to take care of his men. Top was flying back the next evening to be around for the missions on 13 May, but I signed in at replacement company to get a flight the following morning to Cam-ranh Bay, where I would be taking tests for helicopter flight school the next day.

After signing in at replacement company, I walked back through the P training area to meet with Dave "Mad Dog" Dolby. On the way, I passed a group of cherries attending class inside a tent with the sides up. The instructor's booming voice punctuated by laughter ran through his instructional repertoire. I had been the victim and student of countless hours of army classes, and the main complaint I could field was the difficulty of staying awake during instruction.

This class was different, and it grabbed my attention. I drifted in and stood around near the rear of the tent. Other passers-by were also drawn in. This instructor was a big guy, about 6'4", all rib cage, striding back and forth in front of his class, telling them how important first aid was. Aha, a first aid class—normally I would have been beating feet in another direction, but this guy was funny, which was why other folks were hanging around. One look at Sgt. Alan Cornett, aka "Lurch," the handle he picked up later, revealed he had been around the block: he wore a CMB (combat medic badge) and a 5th Special Forces Group combat patch on his right shoulder. I watched the show. He created different personalities with mannerisms and speech, all of them hilarious. I thought the guy was nuts or possessed, maybe both. One of his special characters was similar to "Ernest P. Worrel," the character played by comedian and actor Jim Varney. Years later in a gush of nostalgia and bullshit, Lurch would complain that Varney had stolen Ernest from him. And I have to admit that the first time I ever saw that character was in Lurch's class, back at Phan-rang. Lurch was our source of entertainment later in Lurps, and would keep us laughing for hours. He had a quick wit and was stomach-hurting funny.

Lurch had all his butter bars (second lieutenants) lined up in the front row, and he was expounding on how the U. S. Army, in all its wisdom, had produced just for them a beautiful item that would save their lives. It was called serum albumin, and everyone—"I mean *everyone!*"—should know the method of administering it. Serum albumin is a blood-volume expander, only used when the casualty has seriously lost some blood. Because of its consistency, it is administered in a drip through a twenty-four gauge needle—the size needle used to give horses shots. People in war tend to acquire huge holes in them and bleed profusely, so knowing how to find a vein, insert the needle, and intravenously administer serum albumin is important. Hitting a vein in an arm is really tricky, and doing exploratory surgery with that huge needle is a tough job.

The whole time he was talking, the guy was walking back and forth, readying his left arm by tying it off above the elbow with a piece of surgical tubing and using his teeth for assistance. He then dramatically brought out a huge syringe with a long, thick needle that looked like a Minuteman missile. Inserting the needle into his left arm, he untied the tubing and let blood flow into the syringe—all the time keeping a running, humorous commentary on the procedure and the subject of blood. He pointed out the difference in color between arterial and venous blood and talked about how people upon seeing blood, copious amounts of blood, and the ravages that the human body undergoes when traumatized by a sudden meeting with metal, go into shock.

Not only was this dude knowledgeable about and very familiar with what he was doing, he also was delivering a very physical message. In the not very distant future, those students would be experiencing the ugliness and violence that only combat can produce. I thought of the old Lurp saying: "War is hell—contact is a motherfucker!" About that time, Lurch finished filling the syringe and pulled it out. As the needle hole in his arm continued to bleed, he looked at the officers in the front row in the eye and said, "Now it's your turn!" He whirled and threw the blood-filled syringe into a homemade dartboard set toward the back of the stage. The syringe hit the dartboard and exploded, throwing blood all over the place. Lurch turned around and told the class that that would not be the last time they saw blood. The cloying heat in the tent added to the atmosphere. People started turning green and dropping like flies. Lurch told me later that he went through a lot of ammonium nitrite reviving people. It was an eye-catching performance and a virtuoso demonstration on the giving of IVs—and on the sight and smell of blood. It also attracted a lot of flies, something only Lurch would think about. Not a student in the class was nodding off during that class.

I was impressed with the guy and thought he was crazy enough to be in Lurps. We could definitely use someone like him in our outfit. He noted my Lurp hat and asked me what outfit I was with, and I told him brigade Lurps. He mentioned having done a little Lurping, and wondered aloud what it took to get into the Lurps. I told him that the Lurps were all volunteers, that you had to be a little nuts, and told him he filled the bill beautifully. His MOS was a shoo-in. We agreed to get together after his work day, to enjoy some beers and talk about Lurps.

Lurch was born Alan Gentry Cornett Jr., in Highland Park, Michigan, in August 1944. His father, Alan Cornett Sr., had received a battlefield commission for distinguished action in battle with the 90th Infantry Division, in Patton's 3rd Army, and was wounded twice in France. A decorated soldier, Alan Sr. chose a career in the army, and the family followed his postings. Lurch attended high school in Ridge Township, Park Forest, Illinois, where he was a three-time state wrestling champ, captain of the football team, and lettered in baseball and football.

After attending college on an athletic scholarship for two years, he was drafted and opted to enlist as "Airborne Unassigned." Lurch went through basic, AIT, and jump school then volunteered for Special Forces. He graduated from the SF medic course, and the next thing he knew he was in Vietnam.

Lurch arrived in Vietnam in August 1966 and was assigned to 5th Special Forces Group. He worked at the SFOB in Nhatrang for one month before being assigned to Detachment B-52, Project Delta, working out of Khe Sanh in the northwestern corner of South Vietnam. Delta, Omega, and Sigma were called the Greek Projects and were basically long range recon units utilized by Corps and MACV J-2 primarily for the gathering of intelligence and information within Vietnam. It was hot Lurping country, and you had to watch your step very carefully because you were hunting khaki-uniformed NVA regulars.

At Khe Sanh, Lurch was met by Sergeant Dyer, one of the Delta team medics. As a replacement team medic, Lurch was given the tour of the underground medical facility that supported all of Khe Sanh at the time. It was run by Special Forces medics—all two of them. When needed, a navy doctor posted on a ship on the South China Sea gave assistance by radio or by flying in.

Lurch said, "I was assigned to Master Sergeant Stamper's team. He was a bear of a man at six feet five inches, and two hundred thirty-five pounds. His arms were huge and muscled, and he had a face chiseled out of stone. I was intimidated and nervous meeting his crew. This was the big leagues, and these people were badasses. I still considered myself a cherry."

To Lurch's surprise Master Sergeant Stamper was a softspoken man, but he radiated an air of authority. Master Sergeant Stamper became Lurch's mentor in learning the fine art of staying alive. Lurch was involved in a mission to recover the bodies of a helicopter crew that had crashed in Laos while trying to extract Team Viper, which was run by Willie Stark and Russ Bott. The Team Viper mission itself should have never been undertaken. Because of bad flying weather, the team had mistakenly been inserted "across the fence" into Laos, close to the DMZ and in the center of an NVA regiment. The team made contact and broke it. But they were compromised and became the hunted. It didn't take the NVA long to relocate Team Viper.

When Team Viper made contact, Willie Stark and several

indigenous team members were wounded. The team was in a very serious situation, so an extraction helicopter was sent out with gunships and a medic, Sergeant Dyer, for assisting the wounded. Lurch was on rotation to go, but because he had a bad case of dysentery and because he was junior in rank and experience, Sergeant Dyer elected to go. The weather made flying extremely dangerous. The rescue attempt was a courageous effort on the part of the helicopter crews and the FAC (forward air controller) that attempted the rescue. But Team Viper was being used as bait, and when the extraction helicopter came in, the NVA shot it down, killing everyone aboard.

Because a U.S. Army helicopter had been shot down outside of South Vietnam, the mission turned into an international incident. A low-profile recovery plan was formulated. Master Sergeant Stamper, medic, and two indigenous personnel were to rappel into the site of the downed helicopter to recover the wounded or the bodies. Lurch was the medic, and it was his first really big mission.

"As I moved onto the skid of the helicopter to rappel down, I could see the bird upside down with debris scattered everywhere," Lurch recalled. "I was scared to death. It was the longest fifty feet I would ever rappel! I made it down in record time; my gloves were smoking when I hit the ground. I watched Stamper move, and he was a treat to watch. For the rest of my six tours in Vietnam, I would use his technique to move through the jungle. Something like a big cat stalking prey.

"But as we approached the helicopter, I could smell death. We got close to the helicopter, and Stamper held me back, pointing to a trip wire that was connected to one of the bodies in the helicopter. There were three other bodies lined up in a perfect row by the NVA, outside the helicopter and wired to blow. Demolition wasn't my forte at the time, and Stamper moved in to remove the wires and booby traps. I was thankful for Sergeant Stamper being there. I wouldn't be alive today if I had been there by myself."

This was Lurch's first encounter with the sight and smell of blood and death in combat. The pilot and copilot were already stiff and hard to remove. A Marine CH-57 was called in and used a hoist cable and basket to remove the bodies, one at a time. As they were removing the second body, heavy incoming fire was brought to bear on the team and helicopter. The recovery team was forced off the site of the downed helicopter, leaving three bodies. They fought their way out, then E&E'd to a more favorable site and got a helicopter Stabo rig* extraction out of the area.

Because of bad weather, it wasn't until five days later that a hatchet team, led by Master Sergeant Campbell and comprised of Rangers from the 33rd Vietnamese Ranger Battalion, was inserted. They recovered the three bodies but never found Team Viper. Two of the indigenous personnel with Team Viper managed to escape and were picked up later. The last person to see Stark and Bott was FAC pilot John Flanagan. In communication with the FAC, Russ Bott refused to leave his good friend and teammate, Willie Stark, who was gravely wounded. The FAC pilot and a Delta person by the name of Tommy Tucker gave what support they could. Using smoke grenades and marking rockets, they attempted to drive the NVA away. Stark and Bott were never seen or heard from again; they are carried as MIAs and named on the Vietnam Veterans' Memorial.

Lurch continued to operate with Project Delta out of Khe Sanh, and he and Sergeant Stamper later went out as a reaction force with the 33rd Vietnamese Ranger Battalion, supporting a Project Delta team that had gotten into an asskick. Working with indigenous people was a new experience for Lurch. They inserted into an area northwest of Khe Sanh, very close to the Laotian border, and started moving toward the team's location when darkness overcame them, so they holed up to wait for daylight. A Mike Force (reaction) element in the area reported movement of large numbers of enemy troops into the team's

---

*LBE harness reconfigured to allow snap linking onto ropes for extraction, allowing free use of hands.

AO. The reaction force linked up with the team, and prepared to be extracted. As the helicopters were approaching, the Rangers initiated an ambush on enemy troops closing in on the LZ, and all hell broke loose. Lurch recalls: "As we left the shelter of the woodline, a B-40 rocket exploded, hitting a tree I was passing, and a piece of shrapnel took my legs out from under me. I felt no pain, but I was bleeding. I got up as fast as I went down, but my left leg wouldn't work properly. The choppers were lifting off, and I ran and tried to jump into the one Stamper had boarded. He pulled me inside and had a big grin on his face as if to tell me it was all right and we were all right. We made it out without anyone losing his life, which was remarkable."

Because of bad visibility and the presence of wounded on board, the helicopters didn't take the reaction force back to Khe Sanh. Instead it continued on to Da-nang. Lurch was taken to a field hospital and was sent from there to 6th Convalescent Hospital in Cam-ranh Bay. After six weeks of recovering on the white beaches, he returned to Nha-trang and Project Delta.

"I was excited to get back to Project Delta," Lurch remembers. "I flew into Nha-trang and went directly to get paid. But my pay was cut almost in half, and I complained. I was told to report to a Master Sergeant Childers, who was in charge of the Mess Association. Childers was six eight or six nine, just a huge guy, and he always intimidated people because he was so big. It seems I had not paid my dues for the months I had been in Khe Sanh and at the hospital. I tried to explain to the clerk that I hadn't been around to use the facilities and shouldn't have to pay. It was bullshit. We didn't get paid all that much, and they wanted to take half my paycheck to pay the Mess Association for food I never got to eat. Sergeant Childers came storming out of his office, calling me every name in the book. Without giving me a chance to defend my stand, he told me I wasn't part of the team and to report to Command Sergeant Major Dunaway. Command Sergeant Major Dunaway carried a swagger stick under his arm everywhere he went. When I reported to Dunaway, he laid the swagger stick on my shoulder and said four words to me, 'You're out of here.' In fifteen minutes they had orders for me to go to the 1st Brigade, 101st Airborne. I went back to the Project Delta compound to collect my belongings and say my good-byes. I couldn't find Stamper or anyone from Delta. They were still up at Khe Sanh. It was an inglorious and chickenshit way to get rid of someone."

Lurch's reassignment was a loss for Special Forces and particularly for Project Delta but a great gain for the Lurps of the 1st Brigade, 101st Airborne. I learned a lot from Lurch that night, and we became fast friends. We went to the NCO club that evening with Sgt. David "Mad Dog" Dolby. I was not an NCO at the time and had borrowed a shirt with buck-sergeant (E-5) stripes sewn on. The three of us were talking together when someone tapped me on the shoulder. I turned around, and Top Smith was right there. I was embarrassed at being busted by Top Smith for impersonating an NCO. Top Smith looked at me and with a slight smile said, "Sergeant Martinez, let me buy you and your friends a drink!" I stammered out a thank you and launched into an explanation about the stripes. He cut me off saying, "It's all right. I've put you in for E-5." During the course of the evening, Lurch talked to Top Smith and was accepted into Lurps. I'm right proud to say that I recruited Lurch. But then again, Lurch recruited Lurch. We served together until the breakup of 1st Brigade LRRPS and then later toward the end of my tour in Vietnam.

The following day, I hopped a flight to Cam-ranh Bay and took my FAST tests for helicopter flight school. I had to wait a day after I got there to take the tests. I was later notified that I had passed with a high score and that I would only have to go before a review board comprised of officers to be accepted. I couldn't catch a flight out of Cam-ranh Bay bound for Phanrang until the following day. I was anxious to get back up to Duc Pho because I knew the missions were going out that day. On 16 May, I finally caught a flight. As I was leaving Phanrang, I ran into someone who broke the bad news to me about Fireball Dixon getting killed and my team getting chewed up. The flight back was a long and lonely one. I decided right then

that my place was with the Lurps, and I turned down flight
school.

## WIA

Jungle Jim Cody and I were sitting around on 17 May, discussing the latest mission briefing, and what had happened on
Cruz's team. We had just been briefed by Lieutenant McIsaac
that Operations and Intelligence planned to move the entire
detachment to Nui Cau, Hill 163, which had a strategic
overview of the mouth of the Song (river) Trau Cau River,
where it ran into the South China Sea. Hill 163 also overlooked
the northern perimeter of the 1st Brigade base camp and the
beach area that served as the brigade's logistical support base.
The brigade was being supported with aviation fuel, beans, and
bullets entirely by sea. But before the LRRP detachment could
move to Nui Cau, a team had to check things out.

The team was picked at random by Lieutenant McIsaac, but
it was a good pick. The team leader was Ron Gartner, with
Rudy Lopez as RTO. Gary "Fannie" Fandel was medic, and
Jungle Jim Cody was a scout. They would be augmented by
two engineers with metal detectors from the 326th Engineers.
Gartner's team would be flown by chopper and inserted on the
top of Nui Cau, and the next morning they were to clear a lane
down from the top of the mountain and link up with our team.
With Bacheck as team leader, we'd be coming up from the
bottom. Lieutenant McIsaac and Gary Fandel would stay to
secure the top of the hill. It was a "walk in the park" mission,
as Cody put it, and he kidded me about how I'd be humping
my ass off getting to the top while all he had to do was walk a
ways downhill to meet us. The mountain was a klick away
from our position, and the hump was no big deal, but we Lurps
had to get our ribbing in, any way we could.

I had been feeling pretty down because I hadn't been with
my team when they got hit on 15 May. The incident was so
fresh in our minds that it dominated everyone's thoughts.

The next morning, we came down off Lurp hill, exited the
wire, and patrolled toward the base of Nui Cau hill. I was car-

rying a radio and informed Lopez that we had arrived at the base of the hill and were ready to start the linkup. The word was out to be careful, that there were a lot of booby traps . . .

We had been moving about thirty minutes when we heard an explosion three or four hundred meters uphill from us.

Ron Gartner had inserted on top of the hill, midafternoon on 18 May. The team found a bunker complex that had been built by the marines and based up there for the night. The bunker complex was well built, with a sandbagged wall all around the top that could easily hold a platoon, and the field of fire was phenomenal. There wouldn't be any problem defending it, unless the Lurps were mortared. In the early evening, a firefight started at the southeast foot of the hill, and the Lurps watched the tracers go back and forth. North of them was a small beach, where during the daylight hours they saw a tank upside down, burning, and at night they could see and hear naval gunfire from ships at sea. All night long, the artillery was firing illuminating rounds, and as they watched the firefights below the hill toward their base camp, Gartner's team heard the canisters from the flares landing nearby.

For Cody, the firefight at the base of the hill brought back memories of his days with a line company. Starting about 1600 hours, and lasting well into the night, the fight involved a small element from the 2/502, who didn't have enough strength to press it, and Chuck, who wasn't running. It was a nice, vicious little firefight. Cody was watching from a box seat, glad he wasn't down there. The tracers were flowing back and forth, and to the experienced ear, the sounds and explosions of the firefight were like a book about what was happening down there.

Ron Gartner didn't sleep very well that night. There were a lot of mongooses so he figured cobras were also close. He visited with the two engineers and found out that they had both been in country only two weeks and didn't know much about what was going on. Knowing he had to follow those two guys down the hill made him very nervous. That was only the second time he'd been out as a team leader, and he felt the pressure of the responsibility.

The next morning Gartner's team started down the southwest side of the hill. The two engineers were leading, followed by Jim Cody, Ron Gartner, and, bringing up the rear, Rudy Lopez with the radio. The trail zigzagged through head-high shrubbery and brush. It was hard to see, and harder to keep an interval. The switchbacks were so tight, the men were forced to bunch up, even though they tried to stay spread out. The engineers were even closer together because of the cord connecting the power pack to the wand unit of their metal detector.

Ron was talking with the engineer carrying the power pack, and for ease of conversation he traded places with Cody en route. After about a half hour on the trail, they came to what looked like an old garden fence with concertina wire draped on it. The fence had been blown up and torn apart, but it had a gate that they could go through. Ron got to the gate with the engineers about eight meters to his left front, Cody six meters to his left rear, and Rudy six meters behind Cody. As Ron entered the gatelike area, he looked up and saw the first engineer, who was carrying the mine-detecting wand, reach out for what looked like cat gut or fishing line. Ron hollered, "Don't grab!" and as he said "grab," there was one hell of a flash and explosion. The next thing he knew, he was landing, hitting hard on the ground.

Cody never anticipated the blast. He remembers the explosion, but he never heard it. "It was too much; your ears shut down." He remembers sailing back in the air, and landing on his back. "It's like you have just been coldcocked. I was lying there dazed, wondering what the hell had happened. I looked over, and because of the way we were zigzagged, the engineer with the pack had gotten blown back toward me. He was on his side. He tried to sit up, looked over at me, and asked me to help him. All I could see was that he was bleeding from his nose, his eyes, and his ears. At that point I rationalized that I couldn't help him, he was too far gone. My first sensation, the first thought that came to mind was, 'Oh fuck! It's finally happened!' It was the reality—dodge the BB after all this time, and it finally caught me. I tried to sit up, and my legs hurt. It was excruciating pain trying to sit up. I got to one elbow and looked down. I saw my hand, and what was left of my finger was still smoking. I looked over and saw Gartner. He had gotten blown back into the concertina wire, and he was wrapped up in this wire. He was lying in the wire and moaning, just that sound of agony. I looked back over my shoulder. Rudy Lopez was down, and not moving much. I flashed on taking this Charlie down one time, walking up on him after I had taken him down, and he was still alive. I'd stood over him and looked down at him. There was this nonverbal communication, he knew what was about to happen. He knew I was going to wax him, and I knew I was going to wax him. It was that reality. I flashed immediately to that, and thought about looking up and having somebody wax me, and I thought, 'No, I'm not going that way.' I crawled and reached over somehow, and got my weapon with my left hand. I couldn't fire with my right. At that point, I thought, 'We got ambushed.' That's what was going through my head. I started laying out rounds on semiautomatic. I was waiting for the wave to start to come in. In all my training—everything from day one, but especially in the line outfit—it was always fire superiority that mattered. Whoever could get the most punch out the fastest, got the upper hand. All I thought about was getting that return fire out."

Rudy Lopez had attended the briefing and knew there was supposed to be some heavy booby trapping in that area. That thought was scary enough. But there it was—it had happened. He was about to perform one of the most noble and courageous acts any brother Lurp could ask for, thinking of someone else's pain more than his own. He wouldn't receive any medals for his actions, even though he deserved them. All he could do was suck up the pain and push himself to perform. He had been farthest from the blast, but it had hurled him straight back. He was lying on his back, totally numb, as dirt, rocks, and debris rained down on him. Then what had happened dawned on him. He watched Cody roll to his side and look at the smoking remains of what had been his finger. Cody was shaking his head and

saying something, but Rudy wasn't hearing very well at the
moment. Suddenly, one of the engineers came running at him
from the front. Rudy reached out and pulled him down and the
man passed out. Rudy could now hear firing. Despite the
danger of other booby traps and mines, Rudy crawled and
hopped toward the first engineer, who was trying to drag himself forward. The engineer's upper torso moved a little, but his
lower torso wouldn't. He was a mess, and Rudy knew there
wasn't anything he could do for him. He then moved to Ron
Gartner and rolled him on his back. Gartner was bleeding from
the head, ears, nose, face, right arm, and hand. When Rudy got
to Ron's leg he thought, "Oh, God, his leg is complete hamburger!" It was ripped wide open, little tendrils of smoke
curling out of the numerous holes, and Rudy had to fight back
panic. The only thing he could do was put a tourniquet on
Gartner's leg.

Ron Gartner, meanwhile, had one overriding determination:
not to die there. "My body was just on fire," he says. "I was
burning so badly, I really didn't have much hurting pain—I
was just burning. I couldn't move either leg. My right hand and
forearm had been hit, and savaged badly. I couldn't see out of
my right eye because it was bleeding. I hollered, and I got
Cody's attention. About that time, the engineer who was carrying the power pack came and ran right over the top of me. He
ran past Cody, and the next time I saw him, he was lying beside
Lopez. Rudy was just getting up on the one foot that he could
walk on. He hopped over to me, took my knife, and cut my
pant legs open. You just couldn't imagine the sight of blood,
bone, and holes in both my legs. At that time, I felt blood running down over my testicles—and, boy, I immediately
checked things out! They were all right, but I had wounds in
my groin, within an inch or two of my penis on both sides. I
was sitting in a pool of blood, and when Lopez hopped down
to me, I turned around and saw that his pant leg was open on
his left leg. It looked like a dog had bitten a chunk out of his
calf. I had been hollering at him to call for help on the radio.
When he got down next to me, the handset was hanging on his

web gear, but it was just the earpiece. Everything else had been blown away, and the wire was hanging by his side. Rudy put a tourniquet on my left leg, which I credit with saving my life because I was bleeding badly. He covered my legs so we wouldn't look at them, then went to help Cody. As he was working on Cody, he was starting to pass out. We were both talking to Rudy, trying to keep him awake."

"I was getting light-headed, and I didn't know why," Rudy Lopez recalls. "I tried to get up, stumbled, and found myself on all fours. I couldn't maintain my balance. I remember that either Ronnie's or Jimmie's rifle had jammed. I crawled over and got another rifle and gave it to him to keep fighting. And then I started to pass out. I said, 'I'm passing out, I'm passing out,' and one of the guys was yelling back at me, 'You can't! You're the only one who can move around!' I was on all fours. I lost my balance and fell on my side. I scooted on my back to lean up against a rock, and then the first thing I knew, the pain started to set in. I couldn't breathe, and I didn't know why. My leg started to hurt, and then I looked at my leg, and my boot was covered with blood. I looked at my left calf, and my left calf was gone—completely gone. I pulled out a big bandage, and put it on my calf. I still couldn't breathe. I tried to tell myself, 'Something is wrong, don't panic, just take short breaths, just stay awake, keep your head clear.' Then I noticed that there were two holes in my stomach and another hole in my side. I put bandages on my stomach, but I still couldn't breathe. I was very woozy, I couldn't move, and I just don't remember what happened after that."

At about this time, Gartner recalls, "I got to talking to Cody, and we started firing bursts, three bursts apiece, trying to get an SOS signal out, trying to get help. About the time we started firing for help, Fandel and McIsaac came down to us. Fandel came over to me and took morphine from my shoulder pocket. He gave it to the first engineer, who was still lying in front of me on his side. He was in real bad shape, bleeding out of his eyes, ears, and nose. He had wounds in the back of his head and in his back. We knew we couldn't help him, and so we gave him all the morphine I had. Then Fandel worked on me, then he worked on Lopez and Cody both. I don't know how long we were up there. Fandel did a terrific job. He just . . . the poor man working on us felt as if . . . I know it was a hell of a strain for him. . . . Then the choppers came, and that was the most wonderful sound I ever heard—that steady *whop-whop-whop* of those rotor blades coming. We knew we were getting help."

When Lieutenant McIsaac and Gary Fandel were running down the hill to assist the team, Fandel recalls that Mac, who was in front, tripped another booby trap, but it failed to detonate. Mac called for aircraft assistance and was answered by a resupply chopper that happened to be flying by the area. It extracted Gartner, Lopez, and one engineer and flew them right to the brigade aid tent. A second helicopter picked up Cody, the by-then dead engineer, Fandel, and Lieutenant McIsaac. The quick response by the helicopters and the proximity to the brigade area kept Ron Gartner and Rudy Lopez alive.

Gartner recalls that when he got to the brigade aid tent, a chaplain wanted to give him last rites. He told the chaplain, "Don't even talk to me! I'm not dying here—talk to this fella over there!" Ron indicated the engineer who had been flown in with him. The engineer died as the chaplain was giving him last rites. Ron spoke with Lieutenant McIsaac and S.Sgt. Larry Beauchamp at the aid tent. After being stabilized, all three Lurps were transported to Qui-nhon hospital.

Gartner came to in the hospital in Qui-nhon after surgery. "I only remember being there two or three days before I was put on a plane to Japan. On the airplane, another fella and I got so bad, they rerouted the airplane to the Philippines, to Clark Air Force Base. I went through surgery immediately upon arriving and almost died there and then, right after surgery, I had a bad reaction to the blood pumped into me, and it almost killed me. I was shipped to Camp Zama, Japan, where I got to see Cruz, Kolarik, Cody, and Lopez. I was there one month, and then sent to Denver, Colorado, where I spent a year at Fitzsimmons Army Hospital."

Rudy Lopez recalls being pulled off the litter and seeing medics all around him. "By the time we had gone about ten steps from the helicopter, they had my clothes all cut away with scissors, and a towel over my *chorizo* (penis) and *pelotas* (balls). They took off all the bandages that Fannie had put on me and replaced them. I don't remember much after that. I don't remember the first surgery, but I do remember waking up from the second surgery. They were telling me I was going into surgery again because I had so much internal damage. That's when I just wanted to die. It hurt, it hurt like hell. A third of my liver had been damaged and removed. My pancreas had been damaged. I had five wire sutures that the doctor had used to attach my two bottom ribs to my rib cage on the left side. I had a hole in my right side that collapsed my right lung. I've had five surgeries since then, and my pancreas has a cyst the size of a baseball that the doctors don't want to mess with."

Cody felt he was stable enough that they should take out the more seriously wounded. By this time, he was under the morphine, but he remembers that it felt like all of his wounds were open. He was up in the air and was freezing and shaking. "We got to the aid station, and they had me on this stainless-steel slab. They're cutting clothes away and trying to take my hat. I was holding on to it with my good hand. I was trying to save it. It was my Lurp hat. They kept saying, 'You don't need it,' but it was special to me. They gave me a shot, and I quit battling with them. They took my Lurp hat. They also took the tiger tooth I always wore around my neck."

While that was going on, Bachek's team was on hold, about one hundred meters up Nui Cau, on orders from Lieutenant McIsaac. From the radio we could just grab snatches of conversation about what was happening, and that fed our anxieties about who was hurt and how badly, but we were too professional to get on the radio and ask for details because airtime is valuable in an emergency like that. In the meantime, Bacheck and I did a small recon up toward the top to see if we could get close enough to help. About forty meters uphill from where we left the rest of the patrol, we came upon a U.S. military canvas-sided boot with a foot still in it.* At first we thought it might belong to one of the guys who had been hit. But it was old, maggots had been at it, and you could see the flesh had been cleaned off by them, but it was still mushy inside. It was the weirdest sight. We should have turned it in, but we let it lie where it was.

We received orders over the radio recalling us to base camp. I had to control myself to keep from running all the way back to find out how the wounded were. We had heard there was a KIA. The results of this mission, on top of what had happened to Cruz's team on the 15th, really set me on edge. It was a hard blow for all of us. As soon as I got back to the base, I ran down

---

*The marines also had an experience on this hill. Ironically it was a recon team from 1st Recon Battalion, First Marine Division, that discovered just how nasty Nui Cau was.

On 25 February 1967, 0930 hours, three months before Gartner's team was hit on Nui Cau, Team Duckbill, a twelve-man team under the command of Lt. Ron Benoit was inserted on the top of Nui Cau. The first bird with six men had just landed when the VC took them under fire with machine guns zeroed on the LZ. As the team ran for cover, a booby-trapped 155 howitzer round was set off, injuring two of the team. Airstrikes were employed to silence the machine guns. As soon as the area was quiet, the other bird with the rest of the team was inserted. When the second half landed, more booby traps went off. Then a 250-pound bomb detonated, and the platoon sergeant, Sgt. Joe Barnes, virtually disappeared and several men were wounded, including the patrol leader, Lieutenant Benoit. Their positions were once again taken under machine-gun fire.

Then Hospitalman Brodie, the corpsman, was seriously wounded by another booby-trapped 155 round, adding to the confusion and striking fear into the men. Heavy fighting continued on the hill, the men wondering who was going to set off the next booby trap.

Before being extracted, the team did find one of Sergeant Barnes's legs and was able to bring it back. A few weeks later, a grunt unit found what was believed to be his jawbone.

For his actions, Lt. Ron Benoit was awarded the Navy Cross.

The next day, after sweeping Hill 163, the marines found that the enemy had liberally sown it with explosives and had laid over a quarter mile of commo wire to command-detonate them. The recon marines had not actually triggered a single booby trap.

Team Duckbill had been on Nui Cau for forty-five minutes and had taken one KIA and nine wounded.

I believe the boot with the foot in it that Staff Sergeant Bacheck and I found belonged to Sgt. Joe Barnes.

to the med station, but the wounded had already been transported to Qui-nhon. I never saw Gartner and Cody again. Rudy
returned to us in December, but they should never have
brought him back in country. He had been hit too hard.

Cody says that while in Camp Zama, Japan, Rudy Lopez
came down to his floor and picked him up in a wheelchair, and
they got to see Sid Tolson, Elmer Kolarik, and Ron Gartner. It
was an emotional reunion. Cody really felt for Sid. In the bed
next to Cody was a fellow from the 101st who had been
wounded in the firefight Cody watched off Nui Cau the night
before he was wounded. One year later, Cody was in a car
wreck while stationed with the 82nd Airborne at Fort Bragg,
North Carolina. He awoke in the hospital, and the same fellow
was again in the bed next to him.

Seven months later, Sid Tolson was in his hospital bed in the
States one night, and he kept feeling a lump under the skin in
his left shoulder blade. After working the lump with his fingers
for a while, he finally asked the medic on duty to take a look.
Using a scalpel, the medic made a small incision and out
popped an AK-47 round. Sid Tolson still carries it, on a gold
chain, as a memento of that horrible day on 15 May 1967.

### Mother's Day 1967

Before a mission in the Song Ve Valley, Staff Sergeant
Beauchamp's team was told that there were no friendlies in the
area. Not long after inserting, Bruce Redmer was in a tree
when he spotted about thirty people, walking, two klicks away.
Redmer gave Sullivan the grid coordinates and told him to
check for friendlies in the area. Sullivan called it in, and was
again told no friendlies were in the area. Redmer couldn't tell
who the people were, but they were walking like friendlies.
They were not in single file the way the NVA normally moved.
But the rear informed the team that no friendlies were in their
AO, so they called in gunships. The guns made a quick pass,
and hit a couple of guys—and all of a sudden, the orange
panels came out. It was part of the 327th. Beauchamp's team
had called gunships on Americans. The team was angry; they

had checked with everyone. There were not supposed to be friendlies in the area.

The 327th brought in medevacs and took out several of the men who had been hit. After the medevacs left, the group ran right into an NVA ambush, no more than 250 yards away, which had probably been alerted by the gunships and the medevac. The Lurps were sitting on the hilltop, watching all that happen, and the men were disgusted. Beauchamp's team also saw a number of choppers shot down that day, and bodies floating in the river. The team observed all that and overheard the furious battalion commander on the radio. "We'll be back. We'll be back," he swore. It was like a ringside seat at a major battle.

Nothing was ever said about the team calling in the gunships, or that the 327th had made a mistake and shouldn't have been in that location. Sullivan says they had checked with the Lurp base, which was manned by Len Abate, and that before calling the gunships in the team had Len Abate check with the marines, ARVNs, and any other unit that might have been close to the area. By then Sullivan and Redmer were short, tired of the war and its stupidity.

# 7

# LONG RANGE RECON
## 1     101
## Foul Dudes

### The Third Generation of LRRPs

Due to the loss of two teams and because the second set of Lurps was rotating home, the LRRP detachment had to recruit once more. It was the second transition in our Lurps, and younger people with a different set of values and a different mind-set came with the new group. The senior NCO corps of the army was being ground down by the demands of the war and many of the older NCOs, seeing death or maiming as their inevitable retirement pay, had worked their way either out of the army or out of harm's way. All of a sudden, the twenty-one-year-olds were the older NCOs. The old, by-the-book, NCO way of seeing things was replaced. In the LRRP detachment we got into "growing our own NCOs." It was June 1967, and the people coming into the war represented what was happening in the States. And with them came the Doors and Sgt. Pepper's Lonely Hearts Club Band. They liked to smoke pot rather than drink—though some did both.

New volunteers came to fill our depleted ranks, a large contingent moving over from the MPs. Sandy "Boss" Weisberger, Harvey "Beaver" Bieber, Tom "Greek" Dokos, Mike "Sweet-pea" Kinnan, Jim "Limey" Walker, Donald Braun, Paul Dufresne, and David Sinclair were all "MP Lurps." From the Brigade Security Platoon came Dirk Sasso, who had enlisted with Harvey Bieber, Eddie Cecena, Thomas Melton, and

Michael Matheny. Marty Dostal, Lurch Cornett, and Fannie
Fandel came in as medics. Mike Worrell, Jack Kinney, John
"Big Chad" Chadwick, Joe "Pizza Joe" Remiro, Gene Van-
ditti, Rob Land, Eddie Mounts, John Matvay, Gunther
Bengston, Buster Sullens, Lawton, Joe Marks from a line com-
pany. Craig Vega from Cutoff, Louisiana, had previously
served with a Long Range Patrol Company in Germany. Jim
Brandt, about the only Sp4. with a ranger tab anyone had ever
seen, came from the States. Two men who had been in
Vietnam for some time came from the engineers, Mark
"Wolverine" Thompson, who had extended for Lurps, and
Ernest "Dirty Ernie" Winston, who had come over with the
brigade in 1965. Another man was Bill Scanlan, who arrived
in Vietnam in December 1965, and had been trying to get into
the Lurps for a year. Communications trained, he got into the
Headquarters commo section of the Lurps, eventually working
his way on to S.Sgt. Ronald "Brother" Weems's team. It was a
diverse group, some having combat experience and others just
having the nerve to try it.

S.Sgt. Lester "Superspade" Hite joined us right after the two
teams were hit. Hite was a career NCO. Born in Centralia, Illinois, and raised in St. Louis, Missouri, he volunteered for the
draft after high school, went through training, and spent his
two years with the 41st Infantry Armory in Germany. Coming
back to the States, he served two years with the National
Guard, then enlisted Airborne for active duty. Upon graduation from jump school, he was shipped to the Panama Canal
Zone with the 3/508. Superspade did some extensive training in insurgency, counterinsurgency, and clandestine operations. He loved the jungle and eventually joined the cadre of
the JWTC (Jungle Warfare Training Center). After four years
in the jungles of the Canal Zone, he was sent to Fort Campbell
with the 101st Airborne, then levied to the 1/101 in Vietnam.
Arriving at Phan-rang, he was sitting in the AG personnel
office, on his first day there, when S.Sgt. Ronald Weems happened in. They called each other cousin because while serving
in the JWTC in Panama, they had married girls who were
cousins. After a brief reunion of hugs, back slaps, and laughs,

Weems asked Superspade how his wife was and where was he getting assigned to. Superspade answered he was going to the 2/327. Abruptly, Weems told Superspade he would be right back, and he left. He returned in fifteen minutes, with Lt. Dan McIsaac in tow. Lieutenant McIsaac told the AG personnel that he wanted Superspade assigned to the LRRP detachment, then told Superspade to grab his stuff. The Lurps had just recruited a real stud.

Cadred by the older members, the LRRP detachment went into a flurry of training. Staff Sergeant Tauffer was doing the communications training. Top Smith, Lieutenant McIsaac, Staff Sergeant Beauchamp, S.Sgt. Ronald Weems, Larry Christian, Teddy Bear Gaskell, Bruce Redmer, Gene Sullivan, Danny Williams, Derby Jones, and I all pitched in with the training. Lurch Cornett did the medical training. But the training had to be done in a short time; it was two and a half weeks of very thorough training, starting early in the morning, and going late into the night. All of us benefited from it. The subjects covered were map reading; orientation and navigating with a compass; condensed medical training; all facets of communications and radio procedures, including the calling in of aerial and artillery support; and demolition work, including booby traps, claymores, and other explosive devices that Lurps used in the field. Identification and use of enemy weapons was covered, as well as familiarization with the weapons that we used. Patroling techniques, including interteam movements and SOPs relating to immediate reaction drills to different points of contacts, were all covered. We taught how to call in helicopters, enter and exit them, and where to sit. Lieutenant McIsaac instructed a good portion of the hand-to-hand combat and killing techniques using a garrotte or knife.

Tom Dokos, who went through this training, says, "It was jam-packed and thorough. What was covered was covered well. The way it was presented was excellent. We cherries were there to learn and absorb what was told and shown. These weren't just classes we had to take. This was for real, and we knew that what was being given to us was for our own good—

and the team's. It came down to the same thing: desire. We all had the desire to be Lurps, and prove ourselves."

Another Lurp who went through this training was Sandy "Boss" Weisberger from Perth Amboy, New Jersey. Boss entered the service in October 1965, went through basic, AIT as an MP, jump school, and then on to the 82nd. After three 1049s requesting service in Vietnam, his wish was finally granted, and he went to the 101st. "The first day with the Lurps, Sweetpea Kinnan and I went to the main tent to hang out and meet our new comrades. Derby Jones came up and said something about introductions and shook my hand. It was my first experience of 'belonging'—something I had never felt with the MPs, either in the 82nd or the 101st. It was a feeling that never stopped growing stronger throughout my life. The following days were filled with equipment scrounging and in-unit training. During communications training, Staff Sergeant Tauffer, the commo sergeant, recited a poem written by one of the battalion commanders. It emphasized the importance of the RTO, the life link of the unit. It really stuck with me. We were taught little tricks to keep quiet and all the hundreds of tips on surviving as a Lurp—all the things we as MPs had never been exposed to. Early on, a couple of other guys and I were in front of our hootch discussing our training. One of the older Lurps, who had been there for a while, came by and was explaining things to us. This was Sgt. Rey Martinez, and he explained that we would learn to do a field-expedient tracheotomy. I made the comment that I wasn't sure I could do that. Sergeant Martinez looked at me and said that if a Lurp wouldn't help you when you couldn't do for yourself, he would kill him. I learned more about Lurps from that statement. I learned that this was the real thing, that my purpose was to be a capable member of a team, that the Lurps *never* left a man behind. Looking back on it, that was the strength of our unit."

The training bonded the new recruits to the old guys because it was done as a unit. After training, those who couldn't operate the way we did were weeded out. The next step to take was training missions outside the wire, right there at Duc Pho.

Greek Dokos remembers that Bruce Redmer was his

training team leader. Redmer worked with the new guys, squaring everyone away, explaining what was expected of each position, what areas to cover when moving and stopping, what each person was to do on the mission. They went on their first training patrol on a hot sunny day. After a while, Redmer put Greek on point, gave him some brief instructions, and told him to lead the team to the designated destination.

Greek Dokos recalls: "I was the man, and the pressure was on! When you want to do well, it's extremely important to perform the best you ever have. You tend to place too much pressure on yourself. Too much isn't good; you tighten up, mentally and physically. I was sweating like a big dog. I had never been in heavy brush with a rucksack on, all the equipment, ammo load, and rifle. My thoughts of slipping through the bush like a snake vanished after fifty meters into the thick stuff. Wait-a-minute vines seeming to grab my rucksack, my rifle, or me and hold on. I was getting frustrated, hot, and sweating buckets. At first I would stop and slip the wait-a-minute vines off me. After a while I started plowing through them. I came to one NVA vine that really grabbed on to me. I kept struggling; then all of a sudden, damned if that vine didn't just straighten my ass up! It jerked me right back. I turned around and there was Redmer, holding on to my rucksack, trying to get my attention. He had this look on his face like, 'Damn, boy! Get control of yourself!' It was embarrassing. We got back, and Redmer sat us down and discussed the whole mission. He was cool about it, just pointed out things we did that needed to be corrected and also areas we did okay in—which was important for us. He told us that on the next patrol we would get more comfortable, more in sync, but we'd never stop learning. He was right. The next one went smoother. It was easier after that, and I knew I was going to be a Lurp. I felt more capable, physically and mentally. And most of all, I had the desire to be one of these guys—the best."

Pizza Joe Remiro and Joe Marks were on one of the training missions together. It was to be a night ambush, and the team was just getting into the ambush site, which was a rice paddy dike. Suddenly, they heard two VC walking toward them, talking. The team opened up and dropped them.

Pizza Joe recalls, "We were on the same team on an ambush across the small stream at Duc Pho. We ambushed two VC and killed one. The sergeant sent the two of us over the dike to check the body. What I've never forgotten was that just as the two of us were going over, Joe Marks, who had line time, held me up, told me to be careful. He said that we couldn't be sure the second VC wasn't out there waiting for us. That body could be his brother, his father, or his son. He got my attention with that."

On the same training mission, one of the other guys on the team was carrying a radio. The team leader wanted the radio and called the other man's name several times so that he could use the radio. Pizza Joe found the man crouched down, shaking and unable to function. Pizza Joe grabbed the radio and took it to the team leader. After the mission, Pizza Joe went over and talked to the guy. The man confided that he didn't think he was capable of being a Lurp. Pizza Joe suggested to him that maybe he should leave the unit. The man left the next day.

## First Raid

On 9 June 1967, the LRRP detachment was given a carefully planned mission by Operations and Intelligence. The mission was a raid to capture enemy personnel who'd been identified in a small village controlled by the Vietcong. The initial planning was done by Maj. Richard Morton, the brigade intelligence (S-2) officer and the LRRP detachment commander, 1st Lieutenant McIsaac, who would be leading the raid. The objective was a small village nestled on the east bank of the broad, shallow, slow-flowing Song Ve and the northwest flanks of Nui Ngang (Nui means mountain in Vietnamese), coordinates 630423 on map sheet Mo Duc. The village consisted of ten to twelve bamboo-frame hootches. We would be using five fire teams, "five men per team," plus a headquarters control team, including an interpreter and a PIO (Public Information Office) person by the name of William Singley. We were going in to take prisoners, and had orders not to shoot anyone unless we absolutely had to.

I was picked by Lieutenant McIsaac to be his RTO in charge of air assets—the gunships and slicks of the 176th Aviation Company, the Minutemen and the Muskets. Sp4. Patrick "Mother" Henshaw was to be the RTO for interteam communication. We had forty-eight hours to prepare for the mission and started planning feverishly. We used an abandoned village within the brigade rear area to rehearse each man's actions inside the village. We broke the chopper loads down and had walk-throughs on everything from inserting into the village to the extraction. The Lurps were to use six helicopters for the raiding force and would have three additional helicopters for prisoner loads. The raiding force would contour fly into the objective and come over a hill and ridgeline at the village's back side. The first helicopter would land at the rear of the village and act as a blocking force team to prevent escape. The other five helicopters would land in trail in front of the length of the village. The third helicopter in trail would be the headquarters element. The two fire teams on each side of the headquarters helicopter would pinch in to the middle, securing prisoners as they went. Prisoner extraction points were designated. Two M-60 machine gun fire teams were incorporated within the raiding force. One of the M-60 machine guns would be manned by S.Sgt. Ronald "Brother" Weems and would be on the blocking force team. The other machine gun would be on the first helicopter, in front of the village. Each fire team was further broken down, and three men within each fire team were designated to secure and handle prisoners; the other two would provide security. We had thoroughly discussed what each team and each team member's responsibility would be on this mission. We went over and over each team's assignment and what every man would do within the concept of the whole raid. We would be taking only ammunition and grenades, traveling light and fast with a big-assed punch. We were to take prisoners and not shoot people unless we were fired upon. We would have to be very forceful in order to obtain cooperation rapidly. It was a different and rather

difficult mission because of the no-shooting order and the fact
that we had never performed a raid like that as a group. And
ours was a newly trained unit; this was actually our first mission together as a group.

All of us were at the chopper pad in Duc Pho about an hour
before sundown. Everyone had a painted face, and there wasn't
any ass grabbing or bullshitting. Pretty serious business was
about to come down, and the mission had everyone's attention.
I loaded in with the headquarters group: Top Smith, an ARVN
interpreter, Larry Christian, William Singley (PIO), brigade
reporter, and me. I happened to glance at the reporter and
noticed that he had a camera and no weapon. I asked him
where his weapon was, and he replied that he didn't have one.
I thought that was bullshit and told him so. He was taking the
space of someone who would have the ability to kick Chuck's
ass if it came down to that. I handed him my .45 pistol and told
him I wanted it back.

All nine helicopters started up, and the adrenaline really
began to pump. After the radio checks were completed, we
lifted off, heading directly west. The golden light of the setting
sun bathed the countryside below in beautifully vivid colors.
Looking across the sky, we could see the other Lurps as we
flew in a diamond formation into the setting sun. The four gunships flew two in trail, flying with us on each side of the
formation. The sound and wind added to the incredible nerve-
quivering physical rush we were experiencing. As we came in
sight of the eastside mass of Ngang Mountain, we started
bleeding off elevation, crossing the heavily jungled north flank
of the mountain at contour-flight elevation. You could actually
*see* the speed of the helicopter as we crossed the ridge,
screaming downhill toward a small hill that overlooked the
back side of the hamlet two miles distant. The canopied ridge
looked as if we were sliding down a broccoli-headed slide. We
came in on the village from the west side, banking around the
small hill, and with the setting sun in the enemy's eyes, we
rushed in, flaring into a stomach-stopping landing. They never
heard us or saw us coming.

Our helicopter came in third in trail to land in front of the hamlet. I have a strong visual image of the helicopter flaring in to land. We were passing hootches, and in the brutal rotor wash, dirt, dried grass, and brush were being blown around. The palm fronds on the roofs were coming loose and adding to the movement. Shrubbery and foliage were being blown down and held flat by the violent slap of the rotors. And people were spilling out of the hootches, scrambling for an avenue of escape, a lot of them carrying weapons. We were settling to land in a vegetable garden, and across from me was a large hootch, with a raised porch, at the edge of the garden. On the porch an enemy soldier was reclining in a hammock; startled awake, he jumped out of the hammock, grabbed his web gear and AK-47 rifle, and ran toward us down three steps made out of halved bamboo. I spotted him coming out of the hammock and raised my rifle as he hit the steps. I was going to start shooting when Top Smith pushed my barrel down and mouthed the words "no shooting." The door gunner on my side, the starboard side of the aircraft, also had trained his machine gun on him. As Top Smith was telling the both of us not to shoot him, I was watching the Charlie, and suddenly he went down in a hail of bullets. So much for the no-shooting clause. Top just kind of shrugged his shoulders. Sgt. Clay Wentworth and several other animals on Weems's team had opened up on him.

"I know we trained hard to go out on that raid," says Clay Wentworth. "I was on the lead ship with Lt. Dan McIsaac. We were supposed to come through the hedgerow and cut off the back side of that hamlet. The rest of the guys, a twenty-five man raiding force, were going to hit it from the front. I remember we contour-flew up there, and then we popped over that ridgeline and came right down on that hamlet. We got right down about fifty feet above the ground, and all these dudes starting running out there with rifles and stuff. I opened fire on the first one I saw, and so did the door gunner and the rest of the guys on my side of the ship. We knocked him down, and when we hit the ground, we went through the hedgerow and secured our positions while everybody else did the searching and capturing."

I was told later by other members of the raiding party that they had to kill more individuals as we were landing. It was very hard keeping track of them because everything was happening so fast. These dudes had weapons in their hands, and there was no doubt in anyone's mind what they would do as soon as they could set up a defense against us. People were running all over the place. The village was just like an anthill that had been stirred up. We rounded people up then had prisoner security teams tie them up and escort them to a chopper. We picked up as many documents as we could and prepared to get out of there because we were starting to receive incoming from the hillside behind the village. Sergeant Weems and Sgt. Joe Marks, who were both carrying M-60s, saw the twinkle of muzzle flashes in the ridge and the draw directly behind the village. It was getting dark enough to see them clearly. We had come in very fast and taken the enemy by surprise, but the VC were starting to get their act together. Only five minutes had gone by. The M-60s started chattering, laying down fire, and Mac called in the gunships to strafe targets as we were extracted.

"I helped tie the prisoners up and was trying to keep them segregated, making sure they didn't talk to each other," remembers Brian "Wolfman" Kraft. "There was some sporadic fire when we landed, but I think it was quickly suppressed. It was pretty much grab them and get out of there before the enemy could regroup. But if we had been there twenty or thirty minutes longer, I think we would have gotten into the deep do-do. We didn't have any wounded, and there was a lot of outgoing fire as we were leaving. I don't think we were on the ground more than ten minutes. I remember it was going real quick, and I was in a real hurry to leave and my mind frame was, 'Let's get these people, and get the hell out of here.' I don't think we were strong enough in that unit to do what we did."

Pizza Joe was on the prisoner security team, and he escorted some prisoners to the extraction point. One of them was a young good-looking woman. He was smitten with her looks and started flirting with her. She seemed very receptive and was maybe the only prisoner actually happy to see us. As it turned out, she was the fiancée of a South Vietnamese soldier who had been kidnapped while she was visiting relatives. When we rescued her, she was being forced to undergo political indoctrination by an NVA officer who wanted to use her as a spy.*

We captured sixteen prisoners, who were hustled to the extraction points, where they were loaded four to a helicopter, with two bodyguards. When we were inserted, the two helicopters on either end of the trail formation had flown off. The sixteen prisoners were loaded on the four helicopters that had waited on the ground. They took off as the mission approached eight minutes on the ground. The five other helicopters swooped in as the gunships started raking the ridge and draw with fire. The blocking team with Brother Weems and Clay Wentworth fell through the hootches to our side. We ran to the helicopters as they flew in, and we came out in our assigned helicopter loads.

The mission was a total success. No one was injured, no one was left behind. It had taken ten minutes to execute the raid. In the group of prisoners we snatched was the identified high-ranking Vietcong political action officer. That was the fastest, best-executed raid I had ever been on. The element of surprise was in our favor, and the boldness of the plan contributed to its success. Top Smith and Lieutenant McIsaac were instrumental to the raid's success. With their methodical and meticulous planning and timing, they had shown us how to operate like a precision machine. This was the newly trained unit's first mission and, to my mind, the birth of the Foul Dudes. The mission made it possible for everyone to believe in each other; the detachment's Lurp brotherhood was forged in this raid. After the raid, we walked with our heads just a little higher, and we were ten times as cocky. The raid could have turned into a bloody disaster if the enemy had been waiting for us or

*1st Brigade, 101st Airborne Division. After Action Report, dated 19 June 1967, page 3. National Archives, Suitland, Maryland.

if we had lingered around. But the Foul Dudes didn't believe in "ifs."

## Second Raid

Emboldened by the success of the first raid, two days later, the LRRP detachment was once again alerted for a mission into the Song Ve Valley. This time we would be raiding a target about ten miles from the area of the previous mission. Once again, high-ranking enemy officers had been linked to a hamlet of fifteen to twenty hootches. The hamlet was close to the eastern bank of the Song Ve, near where it started a large meandering curve around the mouth of a wide stream plain that emptied from the hills and mountains to the east. There were five or six hundred meters of abandoned rice paddies on the east side of the village, and there paddies ran up against a large ridge that paralleled the valley floor. To the west, across the river, were eight or so hootches in line against the river, with about two hundred meters of old rice paddies behind them. Nosing onto these paddies was a ridge that came in from the west and was part of a larger hill mass.

The Lurps used the old hootches in our brigade perimeter to approximate the new target. Our plan this time was to land in trail formation on the east side of the valley, coming in on a south-to-north approach. We would sweep, on line, west through the village, pushing the enemy into the open, broad, shallow river. The gunships would take care of any enemy who reached that area. This time anyone spotted carrying a weapon would be shot immediately. All the Foul Dudes were pleased at not being hampered by rules of engagement. We would attempt to take prisoners, but any prisoner taken this time would in all probability be wounded.

I would be going with Lieutenant McIsaac's fire team. Our team would consist of Clay Wentworth, John "Big Chad" Chadwick, Lurch Cornett, and Patrick "Mother" Henshaw, who would be handling interteam communications. I was also humping a radio and would be handling air assets once again. We were the controlling, or headquarters, element, but this time we wouldn't have any dead weight hanging around and would act as a fire team.

One of the young men who was going hadn't been in Lurps very long. Sandy "Boss" Weisberger still remembers the gut-churning rush of excitement he experienced when the detachment was alerted to the mission. A raid! That meant sure contact with the enemy. Boss was a member of S.Sgt. Ron "Brother" Weems's team, and was the AG (assistant gunner) to Joe Marks's M-60 machine gun. The other members were Bill Scanlan and Mike "Sweetpea" Kinnan.

Boss wore tiger fatigues, web gear, carried his own M-16, and two combat packs with linked 7.62 ammo for the machine gun. He belted more of the ammo over a shoulder and was carrying a total of about seven hundred rounds. Canteens and grenades completed his load. But there was one exception—his Lurp hat.

"I still hadn't gotten one at the time," Boss explained. "I suppose it was late morning before I was pretty well organized. One of the 'old guys' (pre–Foul Dude), Bruce Redmer, came by to check me out. He was a Jersey boy like myself, and when he saw I had no Lurp hat, he loaned me his, saying something to the effect of 'not having a Jersey boy go out on a mission without a Lurp hat. . . . Don't come back without it.' The words may have been different, but the tone of voice and expression on his face are still clear in my memory. The message was clear: I had been trusted by a proven warrior and sternly tasked to complete the mission at any cost."

The choppers landed with the village hard to our left. Facing north, Brother Weems's helicopter was the last in line. Gunfire broke out almost immediately as Weems opened up on a group of khaki-clothed men.

"The initial image I still retain is of mass confusion in the village," remembers Boss. "I threw myself down beside Joe Marks. He was hammering away with the machine gun. I experienced some personal confusion of my own as I tried to watch the action toward our front, keep my 16 in my hand, and move the belt of the 7.62 from over my shoulder to the belt of ammo rapidly disappearing into the gun. With every burst, the end lashed like an angry snake as I used fingers, now sausage-like, to snap the ends together. Marks yelled to get the belt straightened out and kept up his fire. I hooked the end of the second belt to the one inside the combat pack on my web belt. Like an umbilical cord, we were linked together, birthing death."

Marks and Boss got up from behind the low berm they had been behind and moved toward their right. There they stood up on a berm at a right angle to the one they had fired from and moved a short way into the village. For a period of time, things seemed to calm down. There was no movement toward their front, so they moved back to their original position, then opened up on the village again. Boss noticed that Top was standing slightly to his rear, firing his CAR-15. As always, Top was dead calm. He heard a voice saying that we were taking rounds from a heavy machine gun from "the ridge" and that we were being pulled out. Marks asked for the last belt, and Boss gave it to him. As the choppers landed, Boss and Marks started toward them. In the excitement, Boss forgot to take his hat off and cram it down his shirt or hold it in his teeth. As they moved out, he spotted a large watermelon lying on the ground and scooped it up. With the melon in one hand and his 16 in the other, he ran toward the helicopter. But the rotor wash lifted the hat off his head. He stood rooted to the ground as it flew up and over a fence, back into the village. Boss threw the melon at a faceless body and ran for the hat. He went down into a slight hollow, fought his way through brush, over a bamboo and wire fence, and grabbed the hat. His throat was parched, he was sucking wind, and his pulse was pounding so loud, he heard nothing else. Boss knew his shit was weak and that he had done a world-famous-stupid stunt. But for his life, he couldn't have left the hat in the village. In that situation, as a green Lurp and an ex-MP, Boss was willing to risk everything to fulfill his personal sense of obligation. He never considered the possibility of being left behind.

Boss ran back to the choppers and such was his timing and position that he headed for the last one in line as the others were then taking off. He recalls, "I saw Lurps sitting in the open doors, legs hanging out, yelling to get my ass in gear. I ran up to the slick, and for an unexplainable reason did not leap into the port side, but ran around the front of the ship to the opposite door. I figure both pilot and copilot were cursing me to the original ancestor from which I sprang. I threw my M-16 inside, made a grab for something solid, and got two handfuls of skid. Weems was yelling and leering at me, I was running with the movement of the ship and thinking we were still ground level. Weems grabbed my harness, poked me in the chest with his finger, and said, 'You fucked up, you fucked up.' He grinned, rolling his eyes, and pointed down. I looked: the hostile territory we had just left was far below. My asshole slammed shut, and my heart crawled into my throat. Obviously these involuntary muscle spasms caused my eyes to 'get as big as dinner plates,' as Sweetpea Kinnan said. My legs were still running in the air as they pulled me in."

As the raid went into the LZ in trail formation, the choppers received fire from the west of the village, across the river itself, and from the other valley. Lieutenant McIsaac recalls that we landed in trail formation, going from south to north, and, as in rehearsals, everybody exited the choppers, moved through the village to sweep the enemy toward the shore and the open area where the gunships would get them.

"We ended up in an intense firefight," Lieutenant McIsaac says. "In fact, we had our helicopter shot down, and, if I'm not mistaken, Marty and I were in the chopper when an enemy 12.7 (.51 cal.) round went in one door and out the other without hitting anyone."

But a humorous incident is the one that Mac most remembers from that raid. It concerns Mother Henshaw, who later transferred out of the outfit, went to II Corps LRRPs, and was eventually killed in action.

"In the middle of the raid we were taking a lot of fire from around the clock, and I was trying to coordinate to bring in gunships and direct everybody on the ground at the same time. Mother Henshaw, however, had one of the new XM-148s, which is the M-16 with a grenade launcher underneath it. I had the gunships coming in on short final for a hot run and had talked through both of the RTOs and had moved all of the teams back. Mother, carrying the interteam radio, was slightly to my left and front. During all of the conversation on the radios, when I was talking to the gunships and calling in artillery and communicating with the different team leaders to make sure everybody was pulled back for the first hot run, I could hear *brrrrt, brrrrrrt, thwump, thwump, thwump*. Mother was over there firing up a storm at the enemy. All of a sudden it gets quiet, and I hear him say, 'Oh, shit, are we in trouble now!' That got my attention, and I looked up and I said, 'Jesus Christ! What do you see, a tank out there or something?' Mother looked at me and said, 'No, Lieutenant. I'm out of M-79 rounds.' I started laughing. You know, everything was so hectic at the time, it was humorous that he thought at that particular moment that we were really in deep trouble just because he was out of M-79 rounds. The gunships came in firing so that they could also fire up the valley and the mountain ranges across from us. The gunship overflew our position, firing across the river, and some hot brass got down Mother's back. That got him dancing like a puppet on a string."

Clay Jay Wentworth recalls getting ready for the raid. He was going to sport some brand new tigers for the occasion. He was proud of his new tigers and figured on pulling the raid and being back in a couple of hours, looking good. The successful raid four days before had made the Foul Dudes complacent and cocky. Wentworth boarded his chopper and landed on the east side of the river. It was around 1500 hours, and the time difference from the previous raid had a tremendous impact on the Lurps. Most of the enemy sentinels and LZ watchers had not left their positions yet, which they would have done as dusk approached. The Lurps came in and immediately started taking fire. The longer they were there, the more fire they were getting, some of it coming down from the mountain. McIsaac's team had never gone far from the LZ because he was trying to get the teams together while coordinating the gunship runs.

"We kept going up and down the edge of the LZ, and there was a big ditch bank there and a barbed-wire fence separating it from the field," Wentworth recalls. "We had gone back and forth a couple of times, and the last time we came out across, preparing for extraction. We received heavy fire, and everybody dove over that barbed-wire fence and down into that ditch. When I went to go over the barbed-wire fence, I got hung up in it. Got my tigers all hooked up on the fence, and I was looking at all them dudes lying down under that cover, looking up at me, while all these bullets are cracking at my feet and around me. Going over that fence, I ripped my tigers to shreds. When we moved out for extraction, I jumped over that barbed-wire fence, and again I got hung up in it! I tore my tigers up even worse. I dove into the left side of the ship, and slid all the way across to the door on the right side, facing the mountain. Marty Jay Martinez was Lieutenant McIsaac's RTO. He had been ahead of me, and when he jumped into the helicopter, he slid all the way across, falling out the starboard side of the helicopter. I helped him back into the helicopter, and we started receiving rounds right through the chopper. I could see gooks down in the line of bushes, and they were shooting at the choppers. We opened up on them. In the meantime, they had shot all the glass out of the chopper. We were lucky with all those rounds going through the helicopter. No one was ever hit, which was very remarkable."

After being helped back into the helicopter by Wentworth, I leaned back against the copilot's seat. We were lifting off in the nose-down attitude, when a 12.7 round hit the doorframe above my head. Another round hit above Lurch's head. He was sitting with his back against the pilot's seat, in the port-side doorway. I saw a green tracer go through the helicopter, between all six of us, and exit heading into the village. During that whole time, the helicopter was picking up speed, almost going into translational lift. The enemy machine gunner had us pegged with his big gun, and he wasn't letting off. The next round hit on the forward post near the starboard door gunner. Another hit right next to him. The rest of the rounds were smacking into the engine cowlings and aft of the starboard door gunner. These were 802-grain, big-ass 12.7mm rounds. The helicopter started shuddering the way a car does when it's running out of gas. By that point, the chopper's nose had come up, and we were about nine hundred meters from the LZ we had just left, about 100 feet in the air. But the copilot was frantically signaling McIsaac that he was going to put it back down. The helicopter started dropping toward the ground. Suddenly the pilot popped the nose almost straight up, and we slammed into the ground. We bounced hard off the dry paddy once, then slid, bouncing, to a stop. I jumped out of the helicopter. The skids were splayed out to the sides. The copilot's door was tweaked shut, and I helped wrench it open. Some of the other Lurps helped the door gunners get their machine guns and ammo out to the security wheel we were throwing up around the helicopter.

"We were advised that one of our ships had gone down and we were going back to support it," Boss Weisberger remembers. "The slight after-action letdown disappeared in a flash. Weems looked at me and said, 'Give me some shit!' I told him I had given Marks the rest of my ammo, but he was hearing none of it. He scowled at me, and raised his voice: *'Give me some shit!'* I turned. By my right hand the door gunner had a large wooden box filled with belted 7.62 ammo. The gunner looked at me and tried to wave me off, but you just don't say no to Weems. I grabbed a belt and broke a good bit off as we started down. Weems was pumping us up, running down how he was going to kill some of the motherfuckers. It was contagious. By the time we hit the ground, I was hooked up to him and the 60, telling him, 'Yeah! We're gonna kill, and I am right with you!' "

Landing, Boss moved out in front of Weems, clearing brush for his field of fire. He thought he heard movement in the high grass to their left. He sat with a grenade in hand waiting to pinpoint the noise. We took sporadic fire the whole time there, suppressing it with gunship fire when we extracted the downed helicopter.

"I remember the machine-gun fire on that second raid," recalls Pizza Joe. "When they first pulled us out, I was hugging the deck of the chopper while rounds cracked over our heads, in one door and out the other. Finally we were out of range and able to take a deep breath; then someone told us we were going back in, we had a chopper down. The helicopter banked and went in and landed, and we unassed the chopper. We laid in that field under grazing fire late into the day. At one point Clay yelled, 'Pizza Joe, Pizza Joe,' like he was hit or something. I yelled back, 'What? What?' and he answers with, *'Wooooow!'* "

The Lurps waited for about an hour and a half, and just as it was starting to get dark, a CH-47 (Chinook) came in to pick up the downed helicopter. The Chinook came in, dropped a bunch of rigging straps, lifted off, and circled as the crewmen rigged the helicopter. The Chinook came back in and opened its ramp door, and two teams went on board. I was part of that crowd, and we hovered over the helicopter as it was hooked up. We could hear the *slap* of rounds hitting the Chinook. We rose straight up, picking up the helicopter, and started flying down the valley, gaining elevation. There was a small trapdoor in the belly of the Chinook through which the crew chief could look down and give instructions to the pilot. They call it the hellhole. It is also where they operate the winch when slinging loads. Well, I saw it as a good place to watch the proceedings. The crew chief warned me to give him some space so he could see what was happening to the slung aircraft. I told him okay but still crowded in to get a view. We had gained about 1500 feet of altitude and were heading east. It was getting near twilight, and the helicopter we had slung was starting to oscillate violently underneath the Chinook. I could see the crew chief talking over his helmet set with the pilot. He looked at me and gave me the cutting motion across his throat with his hand. He hit a lever and the Chinook bucked up sharply from the release of the slung load. The crew chief and I had the best view as the helicopter dropped like a rock, rolling over on its back. When it hit the ground far below, there was a huge orange explosion. Well, so much for spending half the day defending the helicopter. We flew east, into the dark, back to Duc Pho. Boss never did see his captured watermelon again—but he did give Bruce Redmer back his Lurp hat.

## Lurp Hill

Our rear camp at Duc Pho was on the northwest edge of the brigade perimeter, on a little knob we called Lurp Hill. A small stream ran north, contouring the base of the hill and separating us from an expanse of rice paddies that stretched to the west. To the northwest about 2500 meters was Nui Dang, a solitary hill that jutted straight up from all the paddies around it. On the west side of Nui Dang was the airstrip, where the 3/25 was stationed. The marines had gotten involved in some very heavy fighting in that area. To the north about two thousand meters away from Lurp hill was Nui Cua, Hill 163, where Cody, Gartner, and Lopez had gotten hit. To the east, below Lurp Hill, was the brigade forward rear area, extending east and south toward the beach twelve hundred meters away. All that could be seen from atop Lurp Hill.

Our sleeping areas were small hootches made of tent ("shelter") halves, two men to a hootch. Dotting Lurp hill among the scrub brush, it was like a gypsy encampment. Some of the hootches were dug in and sandbagged. That was where we left our gear when we went out in the bush. It was home. Bacheck and Rudy had stolen some tents in Phan-thiet, and we set up one that we used as a training tent. Later, people slept in it.

Other than when we went out to hunt them, we didn't have much to do with the Vietnamese while we were on Lurp Hill. The 1st Brigade was geographically isolated from the Vietnamese populace. When we were in the rear area, we got to where we wouldn't walk down to the assigned headquarters company chow tent to eat, preferring instead to eat C and LRRP rations in our own area. Nobody bothered us on Lurp Hill. It was out of the way, and when we had visitors, the first tent they saw was the TOC tent and Top Smith's tent. Top shielded us very well from the headquarters people.

We matured in the way only war can make people grow up. The Foul Dudes were born on Lurp Hill. Brother Weems, our elder statesman, coined it when he labeled Doc Kraft the "Foul Ogre Wolf" for his ability to eat while simultaneously suffering the worst—and most offensive—symptoms of a bad case of dysentery. Doc Kraft was a Foul Dude. Brother Weems also established the law about not smoking pot in the field. The "Five High Saving Steps" were formed on Lurp Hill. The first high saving step was: Don't let it bring you down. Pizza Joe remembers when Rob Land got sick, and they told everyone he had tried to eat his boot. He comments, "While we were all smoking, Land was eating a Lurp ration dry. Then he chugged a canteen of water. It must have swelled up in his stomach. Anyway, he fell to the ground, groaning in pain. Lurch ran over to him, and I guess we expected him to do some spectacular medic stuff. Instead, Lurch leaned over Land, and yelled, 'Don't let it bring you down!' "

That became our motto afterward. Whatever happened, it was always, "Don't let it bring you down!"

Every night while in the rear area we were treated to some display of fireworks, violently beautiful. We would sit on Lurp Hill and look across toward Nui Dang and groove on Puff the Magic Dragon, whose tracers, like a waving red waterfall, would splash onto the paddies, sometimes rebounding back up into the air, eliciting a comment from one of the Lurps: "I wonder what Charlie is doing right now?" Someone else would reply, "Charlie is a bad motherfucker. He's probably policing up the brass!"

We weren't being sympathetic; we understood and recognized a kindred spirit, even if it was the enemy. Sometimes we saw tracers fired upward by some brave soul. Sometimes we'd see such things while listening to the Doors, Jim Morrison singing, "The killer awoke before dawn, he put his boots on. . . ." I remember one Lurp wondering out loud, "Why did he take them off?" It was a coming of age for most of us, acceptance into a warrior class. We knew we were a special breed, and we developed our own way of looking at things. Wolverine said we were the James Deans of the war; we were the rebels. It showed in the way we preferred to go out in the scrub brush at night and sit in a circle doing a pipe, words from fellow paratrooper Jimi Hendrix going through us: "Are you experienced?" It was like stepping back in time to the Indian

warrior society. People were attracted to Lurps for special reasons. It was the same for other recon units, including the SOG
teams that ran with montagnards. War is a great personal
reality check. You know if you can't make the grade, and if
you don't know, the people around you will let you know. We
suffered no punks in Lurps. A Lurp didn't have to be the most
muscle bound or toughest. He just had to have the right heart
and mind. The most important realization with which we had
to come to grips, and which bonded us, was knowing that when
fate shit on you in Lurps, the probability of being taken prisoner and of enduring all the horrors that came with captivity
was extremely high. It was a silent pact among the Lurps that
we wouldn't be taken alive, nor would we let our friends be
taken alive.

Not everyone was suited to being out in the bush with only
five other people. Where we went, most would feel unsafe with
120 people. As the war ground on, certain types of people
gravitated to the special units. More and more people were
doing multiextensions in Lurps, which added to experience
and professionalism. In the infantry line companies, some
extended to stay on the line, but the percentage was glaringly
low. Infantrymen almost always ended up extending into some
special operations unit or out of harm's way. We were all volunteers, and we weren't running away from the war, but right
into it. We were definitely not the "poor me" crowd. It was our
choice, and people took notice of this. In the rear areas, where
we ran into REMFs (rear echelon motherfuckers), they could
sense us when we came into a place. Death was our com-
panion, and they felt it. We radiated an aura of contained violence. We didn't act bad. We *were* bad. As the Lurp said,
"Lurping is not an attitude, but a way of life. If you're going to
run with the big dogs, you damn well better get off the front
porch and be able to piss on tall trees."

We'd graduated out of the panic shots and had experienced
mind-numbing fear, the kind that leaves a person feeling like
he's swallowed a ten-pound block of ice, hyperventilating and
sweating buckets, wanting to puke. We learned how to let it go
and control it, and our brotherhood was forged in a baptism of

fire. It was totally a man's world, and the baseness of war brought out the best and the worst in all of us.

"On 8 June 1967, Operation MALHEUR II was launched and was the largest civil affairs operation in the history of Quang-ngai Province. In addition to fighting the enemy, the 1st Brigade relocated the population and livestock of the Song Ve Valley to Nghia Hanh, the district refugee center. On 22 June the relocation and cattle drive were completed. Exactly 6,256 villagers and 1,341 head of cattle and water buffalo had been moved. The valley, then cleared of civilians, was the object of intensive search and destroy operations. When MALHEUR II ended on 1 August, the Screaming Eagles had killed 470 enemy in the bitter fighting."
*Operational Report*, 1st Brigade, 101st Airborne Division

One of the first missions pulled after the raids was by S.Sgt. Ronald "Brother" Weems, commanding a heavy team. In the team were Boss Weisberger, Greek Dokos, Eddie Cecena, Doc Kraft, Lurch Cornett, Sweetpea Kinnan, Clay Wentworth, Beaver Bieber, Bill Scanlan, Paul Dufresne, Top Smith, and me. It was a stay-behind mission. We would be inserted on a landing zone where a line company was to be extracted. The heavy team was inserted on the same helicopters that were to pull the line company out. In the confusion caused by all the troops on the LZ, the heavy team worked its way to the edge of the LZ and into the jungle bordering it. We were laying dog, waiting for the line company to leave, when suddenly one of the helicopters that was with us when we flew in exploded. It had just taken the weight off its skids and was starting to fly when it happened. One of the line doggies must have had a loose pin on one of his grenades. It was an ugly, horrible sight. We Lurps could only sit and watch as it happened. Six line doggies plus the helicopter crew of four were killed—ten people killed in just seconds. The other line doggies thought they were taking fire and started firing up the area, including the hillside we were on. After a couple of hours' delay, the rest of the line company lifted off.

In the late afternoon, aided by the confusion on the LZ, we silently climbed up out of the valley floor, using a ridgeline. It should be noted that Top Smith impressed the "Young Foul Dudes" by easily outhumping them up the hill, his advanced age notwithstanding. We set up for the night in a large oval perimeter to accommodate all twelve of us. Beaver was close to my feet, and Clay Wentworth was next to him. We were sleeping in the perimeter, and around 0300 hours, I was awakened by a voice yelling, "Charlie! Charlie!" I always wore a survival knife taped upside down on my LBE harness that connected with my pistol belt. To make it easier to sleep, I would unclasp my pistol belt and lay the ammo pouches attached to the belt to each side. I never took my arms out of the straps and kept the LBE on my person. I would remove the knife from its scabbard and stick it into the ground next to me because while on the LBE harness it usually lay against the side of my face when I went to sleep, and that was uncomfortable. Through the dim light I saw a figure crouched over Beaver, and my first thought was that Charlie was in our small perimeter. As I was raising up, my hand brushed the knife, so I grabbed it instinctively and was lunging to stick it into the shadowy figure looming over Beaver when suddenly the figure yelled, and I realized that it was Clay Jay Wentworth. I had come really close to knifing my good friend. Clay Jay later told me that he was on guard, and Beaver started to talk in his sleep. Clay grabbed him by the foot to shake him awake, but when Clay grabbed his foot, Beaver yelled, "Charlie! Charlie's got me by my foot!" The next thing Clay knew, all these Lurps were around him with knives and me about to stab him. Brother Weems later told me he had been lying behind his rucksack with his rifle and clacker in his hand, ready to blow the claymores.

Well, so much for noise security. All that yelling and milling around had everyone pretty much on edge. It was actually rather hilarious, but no one slept the rest of the night. We reconned around there, but I don't remember seeing anything.

### Cattle Drive

The next mission handed to us involved the whole detachment. They were going to relocate the entire population, including all the livestock, out of the Song Ve Valley. Our mission was to screen and provide security on the outer edges of the valley for an ARVN unit. The ARVNs were to collect all the livestock and herd them down to a shipment point where they would be evacuated. The Lurps were inserted at the very head of the valley and stayed away from a little village located there. The ARVN unit was inserted by Chinooks, and when they unloaded out of the choppers, they had their wives and cooking gear. It looked like they were on a camping trip. The ARVNs went through the village and started killing all the livestock, and looting the village. They set up a couple of BARs (Browning Automatic Rifles, a World War II–era .30-caliber weapon), and started firing at the cattle and water buffalo in the fields—thirty or forty head of cattle, and they shot them all! I remember seeing the water buffaloes taking round after round, standing there, and then they would fall over. The Lurps were disgusted, and we called Operations and Intelligence to inform them what was happening. It's a credit to the commanding force of the 1st Brigade that they immediately had the ARVNs extracted. They decided the Lurps would be doing the cattle drive. They brought in a veterinarian, but I don't know where they found him. With the veterinarian came five Vietnamese who would actually be doing the herding. By then, it was late in the afternoon.

We were still looking out over the field where the cattle and water buffalo had been shot when out of the jungle up on the ridgeline came a tiger. I guess he had smelled all that blood. He showed himself for about thirty seconds or so and then popped back into the woods. We set up a defensive position for the night above the small village, and the next morning we moved down and started the cattle drive. We hadn't gone more than two or three klicks when Clay Wentworth, Pigpen Johnson, and Bob McKinnon saw some Charlies over in a tree line. They followed them, and the VC ended up entering a big ditch with tunnellike bunkers dug into the side of the bank. The Lurps went in to investigate. They yelled for the people to "Lai dai" (come here) out of the bunkers, but nothing happened, so McKinnon and a couple of other guys threw grenades into the bunkers. After the smoke had cleared, they went in and pulled out three Charlies. Two of them were dead, and the third was about to die. We stayed there for a few minutes because Pigpen was a medic, and he was trying to patch the guy up. But then Lieutenant McIsaac called us on the radio and told us to move out, so we left him. We moved down about 150 meters or so, walking in a file, and a water buffalo came up and tried to attack us. It was a bull, and he was only defending his territory, but all the guys opened up on him. That water buffalo took numerous rounds from the M-16s, and it took him about five minutes to go down. Not wanting it to suffer, Lieutenant McIsaac ordered someone to kill it. Sinclair walked up, knelt, carefully sighted on the creature's head, and shot it. A lot of the Foul Dudes were touched by the proud display of defiance from the bull. We moved up about another hundred meters and found some hootches, which we searched. Sgt. Clay Wentworth found a .51-caliber machine-gun barrel, which, heavy as it was, he kept as a souvenir and humped.

Boss Weisberger and Beaver Bieber were alternating at point and slack, with some of the Vietnamese soldiers close to them. When the Viets started yelling and doing the "VC! VC!" thing, pointing at a shelter, Weems told Boss and Beaver to check it out, so they each stood on either side of the opening. Boss was supposed to tell whoever was inside to come out. He got his words confused and yelled, "Dong lai," meaning "halt," instead of "Lai dai," meaning "come here." Weems told Boss to get his shit together. Just as Boss was about to toss a grenade, he heard some noise, and two Vietnamese came out. Boss was glad he hadn't thrown the grenade.

The Lurps moved on down the valley with Limey Walker on point. We hadn't gone much farther when we found a wounded Charlie. He came out of a hootch, his arm bandaged with a dirty rag. Doc Kraft removed the bandage, and there was a huge hole in the Charlie's right bicep and down toward his elbow. The hole was filled with maggots, and the maggots had eaten all the muscle tissue so that you could see the sinews and tendons in his arm. The stench from the wound was horrible. He kept saying the VC did it, but we believed *he* was the VC. We radioed in for a dustoff and sent him off on a medevac chopper. We then continued downriver, driving the cattle. Suddenly we encountered dead bodies lying everywhere. We had been filling our canteens upstream from where about six dead gooks were lying. Lieutenant McIsaac had refilled his canteen farther downstream, and was drinking from it when Pat "Mother" Henshaw and Bill Scanlan advised him about the Charlies lying in the river. The lieutenant did some fancy projectile puking as he got rid of the water.

As we moved down the valley, we kept finding pieces of helicopters that had been shot down littering the valley floor. Years later an incident was related to me by CWO Gary Sauer, a helicopter pilot with the 101st Aviation Section. He told me that he would sometimes fly with one of his friends, a captain, who flew with the 176th Muskets, the gunship platoon. One day when the captain had only a week left in country, they were flying a mission in the Song Ve Valley when the 1st Brigade first moved into that new area of operation. Flying in a daisy chain, attacking and prepping the area, they were taken under fire by a 12.7 machine gun (.51 cal.). They hadn't known that there were fifties in the area. The pilot was hit in the head by one of the rounds and instantly killed. When the large round hit the pilot, it took both his head and helmet off, but his heart kept pumping, spraying blood all over the cockpit. The wind inside the cockpit blew the pilot's blood all over Gary Sauer's helmet visors—both the tinted visor and the clear. The spray also covered the inside of the helicopter windshield. Gary was breathing and swallowing the blood and was scared shitless. It was a traumatic, horrible incident, compounded by making it almost impossible for him to see out of the helicopter to fly it. One of the gunners in the back was also hit and killed instantly. Riddled with holes, the aircraft managed to limp back to base. The brigade lost several helicopters to the same fifty that day. To the Lurps, the pilots had always performed above and beyond what was expected of them. I've yet to encounter a former Lurp who has anything but praise for those Knights of the Air.

CWO Gary Sauer also related a humorous incident about his transformation from pilot to pilot-cowboy during the cattle drive. We were having difficulty getting one water buffalo out of a bomb crater filled with water. The water buffalo had taken a liking to the makeshift swimming pool. Gary Sauer brought his UH1D Huey directly over the bomb crater, and, hovering, started bringing the helicopter down into the crater. He flushed the water buffalo out of the water-filled bomb crater, but when he started pulling pitch, he couldn't get the helicopter out because it was so hot that he couldn't get enough lift. He was in a very funny but very serious predicament; landing in the crater would have caused a blade strike on the sides of the crater, making for a very bad day. He had to hover for over ten minutes before a small breeze finally came to his aid, and he was able to lift off. After that incident, he decided that helicopters were not the best horses for cattle drives.

Clay Wentworth remembers moving down the valley and going into a little hootch complex. Pappy Lynch was with him, and he wanted to have some chicken and rice. A mammasan was there calling her chickens, and as they came, the Lurps would shoot off their heads. They gathered the dead chickens up and liberated some of the hootches of their pots and pans, some rice and peppers, etcetera. Pappy Lynch made us a big chicken stew. They were some pretty hard chickens. When we were done cooking them, they were still tough as shoe leather.

Another thing Wentworth remembers was that one afternoon we had stopped and he got up against a berm, lying back on his rucksack to take a little break. He looked over to his left, where a certain Lurp sat cleaning his rifle. Wentworth didn't trust this Lurp, and he was watching him. The Lurp laid the rifle he was wiping down across his lap, the barrel pointed at Wentworth. Wentworth watched as the guy cocked the rifle, chambering a round. Then he must have pulled the trigger, and it went off. The bullet came right over Wentworth's stomach.

Pigpen Johnson went over and snatched the rifle away from the guy. Wentworth knew it was coming and could see it coming. It was one of those deals where you watch it happen, but can't do anything about it.

It took the Foul Dudes five days to work their way down the valley collecting the livestock. We reached the collection point on the last evening, linking up with an ARVN company that had an American adviser. We stayed in their perimeter that night, and in the middle of the night the perimeter was probed. Tracers and rounds were flying back and forth. Funny thing was, throughout the entire firefight, Sgt. Clay Wentworth never woke up. He slept through the night, and we had to tell him about it the next morning.

The Foul Dudes were extracted and moved back to Duc Pho, their cowboy days at an end.

Right after the cattle drive, the LRRP detachment received a new Lurp by the name of Sgt. David Sloan. He had transferred from the 1st Infantry Division LRRPs to the 101st. The 1st Infantry LRRPs operated in five-man teams without the benefit of a medic, and Sergeant Sloan liked the feeling of security of having one on a team. One of his memorable missions with the 1st Infantry Lurps was when his team called in a sighting of "pink elephants." The elephants were being used for transport and must have lain in some red mud. Sloan had his controlling element doing a double take on the description of the sighting. Assigned to Pappy Lynch's team, Sergeant Sloan pulled a mission close to the lighthouse, which was located north of the mouth of the Song Tra Cau. The river emptied into the South China Sea near Duc Pho. Operations and Intelligence wanted a prisoner.

Around 0100 hours the team watched a sampan motor into the small bay formed by the river. The VC were using the lighthouse as an off-loading point on the coast because they had access to it by road. They watched the VC break out lanterns, then start to unload the sampan. The team called in a gunship to sink the sampan and ended up seizing some RPGs and crated weapons. On another mission pulled by Pappy Lynch's team, Sergeant Sloan recalls that the Lurps set an ambush on a dirt road that led to the lighthouse. Around 0200 hours, a group of people who looked like nuns and priests, in robes and carrying torches, walked right into the team's ambush. Sloan called it in and was informed by the rear not to engage them and that they would check it out. A few minutes later they called back and told the team to fire them up. Of course, by that time the group had walked past the kill zone. About five minutes later a lambretta came by, and the team detonated the claymores, which wrecked the lambretta but never touched the driver. In the ensuing firefight, the driver was killed along with four other VC. The Lurps confiscated an RPG* and two AK-47s from the wreckage of the lambretta. The team realized that the lambretta was part of the group that had passed earlier and felt they should have just fired the group up. But they had been concerned with the group's appearance and did not want to kill who they feared might be nuns and priests. Even so, the Lurps had scored again.

In late June 1967, the 1st Brigade of the 101st Airborne Division pulled its infantry battalions in from the field for a stand-down and a change in mission. The purpose of the stand-down was to refit and reorganize due to casualties sustained in previous operations and personnel lost through normal rotation. The refitting and reorganization were accomplished at their forward operating base, near the village of Duc Pho, Quang-ngai Province, South Vietnam.

Stand-downs gave the infantry troops a chance to relax, catch up on mail, drink beer, and look up friends in other units. I went searching for a good friend of mine, Sgt. David Charles Dolby, better known as "Mad Dog." I found him with his unit, Bravo Company, 2/327. After talking briefly, we agreed to get together later that evening on "Lurp Hill." The Foul Dudes had scored a pallet of beer through the usual questionable but entirely honorable methods, and the evidence needed to be disposed of. Mad Dog was more than willing to help.

---

*A Soviet-designed antitank weapon firing an 82mm rocket, a "rocket-propelled grenade."

Just as the sun was setting, Mad Dog arrived with his friend Charles "Wildman" Romig. Both had served together with the 1st Cavalry Division in 1966.

Lurch, Jaybird, Pizza Joe, and I, along with several other Lurps, sat in a circle, as was the custom, enjoying the beer, the friendships, and the night. It felt good. Earlier, Dolby and Romig had talked to Top Smith and Lt. Dan McIsaac, our platoon leader, about joining us. They were interested in transferring to the Lurps. We were discussing everything ground pounders talk about. The conversation wandered into Dolby and Romig's tour with the First Cav.

Mad Dog had told me that he'd been put in for the Medal of Honor during his previous tour with the Cav. I knew some of the story, but Dave had never gone into detail on what had really come down. I wanted to know but had too much respect for him to ask the details. Everyone in that circle felt the same way: nobody wanted to be a punk and ask a Medal of Honor nominee to recite a war story. The telling of a war story is a very personal matter. It has to be offered. Real, honest war stories almost always deal with adrenaline rushes; moments of sheer, naked terror; and the suffering and death of good friends. Oh, fun can be had with a war story, but you knew the line you weren't supposed to cross. When Mad Dog suddenly started telling us the story that night, we were honored and felt the weight he carried. You could hear it in his voice.

"Well, you see," he began, "we were on this operation, called Operation CRAZY HORSE. . . ." It was a story of the death and wounding of most of Mad Dog's platoon in an ambush. His platoon in a death trap, Mad Dog had charged and knocked out several machine-gun bunkers. The incredible part was that he had to do that several times, because the enemy kept reinforcing the machine-gun bunkers through underground tunnels.

We were sitting spellbound by what we heard from Mad Dog. Hearing a horror war story in the middle of a combat zone catches your undivided attention. In our line of work, the next such mission could very well be your own.

But it was obvious that Mad Dog was emotionally redlined,

and we could see he was at the breaking point. Wildman
Romig sensed his friend's discomfort, and came to his rescue
quickly. As Mad Dog finished speaking and in the silence that
followed, a frog came hopping into the circle. Wildman, living
up to his name, snatched up the frog, bit its head off, and
offered it to Mad Dog saying, "Hey, Mad Dog, look here's
some fresh meat!" It broke the tension and Mad Dog started to
laugh. As we all joined in the laughter, the night sky suddenly
went pure white, and you could see the whole surrounding
area. Somebody yelled, "It's a nuke!" It was coming from the
beach area and looked very much like a nuclear fireball. The
sound of the tremendous explosion hit us seconds later; we
could hear and feel it.

Well, Mr. Charles was out trying to win his own Medal of
Honor from his country by blowing up the ammo and aviation
fuel stored on the beach. Doing a damn good job of it, I might
add. God bless them little guys! Nothing like something dramatic to end a good party. Mad Dog and Wildman decided
they better get back to their company area. Mad Dog said to
me, "Take care, my friend, and get some."

I never saw Mad Dog or Romig after that night. All of us
went back out in the field. With his pending nomination for the
medal, Mad Dog was not allowed into 1st Brigade Lurps
because of the nature of our work. It was our loss.

On 28 September 1967, President Lyndon Johnson presented the nation's highest award, the Congressional Medal of
Honor, to David "Mad Dog" Dolby.

I will always remember that night; I was touched by Mad
Dog's story. It gave me a reference to the caliber of courage
and unselfish devotion he had shown. Truly, his was an accomplishment "above and beyond the call of duty," as such things
are worded. It was a measure to set for oneself—resolving
always to put my friends above myself and hoping never to fail
them. We all knew why Mad Dog had done this extraordinarily
brave thing. He didn't do it for glory, or country, or for a
medal. He had done it for his friends. . . .

### Fourth of July

On 30 June, the LRRP detachment was given a Warning Order to insert a team onto the west side of the Song Ve Valley to monitor any enemy troops who might be infiltrating back into the valley. The team members were Larry Christian, Paul Dufresne, Lurch Cornett, Top Smith, Jaybird Magill, and me. We were inserted at last light on 2 July. The LZ was located inside of a bowl of the mountain that hid us from the valley floor. We "side-hilled" up to a finger and then moved parallel to the ridge, down toward the valley floor, eventually finding a really nice observation point that was situated on a little knob. There was heavy vegetation, and we had to climb up into a tree in order to get a good view. The ridge abutted the river, causing it to make a slight bend. From our position we could see both ways up the valley. Road 516 ran the entire length of the valley, crossing the river directly below and a little north of us at a bridge that had been blown down* at coordinates 549610 on map name Mo Duc. The supports were the only part of the bridge left standing. On the east side of the river, right on the bank, and about seventy-five meters north, was a small village or hootch complex that extended about seventy-five meters east from the river-bank. The map called it Ngoc Da, and its people had been relocated along with most everyone else in the Song Ve Valley. The eastern edge of the hootch complex ended at dry rice paddies, and trees and bushes ended where the paddies began. On the west bank of the river, trees and vegetation crowded the river. Contouring next to the river was a good-sized trail. The river flowed northeast, centering itself in the valley, with unused rice paddies terracing the valley floor. Jungle vegetation grew on the banks, as the river slowly meandered northward. Road 516 took off due north, and disappeared up a narrow valley climbing the east flank of Nui Ban Co and dropping back down on the north side.

*Map name, Mo Duc, Sheet #67381—1/50,000—Coordinate 549610.

We did not see a single soul the first day and night, but we didn't expect to because the 1st Brigade had spent the previous two weeks relocating the valley's population. It was now the third of July, it was getting late, and the sun had gone down behind the ridge we were on. The ridgeline that formed the other side of the valley was still bathed in the glow of the setting sun. As we were glassing the area below us, we spotted people on the west bank of the river traveling south on the trail, heading in our direction. They were about two thousand meters downriver from us, coming into view in the occasional small clearings through which the trail ran. They were hard to spot, but as they drew closer, they passed through an open area of the trail, and we could count them: eighty or ninety people, the majority of them wearing black PJs, though some of them had on light-blue uniforms. Some wore pith helmets, but most were wearing the traditional conical hat. A whole damn VC company was on the move.

It was getting on dusk when they stopped downriver of the bridge to case the east side of the river. After a few minutes they sent a squad across to recon the hootch complex. Looking very professional, seven VC crossed the river in a staggered, spread formation. Meanwhile we had sent in a SALUTE (size, activity, location, unit, time, equipment) report. This was shit hot. You didn't very often get the drop on Chuck, and when you did, you exploited it. It's like being on an elk hunt, and a six-point bull elk walks into your AO, totally unaware of your presence. We wanted to engage these people. We had access to artillery and gunships, but conditions were getting marginal with the light remaining. We had to make our move on them the best way possible. The enemy recon squad cloverleafed to the outside from the man in the center, who must have been the squad leader. This squad swept the area with coordination and minimum use of time and ended with three-man elements 150 meters up- and downriver, covering the flanks of the company movement across the river. These guys knew what they were doing, and it was pretty neat to see the enemy operate. Although they were barely visible because of the encroaching darkness, it was still quite a sight to see so many enemy in that wide, shallow river, as they crossed in a two-file formation.

Top Smith had started to call artillery on the VC when they were crossing the river. It was a bad option in that the enemy would have immediately deduced the area from which they were being eyeballed. Top abruptly canceled the fire mission because while glassing the VC, he realized they were starting to break for the night. As it got dark, we could see the winking of numerous little fires down in the hootch complex. The fires weren't burning on the open ground, but inside the hootches. We had plenty of time to discuss the best way to make our move. If there ever was a perfect Lurp mission in Nam, this was the one. It was dark already, and gunships were out of the question. Artillery could be used, but it would be hard to adjust on the target because of the darkness. We decided that we would wait until first light and bring in a two-battery (twelve guns, six per battery) TOT (time on target) artillery barrage. To a "redleg" (artillery man) you couldn't find a better fire mission. A TOT brings a multibattery concentration on the target at the same time. You can grid your target by centering each gun tube of the batteries to hit a certain point. You can cover a twenty-five-meter square with one round; multiply that by twelve and the ground gets saturated with shrapnel in a hurry. A box is formed with all the rounds, and then you move the box by adjusting the next firing. Our box grid was three rounds wide and four rounds long—or seventy-five meters by one hundred meters. We would adjust fire twenty-five meters at a time added consecutively, with a three-round barrage. That meant that each gun would fire a round, adjust twenty-five meters north of where the last round had exploded, fire-adjusting twice without stopping. That's thirty-six rounds in less than a minute and a half! We would start on the south end of the hootch complex, then work the barrage north. After the third round, the two batteries would adjust to fire in a column on a north-south orientation, paralleling the hootch complex. The guns would wait for our adjustment before firing again. To handle a TOT properly, the forward observer had to know how to use gun batteries. Top definitely knew what he was doing.

When firing a box grid and column fire, both batteries fire as one unit. Having been trained as a cannon cocker, and having worked in the FDC (fire direction center) as a computer, I considered this mission really special to me. We would have to use one spotter round from each battery before we could bring in the TOT. Top really appreciated the fire mission. You can't have a better fire mission for "troops in the open."

In the predawn darkness, on the Fourth of July 1967, we saw morning fires being lit. Being anxious for the morning and worrying that the company would leave, we hadn't slept much that night. We planned that the barrage would come in, and an infantry platoon reaction force would be airborne and ready to insert as soon as we had lifted the fire mission. They would box the hootch complex from the paddies while using artillery on the river to keep the VC trapped. Top was to do the spotting and adjusting, and I would be working the radio. Soon it was first light, and we could just barely see. We got word that the reaction force was ready, and the cannon cockers were standing by their guns. Top had picked a spot two hundred meters to the right of the hootch complex and behind a line of trees for the spotter rounds. We gave the word for the spotter rounds to be fired, and I got the "on the way, over," from the redlegs. The two willie peter (white phosphorous) rounds exploded exactly where they should. I gave the adjustment of "left two hundred, fire for effect," on the TOT fire mission. It took the redlegs about a minute and a half to adjust their base guns, and then I got "on the way, over." Top and Christian had their binos out and could see the Charlies milling around as soon as the two spotter rounds went off, not really moving anywhere, hesitating. Because of our position on the gun-target line, we couldn't hear the rounds approaching. But Chuck heard them. He just heard them way too late.

We saw several people running, reacting to the rounds coming in. The barrage came in as one big twelve-round huge orange *crruump!* Through our binos, we could see bodies and hootches flying through the air. Very quickly, I got the second, and then the third, radio transmission that the rounds were on the way. A concentrated mass artillery barrage is really something to witness. But to be on the receiving end is a nightmare out of hell. The left side of the grid box was a little into the river, but overall it was dead-on. I had been part of a battalion TOT fire mission in Germany once, but this was totally different. In Germany it had been against basic range truck targets, but these were human, and we could clearly see our handiwork. After the third round, each battery adjusted to shoot a column fire. After just a little bit, they told me they were ready, and we had them fire. The rounds impacted on both edges of the hootch complex. We adjusted the rounds left, and then right, firing twice more. It was devastating to watch. In a space of five to seven minutes, we had put seventy-two 105mm rounds in a space roughly seventy-five meters wide by 125 meters long. We had been told to move out to our extraction point on the backside of the ridge finger as soon as the last rounds from the fire mission impacted. We released our command of the artillery, which was taken over by the infantry platoon leader.

An interesting side note to this fire mission was that I had known Pete "Crazy Pete" Peterson from Philadelphia, Pennsylvania, when we were both in the artillery stationed at Rhine Kaserne in Biebrich, Germany. Top Smith had served in the same place in 1955. Crazy Pete followed me to Vietnam later on and eventually transferred to Lurps, and we served together. Crazy Pete was on one of the guns firing that morning. He still remembers it. "We stood to our guns early that morning and fired round after round, then waited around our guns in case more was needed. I had heard it was a Lurp team we were supporting. It kind of pissed us off because we never got anything back. We fired beaucoup rounds and worked our asses off and no results or a 'thank you' from you guys. I figured you guys were having your own private Fourth of July celebration."

As we moved back to our LZ, we turned over control of the artillery. S-2/S-3 wanted to insert the infantry platoon and extract us right away with one of the helicopters from the infantry platoon's flight. I saw six or seven bodies lying in view through the smoke and dust that covered the shattered hootch complex, and radioed that in. There had to have been a higher body count, but we were under pressure to be at the LZ for extraction. We all would have liked to hang around and enjoy the show, but we didn't stay more than seven minutes after we had called in the barrage. The infantry platoon's C&C (command and control) chopper that was overseeing the operation called us and said, "Job well done," and that they would take over. The chopper extracted us, and flew us twenty-five miles southeast back to Duc Pho, and way out of the operation range. Top got in touch with the artillery after we got back to Duc Pho, but that was hours after the action. We also wanted to know the results, but I don't recall ever hearing what happened. It's hard work being a cannon cocker, and there hasn't been enough said of what those guys went through to support any ground pounder who needed their help. I remember later on at a firebase watching those guys hanging on to their barrels as they displaced and moved the howitzers for direct fire, and all the time we were getting mortared and rocketed. As a Lurp I learned to appreciate artillery more than I ever really did when I was a redleg myself.

This was a mission that exemplified to me what a Long Range Reconnaissance Patrol was all about: we found them; brought the wrath of God on them; then beat feet. All without loss or injury to any member of the team. My only regret was that we should have been left in the action so we could have had a better view of the infantry platoon sweep. It was definitely the most memorable Fourth of July fireworks display I've ever seen.

## Last Mission

On 4 July, a Lurp team with Gene Sullivan as team leader was inserted into the western side of the Song Ve Valley. Most of the team was made up of new members. It was a last-light insertion, and the LZ was about twenty miles upriver from where our team had been extracted that morning. Sullivan went in and soon after spotted about forty VC two or three klicks away from them. He could see them pretty well through the binoculars, and he called the sighting in. For the next five days the team pretty much stayed stationary, observing the valley. On the third day of the mission, Sullivan called artillery in on a group of VC that was fording the Song Ve. The VC were caught in midriver, and the artillery hit at least one man; the Lurps saw the body floating. Everybody else seemed to scatter. The team ran out of water on the last day of the mission and couldn't go down to the river for more. When the helicopters came, Sullivan thought they were going to get extracted. Instead, the ships flew right over him and dropped a five-gallon water can. When a helicopter comes in, the last thing you want is for them to come near you and pinpoint your location to the enemy. The rear wanted the team in for an extra day. But by dropping that can on their position, the helicopter scared the hell out of Sullivan. When the time finally came to extract all the teams, Sullivan's team was the one that had the most activity, and yet they were the last to be picked up. His LZ was in a little valley, and the Lurps couldn't establish commo. Fueling his anxiety were the many footprints to be seen in his RZ, only 125 meters from where the team had been set up for five days. It bothered Sullivan that the enemy could have been so close. What bothered him even more was that he was out of communications with anybody from the LZ. Fifteen minutes after it was supposed to, the chopper finally came in. Sullivan was pissed when he got back to base camp. Top Smith was there, and Sullivan blistered him. All Top could do was stand and listen. It wasn't Top's fault, but by then Sullivan's nerves were shot. He had four or five weeks to go, and that was his last mission. Bruce Redmer, Freddy Hernandez, and Sullivan left and went to security platoon for their last weeks in country.

I got a glimpse of what went on in officer country when I talked with Gary Sauer, a warrant officer who flew for 101st Aviation Section. He met Lieutenant McIsaac through flying us in on insertions and later at the makeshift officers' club in Duc Pho. The officers' club was a GP Medium tent, with wooden ammo crates at one end forming the bar. Air Force FAC (forward air control) personnel were regular fixtures in the bar. Gary Sauer says that the FACs elicited good-natured ribbing from the rest of the officers. The aviation unit went into the bar quite often. Lieutenant McIsaac frequented the bar when he could, and everyone liked him because he was a lot of laughs. According to Sauer, Mac was a very funny person. He had a ritual with his VC bird that he would carry around on his shoulder. When Mac would enter the officers' bar, he would stand straddle-legged, John Wayne style, in the entrance. He would step in, and everyone would turn around and yell, "Yeah, yeah, let's sing him a hymn: Him, him, fuck him!"

Mac would stand there with his hands on his hips and this bird on his shoulder, then point and yell, "Kill!" The bird would run down his arm and make a racket and try to peck anyone who was close. Mac's bird was black with an orange beak—God knows where Mac had found him. He liked to put the bird down on the bar and buy it a drink, then order himself one. They would put a little popcorn in the shot of whiskey for Mac's bird. The bird would put his beak in the drink, and when he came up his eyes would be rolling, and he'd be shaking his head. Sometimes his legs would go out from under him and he'd lie down. If for some reason the bird spilled a part of his drink, Mac would take out his .45, turn it around, and pretend to hit the bird on the head with the butt of his pistol, admonishing it for pissing on the bar. If Mac's bird shit on the bar, Mac really dressed it down, standing it at attention. The bird would be shit-faced, and Mac would be carrying on.

Gray Sauer recalls that McIsaac's walking in was the highlight of any evening. Congress might have commissioned him an officer and a gentleman, but in his own way, Mac was a Foul Dude.

## Bicycle Mission

Around the first week in August, a twelve-man team was assigned to screen one of the main dirt roads that headed west out of Tam-ky. The two teams were S.Sgt. Larry Christian's and S.Sgt. Pappy Lynch's, with Lieutenant McIsaac in overall charge. The second day in, Pizza Joe Remiro was walking point for Christian's team with Sullens walking his slack. Pizza Joe came upon a chicken, right in the large trail they were walking. Sully told Pizza Joe to shoot it so they could cook him, and Pizza Joe popped it. But being a city boy, instead of shooting it in the head, Pizza Joe shot the chicken in the body, which left nothing but a bunch of feathers to cook. Sully thought that was really funny, since he was from the country.

About the fourth day out, early in the morning, they heard talking close to the river's edge along the road. The Lurps crept in closer to investigate, and discovered a Vietnamese lady using her conical hat as a large cup, drinking water she had just dipped out of the river. Two men were with her, probably guards. When they realized the Foul Dudes were close by, the men tried to open fire with their weapons but were cut down immediately. The Lurps found a transshipment point off the side of the trail. From outward appearances, it appeared to be a thicket, but on closer examination, it was framed by bamboo poles and covered by a woven mat with foliage growing on it. From the air it looked like normal growth, but underneath it was a big warehouse, about forty feet square, fifteen to twenty meters off a well-worn trail on which the enemy had been ferrying supplies in and out.

Inside the warehouse, loaded with supplies, were twenty-seven bicycles, heavy-duty machines specifically designed for hauling supplies, and rigged to be pushed from the side. While the Lurps were inside the warehouse, more people showed up, but they were on mopeds. As soon as they realized Americans were in the area, they tried to put up resistance and escape but were promptly shot. The mopeds had large sticks tied to the handlebars so the Charlies could walk on the side and push them. They were loaded with rice, Ruby Queen cigarettes, and a liquor of some kind that tasted like red licorice. There was a lot of money, including greenbacks. Clearly the Lurps had stumbled upon some sort of VC transportation company. When confronted with armed Americans, most Vietnamese civilians would have just passively held their ground because it was common knowledge that most Americans wouldn't shoot unless threatened. But we were way out in the countryside, and who was and who wasn't enemy was pretty much cut-and-dried.

Lieutenant McIsaac called in a CH-47 Chinook to extract the large cache. Doc "Wolfman" Kraft says that it started getting real hot as they were leaving. The enemy was gathering and the incoming fire picked up. The situation started to deteriorate while the Lurps and Chinook crew loaded the goods aboard, so an infantry company was brought in to deal with the concentration of enemy forces in the area. While it was just the two Lurp teams and the Chinook crew, things were getting a little tight.

When the Lurps got back to the rear, the brigade made the mistake of letting us keep the mopeds and a couple of bikes. A day later, Lurch was driving one of the mopeds with Wolfman on the back. They were both drinking, and they took off down Lurp Hill. As they picked up speed, they discovered that the mopeds didn't have any brakes. Lurch lost control and ran right into the sergeant major's tent, hitting all the guide ropes that held the tent up and causing it to fall in on him. Leaving the motor scooter behind, Lurch and Wolfman escaped and evaded back to the Lurp area. The brigade knew the perpetrators had to be the Lurps, because we were the ones who had brought the equipment in. But despite their having scrapes and bruises from the crash, Lurch and Wolfman were never caught.

Of course the brigade promptly ordered that all the bikes and mopeds be turned in immediately, and that was the end of our two-wheeled transportation.

Around mid-July, three teams from the LRRP detachment were dispatched by Caribou aircraft to land at the Special Forces CIDG A-camp at Tra Bong. I was the team leader, Top Smith the ATL. Others on the team were Limey Walker, Paul Dufresne, Ed Mounts, and Wolfman Kraft. In support of one of the line battalions, we were being used to monitor enemy movements in and out of the operational area. Because of the short runway at Tra Bong, the gangly looking Caribou was used to transport us in. The camp was a fortress in the middle of the jungle. The CIDG were enlisted montagnards nominally led by Vietnamese officers. A marine artillery 105 howitzer battery was also stationed there. We landed around midday and went into the camp. Top Smith, the rest of the team leaders, and I went to the A-camp operations shack to coordinate the operation. We would be walking out of the camp with the CIDG company and their two Special Forces advisers. We would drop off from the tail end of the column then insert on foot. During the briefing we noticed an undercurrent of tension between the senior Montagnard NCOs and the Vietnamese officers. At first, I thought it might be directed at the Lurps, but the Yards seemed friendly enough to us. After the briefing, we told the teams what was going to come down, and that we had some time to kill. We wouldn't be leaving until that evening.

At one point, Limey was watching a three-quarter-ton truck from the marine artillery battery back up to a trash pit that was located outside the camp perimeter. Two marines started throwing trash from the back of the truck when the pit suddenly flashed and the truck caught fire. The marines must have been dumping excess powder charges from previous fire missions and had thrown the powder on something smoldering in the pit. The flash explosion burned the two men on the dumping detail pretty badly.

I traded some Lurp rations with Montagnard soldiers for indigenous rations, getting fish heads and rice. The packet included dried, ground red pepper, which is what I really liked. After a bit, you got used to the little eyeballs in the fish staring at you, and they didn't taste too bad.

That evening we left the A-camp with the company of CIDG and their two Special Forces advisers. The three Lurp teams were at the back of the column. We walked for a good mile; then we started dropping off by teams and inserting into the bush. Our team was the last to drop off. We grabbed a small ridgeline and started gaining elevation. For quite a ways we could hear the CIDG chattering away like magpies as they moved down the shallow, narrow valley we had been walking.

We selected an NDP (night defensive position) about fifty meters downhill from the ridge and about five hundred meters from the indigenous company. At about 2200 hours, we heard shooting from the direction of the CIDG company. Fifteen minutes later we received a whispered transmission on the Lurp net from the Special Forces advisers, who informed us that they had a small problem and wanted to link up with us.

They had called us because Top Smith was the senior NCO from all three teams. It kind of showed who really was team leader on my team. We went down the ridge in the dark and managed to link up with the two SF advisers. One was a first lieutenant, the other a staff sergeant. After arriving and setting up in our NDP, they whispered to us that they had reached an area where they were supposed to pull several platoon-sized ambushes. Somewhere in there, the Yards had shot and killed both Vietnamese officers. The SF advisers said that the murders stemmed from a long-running dispute over their pay. In addition, one of the senior Yard NCOs felt the company had been infiltrated by VC and, worried about their safety, he had confided in the two advisers. That is why they had linked up with us. That was the Special Forces nightmare they always had to worry about and contend with.

The next morning we dropped off the advisers at the A-camp. We went back out that evening and patrolled for three more days. During our three weeks at the A-camp, we performed various missions. After linking up with another team, we worked as a heavy team, and when we came back to the camp, I think the Green Berets were glad to have us around.

**On 13 August the 1st Brigade deployed southwest of Chu Lai in Operation BENTON. The brigade was assigned the task of locating and destroying what were believed to be the 21st NVA Regiment and the elusive 2nd NVA Division. Intelligence also showed the probable presence of the 70th Battalion of the 1st VC Regiment. When Operation BENTON officially ended on 29 August, the Screaming Eagle paratroopers accounted for 303 enemy killed, with 131 weapons, thirty-one tons of rice, and four tons of tea captured. A side benefit of the brigade's presence in heavily populated Quang-ngai Province during Operation**

BENTON was that the Vietcong infrastructure was prevented from affecting the Vietnamese national elections.
The brigade was extracted from the mountains southwest
of Chu Lai and transported by C-130s to the brigade base
camp at Duc Pho for stand-down.

## Painted Faces and Scary Places

It was mid-August, and a fast mission was laid on the LRRP
detachment by brigade Operations and Intelligence. We were
given the Patrol Warning Order in the morning and were
scheduled to be inserted that evening. The recon zone was
located northwest of the Song Ve Valley. The S-2/S-3's attention had been drawn to that location by information obtained
from enemy prisoners. Due to the urgency of the mission, our
reaction force would consist of the brigade "security platoon."
We were not too happy with that part of the operation.

A "patch-together" team was formed by Lt. Dan McIsaac. I
was the probationary team leader. I also carried a radio. The
team consisted of S.Sgt. Larry Christian, senior scout; Jim
"Limey" Walker, junior scout; Jay "Jaybird" Magill, RTO; Lt.
Dan "Mac" McIsaac, ATL; and Brian "Wolfman" Kraft, the
medic.

Lt. Dan McIsaac and I went on an aerial recon of the area to
pick the LZs. The recon zone consisted of one big mountain
with a fairly well defined high point that spread out into a flat,
heavily jungled bowl funneling into three drainages that ran
into the valley below. Two ridgelines flanked the bowl, and
patches of elephant grass dotted the ridges where they dropped
to lower elevations. The primary LZ was on a finger of a ridge
that ran off the back side of the southeast ridgeline bordering
the park. It was a good LZ in that it was hidden from view of
the designated RZ.

We boarded the helicopter and headed northwest into
the setting sun. We flared above our LZ and jumped in. As
I exited the chopper and was falling toward the ground, the
elephant grass was moving around violently from the rotor
wash, and I suddenly realized I was staring at the top of a

sharpened bamboo punji stake two or three feet tall. I did some
unbelievably crazy body english in midair and landed with
the stake going through the bottom of my rucksack, right
beside my back, then hitting a pound-cake can that deflected it
toward the middle of my rucksack, before exiting out the top.
Amazed that I wasn't skewered like a chicken, I briefly sat on
the ground. When I tried to run for the wood line, I couldn't
move; I was stuck fast. I hurriedly slipped out of my rucksack
straps, and with Limey's help got the punji stake out of my
rucksack. The fire-hardened bamboo had been sharpened to a
point and was tough as a crowbar.

We started moving out and discovered that the LZ had been
laced with punji stakes two to three feet tall and sticking
straight up. We had been lucky in that our helicopter had
landed on the outer edge of the LZ. That LZ had been defended
against air assault, so there was no question that we were in
hunting country. With S.Sgt. Larry Christian on point, we
moved toward the main southeast ridgeline and crossed it,
dropping into the east edge of the bowl. From there we moved
parallel with, and about forty meters below, the ridgeline, then
traveled toward the high ground. The undergrowth and wait-a-
minute vines made the patrol tough going. Limey relieved
Christian on point, and we took off again.

"I had just taken over point from Christian when I had an
uneasy feeling and signaled the patrol to a halt," Limey says.
"Something up front just didn't match up. The vegetation
appeared to change hue. Or maybe it was just a gut feeling. I
crawled up a few feet and peeked through some bushes. There
it was. It was a trail, and a well-used one. Fresh sneaker prints
were liberally scattered on it."

The team backed off from the trail, and we started paralleling it. About fifty meters farther up the ridgeline, the trail
veered to the right, toward the heart of the bowl. Then it split,
and the left-hand fork continued on, following the contour of
the ridgeline. About ten feet off the trail, we stopped alongside
two huge trees that were perched on their roots, with a big
undercut exposing the roots. At the rear of these trees the
ground dropped away from the trail. We stayed in a line and

dropped into the undercut. We didn't pick it; it just happened to be there. Our attention was concentrated on the trail, which was ten to fifteen feet from us. Since it was getting dark, we had to find an NDP, but that decision was made for us when suddenly a lone NVA soldier, clad in what appeared to be a new khaki uniform, came bopping down the trail toward us, an AK-47 balanced on his shoulder, his right hand holding the barrel. We silently watched him go by. Using silent hand communication, Mac and I decided to stay in place. We had good cover and concealment. The NDP was a little too close to the trail, but we might have gotten in more trouble trying to get out of there.

Limey remembers this well. "As the darkness overtook us, we heard a tremendous racket. It sounded like the entire population of North Vietnam was plodding down this small obscure trail. Mess kits and canteens were banging together, and the sing-song chatter of the enemy could be heard clearly. I wished I could understand Vietnamese. Chuck didn't give a damn about noise discipline. I caught glimpses of shadows as they passed and began to count. I had reached twenty-six when I gave up. My gut was in a knot, and steady breathing had become hard labor. I calmed myself down by thinking of childhood games like 'Peek-a-boo, I see you!' No one rested; we just lay in place and watched the parade. About five hours after the first sighting, we began to see lights. My heart skipped a beat. Were we being searched for? The lanterns were not in line and appeared somewhat disorganized. The lights gave the impression that the area was infested by gigantic fireflies. There must have been forty or more of them. At times they came too close for comfort, and one was actually no more than ten feet away on the trail."

About twenty-five minutes after the lone NVA had gone by, groups of NVA went by us, traveling toward the center of the big park. They were moving in groups of twenty to thirty people. At least 125 enemy soldiers had passed not ten feet away from us. It was nerve-racking, and Mac later confided to me that at one point during the movement, one of the NVA had actually stepped away from the trail and had stopped beside one of the big trees. What he was doing we didn't know, but he stepped on Mac's pinkie and the ring finger of his left hand where Mac had been holding on to one of the roots to keep from falling farther into the tree's undercut. That it was pitch black had saved our asses. After the lone NVA had gone by, we radioed in a coded message and reported the trail and that we were turning our communications off. We then turned off both radios for fear of having a squelch break or static hiss give our position away. Most of the lights we saw were toward the center of the bowl. The great thing was that Chuck didn't know we were in the area—at least they weren't acting like they knew. Things started to quiet down about 0200 hours.

"Around 0300 hours," Limey recalls, "Martinez tapped me on the shoulder and whispered in my ear that we were going to back out of there. The noise and lights faded as we backed away. I bumped into some foreign objects as I moved. When I ran my hand over one, I saw it was one of many punji stakes pointing in the same direction we were traveling. Apparently, we had penetrated the edge of an enemy perimeter without fully realizing it. After what seemed like forever, we made it to the edge of the tree line that would be our LZ. Lying in the brush, I edged over to Jaybird and told him I had given up counting the enemy at twenty-six. Jaybird whispered, 'Limey, at ninety I was so scared I lost count.' Like a ton of bricks it hit me. Fear, I loved it! It made me feel good to conquer something that had haunted me for years. Lurps had to be adrenaline junkies. We were still not safe, yet I felt secure. If I went down, I wanted to do it with these guys, doing the job I loved best. We waited for first light."

As we worked our way downhill, staying away from the trail, it was pitch black. We moved about 200 meters down, then set up communication with the rear, sending in a coded message on what we had observed and that we wanted an extraction. Shortly after, we got permission to move to an LZ and were informed that we would be extracted at first light. We moved another 100 meters downhill and then crossed the ridgeline. We had been thinking of using our insertion LZ but decided against it when we came out below it on the ridgeline.

Mac recalled from the insertion that another ridgeline with ele-phant grass was located farther south. We dropped into a small draw, crossed it, worked our way up to the ridgeline, and waited in the tree line for daylight. Just when it was light enough to see, we sent Limey and Christian to do a 360 around the LZ. They reported that everything looked good, and we radioed in our LZ coordinates.

Limey remembers: "We waited, and finally I heard the dis-tinct thumping sound of a Huey. The noise became louder. Suddenly the chopper was there flaring onto the LZ. The bird came in quickly, and we dived aboard so fast that the rotor pitch didn't appear to change. We were all aboard yelling for the pilot to go. The copilot turned around and gave us the thumbs-up. I could have kissed that smiling face. We were off and away. I looked back toward the LZ and saw clouds of smoke rise up from where we had been just seconds ago. With a look of bewilderment, I looked at Lieutenant McIsaac. With that grin on his face, he yelled, 'The fucking dinks are a dollar short and seconds too late with that mortar fire!' The mission had lasted less than fourteen hours. It would take me twice that long to come down from the high I was riding on! The near miss with the NVA was history within the Lurp ranks. The story was told and retold six different ways. The only thing we completely agreed on was that we had been lucky sons of bitches!"

Lieutenant McIsaac and I went down to the S-2/S-3 TOC to debrief. They listened to all we had to say and asked some questions. It was in their hands, but I felt strongly that a bombing mission should be put in, though I never really found out what came of that mission. I felt it typified a perfect Lurp mission, and the intelligence gathered should have been acted on quickly. In all fairness to brigade Operations and Intelli-gence, I always felt they did a decent job. But I do not know if information was passed on regarding that area.

It is possible that the information we gathered on that mis-sion was used to plan a mission for the 1/327th Tiger Force because several days later Limey Walker ran into one of his Tiger Force friends, Sam "Chief" Samora, in the makeshift club at the brigade base camp at Duc Pho. I also knew Sam, who was a Mexican Indian from Arizona. According to Limey, Chief Samora was in a despondent and sullen mood. Eventually, with tears in his eyes, Chief Samora confided to Limey that he felt Tiger Force had been screwed over by the command structure. Tiger Force had inserted into an LZ that had been heavily booby-trapped with punji stakes emplaced in the elephant grass, and they had taken a few injuries on the insertion. After the wounded men had been evacuated, Tiger Force moved into the jungle. They hadn't progressed 200 meters into the jungle before they were taken under fire by automatic weapons emplaced in well-camouflaged bunkers. Unable to move, they were getting systematically hit, one at a time. With the rallying cry of "Tiger Force!" what remained of the unit charged the bunkers. A bloody fight ensued, with some of the fighting hand-to-hand combat. The Tigers were victorious, but at a bloody price. Chief Samora told Limey that the mission was supposed to have been a routine sweep in an area of limited enemy activity. Instead, it had turned out to be what Teddy Bear called a real pork chop. Limey thought Chief Samora's description of the terrain strongly resembled the area we had been extracted from two days before.

## Bacheck

Stories abound about Bacheck. His passion for eating insects and bugs was staggering. Brother Christian, the ultimate Lurp gambler, would set the stage. Sitting in on a card game with some headquarters people, he would start to gamble on off-the-wall stuff. Then Bacheck would conveniently show up with an insect or pluck one off an indoor tent pole, the insect's favorite roosting spot. He would grab it and throw it on the table. Usually the insect was big and grotesque. Then Christian would throw out some bills and bet Bacheck that he couldn't eat it. They'd get to arguing, escalating the terms of the bet. Encouraged, other people would soon start throwing down their money. The whole scene was carefully crafted to entice the rest of the players to lay out *real* money. Bacheck wouldn't agree to eat the whole thing, just the legs or some portion of it. After what Bacheck and Christian thought was a sizeable sum had been anteed up, Bacheck would pick the insect up, roll his eyes, then delicately chew off a portion. By that time, the gamblers would want more action, so more money would be wagered, this time on Bacheck's eating the whole insect. Now, Bacheck's favorite insect wasn't some little bug. It was about two inches long and thick bodied. He particularly liked it because it made for very crunchy sound effects. More money would be thrown in the pot. What the gamblers never understood was that Bacheck liked the perfor-mance. He would pick the insect up, place it between his teeth delicately, and then start loudly chewing on it. It always sounded loud and crunchy, yet a little squishy, like a corn chip filled with ripe grapes. Bacheck had an unusually long tongue, with which he could lick his eyebrows, and he was probably some woman's dream. A little masticating and shearing action with his teeth, then Bacheck would place the whole green, oozing mess on his tongue, rolling it out of his mouth like a ser-pent slithering partway out of a cave, momentarily offer the prize for inspection, then swallow it before licking his fingers as if he had just finished a sumptuous basket of shrimp. That always created quite a stir! I've never ever met another person as gross as Waldo Bacheck—nor one with so much class.

Puke Palk told me about a Bacheck insect incident that hap-pened in late January in Phan-rang. They had both gone to the Finance Section about a pay matter regarding Puke Palk. The REMF clerk was exerting some power-play pressure on Puke about his pay problems, when Waldo gave him a dose of shock therapy. He grabbed a large insect off the wall, deliberately nibbled off all the legs except one, broke the insect's stomach open with his teeth, and laid it delicately on the paperwork in front of the clerk. The one-legged insect pushed itself around and around, oozing green slime all over Puke's finance records. The clerk promptly threw up. Puke's problem was resolved in a timely fashion by the senior NCO in the Finance Section, who apologized for the misunderstanding.

During our stand-down in Duc Pho one evening, Bacheck

suckered one of the new Lurps into a bet. Waldo bet him that he could piss over the width of a deuce-and-a-half truck. The word had quickly spread throughout the detachment, and a crowded had gathered. We all walked en masse down Lurp Hill and found the truck we needed. This was entertainment. At seven feet high with side boards, and a ten-foot-wide bed, a deuce-and-a-half was a formidable obstacle, even for Waldo. After the healthy sum was collected, Waldo applied himself to the problem with a quiet and fierce concentration. He chug-a-lugged several beers as he scoped out the problem. Moving around, figuring throw weights, distance, and dimensions, and centering in around the dual-wheeled axle of the truck as a reference, Waldo finally concluded he was ready. He placed the new Lurp about three feet out to the side of the rear dual tires and admonished him to stand right there. Jaybird Magill was placed toward the rear of the truck to observe him and make sure he didn't move. Waldo moved around to the opposite side of the truck. It was like a damn circus act. Ole Waldo dropped his jungle utilities, massaged his dick a few times, pinched his uncircumcised foreskin closed with his fingers, and pissed. His foreskin ballooned outward, then with a loud grunt and strain, he released it. A big yellow water ball went sailing over the truck, landing squarely on the new Lurp. A Lurp golden shower! It left all of us rolling on the ground in laughter. None of us, including the new Lurp, had even thought about his placement. Waldo collected his money, arched his eyebrows, and rolled his eyes, and we knew he'd done this before. We all walked back up Lurp Hill following a true Foul Dude.

# 8

## LONG RANGE RECON
### 1 101
## Chu Lai

Still under operational control of Task Force OREGON (now designated the Americal Division), the 1st Brigade returned to Chu Lai to embark on Operation WHEELER. Underway on 11 September, the brigade finally encountered elements of the 2nd NVA Division west of Tam-ky. With estimated strength of nearly 5,000 men, the 2nd NVA Division was made up of the 1st, 3rd, and 21st NVA Regiments. Also included were various support groups like engineer, artillery, antiaircraft, and signal battalions. Other enemy forces in the area were: the 70th VC Battalion, attached to the Quang Nam Province headquarters; the 72nd Local Force Battalion, and seven local force companies. The population of the province's districts had been under communist control for the past twenty years, making the enemy forces in the area even more formidable.

When Operation WHEELER came to a successful close on 23 November, brigade intelligence estimated that approximately 1100 enemy soldiers had been killed during the operation. It was the 1st Brigade's most significant action of 1967.

### MACV Recondo School

The last week of August, Ed Mounts and I received orders to attend the MACV Recondo school in Nha-trang. The school was staffed by members of Project Delta. It was a finishing school for me and prepared me to become a team leader.

The school taught an excellent course on map reading and everything related to it, setting up and adjusting fires both aerial and artillery, basic first aid, and how to plan and execute a mission from beginning to end. Immediate action drills, patrolling, rappelling, radio procedures, and all the other intricacies of long range patroling were also covered.

After having spent nine months as a member of a LRRP team, I thought I was in top physical shape. I was, but those Delta people really knew how to push a guy. Running ten miles with a forty-pound rucksack plus your basic load and rifle made for a very tired pup.

On our training mission my team adviser, a warrant officer from the Australian SAS, was a hard man but fair—and crazy, the way all special operations people and most Aussies tend to be. I was appointed the team leader and had with me four Filipino Special Forces soldiers, two officers, and two NCOs. We were teamed up because I was fluent in Spanish. It was an interesting learning experience for me, and I was working with some very capable and professional soldiers. The Filipino soldiers had been involved in the fight against the Huk rebellion back in the Philippines. Nothing of any real interest happened on our mission, but I got a good chance to see firsthand how "my" people operated, a barometer against which to measure where we in the 1st Brigade fit on the Lurp scale. We were every bit as good.

We graduated on 22 September, and I was number 662. I finished second in the class. We then had a steak fry to celebrate our graduation. Recondo was the best school I had ever attended in the army, and the NCOs who staffed the school were the best I had ever encountered. I was seriously recruited by Special Forces Project Delta and was told that if I wanted, I could join them immediately without even going back to the "One-Oh-Worst." I felt honored to be considered, and was tempted, but I had some good friends in Lurps, and at that stage in my young life they were my family, closer than my blood family.

After graduation, Eddie Mounts and I flew back north to Chu Lai to rejoin the brigade. We were in the middle of the monsoon and it was very wet, but we were looking forward to seeing our friends. While we were gone, we had lost a brother Lurp. John Lester Hines from Virginia Beach, Virginia, had been killed in action west of Chu Lai on 15 September. John had come to us just before the detachment left Duc Pho in late July. I had gotten to know him, and it was a big loss to all of us. Lurch, Limey, Danny Williams, Waldo Bacheck, and Wolfman Kraft had been involved in the mission, and they filled us in on what had gone down.

## John Lester Hines, KIA

While under operational control of 2/327 Infantry Battalion, the Lurps were given a mission west of Chu Lai. Having observed lights in the valley below the 2/327 firebase on several consecutive nights and concerned for the safety of his firebase, the commanding officer of 2/327 had handed the mission to the Lurps because his recon unit (Hawk Platoon) was tasked with the security of the firebase and was unavailable. The heavy team (two six-man teams) was led by S.Sgt. Walt Bachek. Walt's team consisted of Bob McKinnon, Limey Walker, David Wofford, Paul Dufresne, and Lurch Cornett. The other team would be Sgt. Danny Williams's team and consisted of John Hines, Wolfman Kraft, Jimmy McCormack, Fred Wyche, team medic, and the other team members.

Sgt. Danny Williams recalls: "The day before the mission, I boarded a Huey with Jimmy McCormack and Walt Bachek and selected our primary and secondary LZs. There was nothing really special about this mission other than the fact that the 101st Airborne was working with the Americal Division. Our AO was reported as having extensive NVA/VC activity. I guess that I did give some thought to the fact that we would be operating as a twelve-man team and that it must be a hot area. We were getting a fancy sendoff on the day of the mission, and the 101st public relations people were to photograph us as we got on the choppers. But when they took our picture, John

Hines was not there yet, an irony in itself. En route, we were radioed a change of mission: both teams would be landing at the 2/327 firebase. On landing, we found out that we would be walking off the hilltop and inserting by foot into our AO. I started to have strange feelings about this mission."

"I had been bullshitting with some of the Hawks on the firebase hilltop, and they told me to watch my ass," Limey Walker says. "I was told that a couple of days before they had pulled a short patrol, and not two hundred meters into the jungle they had killed two trail watchers right in the area we would be passing through. The only time Charlie would bother using trail watchers was when he had something to protect or to monitor our movements.

"We waited around for three hours for a briefing. Finally Walt Bachek came back and gave us the scoop. Lights had been seen in the valley and we were to check that out and possibly lay an ambush. We waited for more but that was it! Hell, we were in a free-fire zone. If they wanted the lights out they could have used an airstrike or, better yet, given the redlegs (artillerymen) some target practice. The lights wouldn't have stayed on long!

"We moved out early in the afternoon, traveling at a forced march in the open, for five hundred meters down the hilltop until we entered the jungle. I began to feel a little easier with the protection the bush offered. We came across a trail and because of the late start we did the unthinkable: we walked it. Assigned to pull drag, I became extremely cautious, stopping every one hundred meters and letting the rest of the team continue. Crouching under concealment, Wofford and I waited and watched for a few minutes to make sure we weren't being followed. This continued for three hours until the patrol stopped. Leaving Wofford as rear security, I worked my way to the front of the patrol to find Bachek and McKinnon scanning the valley floor with binoculars. We had come to the end of the vegetation, which was the reason the patrol had stopped. Bachek handed me the binoculars and turned to talk to McKinnon. Adjusting the binoculars, I could plainly see two Vietnamese bent over a dike less than ten meters from a hootch.

While observing them, I suddenly saw a puff of smoke. I couldn't believe what I witnessed. As I was watching, I saw the dinks get blown to bits; parts of their bodies were flying in all directions. Even the side of the hootch disappeared. They must have been planting a mine, and it had detonated. The sound of the explosion reached us and got Bachek's attention. He grabbed the binos back and started scanning the area. He whispered to me, 'Where the hell are the dinks, Limey? Where did they go?'

"Unable to tell a lie I replied, 'All over the place, Walt—here, there, and everywhere!'

"With that, I told him I was going to move a couple hundred meters back down the trail to make sure we hadn't been followed. Just before dark we made our way back to the team and moved to our night defensive position. In the security wheel facing out, John Hines was to my right, and Danny Williams was on Hines's right. Lurch was on my left. I had been assigned watch from 0300 hours to 0400 hours, so I pulled the poncho liner out of my rucksack and sacked out. Just as I was dozing off, I was startled by an ungodly racket coming from Hines. I watched him pulling out a canvas tarp, a noisy one at that. I couldn't believe it.

" 'What's your problem, Hines? You know better than that,' I growled. Hines replied, 'Sorry, Limey, I didn't realize it was so noisy.'

"Instead of putting it away, he wrapped himself in it and went directly to sleep. I guess since John was a cherry, he didn't fully realize what a mistake he had made by bringing the tarp into the field. I promised myself that I would burn the damn thing at the first opportunity. Then I went to sleep."

Bob McKinnon recalls, "I remember waking up to green tracers coming into the perimeter. I rolled to my left and commenced firing. Someone was yelling that Hines had been hit. I almost shot Limey because when he opened up with his grease gun (WW II–era .45 cal. submachine gun), it didn't sound like an M-16. That grease gun almost got him shot! I remember Danny Williams yelling that Hines was dead."

Danny Williams adds: "Around 0045 hours, 15 September,

I opened my eyes and looked toward John Hines because I had felt him move. He was on his knees, bending over his radio. I asked him, 'John, what are you doing?' He answered that he was getting his radio ready to make the sit-rep call at 0100 hours. I had just shut my eyes when the shots started. Before I could move, John fell over on top of me, and he called out to the team, 'Look out!' I felt another round hit John as he was lying on top of me. If he had not been lying on me, the round would have hit me. My team medic, Doc Kraft, Bachek's medic (Lurch) and me (an ex-medic) all tried to save Hines's life, but it just wasn't to be. He had been killed instantly.

"We had artillery support from the firebase we had walked out of. We also had two gunships on call, but because of the nighttime we could not utilize them."

Limey adds to the story. "I was startled awake. Automatic weapons fire was coming into our perimeter. I tried to dig my ass into the ground as green tracers crossed my chest and face not more than a few inches away. I grabbed for my grease gun and instead grabbed someone's ass. Yelling for my weapon, I was met with an apology from Lurch. Bachek yelled for a 'mad minute' and we did it—I heard spoons fly off grenades and then a grenade hit a tree and bounced back close to our position. Calling first for a cease-fire, Bachek yelled for me to secure Hines's radio. Crawling over to his pack, I attempted to quick release the straps then realized that they had been tied in a knot so I cut them away and passed the radio to Walter. Returning to my position, I heard movement to my front. Holding my fire, I whispered to Lurch that I could hear them out there. Lurch replied, 'Yeah, and they stink like shit, too!' He was right; the smell of the dinks was overwhelming. I pulled loose ammunition from my pack and reloaded the two magazines I had fired earlier. I began to wonder why the dinks didn't attack us again. Maybe by some freak accident we had dusted their commander in our mad minute, and they were at a loss as to what to do. Bachek yelled for us to keep our heads down."

Bob McKinnon remembers, "Bachek called in artillery and got it crumping fifty meters outside our perimeter. It was a good display of adjusting artillery in close. Earlier I was next to

Bachek as he started throwing hand grenades. That went on OK for awhile; then he threw one and it hit a tree right to our front and bounced back. I yelled, 'Aw, shit!' it went off right in our faces. We were there all night and had several mad minutes. The gooks didn't seem to want to attack our position. A reaction force from the Hawks came in and linked up with us when it got light. We walked out carrying the body."

Limey remembers: "Finally, before first light, the stench and the noise vanished. The jungle was quiet again. At first light the point element from the Hawks entered our position. Looking in front of my position, I realized how powerful the grease gun was. Not a bush or limb had been left standing. I had cleared a perfect firing lane. Wofford drew my attention to his rucksack. The top of the metal frame had almost been cut away by small-arms fire. Even so, he had been luckier than Hines. We carried the body of our good friend John Lester Hines, wrapped in the same tarp he had brought with him, from the bush to the LZ. After less than ten minutes we were extracted. Our mood was grim. Another Lurp had been taken from us on a humbug mission. I recovered the tarp from Graves and Registration, promptly found an open area, and burned it."

Danny Williams adds to the telling: "Many times I have thought about that night and wondered what I could have done differently, that might have made a difference where John Hines was concerned. John Hines was awarded the Silver Star. The U.S. Army lost a good soldier, the LRRP detachment lost an outstanding radio operator, and I lost a good, close friend. My team took John's loss very hard. I wrote a letter to John's parents, as a team leader and as a family friend. John's name is on the wall in Washington, D.C. He will never be forgotten, at least never by me."

A truly sad thing besides the death of John Lester Hines was that on arriving in the rear in Chu Lai, Charles Wofford left the LRRP detachment thinking that he might have played a part in Hines's death. Bob McKinnon says that it had stopped raining that morning and Hines had just got off watch and was putting his tarp away. Wofford speculated he had been having a dream, woke up, and fired off a burst that might have hit Hines. But Bob McKinnon adds: "I still say, I woke up to green tracers coming into our perimeter, and David Wofford had no part in John Hines's death."

So to our brother Lurp, Charles Wofford, wherever you may be: We love you like the brother you were, and nothing will ever change that. . . .

**New intelligence received by the brigade indicated that large enemy forces, including the 2nd NVA Division headquarters, were located ten miles west of the brigade's present area of operation, making use of the mountainous region in this area. On 27 September, the brigade redeployed its three line battalions to exploit the new situation.**

## Forty-Day Mission

The brigade LRRP detachment was tasked with three team missions on 25 September. Two six-man teams were to insert on 25 September, and a heavy team was going in on 26 September. The monsoon season was there in all its glory. I had experienced the spring monsoon, but the winter monsoon is a totally different climatic phenomenon in Southeast Asia. The rains came in late September, and we would end up doing a lengthy mission that stretched over forty days. Thus the "Forty-Day Mission." Fannie Fandel once told me that it was actually fifty-four days. It involved long-range patrolling, static deployment on several hilltops, as well as providing security and running search-and-destroy patrols off firebases.

The night before we took off on our mission, I went to bed early. I was awakened by Larry Christian, who said he needed some money. He was in a heavy poker game and knew I had just recently arrived from the rear with MPC (military pay certificates). I sleepily rustled through my pockets and gave him what I had without counting it. Later on he said it was $86.00. He kept telling me he was hot and needed some money to stay in the game. I figured, "Yeah, right, that's why you're borrowing," and promptly went back to sleep. He woke me up as it was getting light and handed me a bunch of very illegal greenbacks. Brother Christian had gotten involved in a high-stakes poker game with some marines and he had won $1200.00! He gave me back $190.00. Not bad interest, doubling my money while I slept!

We started our mission on 25 September as a heavy (i.e., double) team. It was a reconnaissance mission on which, if we found something, we were supposed to "develop the situation." All the Foul Dudes were enamored of that catchy phrase. We were packed for a six-day mission. It was raining when we left Chu Lai, but as the duration of the mission increased, so did the severity of the foul weather. Can you recall how it is when it rains, the sounds, the wetness, the smells, and the discomfort, after an extended time in the rain? I mean a continual steady, heavy rain, not a drizzle. How much time have you spent in the rain without rain gear or getting into a shelter such as a tent and feeling how great it is? An hour, a day, a week? Try four weeks without a letup in sight. It rained the likes of which I have never experienced, not since then. I remember that the water constantly dripping off my Lurp hat on the fourth day, surrounding my face like a wet veil, bugged the shit out of me. None of us normally carried ponchos because in Lurps that was a mortal sin, but being in the field for so long during the monsoon made the perils of hell seem somehow less terrible. We gave in and tried to requisition them. However, our request for ponchos could not be filled for over two weeks, and even then some of us never got one. Not that our rear people were slacking on their job. The demands for ponchos from the brigade simply swamped brigade supply. Every afternoon at 1400 hours, it would be as if someone had turned off the faucet. The sun seldom showed its face during that period and so we just tried to find the driest place, which was usually sitting on our rucksacks. If possible, we tried to spread our poncho liners out to dry. If the sun briefly broke through the leaden clouds, the countryside would be enveloped in a sauna-like steamy mist. It was very beautiful. Promptly at 1600 hours, like clockwork, it would start raining again, and sometimes you could see and hear the rain coming up a valley or down a ridgeline. All those raindrops hitting all that vegetation produced a sound that started as a whisper but got louder as it got closer until it literally washed over you when it reached you.

The full monsoon was a very miserable experience until we adapted. At night we would drink lots of water just before we wrapped ourselves in wet poncho liners to try to get some sleep. Lying on the mud, wrapped in a poncho liner, with no ground pad, the rainwater soon found its way into the side you were lying on. So taking a leak was the only time we ever became warm. You would point your dick up your stomach, and the urine warmed your stomach and chest area, an exquisite feeling that lasted only until it cooled. It rained so much, it didn't take long for body and clothes to be washed thoroughly.

During the daylight we would patrol and keep on the move simply to stay warm. There was a plant called an "elephant ear," a common indoor plant here in America, which grew there in the draws and bowls of the mountainsides and valleys. Elephant ears grew on stalks about two inches thick and four feet tall, and a single leaf was three or four feet wide, in the shape of a heart or an elephant ear tapering to a point. We would cut several of its leaves and make a temporary shelter by using them as umbrellas. The only problem was that the raindrops falling on the leaves reduced our ability to hear what was going on around us. We also used an elephant ear to fill our canteens by tying the bottom sides of the leaf together with a twig, creating a funnel for the water to drain into our canteens. During the monsoon, it didn't take long to fill a canteen with fresh water.

It was vitally necessary to keep three things dry: the handset on the radio, coffee and the condiments for it, and cigarettes and matches. I know smoking is bad for your health, but so is war. A cigarette had a calming effect that would take the edge off; more important, it was a luxury, a touch of something personal. In the monsoon, once a cigarette was lit, we needed to use ingenious methods to get some puffs off it. A couple of drags, and it would be running down your chin. There were some missions where we wouldn't smoke cigarettes in the field. But that fall, operating sometimes with three teams, the security of numbers afforded us that luxury.

Another thing we had to contend with was the proliferation of leeches. When wearing wet clothing, they were hard to feel on your body; we couldn't really feel them until they were firmly attached. We squirted mosquito repellent on the tops of our boots, where the pants bloused into the boot. That was effective for a short time, but with all the rain, the repellent soon washed away. After it was light, we would perform a visual recon of the groin and inside of thighs, areas that they seemed to particularly like. During the spring monsoon, when we were operating out of Khanh Duong, I found a leech on my right testicle, and on the suggestion of another Lurp I squirted some mosquito repellent onto the leech. Man, was that a mistake! It felt like someone had put a blow torch to my testicles—which was very painful for me and very entertaining to the rest of the guys! The best way to remove a leech from your body is with a lit cigarette—another reason for smoking.

We ate our meals using the rapid spoon-shoveling method. Teddy Bear always took great pains in fixing his meal, laying out his cans of food like a chef preparing a twelve-course meal. Sharing a cup of mocha was a ritual that I looked forward to every evening. We mixed cocoa powder, coffee, creamer, and sugar from a C ration unit. Teddy Bear always carried a canteen cup, which made enough coffee to split. We improvised stoves out of B-1 cans, which held the crackers, and a thumb-sized piece of C-4 would heat a steaming cup of mocha. The beauty of C-4 was that it burned even when it was wet, and a huge amount of heat was generated by a small piece. A cup of steaming mocha and a cigarette were small pleasures that we treasured during the wet period, but they were themselves dangerous.

Humping in the monsoon is hard on the body. The suspenders on the rucksack and LBE are always wet, and the constant rubbing on a wet tiger shirt irritates the skin around the clavicle and the small of the back where the rucksack rests. Other hot spots are around the waist from the LBE web belt, the inside of the thighs close to the groin, and around the bottoms of the calf muscles on the inside of the lower legs. Once a sore is produced, an infection can develop and then combating the infection and still being able to function becomes an uphill battle. Keeping our feet in good shape was also very important. We never wore socks or underwear, as that was a sure way to trash our feet or crotch. I watched one inexperienced Lurp peel off his socks, leaving the skin from the soles of his feet in the socks. It was even painful to watch. Our clothes didn't last very long, and the first thing that went was the crotch in the pants. When that happened we used cravats, triangular bandages, to keep testicles and *chorizo* from hanging up on the vegetation.

It wouldn't have taken much to set up a small camp to get out of the elements, but we just couldn't stick around an area for any length of time. The weather was an inconvenience, but Chuck could turn into a major problem with the weather in his favor. He wasn't moving around a lot because the weather gave him some security from the air. It reminded me of hunting elk or deer. Game doesn't move much when it's raining; it mostly lays dog. During the first week out we saw Chuck once and called artillery on him. We never physically inspected the area of the strike to get a body count. We were resupplied in the field and continued our mission.

## Mission out of Chu Lai with Top Smith

About this same time M.Sgt. Lloyd "Top" Smith, as the unofficial team leader of a six-man team, was inserted northwest of our recon zone. With Top Smith were Sp4. Thomas "Greek" Dokos and Sp4. Harvey "Beaver" Bieber. Their mission was to monitor a small valley that was suspected of being a staging and movement area for the NVA. The team was inserted on the back side of a hilltop from their objective. They followed a wet, heavily vegetated ridgeline down to a position where they could effectively watch the valley floor. Another team had been inserted about three klicks farther down the valley, but on the opposite side. The valley floor was only about one hundred fifty meters wide. It was green and there were several crops being grown on it. There were three or four hootches on one side of the valley and seven or eight men tending the fields at any given time. That seemed weird to the team because there were no women or children around, and the men tending the fields were not really working—just trying to look like they were. Watching them with binoculars, the team quickly caught on to the scene being staged by them.

Greek Dokos remembers: "Top was kind of neat right from the get-go. 'What do you think?' he asked. 'You think this is a good area, or should we move down?' I mean, he gave us options; he didn't put us on the spot. We would say, 'Well this looks like a good area,' and so Top would say, 'OK, if you think so, we'll stay here.' That's how the whole mission started off; everybody had a say in everything we did. Top let *us* do things. He was in command, but in the background, and he conferred with all of us before any decision was made. We set up the first position and watched the valley floor using binoculars the first day. Top suggested a perimeter recon and at the same time found a better observation point for the following day. The next morning Top asked us if we should get a little closer. 'Yeah,' we said, 'let's get closer'."

The team worked its way slowly and silently to a position they had found the previous day and made a place in the vegetation that had a great view of the valley floor but where they couldn't be seen by Chuck. Because of their close proximity, this time they didn't need binoculars to view the activity in the valley; they could actually tell what individuals were doing. Greek Dokos said that when the Charlies started moving stuff out of the hootches, they would always look around a lot. They started going out into the fields carrying packs and bundles but no weapons, and they would lift a hatch that seemed to be part of the paddy. Even with binoculars you couldn't begin to see it. Apparently they had underground storage places throughout the fields. Some Chuck would come into the area carrying a bundle or pack and leave with something out of one of the holes. Top's team radioed in the sightings throughout the day, but the other team hadn't seen much if any activity. Everything was happening in front of Top's team.

On the third day, as part of the operation, one of the line companies was walking down the valley, clearing it out and approaching the sector that the team had been monitoring. Top Smith had wanted to use artillery but was waiting for the approach of the line company. There was a bend in the valley to the right of the team, and the team could hear the approach of the line company. Greek Dokos was amazed at how the sound carried down the valley. The line company was quite distant; yet the clanging and voices could be heard very clearly. When they heard the line company approaching, the Charlies in the field started running from hootch to hootch carrying things and stashing them in the underground storage places in the fields.

Greek Dokos recalls the incident: "Top decided right then, 'Hey, they're going to be gone soon; it's time for Arty.' It was pretty neat; he left it up to us. We talked real briefly about the grid coordinates and called it in. Top asked for willie peter as the opening round. A brief adjustment and the fire for effect with HE (high explosives) came in right after. Top didn't have anything to do with using the radio. He let us do it all; it was our show. Top Smith was there to make a suggestion, but it wasn't like, 'I don't think you should do that.' He was always saying, 'What do you think about if we did this?' God, it was just a neat feeling; it was a real close time with Top. It was like we saw him at his finest, just how good a leader he was. It got to the point where we didn't feel like he was the leader. I mean, we knew he was, but he left it to us. I remember two Charlies were running, they were out in the fields where the underground storage areas were and were trying to get back toward the hootches. Not far from the hootches to our left was our tree line, which fed into the valley at that end, but at the other end, where the line company was approaching, it was more open. The gooks were just hauling ass after that first round, and when the HE came in, man, we were just walking it everywhere through the valley. A couple of rounds went off by these Charlies while they were running. One of them got blown into the air the way you see in cartoons—legs still running. We totally destroyed the hootches. The line company took care of going through all the stashes. We pretty much got all the enemy that were down there that we had seen. We just covered the valley with artillery rounds."

The team made its way back up to the top of the ridge. The Lurps had received word that they would be extracted and reinserted farther down the valley the following morning, at which time they would be resupplied with food and water. As I gathered this material, I came across numerous recollections from various members of the LRRP detachment about Top Smith. It all involved "the look" Top would give the poor soul who "stepped on his dick." Here is a variation of such an incident and a glimpse of Top's command presence.

The team moved into the night site, and two short shifts on the radio were to be pulled by each man. Greek Dokos says, "I had the last shift on radio watch and was sitting up with my poncho liner wrapped around my shoulders. It was wet and cool. Because of being so wet, I hadn't been sleeping very well nor had anyone else. I didn't have much time left on my guard, fifteen or twenty minutes. At the end of my shift, on the hour, I was supposed to report in. I was sitting there not even nodding off, and, fuck, the next thing I heard was squelch breaking on the radio! I bolted upright and knew what had happened—I couldn't believe I had drifted off. It woke up Top also, who was to the right of the radio. I freaked and, grabbing the handset, looked over at Top. Top Smith sat up and just *looked* at me. He gave a shake of his head is all he did. I thought, 'Oh man, you fucked up!' I felt like dying, and if I could have evaporated off the face of the earth at that moment, I would have done it. I could have put the muzzle of my sixteen in my mouth and fired a full automatic burst. I mean, it was the only noble thing to do. It sounds extreme, but that's how I felt. That's how much Top and being a good Lurp meant to me. It had been such a good mission, and we all were enjoying the really good feeling of that bonding amongst us. That mission was a special one because Top had presence, a radiation of authority. He was a special person, and when he had to, he

would just look at you, just kind of give you that look. He usually wouldn't chew your ass out; all it took was the look;
because nobody wanted to disappoint Top. He was so
respected, not just as a soldier but as a person. On this mission
I saw Top a little differently. He seemed at ease, and I think he
was really enjoying himself. He wasn't laughing but sometimes you would catch that glint in his eye. He just looked
pleased he was having a good time. It was the best mission I
was ever on. I really wanted to see Top and talk to him and just
tell him what a special person he was, what he meant to everybody and you know unfortunately I didn't get the opportunity.
Up to that point it was a special mission, it was the best one I
had. Kind of ended bad, but that didn't overshadow what happened before."

Wandering around, not getting much results for our efforts,
frustrated us. Lester "Superspade" Hite came up with the idea
of making a snatch. The previous evening we had spotted four
Charlies with weapons enter a three-hootch complex at the
bottom of the drainage. We decided we would sneak down
early in the morning, kick ass, and—hopefully—take a prisoner. That should earn us extraction. We dropped our rucksacks and left a small element to watch Chuck as the rest of us
worked our way down into position by the hootches. We
moved in, but the Charlies we saw the previous evening had
split. Instead we found a middle-aged woman and young man
around seventeen years old. We found some rucksacks but
never located any weapons. We did a really quick search and
then hauled ass with our prisoners back to our rucksacks. We
moved over a ridgeline and about two klicks away from the
hootches and sent in a report that we had some prisoners to get
extracted. That afternoon during the rain break a slick and two
gunships flew out, extracted our prisoners, and left us with a
job well done and scratching our heads. We beat feet getting
away from the LZ we had used.

On the tenth day of our extended mission, in the late afternoon, we put the twelve-man team in a security wheel in a
copse of trees just on the back side of a small saddle situated on

a long ridgeline that paralleled a small valley we had been monitoring for several days. It was about seven klicks away from where we had taken the two prisoners. During the afternoon rain break, as it was starting to drizzle, Jaybird Magill, Superspade, and I had crossed the saddle and found a good spot to glass the valley. We could still see the valley, but eventually it would start raining hard and we would lose sight of it. We spotted a group of Charlies, about platoon size, thirty to thirty-five people. They were about eight hundred meters away moving south down the valley toward us. They were mixed clothing of black PJs and khakis, the khakis looking darker because they were wet. They were traveling in a single column and one individual stood out from the rest of the group, right in the middle. He towered over the rest of them. He was wearing black PJs, and as he got closer, we realized he was a Caucasian. We coded a SALUTE report and sent it in.

As the Charlies got closer and directly below us, with the binoculars we could make out his features and thought he looked Slavic so we pegged him as being from some "Combloc" country, East Germany or possibly Poland, but we believed it more likely that he was a Russian. He carried the standard canvas rucksack with canvas LBE of the communist countries. His weapon was an AK-47, and his size made it look small in his hands. He carried himself with the air of confidence that professional soldiers exude. "Spetnaz" (Soviet special forces troops) crossed our minds. This was exciting and a pretty special observation for us. This was shit hot! We had received "unofficial" intelligence summaries that Russian advisers were suspected of operating in South Vietnam with the North Vietnamese. We received an excited message from the rear saying they wanted us to snatch this individual, a very interesting decision seeing as how it had been made in the comfort of some dry tent in the rear. It was a tempting and exciting proposition but not very realistic; prisoner snatches are extremely hard to carry out. The enemy wasn't inclined to be taken prisoner, and usually the team ended up with a very dead or severely wounded prisoner. Getting the drop on these guys was going to be dicey.

As we hashed over ideas on the best method of getting down into the valley to engage the Charlies, they disappeared into a vegetated island in the unused rice paddies a little south and directly below us, where a couple of hootches were visible in the vegetation. Since it was late in the day, we figured they were basing for the night. We couldn't really walk down the exposed hillside from our position toward them. It was starting to rain harder, and visibility down into the valley was getting poor. We were running out of daylight. Superspade decided to send a two-man recon element south on the back side of the ridgeline to find a suitable way to sneak into the valley. About fifteen minutes later they contacted us to say they had found a vegetated draw that offered concealment and led down into the valley.

It started raining like a cow pissing on a flat rock as we moved south down the ridgeline, and we joined our two-man recon element as it was almost getting dark. Superspade, Jaybird, and I crossed the ridgeline to check the area out. The valley was obscured by the rain and clouds settling down on us. It was a bummer in that the odds were stacking up against us on making a move on the group. The worst part was we could have just called artillery in on the group instead of trying to take the guy prisoner. There was over two to one odds in manpower against us, and we were running out of daylight and the weather, so we should have just kicked ass with artillery the way we had originally intended. The Caucasian was a rare intelligence opportunity and extremely tempting but oh so unrealistic.

Superspade decided to find an NDP and get something going in the early morning. We found an NDP about seventy meters farther south on the ridge and sixty meters down from the crest. We moved into the NDP in the dark, set out our claymores, and started eating the evening meal in shifts. Superspade joined me just as I was finishing my Lurp ration. Superspade whispered, "Marty, I got a bad feeling about this place." Jaybird, TB, and I had just been talking about those same feelings. We all answered Superspade by saying, "Let's get the fuck out of here."

As I hurriedly packed my ruck and brought in my claymore, Superspade went to every member of the team and urgently informed them we were saddling up and moving to a different location. Then he rejoined me and asked me to help him set up a couple of booby traps. We moved uphill about twenty meters in the direction from which we had entered the NDP and set up three booby-trapped grenades spaced out and on line. In Lurps we carried preprepared booby-trapped grenades made by emptying the charges out of the MKII A-1 (pineapple) grenades and filling them chock-full of C-4, exchanging the four-second fuse cap for a one-second smoke grenade fuse cap. It made one hell of a powerful explosion. We cut a length of ten-pound test fishing line and attached it to the neck under the spoon of the grenade. To identify the booby-trapped grenades, we wrapped a piece of "go to hell tape" (duct tape) around the grenade pin. When it was prepared like that, all we had to do was tie the end of the fishing line to the base of a tree or shrub about five to six inches off the ground, stretch the line out and insert the grenade into a B-3 can or the notch of a tree or shrub until the inside of the can or notch held the spoon in place, and pull the pin. Tripping the line would jerk the grenade free, the spoon would fly loose, and some Chuck's day would just be ruined. That type of booby trap was handy when you were in a hurry and wanted to slow down someone who was on your ass. It was a simple, effective, and deadly tool.

Superspade and I rejoined the team, and he led us straight down the hillside about one hundred meters and then to the left, paralleling the ridge about two hundred meters north to a little rock spur that jutted from the hillside we had passed earlier that evening. We passed under the downhill side of the spur and moved into the new NDP from the back side. We had lucked out on an easily defensible position, one that was especially good in the dark. I placed my claymore and was reeling the wire back to my position when mortar rounds started going off at the NDP we had just hastily vacated. After a bit one of the booby traps went off and numerous AKs fought a horrific, one-sided firefight. Eventually we heard the other two grenades explode. We were laughing into our Lurp hats as the one-sided firefight went on. Our common thought was, "That's a lick on you, Chuck!" Superspade called in artillery on the old NDP site and the vegetated side of the draw leading down into that small valley. We figured we had been seen by the folks down in the valley or else Chuck had someone walking the ridgeline who had spotted us. Whichever, Superspade's intuition had saved us. It paid to listen to the reptile that whispered in your ear and made your hair stand on end.

After the "white dude" incident, we got a call to hump six klicks or so to the northeast and go into static deployment on a strategically located hilltop overlooking a three-valley junction at its west base (number 403 on the map). The 2/502 was making a battalion sweep, line companies pushing north up the three valleys to their junction. We were to monitor the junction and engage the enemy with artillery. A hill to the north of us, occupied by Battery A 2/320th Artillery*, overlooked a valley we could not see because of an extended ridgeline that dropped into it. Our hill had previously been occupied by marines, who had laid some concertina wire on its east side where vegetation grew up a draw abutting the hilltop. It had also been heavily booby-trapped by the marines. That was the weakest point in our defense of the hill, and we had to adjust accordingly. Brother Weems, who was in overall charge, had joined us shortly before the hump to the hill. Superspade and Weems were both staff sergeants but in the Lurps, experience usually commanded. Brother Weems had gaggles of experience, and the beauty of Lurps was that everyone knew his limitations and his place. Whenever Top Smith or Lieutenant McIsaac joined us in the field, they deferred to whoever was in charge. Of course, we still listened to their suggestions. Top and Mac tried to have one of them in the field as often as possible. During this lengthy deployment, people joined and left us in the field. We had over three teams on the hill, and Weems thought it wise to bring in an M-2 .50 caliber machine gun to snipe with and to mark targets. We dug two-man fighting holes, with two layers

---

*S.Sgt. Webster Anderson was awarded the Medal of Honor for his actions in defense of this firebase against a large NVA ground assault.

of sandbags around each hole encircling our perimeter. We positioned claymores to ring our perimeter and set booby traps and trip flares on the most likely avenues of approach. Directly to our west was a bald ridge that dropped down into the three-valley junction. We placed the fifty to cover the bald ridge and a draw that came in from the north. To our south was a valley that ran east-west into the valley junction and formed the base of our hill.

Clay Wentworth joined us on the hilltop after returning from extension leave. As he describes it, around 15 October 1967, "We were supposed to be observers and call artillery down on those people in the valley going up the trails. Right across, I guess it was up to the northeast, we could see another barren hill, and there was a firebase set up on that hill. I remember one morning we woke up at about 0300. Chuck had attacked the firebase up on that hill. They were really getting into it, a good firefight that lasted twenty or thirty minutes; then they retreated down the hill, and Puff came along and fired the place up. Later on in the day, on the south side of our hill, we could see another little valley, and in the middle of the rice paddies there were maybe fifteen acres of jungle, and some marine F-4 phantoms were bombing that little island. We were observing through the glasses and I watched these Charlies run out of the cover of this little island and the jet pilot got one with his twenty mike mike (20mm). A chopper pilot who came out to resupply us saw a couple of gooks around our perimeter to the east, and we went to check them out. We didn't get very far because that place had really been well booby-trapped by the marines who had occupied our hill before us."

About the third day on the hill, Top Smith, who had come in the evening before, led a seven-man team into the valley on the south side of our hill. The team consisted of Limey, carrying a radio, Pizza Joe, Jaybird, Thomas Melton, me, and another member from my team, plus a couple of men from a different team. We walked out the south side of the perimeter, worked east, and crossed onto the back side of a ridge that dropped east off the hill. When we got to the bottom of the hill and into the valley, we worked west toward the three-valley junction. We were finding a lot of sign that indicated that many people were using the trails lacing the small valley. Toward the center of the valley vegetation was encroaching on old rice paddies. The edges of the valley were vegetated, and we were using the bush to mask our movement. We patrolled west, paralleling the base of the hill. I was walking point and had moved about four hundred meters when we took a burst of AK-47 fire directly from the south. Our patrol laid suppressive fire in the direction of the enemy fire. I had just passed a semiopen area and was in vegetation, so I low-crawled toward the edge of the bushes that opened onto the old paddies. Our patrol had taken only the one burst of fire. Word reached me that someone had been hit. I worked my way back and found Top Smith helping Thomas Melton. One round had struck him directly under his left armpit, striking a rib, breaking it, and then miraculously deflecting off the rib, traveling down the outside of his rib cage, under the skin, before exiting above his hip. It was a nasty-looking wound hole, but the round had not penetrated his chest. Melton had been damn lucky. The sniper had been right on target, but luck had been on Melton's side.

While in Duc Pho, Thomas Melton had received a stainless-steel forty-four magnum revolver with a six-inch barrel from someone in the States. Those of us who fired that cannon were amazed at the recoil it produced. You had to shoot it two-handed.

We called in a dustoff and gunships, and had the gunships fire up the south end of the paddies as we medevaced Thomas Melton out. Even so, the dustoff took fire as it left.

After Melton was safely off, Top decided that a six-man patrol was a little small to be messing around down in the valley, especially since we had been spotted. Judging by all the recent sign around, we could see it wouldn't take Chuck long to set us up for an ambush. Melton had been carrying one of the radios, so Pizza Joe took it. Limey was carrying the other radio. We backtracked about two hundred meters and took a wooded draw that led back to our hilltop position. The vegetation in the draw ended about seventy-five meters from the top. We set several booby traps at the edge of the wooded draw and worked our way up onto the hilltop. It started raining again.

Craig Vega recalls: "When we first got on the hilltop, one of the men had the runs, so he went outside the wire to take a dump, but he tripped a booby trap while in the process. There was an explosion, and a line of excrement ten feet long described his flight through the air, to where he landed in a heap with his pants around his ankles. I don't mean to make light of the incident because it seriously rattled his cage. It was miraculous that he was not severely injured. Nobody had informed us that the hilltop had been heavily booby-trapped.

"About six days later we were treated to a ringside seat as an infantry company made contact with an entrenched enemy force at the junction of the three valleys to our west. Charlie had moved into preprepared emplacements during the night and ambushed the leading elements as they arrived at the junction. At first we couldn't see into the valley because of the morning ground fog and clouds hovering over the area, but we could hear the firing and switched to their company frequency. They had some people hurt and pinned down and were calling for a dustoff. The firefight raged for a while and then died down. The dustoff and two gunships came on station and were ready to evacuate several casualties. Soon there was a break in the fog and cloud cover, and the choppers went to work. As the first gunship overflew the area and the dustoff was coming in to land, Chuck suddenly opened up with a 12.7 (.51 caliber) heavy machine gun and lots of small-arms fire. The dustoff never stood a chance. It instantly crumpled onto the LZ. One of the gunships flew away but after being shot full of holes, the other had to make an emergency landing in one of the adjoining valleys. Then the line company was once again in a horrific firefight. The heavy machine gun was emplaced on the ridge that came out of the west and nosed down into the junction. It overlooked and commanded the valley the grunts had patrolled down. All of that was taking place at the west base of our hill, and we had an unrestricted view. It was the Super Bowl, and we had seats on the fifty-yard line.

"The cloud cover had improved enough so that the line

company called in an airstrike of marine F-4 Phantom jets.
Their approach to the target was directly over our hilltop. The
F-4s would come screaming in on the bomb runs, releasing
their bombs directly over us at three hundred or four hundred
feet. They were so close we could see the helmets of the pilots
and watch the stabilizing fins pop out on the bombs and the
flight of the bomb as it tracked down to its target. The jet would
increase power as it clawed its way back up. Because of the
moisture in the air, we could see concentric rings emanating
from the explosion. The sound of the explosion reached us a
second or two later. The whole time it was going on, we could
hear the lone gunner continuously firing, even during the
explosions. That gunner had some big nuts and knew how to
lead a jet. Testimony to that fact was that one of the F-4s
departed trailing smoke. The first flight of jets was soon to be
replaced by another flight of two. Those jets followed the same
procedures, and pretty soon we were starting to cheer the lone
enemy gunner on. We were witnessing an incredible display of
bravery, above and beyond the call of duty. Maybe he was
chained to the gun, but that man and crew should have won
their nation's Medal of Honor. The second flight was carrying
bombs and napalm. One of those jets was also hit. The infantry
line company was bogged down with casualties and could not
maneuver. A third flight of jets was called in, and the weather
around our hill and the target was starting to deteriorate.
Clouds were moving in, and the jets were starting to have to
jump down a hole in the sky and release all their bombs at one
time. The enemy gunner kept firing, but the second jet of the
third flight must have got lucky and secured a direct hit
because the heavy machine gun finally went silent. Three
flights of two jets apiece had dropped their ordnance. It had
been an incredible display of flying skills on the part of the
pilots and of bravery and tenacity by the enemy gunner. We
watched as the casualties were extracted by helicopter."

About three days later the weather started to change. They
called us at midday and told us that a typhoon was coming
ashore off the South China Sea, and high winds and rain were
to be expected. That afternoon the horizon to the east started

turning black. As the typhoon got closer, lightning flashed in a huge cloud front that extended as far as we could see. When it got even closer, the air got deathly calm. Then the wind started picking up, and we hurried to secure everything that might get blown away. As the wind increased, it got pitch black, and rain started falling very heavily. The huge cloud enveloped us, and lightning started striking like I had never seen before. We were in our fighting holes, and pretty soon we had our faces in our Lurp hats hugging the east wall of the fighting holes with our mouths and noses close to the top of our holes to breathe. I threw my rucksack into the hole with me simply to displace the water out of my hole and to keep the ruck from being blown away. By this time the rain was falling sideways, and it stung when it hit.

It was terrifying to witness nature in all its glorious fury. The air was so charged with electricity that the hair on our heads and forearms stood on end. Pretty soon the claymores and trip flares started going off, and pieces of trees and shrubs from the east side of our hilltop started flying through the air. As the storm gathered in strength, the size of flying debris increased. Winds in excess of ninety miles per hour actually picked up the "fifty"—despite the sandbags weighting the tripod—and blew it right over the side of the hill. Ozone was strong in the air as electrical discharges went off with a strobe-light effect. The storm continued like that for what must have been four or five hours. I have never felt more vulnerable in the face of nature than I did that night.

An interesting note to this is added by Allen "Teddy Bear" Gaskell: "I had the only radio on the entire hill that was receiving that day, and we got a message just before the full fury of the storm hit. They informed us to expect to be assaulted by a major enemy force that had been spotted assembling at the east base of our hill. That transmission came in several times until the brunt of the storm hit us, and we lost contact with our rear base. Of course all thought of a major enemy assault was forgotten as we dealt with the storm. No doubt Charlie was having his own problems in riding out the storm."

Doc Brian "Wolfman" Kraft recalls: "One of the guys, Paul

Dufresne, had joined us a couple of days before the storm and had brought in a rubber lady (air mattress), and everyone was envious that he had such a comfortable item. The storm blew itself out about 0200 hours, so Paul pulled his air mattress out and inflated it. The wind had died down, but it was still raining strong. Sometime after falling asleep on the air mattress and because there was so much rain falling, he floated off the hilltop and ended up in the concertina wire draped around the downhill side of our perimeter. The air mattress popped on the razor wire and left Paul all entangled in the wire. We got a good laugh out of that one."

During our stay on the hilltop, Derby Jones, Larry Christian, and Jay "Jaybird" Magill went out on a resupply chopper to do some administrative business at Chu Lai. "Just after we lifted off with shit-eating grins on our faces," Jaybird says, "Chuck opened up on us from the east ridgeline, about halfway down the hill. At first we just heard the slapping sounds; then the chopper started to buck and head nose down into the valley. Derby, the ever alert NCO and team leader that he was, left Christian and me looking at each other while he became one with the pilot and copilot. The crew chief was screaming to pull up, and the other door gunner had converted to Hari Krishna! Christian is telling God he will stop gambling and pay me the money he owed everybody. I was totally agreeing with him only if I lived. Of course, this had taken all of 1.2 seconds to transpire. The pilot had somehow gained altitude but felt that was too boring, so he decided to autorotate, and down we go, calmly glued to the floor plate by our assholes. A thousand feet later the chopper jockey regains control, and we start limping into Chu Lai. We landed at a leg outpost and checked the chopper, which had been ripped pretty serious."

Three or four days later we got a coded message that we were to prepare to move overland about four kilometers to another hilltop that was located north-northeast of our present position; as the line companies worked their way north, the area of operation had shifted farther north and east. A helicopter would be coming in to pick up the .50 and any items we wouldn't be humping and bring in maps of the new area. An hour before we were supposed to take off, we received a radio transmission saying that helicopters would move us. That was fine by us.

We helicoptered to our new hilltop position, Hill 488, which from the air looked more like a spiny ridge than a hilltop and actually had one major knob with a ridge connecting two other, lower knobs. Here, too, we were joined by a new man, who some of us hardly noticed at the time: Kenn Miller. A year and a half later, he'd be the last of the Foul Dudes still serving as a 101st Lurp. It was on Hill 488 that an eighteen-man team from Company C, 1st Recon Battalion, USMC, under the leadership of S.Sgt. Jimmie E. Howard, was attacked by an NVA battalion. On 15 June 1966 starting at 2200 hours the marines fought a vicious battle for their lives that lasted all night, and despite the tremendous odds, the enemy never took the hilltop. The team paid a heavy price: six dead and everyone else wounded. S.Sgt. Jimmie Howard was later awarded the Medal of Honor for this action and two of his men received the Navy Cross. The team was serving as a radio relay in support of a marine force recon combat jump. Since then much has been written about the bravery displayed on that hill by the recon marines.

The ridgeline was very narrow with edges dropping off sharply on both sides. On the knobs, bunkers had been built by the marines but were falling apart. The first night on the hilltop we got mortared. The ridge was so narrow that the mortar rounds would fall short or go over and explode on the back side. We called artillery on the suspected mortar positions but could never eyeball their exact location. It rained hard that night and completely filled the bunkers with water, forcing us out of them. We were mortared again the following night, and it was still raining.

The next morning the sun broke out at about 1100 hours. It was great to get sunshine, giving us the chance to dry our poncho liners. Around noon we received a radio transmission that we were to get ready to be extracted off the hill and flown back to Chu Lai. We were elated but suspicious. But sure enough, at 1300 hours we boarded helicopters and flew east to

Chu Lai. We had been in the field for thirty-one days straight, and most of us were on our second pair of tigers, which were coming completely apart. All the Lurps were smiling when we lifted off Hill 488. Thanks to Rommel Murphy and the other Lurps working in the rear at the time, we landed at Chu Lai to cold beer and steaks. We were transported to the shower points. It felt great to shower and use soap to get the grime off, because we stank to high heaven. They informed us then that we would be going back out the following day, so we were to repack our rucksacks, resupply with ammo, and be ready to go back out in the field.

That evening some of us Foul Dudes decided to quench our thirst. The closest place within walking distance was a Korean NCO club in the White Horse Division. Accompanied by some other Lurps, Lurch, Pizza Joe, Jaybird, Wentworth, and I walked over. The club was fairly crowded. It had a plywood bar and plywood tables, with benches to sit on. No other Americans were present, and as soon as we walked in, we got the vibes. We found an empty table and sat down. A couple of Vietnamese ladies were waiting on the tables but they weren't fast enough for Lurch, so he walked over to the bar to order. We could all see it was a big deal for all the Koreans that we were in their bar. We didn't care, we were thirsty. Nearby one husky dude, a Korean sergeant, was karate chopping empty Black Carling beer cans—this was in 1967, when cans were made of light steel, and crushing empty beer cans could still be thought of as a macho man's sport.

I walked up to the bar to help Lurch with the beers and carry them back. As I approached the bar, the beer-can smasher took a position slightly behind and to the left of Lurch's left shoulder, putting his hands on his hips and giving "the stare." The bartender was opening the beer cans with a church key (remember them?), when suddenly the beer-can smasher let out a horrifying scream and smashed the first full beer the bartender had opened. Beer sprayed everywhere, and the can was smashed flat. It kind of took Lurch by surprise. He threw his hands up in exasperation, then turned and looked at the Korean and said, "You stupid fucking gook!" then nailed him with a right. With a sound like the crack of a bat hitting a homer out of Chavez Ravine, Lurch's fist hit the Korean right on the chin, lifting him off his feet, and throwing him into a bunch of Korean soldiers who had crowded up when the can smasher did his act. To the credit of the Korean sergeant's toughness, the blow didn't knock him out, but it had definitely rung his bell. The other Foul Dudes ran up and formed a perimeter in a semicircle with the bar to our backs. It got deadly quiet, and I thought, "Oh, shit, this is going to get ugly real quick." The dude Lurch hit kind of staggered a bit, trying to get his eyeballs working again. He looked at Lurch and the rest of us for a few seconds then broke out in a huge grin. He snatched one of the open cans of beer off the bar, took a huge drink, and offered it to Lurch. Lurch emptied the can, belched, and the party was on. The Korean sergeant said something in Korean, and the soldiers that were crowded around relaxed. Huge grins abounded, and we carried beers to our table. During the remainder of the evening, I don't think we bought very many beers. The Koreans were very friendly, and we managed to communicate with each other by gestures.

At one point during the evening a Korean sergeant who could speak English walked in. He told us that he was surprised to see us in the club because they had never allowed any Americans into it. We found out that a Korean REMF unit ran the joint, and the husky sergeant was a grunt passing through. They had mistaken us for U.S. airmen, but our tiger hats had thrown them; we didn't have any insignia sewn on, and the dude that Lurch hit thought we were from Special Forces. The drunker the Koreans got, the more they started mewing like cats and smashing cans. We smashed a few cans ourselves. We Lurps were glad that Lurch had taken care of business so we didn't have to resolve the issue by fighting. When we had asked around during the early evening about where to go to drink, the REMFs had warned us about the club, saying no one was allowed in with weapons. Even so, all the Foul Dudes were packing pistols that night, and we wouldn't have hesitated to use them.

After midnight we walked back to our area, but Pizza Joe

remembers that some marine MPs stopped us, and we got in a confrontation with them. Soon a marine major was standing up in his jeep and read us the riot act, but when someone yelled out, "Kill that motherfucker," the jarheads took off. God must take care of his Lurps!

The next afternoon at 1300 hours on 27 October 1967, we were helicoptered out to the 1/327 firebase. While we had been in the rear for that brief time, some of the Lurps found and bought pants and jackets made out of poncho material. Some enterprising mamma-san had sewn some of these outfits together. They looked pretty good but lasted about as long as it took to put them on because they had been sewn together with lightweight cotton thread. It was raining once again, when we left. . . .

While the rest of the Lurps were in the field, new people were recruited into the LRRP detachment: Dennis "Keener" Keene; Robert Rawlings; Steve LeGendre; Edward "Peppy" Wanglarez; "Doc" Doug Norton; and Steve "Crazy Pete" Peterson, with whom I had served in Germany with Paneck, a refugee from Czechoslovakia who had fled from that communist country by flying a small plane into West Germany with his brother and sister-in-law. Enlisting into the United States Army in order to acquire citizenship, Paneck ended up serving on my Division Lurps team later on.

## "Sully"

The 1st Brigade AO was still in Quang Tin Province. We landed at the 1/327 firebase, west of Tam-ky, and immediately integrated into the defensive perimeter. The Lurps' mission was to provide security on the firebase at night and do search-and-destroy patrols during the day in the valleys and draws that surrounded the firebase. This was *not* Lurping; it was standard infantry tactics. We hadn't yet gotten the word on the real reason we were at the firebase. That came later.

Clay Wentworth recalls: "The day before the blocking-force mission, we went out on a patrol and were supposed to be looking for a sniper that had been firing up on the artillery base. We went down in the valley with three teams together and walked down a really big trail. We looked around down there but didn't find anything. Top was with us as we came back up through the valley, off the trail, and started up the hill. The patrol took a break, with "Dirty Ernie" Winston walking point for the team that was on point; he was carrying that sawed-off pump shotgun of his. For some reason he decided to walk farther up the hill. He wasn't gone more than two or three minutes when we heard shots. We all ran up the hill, and as we neared the area, I was looking around while running when suddenly I stepped on a big round rock, and I twisted my ankle and went down but got back up. Dirty Ernie was sitting up there with a bullet hole in his knee. Dirty Ernie had been sitting back against his rucksack facing downhill with a draw on his right side about forty meters away. The sniper had shot uphill and from Dirty Ernie's right, aiming at his heart but hitting him in the right kneecap. One inch higher and he would have drilled Ernie through the heart. We fired up the area and went in looking for the sniper but couldn't find him. Dirty Ernie got his tenth Purple Heart, and we medevacked him out of there. Most of the Foul Dudes never saw him again."

Sgt. Ernest Gregory Winston received his incredible thirteenth Purple Heart later when he was killed in action, on 6 June 1968, in the Ashau Valley, RVN, while operating with Tiger Force.

"We headed back to the artillery position," Wentworth continues. "When we got up there, my ankle was in bad shape, and really hurting. We were in a bunker position, and we went outside the perimeter to a very big rock facing the ridgeline and the valley and with a shaving-cream can we found in our position, we wrote on the rock in really big letters SAT CONG ("kill Cong"). We got rocketed and mortared shortly after."

On the evening of 31 October 1967, all the team leaders went to the battalion TOC (tactical operations center) to get mission briefings and maps. They brought some sundries in for us Lurps, and we were also given two beers per man and mail call. At the time my team was on the southern part of the perimeter in two adjoining bunkers. The meeting ended, and I was walking back with all these sundries, beers, mail, and maps, when suddenly the gooks started mortaring and rocketing the firebase. I immediately went into duck-and-scoot mode and the guys ribbed me when I reached the bunker because I had shaken up the beer.

Pizza Joe Remiro recently wrote me about that time. "The night before Chad and I took off was the first time we were all put together as a team. We left on the same chopper that brought our orders, so we had no idea the night before. I remember really liking the idea of finally having a team made up of my closest friends and Foul Dudes. It was a closer group than Weems's team had been. I can remember Chad, Beaver, and Wentworth were there. Our position was the only one that could see where the mortar rounds and rockets were coming from. We could see smoke and flashes from the enemy rounds leaving their barrels. To spot that position, so the artillery could lay a few rounds in, Beaver opened up, and his tracers drew the line. We were not in any danger because the enemy fire was directed at the top of the hill, nowhere near us. It was close to you since you were coming down from up there with our team supplies. That's why you came running and why we were joking about you shaking up the beer. Beaver's M-60 barrel began turning red and the sandbag caught on fire. Chad began pouring water over the sandbag from a five-gallon can. It was humorous because he stood on top of the sandbags to do it, in clear view of where the enemy fire was coming from. While Beaver and Chad were doing their thing, someone popped some beers. We were all laughing and making a party of it."

Meanwhile up on the hilltop, Top Smith, McIsaac, and the redlegs weren't having as much fun. Wentworth recalls looking back toward the hilltop in time to see a rocket impact directly on the FDC (fire direction center) bunker. Later we found out that casualties and deaths resulted from the direct hit. He can also remember the artillery boys out in the middle of the rocket attack, hanging on the barrels of the 105s, swinging them around to shoot at the enemy.

After the excitement, I distributed the mail and sundries and gave the team a rundown on what would be coming down the following morning. We would be airlifted off the mountaintop, inserted northeast of the firebase, and set up a platoon-sized blocking position. It would be a classic infantry "hammer and anvil" operation. We would be the anvil. The terrain was huge expanses of rice paddies with islands of trees situated among the paddies. Sergeant McKinnon's team, Sergeant Gaskell's team, and my team would be on the operation, with Lieutenant McIsaac in overall control. Not having to pack the extra eighty pounds of our rucksacks, just ass-kicking hardware, water, and one ration would be a plus. Beaver would be carrying the M-60, the rest of the team their basic loads. I would be one man short on this operation because Clay Wentworth was injured.

I got involved with reading a couple of letters and then cleaning my rifle and generally getting my gear squared away for the next day's mission. I got a visit late that evening in my hole from George "Sully" Sullens. We sat around and bull-shitted and smoked a cigarette and got down to the reason for his visit. Sully had been put on a medical profile by Doc Alan "Lurch" Cornett because he had a severe case of jungle rot. He wouldn't be allowed to go into the field without being removed from this profile by one of our medics or by the platoon leader. Sully was at my hole doing some politicking. He told me that he had talked to Top Smith and Lieutenant McIsaac about let-ting him go out on this mission. He figured he wouldn't be holding anybody up, and it wasn't an extended mission. Sully knew I was one man short, and wanted to know if I would intercede on his behalf by talking with Top Smith and McIsaac about letting him go out assigned to my team. I knew Sully well, and all I could see was a good man trying to help his friends out by sticking with them. I asked him if he was sure, and he answered me in his Oklahoma twang, "I wouldn't be here ah-asking." That was good enough for me.

I had first met Sully back in July at Duc Pho. We were between missions and were drinking at an EM (enlisted men's) bar, just a tent with the sides rolled up and a bar of wooden ammo cases. At the time, Sully was assigned to a company in the 501st Signal Battalion and had become acquainted with

Limey Walker. He asked Limey about joining Lurps, and for
some reason Limey sent him over to talk to me, as if I had any
pull. Sully introduced himself as George Buster Sullens Jr.,
and we shot the bull for a while. The other Lurps and I asked
him questions basically relating to commo. The man knew his
stuff and impressed us as someone who would be an asset to
the outfit. I told him to go up and talk to Top Smith, that I
would vouch for him.

I later got to know Sully and really liked the man. He was
quiet, soft-spoken, and could play a good guitar and sing really
well. He was from Pryor, Oklahoma, and his music was influ-
enced by his origins—it was pure country. He used to sing a
particular song he made up especially for Pizza Joe. Out of all
the Foul Dudes, Pizza Joe was Sully's best friend; they were
soul mates. Pizza Joe carried an XM 148 under his M-16 and a
.38-caliber revolver. Sully would get a kick out of him carrying
three weapons and thus the song. The lyrics always started,
"Hey, Joe, where you going with that gun in your hand?" He
made up the words as he went and intermixed our names into
the song. Other lyrics followed the opening: "I'm going out to
hunt the man or maybe I'm going to the promised land." We
never tired of the song and asked Sully to play it often. Sully
was a hell-raising party animal but in a laid-back way. He
could and often did entertain by the hour. He'd pluck and sing
and between songs tell jokes and stories. Of course, Lurch was
his backup. They made a good team entertaining us.

It was late evening as I walked up toward the TOC where
Top Smith and Lieutenant McIsaac were. On the way, I had to
cross the one-bird chopper pad, pausing because a chopper was
landing. I shielded my eyes from the dust it was kicking up.
The chopper settled down, the pilot chopped his power to idle,
and then the door gunners and a couple of medics pulled out
four KIAs just lost by one of the battalion's line companies.
The KIAs, wrapped in ponchos or poncho liners and dragged
to the side of the pad, joined those killed by the rocket that had
struck the FDC bunker. The door gunners flushed the chopper
out with three large buckets of water from the uphill side. I
watched the blood and body fluids come washing out of the

downhill side in a pink stream. The chopper's pilot was looking at me the whole time this was going on. He looked at me, and I looked at him, and a silent communication took place between us as we both shook our heads. The crewman loaded cases of ammo, grenades, and some water onto the helicopter and jumped back on board. The pilot gave me a sad, slow, salute/wave, increased power, and took off, going back to wherever the shit was hitting the fan. As I returned his salute, I silently wished that pilot a safe journey through his war.

I walked on past the dead men and found Top and Mac. I told them what Sully had laid on me and said if they didn't mind, I would take him out with me. They agreed, and I went to see Sully, who was in a bunker with Danny Niehuser and some other men. I briefed him on what would be going down the next morning, not knowing that this would have a tremendous impact on him and everyone around him. Later on it only proved that we all work for the same master: Fate.

That 1 November 1967 dawned a gorgeous beautiful day. A sprinkling of puffy, fleecy clouds floated in a deep-blue sky, a pleasant contrast to all the rain we had been receiving. Early that morning, we got word that John Chadwick and Pizza Joe Remiro would be leaving us that morning because they'd volunteered for Tiger Force (Battalion Recon 1/327). Dirty Ernie Winston and Sully had also volunteered, but Dirty Ernie was out of the field because he had been shot in the kneecap the day before. Sully had changed his mind about going to Tiger Force and pulled his 1049; he wanted to stay with the Lurps. Pizza Joe says, "The morning we got our orders for Tiger Force, Sully came to me and he was almost in tears. He explained how his head was together for the first time in his life. He was short (i.e., his assignment to Vietnam was coming to an end) and finally ready to go home and settle matters that had driven him half nuts. He felt more comfortable finishing his time with the Lurps. He felt terrible, as if he was deserting us. Of course I understood, and told him so. He felt better, we said our good-byes, and Chad and I got on the chopper to the rear."

Pizza Joe and Big Chad wanted to go on the mission but were already assigned to Tigers, so they got turned down. They would take the resupply chopper back to forward rear (Chu Lai) to go through their reassignment to Tiger Force. That left my team with only four men, but at the last minute Bengston was shifted onto my team, which then consisted of Harvey "Beaver" Bieber, Sully, Doc "Wolfman" Kraft, Gunther Bengston, and me. We turned over our fighting positions to the folks who would be pulling security, and we walked uphill to the chopper pad, where we were forming up our chopper loads. The first chopper in was the resupply ship with some ammo and C rations for the firebase. Big Chad, Pizza Joe, and Clay Jay Wentworth boarded the resupply ship. I really didn't want to see them go and was upset over their leaving. They were upset, too. All three were studs and damn good recon men, and I didn't like losing that caliber of individual. Clay Jay would be coming back. We all said our good-byes and wished them well, but it was like watching our brothers going away. It was hard to see Big Chad and Pizza Joe leaving; they were Foul Dudes. I never saw them again.

Along with Lieutenant McIsaac and his RTO, my team boarded the next chopper that came in. We took off and orbited, waiting for the other two choppers that made up our combat assault to form up.

We inserted into a cove of trees on a fairly big island. There wasn't any water in the paddies, so it made for a good LZ. We didn't receive any fire coming in. We did a recon around the area, then went and set up a linear ambush facing out across the wet paddies to our front. The paddies extended out about 150 meters, where they ran into a big island of trees and growth. The island ran east and then cut back south with the paddies extending inward for a ways. It was a good place to set down an anvil and a damn good place to die. We did a short recon back into the island behind us about 100 meters, where we found corpses that had been lying there for a few days. We came back to the original ambush about the time the 1/327 hammer was crunching on the other side of the island to our front. Pretty soon people were running our way in an attempt to get away from the infantry push. People with weapons were running across the open paddies about 400 meters away.

Everyone started firing, with Sp4. Harvey Bieber and Sgt. James Gray doing the most good with their M-60s. Gray was knocking the shit out of them, and several were down. There was a lull in the firing; then another group started crossing the paddies, a little closer to our position. We resumed firing.

After a while we were ordered by the battalion headquarters to go check the bodies for weapons and get a body count. Lieutenant McIsaac reluctantly ordered us to do so. My team and Sgt. Bob McKinnon's team would be going out, with one team in reserve as security. We were the point team, and the order of march was Beaver, myself, Sullens, Bengston, and Doc Kraft. Sergeant McKinnon's team was trailing. I remember going across two paddies full of water. Coming up to the second dike, I stepped up with my right foot on the dike and it crumpled, causing me to slip and fall forward, sticking the barrel of my M-16 right into the mud. As I was falling forward, I remember thinking what a stumblebum I was. Suddenly I felt a hot *crack* extremely close to my right cheek and ear, then several other *crack*s almost like just one string of *crack*s together. Stumbling had saved my life. We were getting shot at with automatic weapons. I fell, rolled to my right, grabbed my sawed-off M-79, and fired at a muzzle flash sixty or seventy meters away, at the edge of the tree line I had glimpsed as I was falling. I rolled onto my left side to get another round, rolling the right side of my body out of the water. In doing so, I happened to face to my right rear. Sully was facedown in the paddy water about twenty meters away, air bubbles and a steady spread of bright pink in the water around his body. That pissed me off. Simultaneously, I saw Doc Kraft running toward him. I turned around and fired my M-79 again, thinking I needed to put out some covering fire for Doc. Then I tried to clean the mud out of the barrel of my M-16. It didn't work, so I rolled over to get another M-79 round and saw Doc Kraft with Sully. I loaded the round and fired again. I had to keep rolling my body out of the water to get rounds for my M-79. Each time I glanced over at Doc Kraft again and could see that he was having trouble working on Sully. Doc was looking around for someone to help prop Sully out of the water so he could have his hands free to work.

Doc Kraft recalls: "I was fifty to seventy feet behind Sully and to his right when I saw him go down hard. The fire was coming from our front and to our left. They had one heavy gun per platoon, and I would say not more than thirty or forty men. I remember the splashes and tracers. I unstrapped my first-aid kit off my back and ran toward Sully, having a hard time moving through the paddy because of the deep water. There was about sixteen inches of water in the wet paddy. I pulled him out of the water, rolled him over, and had trouble holding him out of the water and working on him. I yelled for help and started cutting his gear off. Marty ran over and started helping me."

Holstering my M-79, I picked up my rifle, and started running toward Doc Kraft and Sully. I remember it was like slow motion, and I could see splashes around me going *thlooop*, *tholoop*, like the sound a small rock makes when you throw it into water real fast, only more violently. Little geysers of water exploded up every time a bullet hit. I knew I was attracting fire because I was the only one up and moving. Doc Kraft was hunched over small and trying to cover Sully's body with his own. I got to Doc and Sully, grabbed Sully, and, pulling his back and head onto my chest, I cradled him with my arms. I was kind of lying, leaning out of the water, facing in the direction where the fire was coming from. Doc's back was to the fire, and he calmly started working on Sully as I watched green tracers and rounds hitting around us. We were in the middle of the paddy with Doc kneeling over Sully, his whole back exposed to the fire yet calmly working. I was impressed because that took some big-ass nuts. I couldn't believe how many leeches had gotten on us. With Sully bleeding in the water, they were all over us.

"I was looking for wounds in the upper body, looking for the major bleeders," Doc later told me. "I had dressings out and was stuffing holes in his chest. Usually you can feel with your hands if they're breathing. There wasn't any breathing, so I asked Marty, 'Do we have a pulse?' He replied, 'I don't think so.' Well, I said, 'I think he's dead.' I really did. I would never leave anyone unless I absolutely knew he was dead. Those rounds were on both sides of his nipple line and sternum. I can recall tracers and splashes around us as we were working on Sully."

When Doc asked me if he was breathing and had a pulse, I couldn't tell at first. And then I realized I was just trying to prolong what we both already knew. Sully had been dying as Doc was working on him and I was holding him. He had died in my arms. Doc Kraft kept feeling for a pulse and finally said, "Marty, he's gone. Take this serum albumin to the other guy who was hit."

That's how I found out that someone else had been hit. Doc would follow when he got his medical kit bag zipped back up. I slid out from under Sully's body and took off running. Jumping a paddy dike into a dry paddy, I found Lurch and Boss Weisberger working on Bengston, who had been shot in the throat. The firing was still going strong both ways.

Sergeant McKinnon's team had been inserted third and thus was at the rear of the platoon. Boss, a member of that team, remembers: "We were supposed to be on point, and I was frantically trying to get reoriented. I met up with Lieutenant McIsaac, who asked, 'Where the fuck were you? You were supposed to be up front!' I answered, 'Hold for a second and we'll get up front.' The lieutenant answered, 'No, we can't wait; just move in behind everyone else.' We moved into our ambush site and after a while we started seeing the enemy. We started hammering them. We had some bodies out in the paddies and were asked to check them out. We were in the process of moving out when the unmistakable sound of rounds breaking the sound barrier clapped around my head. I slammed myself into the dirt. Raising my head, I saw Bengston lying on his stomach, his rifle lying untouched by his side. His head was turned away from me. Return fire was mounting from the platoon, and I noticed Bengston hadn't moved. I slid forward, poked Bengston with his M-16 and said, 'Hey man, grab your shit.' There was no movement, and I felt a cold knot inside. Grabbing his right shoulder, I rolled him over. An incredibly bright red spout of blood gushed from Bengston's throat. I grabbed his head and tilted it to one side and hollered for Lurch. Tom Dokos had heard me shout and at first thought I had been hit and was calling for help. He passed the word.

"I told Bengston, 'Get it out of your mouth, spit it out, don't choke on it. We have you, and you're gonna be OK.' Bengston made a hacking sound and dribbled some blood weakly from his mouth. Lurch got to us and began opening Bengston's web gear and shirt. I turned and saw Marty jumping the dike with an IV (serum albumin) setup in his hand. 'It's from Sully; he's dead!' he yelled. Then he was gone. I turned back to Bengston, tying off his arm and milking the air from the tube. Bengston was in shock, the veins in his arm flat and impossible to feel. I slid the needle in but found no blood. Lurch was working on Bengston's throat, and he calmly said, 'Boss, slide it in just like I taught you.' I got it on the second try. Doc Kraft showed up and told me, 'I got him, Boss.' He had moved from Sully's body to help. I returned to the fight."

When I arrived with the serum albumin for Bengston, Doc Lurch was really pissed off at what had come down, and he started yelling at me. He was venting some emotion, and there was no specific reason. I just happened to be there and was his target. I took no offense from it; we were all enraged. I returned to the defensive perimeter behind the paddy dike and began firing my M-79. There was still a lot of incoming fire, and Lieutenant McIsaac ordered in some gunships. They made some gun runs on the periphery of the island where the fire had been coming from. That really stopped the incoming fire. During this whole time, Beaver had been out in the paddies by himself, firing. Beaver was a man you could count on in any situation. While the gunships were making their runs, he came back in.

Lieutenant McIsaac told me to get a couple of men and retrieve Sully's body because he was still lying out there in the paddy, about thirty or forty meters in front of where everybody else was. Tom "Greek" Dokos, Dirk Sasso, and I ran out and grabbed Sully's body. Greek and I both had an arm apiece, and Dirk had his legs. I had hold of his left arm, and it felt like it was going to come off. Sully had been smacked hard, and it felt like mush in there. Dirk Sasso commented to Greek later how heavy and awkward it was to carry Sully's body through the paddy water. We cut a beeline right to the perimeter. Shots were still coming into our defensive perimeter, so we were trying to get out of harm's way. When we vaulted over the dike, we were under fire, and we somehow dropped Sully's body. It landed right on top of Teddy Bear Gaskell, who happened to be reloading his rifle. He was taken by surprise when the body landed on him. We pulled Sully off him and took the body farther down the dike, away from the rest of the Lurps.

Teddy Bear recalls: "Sully had that smell of death. I cooked myself a cup of coffee right there. I was just sitting out there and didn't have anything to look at. I had C-4 that I carried in a claymore bag. I kept my canteen, coffee, and stuff—in case I got separated from everybody I would at least have my coffee. You know, I had my priorities and would keep something like a roll or fruit cake in there. I boiled a cup of coffee while that was going on. I was angry, really pissed off. I was pissed off that we were out there and it was a dumb place to be. There we were at ten or eleven o'clock in the morning, on a bright sunny day, in the middle of the biggest fucking rice paddy I ever saw in the world and I mean that was dumb. We were lucky we didn't have more dead men laying around there."

After a while we got control of the situation enough so that we could bring in a dustoff. When the ship arrived, Greek, Sasso, and I grabbed our dead friend and loaded Sully on the chopper. Lurch and Doc Kraft loaded Bengston. While we were loading our friends, we were taking sporadic fire and heard several rounds hit the helicopter. When the dustoff took off, I happened to look down, and there was a .45-caliber pistol lying on the ground. I picked it up and tucked it in my shirt. The dustoff radioed us and said the crew chief had lost his pistol and wanted to know if we had found it. They asked around, and I never volunteered having found it. The standard issue .45 was hard to come by because they were issued only to officers, crew chiefs, machine gunners, and so on. My friends told me not to report it because it would be written off as a combat loss. The dustoff wasn't about to come back into a hot LZ just to retrieve a pistol.

The gunships worked over the large island where the fire had come from. The line companies had received some strong resistance, but the bulk of the enemy force had slipped eastward, between our position and the advancing infantry. Using helicopters, the 1/327 commander leapfrogged one of his line companies eastward, maintaining contact with the enemy force. Battalion sent some choppers in for us and I remember flying over the bodies of the enemy lying on the ground like broken dolls. And we were missing two brother Lurps who had gone in that morning with us. No matter how often we lost one of our friends, that was always hard to adjust to. But we quietly talked about what had happened, who had been where and done what. Stories surfaced that Sully had a premonition that he would not survive the mission. I was deeply troubled on hearing that; if I'd known, I would not have let Sully talk me into letting him come on the operation. Years later, Pizza Joe told me that on arriving at the rear base camp at Chu Lai that day, George "Rommel" Murphy greeted him with a bewildered, troubled look, saying that somehow a message had been received that Pizza Joe had been killed in action. Pizza Joe adds: "I was shocked and saddened to hear of Sully's death. I loved Sully. We shared a hootch; we set booby traps together, we blew up everything we could tie C-4 to, and Sully told me his secrets. Sully was a Foul Dude. Maybe I should have contacted his family. I feel a little guilty, but I was little more than a teenager, and I still had to survive. I guess I fell back on the first High Saving step: Don't let it pull you down. It would be years before I'd really be able to let myself miss Sully. He is my partner and personal Zen exercise."

We landed back at the firebase and once again took positions on the defensive perimeter. We took some sniper fire, probably from the same Chuck who had shot Ernie Winston in the knee. The firebase was mortared and rocketed again that evening, and it started raining again.

After Sully's death, a letter postmarked 18 November 1967 was received by Boss Weisberger. It was written by Mrs. Mary

Leaellen Jones, Sully's sister. A month or two before Sully's death, Boss was going on R&R but had no money, so Sully loaned it to him. Flying out to rejoin us in the field, Boss had no means of paying Sully back. After Sully was killed, Boss came out of the field and sent home the money he owed Sully along with a letter. Boss's mother also wrote to the Sullens family offering her condolences. After he arrived back in the States, Boss spoke with Mrs. Sullens on the telephone about her son's death. Boss's mother was crying as she overheard the conversation and afterward made the comment to Boss, "All of you were our sons." I suppose any mother who had a son in the Nam took a loss with every casualty.

I would like to add this letter to the story because it sheds light on the times as well as the sorrow that the families experienced when one of our friends was killed or injured. We simply couldn't know at the time, but after all these years it still tugs at my heart. Twenty-five years later, I had a telephone conversation with Mrs. Jones. During the conversation, she asked me how her brother had died. I was deeply surprised at the emotional impact relating the facts to her had on me. As I was telling her, I was mentally transported through time, and it was like reliving it all over.

Mrs. Cora Sullens had three sons. The eldest, Harold Sullens, was killed while serving as a combat medic with the 1/5, 1st Cavalry Division on exactly the same day, same month— 1 November—during the Korean War in 1950, seventeen years earlier. Sully was from a long line of men who had served their country. His dad, George Buster Sullens Sr., who also was nicknamed "Sully" while in the army, served during World War II and was wounded. He was at Normandy and in the Battle of the Bulge. Sully's mother had a premonition on the day that Sully was killed. It was Halloween night in the States, and Mrs. Jones and Sully's mom were taking the children trick or treating in Tulsa, Oklahoma. Mrs. Sullens was suddenly overcome with grief and told her daughter that George had just died. She knew as only a mother knows. How many fighting men have heard their friends' last dying words, calling for their mothers. Oh, so many.

This was a letter from the heartland of America. It added humility and kindness to our lives, which were overshadowed by the brutality and viciousness of war. It spoke not of hate but of forgiveness, a noble moral value we could understand, but a luxury we simply could not afford. We were tied into this drama called war, and the price of admission was our lives. I remember hearing about the letter in Vietnam, though I never read it. It was one of those special things that one never forgets. It made all of us realize that someone really cared what was happening to us. It was within the extended family of the Lurps, all of us were tied into this, and the families were an extension of us. It reads:

Dear Sandy,

I am George Sullens' sister and I'm writing to tell you how much your letter to mother was appreciated. Of course it was also read and appreciated by me and our family. At this time it is on our church bulletin board. All of the people loved George and you and your mother's letters were a great consolation, not because of the money but because you were George's friend. I believe we have a picture of you and George together.

I would like for you to know that our church is praying three times a day for you men and we are asking God to strengthen you and comfort you when you're under such a terrible pressure as you all have to face. I guess I really never realized how much so until the Sgt. that escorted George's body home talked to us. He was very nice and let us know where George was hit. We could not tell by looking at him and God was so good to take him quick if he had to go. God knows the future, Sandy, and if your soul is ready then all is well. God has been so good to us through all this and I thought within myself that mother couldn't and wouldn't make it through because George was her baby, but she came through with victory and has a desire to help all the youth she possibly can.

You men will never know what a blessing you are to the people in America and our hearts go out to you. Please don't hold George's death against the "Charlies," as you call them. They are fighting for their country, also, and the one that shot George was some mother's son.

I'm glad you cared that much for him, but please don't let it cause you to hate. It has only caused more love in the States. We loved him dearly and we will miss him terribly, but he died a hero and he would have liked that. He would have been so proud if he could have seen everything that took place because of him. He looked as if he were just asleep with a slight smile on his lips. The embalmer did a wonderful job on the wound and the Sgt. said they had taken special care. (He didn't know why, but we did.)

Excuse me for writing such a lengthy letter but I have been crying and I'm writing to you instead of George. If any of the boys would like for us to write them please send me their addresses. Maybe some have no one to write to, so we would love to write to them if they'd like. I also have some young lady friends in our church that would like to write them on the basis that you're all over there fighting for us back home.

Sandy, thank you for being such a good friend to George and always remember we care and are praying for you. I hope God permits you all to come back home if it is His will. Always trust the giver of life.

Yours Sincerely,
Mrs. Jones

**9**

# LONG RANGE RECON
## 1 101
### Bao-loc

With the successful close of Operation WHEELER, the 1st Brigade redeployed from Chu Lai back to its permanent rear base at Phan-rang. We were on a four-day Thanksgiving holiday stand-down.

The LRRP detachment would be transported back to Phan-rang on a Navy LST. For the administrative purposes of the movement, the Lurps were assigned to the 326 Engineer Company and M.Sgt. Lloyd "Top" Smith was in charge of the Lurps.

"There were two other companies, an engineer, and a line company," Top Smith recalls. "The engineer company commander, a captain, called in all the platoon sergeants and said that the other company was allowing their people to drink beer, but our company would not drink on this movement. He said, 'I want you to know right now that they will not drink.' We were attached to them, so I went back and got everybody together, and told them, regardless of what the other company did, we were under orders that we could not drink on the way back. Everybody fully understood that as long as we were attached to 326 Engineer Company, we had to follow their commander's orders. The Lurps weren't happy about it, but they all understood. So in the afternoon, this captain came down on the deck of the LST. He walked over to me and said, 'Did you get the instructions on no drinking?' I answered, 'Yes.' So he said, 'Come on with me.' I went with him, and

Bachek was just busting open another can. I called Bachek and got a hold of him and reamed his butt out, and I said, 'Now do you understand there is no drinking? We cannot drink on this movement unless the engineer company commander changes his policy?' Bachek understood, so the next morning we had pulled into Phan-rang, where we were to off-load from the LST. The captain called to me and said, 'Come up here.' He told me, 'I want you to get these nondisciplined people that you've got, who cannot follow instructions, and unload from this LST right now!' The tide was out, and we're waiting for it to come in so we could unload the equipment. I told him we weren't completely docked yet, and we wouldn't have our equipment. He said I could leave one man with our equipment, and to get everybody else off. I asked him what the problem was, so he turned around, and there was Bachek with his side-kick Rudy Lopez, sitting right alongside of him, with a can of beer in his hand. I mean, he didn't even bother to hide it; he did it right in front of this captain. I put Walt Bachek on a two-week restriction after arriving in Phan-rang and seriously thought about giving him an Article 15. I made arrangements for transportation of the platoon and stayed with the equipment. While waiting for our equipment to be off-loaded, the engineer captain was in his jeep, and he said, 'Top, you want a ride?' I said, 'No, I'm waiting for my vehicles.' "

While we had been docked in Phan-rang, waiting for our LST to move closer to shore, a bunch of us Lurps were jumping into the water from the decks, which probably added to Top Smith's problems as the man in charge. Walt Bachek was lightly punished, and the rest of us should have had our heels locked right alongside him. But Top Smith really cared for his Lurps.

Operation KLAMATH FALLS in Binh Thuan and Lam Dong Provinces would be the next area of operation for the Puking Buzzards. Lt. Dan McIsaac was leaving us. That didn't sit very well with the platoon, and we all went down to Headquarters Company and talked to the officer in charge of reassignments. We pleaded the case on behalf of Mac, who wasn't thrilled at the idea of leaving, either. We felt we had an extremely capable officer, and the integrity and morale of the unit were at their peak. All the Lurps were extending their tours to stay with the outfit because we were working well as a team. As the commanding officer, Mac had shown genuine concern for our morale and welfare. He had tried to shield us from officers who wanted to use Lurps in operations that weren't geared to our training or manning—we could do them, but it wouldn't have really benefited the brigade. As a unit, we trusted him, and that underscored his ability as an officer. Now our situation was being very seriously threatened. But reversing his reassignment was not to be. In its infinite wisdom, the army transferred Mac out, terming it a "career enhancement" move. Teddy Bear, Jaybird, Doc Kraft, and I left the Lurp platoon at Phanrang to go on extension leaves.

Fortunately the Foul Dudes ended up getting a very capable officer by the name of Lt. Tom K. Kinane, an Irish Catholic from Brooklyn and a rogue rugby player. A graduate of West Point, he came to us from an infantry company in the 1/327, where he had served as a platoon leader. He brought with him two good men from his former platoon, Ralph Duckett and Gene Ackerson. The platoon moved to Phan-thiet when I departed.

Clay Jay Wentworth remembers: "The next place that we went to was Phan-thiet. Lieutenant McIsaac had left, and we got Lieutenant Kinane at Phan-thiet. When they said we were going to Phan-thiet, I knew what that was all about because I had been down there on an operation as a line doggie: it was some nasty country, really hot, dry, and water was so hard to come by that the army had to set up a seawater desalinization depot. We pulled some missions out of there, but they were just normal recon missions, and I don't remember us finding anything down there. I also remember we were out in the field, and we'd come in and Lieutenant Kinane told us we were supposed to go up to have a group picture of the Lurps taken at noontime. He told us everybody had to stay straight, he didn't want anybody messed up, and all that kind of stuff. We partied on anyway, and when we got up there I remember Dennis "Keener" Keene had forgotten his rifle, so he went in and borrowed a souvenir AK from a colonel. I think Keener was drunk. We're standing there and were waiting for Lieutenant Kinane to come up, and he was about ten minutes late. He had told us not to get messed up, not to party too hard. And here comes Lieutenant Kinane. He was so drunk that he was doing one of those deals where he would stagger twenty feet to the left, then stagger twenty feet to the right, and make about two or three feet forward progress."

## Bao-loc

As General Westmoreland's Fire Brigade, the 1st Brigade, 101st Airborne, was next sent to Bao-loc, eighty kilometers north of Phan-thiet, in Lam Dong Province. Bao-lac was one of the few places where the Lurps felt like they were doing something worthwhile. The Foul Dudes partied when they could, and frequented a certain bar boom house. Eddie Cecena, being dark complected, was really popular because the Montagnard women thought he was so handsome. That was the place where an ARVN soldier's girlfriend walked into the bar, and the ARVN soldier, in a fit of jealousy, threw in a grenade. Tom Dokos and another Lurp had luckily just left the bar. One of the most interesting occurrences was when Clay Wentworth and some other Lurps at Bao-loc met a Vietnamese man who was getting married, and he invited them to his wedding reception. They were treated very well, and the Vietnamese were very happy to have them; being South Vietnamese patriots, they thought the Americans were doing a good job. Clay says they ate a lot and drank whatever was there. The reception is one of his most positive memories of Vietnam.

Sgt. David Sloan went to a small Montagnard village on the outskirts of Bao-loc. Sloan, Wentworth, and several other Lurps walked into the village and found a place that served food, so they sat down and ordered some groceries. They were sitting there eating when in walked an armed VC squad. The VC sat down and also ordered food. Of course, the Lurps knew right away those guys were not South Vietnamese soldiers. So both sides sat, nervously eating, as they eyeballed each other.

The VC, finishing first, slipped out the front. As soon as the VC left, the Lurps, not knowing what the VC might have in mind, beat feet out the back.

"We had some interesting things that happened up there," Wentworth recalls. "We had two records, the Beatles' *Sgt. Pepper* and the Doors. Pizza Joe had brought them back from extension leave. We played them on a battery-operated record player that took eight D-sized batteries. We played them over and over, and they got pretty scratched up. One night ol' Superspade was so frustrated that he came walking through the big tent we were in with his pistol out saying, 'I want to hear some *soul music*!'"

During one recon mission out of Bao-loc that Clay was on, Brother Weems was the team leader and he was walking point. They went out on the overflight to choose an LZ and spotted one that looked good from the air. The plan was to insert about an hour before dark. But when the team got off the ship, they discovered that all the grass had been burned, and the LZ was thick with ash. With the helicopters hovering, the rotor blades made the ashes swirl around, and it turned pitch black. When the team unassed the chopper, they couldn't see their hands in front of their face, much less the wood line. Of course the ashes were also flying straight up in the air, and it was like putting out a big smoke signal, saying: 'Here we are!' The ashes finally settled, and Brother Weems set up by the LZ for a few minutes, then decided to move out. Clay hadn't gone more than thirty meters up a hill before he came across a steep trail that went up over the side of the ridgeline. Clay had been a line doggie for six months, and he knew what it looked like when a company goes up a steep hill. This was a trail that looked like a company had recently gone through. The team followed the trail to the top of the ridgeline, and when they arrived, they eyeballed the high-speed trail going both ways. Suddenly, they heard pots and pans rattling and people talking and dogs barking—all moving in their direction. The team knew they had been compromised and the gooks were looking for them, so they went back down the hillside to their LZ, and asked for an extraction. The rear didn't want to extract the team at first, but Brother

Weems demanded extraction because he thought there was probably a company-sized group up there looking for them. After dark, they moved out about 500 meters to a secondary LZ and set up a perimeter. Soon an extraction ship came out for them. They had to use a strobe light to bring the ship in. It came in with the door gunners firing up the wood line. The team knew that rear base was pissed off at them for getting extracted, but they felt they were being hunted and that there was no question about it.

On another recon mission out of Bao-loc, again with Brother Weems as the team leader, Clay recalls they had been heliborne into an LZ at dark and then set up for the night. Waking up the next morning, they got a call from higher up saying that a captured NVA officer had pinpointed a battalion-sized base camp, down at the base of the mountain the team was on. The team went to check it out.

Clay Wentworth was walking point, really slowly. They got about halfway down when base called up to say they'd decided to bring in a line battalion. So they sent the team back up to the top of the hillside to expand the LZ. The Lurps spent the day up there blowing trees and getting the LZ set up. Later in the afternoon, here came the line doggies. Clay remembers that he and Marty Dostal were watching their approach when the command chopper landed and someone talked to Brother Weems. The team got extracted. The Lurps never learned whether or not the line doggies found the base camp.

## The Fight at Bao-loc

The Foul Dudes were alerted for several missions from the Operations and Intelligence S-2/S-3 shop. Two heavy teams (ten or twelve men per team) were to be deployed in two different locations overlooking a shallow valley that ran west to east. On the eastern and northern edge would be a heavy team under the command of Sgt. Dave Sloan. Sgt. Craig Vega's team made up the second half of the heavy team, and he was ATL. A heavy team under S.Sgt. Ronald "Brother" Weems would be inserted on the back side of a hill mass that overlooked a suspected NVA base camp. They would be operating west and on the southern edge of the valley that both teams were monitoring. They were to recon the area and see if Chuck was around. The ATL and senior scout on the mission was Sgt. Clay Wentworth.

The heavy team leaders and ATLs went on an aerial overflight and picked primary and secondary LZs. The two heavy teams were inserted without any problems. Brother Weems's team was inserted on a ridge that ran off a large mountain mass away from the recon zone. They sat up near the top of the mountain overlooking a valley. Pulling two- and three-man patrols, the Lurps reconned the sprawling mountaintop but found no fresh sign of the enemy. A few days later Operations and Intelligence decided to extract the heavy team.

Sergeant Sloan's heavy team had detected and reported various groups of enemy forces moving back and forth through their recon zone. Prompted by these sightings, Operations and Intelligence decided to reinsert Brother Weems's heavy team into the same AO two days later. On 22 December 1967, using a different LZ, Brother Weems's heavy team was again inserted. They worked their way back close to the position they'd occupied two days earlier, then spent two uneventful days monitoring the valley. On the afternoon of the third day, Brother Weems and Clay Wentworth decided to take a closer look in the valley as a two-man recon team. Sergeant Wentworth, walking point, worked his way down slowly through a single-canopy draw. He found sign of the enemy and pointed it out to Brother Weems. They agreed it was fresh and pressed farther into the valley. On the valley floor they saw and heard many people chopping wood. Slowly and silently, they made their way back up to the team. Brother Weems called the information back to Operations and Intelligence. Farther east, on the opposite side of the valley, Sergeant Sloan was reporting large groups of NVA moving around his team.

Feeling they were getting the pulse on the enemy activity, Operations and Intelligence decided to commit two line companies from the 2/327 into the area.

Sp4. Tom "Greek" Dokos could see that the valley was

heavily vegetated, very green, with the thickest vegetation to his left. Directly below him, the vegetation thinned out a bit, becoming thick jungle once again on his right. It was a sunny late afternoon when the line companies swept the valley floor from the west. The line doggies were almost directly below Greek when they made contact. The battle started out as pops and cracks, like popcorn popping, but it didn't take long to get heavier. Suddenly it became a roar, and he could no longer distinguish individual weapons. It was a huge firefight, with a lot of firepower going back and forth. Unlike the area where the team was, the valley was heavily vegetated so all Greek could see of the firefight was the smoke haze from the weapons being discharged, filtering through the tree canopy below. Starting out as a light wisp of smoke, it thickened as the firefight intensified until a thick, smoky haze enveloped the treetops over the area. The firefight raged for two or three hours.

In radio communication with the line companies, Brother Weems received a call telling him that the NVA were breaking contact and that he was to watch to see where they might head. There wasn't much cover on the top of the hillside, and since the heavy team was concealed, they would have to move into the open to better observe the valley. Unable to find a suitable observation point, Brother Weems picked a good defensive position at the top of a vegetated draw. The enemy would be attempting to leave the valley, and that draw was a possible avenue of escape. Starting with Sgt. Clay Wentworth on the right flank, the team set in on a linear position. On line to Sergeant Wentworth's right were Sp4. Eddie Cecena, Sp4. Tyrone Woods, Sp4. Eddie Moroch, Sp4. Peppy Wanglarez, Sgt. Jerry Prouty (RTO), S.Sgt. Ronald "Brother" Weems, Sp4. Doc Jones, Sp4. Tom "Greek" Dokos, and Sp4. Harvey "Beaver" Bieber. The team set up among some boulders. To their front, toward the valley and draw, the terrain was flat and sloped downhill, and covered with short grass forming a small clearing about twenty yards wide with a few boulders strewn about. At the downhill edge of the clearing, the foliage turned into thick, dry, noisy brush about three or four feet high. The noisy part of the brush stretched about thirty yards before

heavier, leafy, moist greenery that would muffle movement
became predominant. The heavy team was overlooking the
mouth of the draw. To the Lurps' back was thick jungle vegetation that abruptly ended on a cliff that fell off the back side of
the ridge. Overhead foliage was sparse at the team's position.
Movement out of the draw would naturally channel toward the
team's position, then slide toward the team's right where a
natural saddle formed. The Lurps set out eight claymore mines,
starting at their right about thirty meters, covering some dry
shrubbery that lipped up to the natural saddle on the ridge, then
following pretty much on line with the end of the dry vegetation before wrapping around the front of the team's position to
the left. To protect the team from the mines' backblast, most of
the claymores were placed on the far side of boulders. The
Lurps had covered any anticipated movement coming out of the
draw. Brother Weems also plotted artillery concentration
points on the natural saddle to their right and down into
the draw.

Around 0400 hours on Christmas morning 1967, something
woke Sergeant Wentworth. He smelled wood smoke. It was
cold that morning on the mountain. Aided by a full moon, he
raised his head to see who was on guard. Moroch was on duty,
and he was hurriedly waking people. Clay could hear faint
movement coming straight up the draw toward the Lurps and
more movement to his right flank.

Because of the cold, Greek Dokos was not sleeping very
well that Christmas morning. He was pissed because he had
brought a wool blanket out on the mission, and it had been fine
till it got wet. Now he had to hump that heavy thing around and
swore it would be the last time. Most of the men were wearing
their woolen sweaters. Beaver and Greek had been awake for
some time, and they woke Brother Weems when they heard
movement. Weems sat up with his poncho liner draped over
his head like a hooded robe, holding the liner under his chin
with his hand. The moon was very bright, and Greek could see
Brother Weems clearly. He sat listening a moment, then
smiled and whispered a classically outrageous Weems statement: "Good, we'll attack them!" The team was awake and

ready. As the enemy entered the noisy brush, the sounds got louder. The enemy wasn't moving in a single or double file, but rather spread out on line through the dry crackling brush. There was a bunch of them, and they were plainly trying to get away from the infantry below.

Brother Weems had knee-crawled over by Sergeant Wentworth to talk with him about his plan of action. Now he slowly stood up and looked downslope into the bright moonlit area of dry growth. He quickly came back down and said to Sergeant Wentworth, "Man, about two platoons are out there, coming our way. Okay, everybody, grab two hand grenades. I'll blow my claymore as a signal, and everyone detonate your claymores, then throw two hand grenades out."

The word was passed to all the team members. Brother Weems wanted to deal the enemy a shocking blow right away and take the initiative away.

The team lay there, waiting silently. Judging by the noise of the movement approaching, the enemy was centered right in front of them in a line, and getting louder. And closer. As the line of NVA soldiers entered the clearing, seven claymores were detonated, followed by twenty hand grenades in quick succession. That shocked and devastated the enemy.

After the claymores and grenades exploded, there was a brief lull. Then moans, cries, and grunts could be heard in front of the team's position. These attracted a flurry of grenades from the Foul Dudes, followed up by full automatic fire from the team's ten M-16s. The team put out massive firepower and kept it up. Any movement or moan was answered by grenades and rifle fire.

On the right flank, Sgt. Clay Wentworth had not detonated his claymore. He had a strong feeling it might serve him well later. But he was pitching hand grenades where he felt they were effective.

Wentworth describes the action: "Fire was starting to come in, and the first thing I saw was a Charlie about three feet away from me. He had crawled up that close. Eddie Cecena's head was positioned off my left boot. That VC was lying there, and he had a carbine. This guy was shooting right past Cecena's head and over my foot. Every time he pulled the trigger, I could see him in his muzzle flash. I promptly fired him up and killed him. I heard an explosion inside the perimeter, and Wanglarez yelled out, 'I'm hit in the head!' The team kept firing, and when the firing tapered off a little, I went over to check out Wanglarez. Doc Jones was working on him. Peppy Wanglarez had taken a small piece of shrapnel in his head, not a very serious wound. He was really more upset about not having any ammunition. He couldn't find any ammo, and I gave him a couple of magazines. I went back to my position. By this time, Brother Weems and Prouty had moved behind us about five meters. They were under a poncho with a flashlight and on the radio, getting artillery set up. I was back out on the right flank by myself and could hear the NVA in the bushes. They had shifted over to the right flank. I don't know how many of them came up, but they assaulted us on the right flank, where I was by myself. When I heard the NVA coming up on the bushes, I detonated my claymore and opened up on them, then threw three more grenades. Next thing I heard the gooks staggering back down the hill, falling over. And then we all heard the gooks out in the clearing, crying and moaning. Everytime I heard a moan, I threw a grenade at the sound."

With his preplotted artillery concentration points, Brother Weems started pounding the draw with 105mm artillery, bringing the artillery fire up the draw to within forty meters of the team's position. He then shifted the fire to the natural saddle and worked it back down into the draw. Having exhausted its supply of hand grenades, the team took blocks of C-4 and imbedded empty brass in them, stuck a blasting cap and fuse into each block, pulled the igniters, and threw them into the dry brush area. Brother Weems called for gunships and was informed the gunships would be at the team's position with first light. By 0500 hours, the action was all but over.

As it was getting light, the enemy started to withdraw. At dawn, Wentworth saw two gunships hanging in the morning light. He also noticed that what had once been an area of dry brush about three feet tall looked as if someone had come in with a rotary lawn mower and cut it down to ankle height.

Sergeant Wentworth had only one magazine and only fifteen rounds in it. The team pulled back right to the cliff's edge, and the gunships went to work, raking the area directly in front of the team's position and really tearing it up. As they made their runs, both pilots of the gunships excitedly radioed the Foul Dudes, and told them that there were a bunch of dead NVA and weapons lying all over the hillside. When they heard this, the heavy team stood up and gave a victory cheer. Behind the gunships came two slicks to extract the Lurps. On the gunship's third pass, the heavy team moved right up the ridgeline, past the natural saddle, to a flat spot that served as the extraction LZ. The TOC wanted the Lurps out if for no reason other than almost everyone was out of ammo. A line company had been moving in their direction up the draw and would sweep the contact area for weapons and packs.

As the two slicks flew back in formation to the base camp, Sergeant Wentworth got a call on the radio. On the other slick was a buddy from Charlie Company, 1/327, who had extended to be a door gunner. Sergeant Wentworth gave him a thumbs-up sign.

Brother Weems's heavy team got back on Christmas morning to find that packages for some of them had just arrived from the States. One of these packages was for Clay Wentworth, from his mother, who had sent him two fifths of hard liquor. One was broken, but the other was still intact. He took the cap off the bottle and threw it away; it was party time, and with the adrenaline still racing, the Lurps started partying down. As the liquor flowed, they sang one of Doc Brian Kraft's favorite Christmas songs:

Jingle Bells
Mortar shells
Charlie's in the grass. You can take your Merry Christmas and shove it up your ass!

While the Lurps had been in the field, Headquarters and Headquarters Company had gotten a new executive officer, a little black dude, a lieutenant. Because the Lurps were attached to Headquarters Company for "beans and bullets," H&HC was a constant source of irritation. The Foul Dudes were in their hootch celebrating the morning's ambush and the fact that they were out of the field, when the black lieutenant walked in and started raising hell. He demanded to know why they were in their tents and not on duty, why no one had called the tent to attention when he walked in—just plain asinine bullshit. The Foul Dudes ignored him and pretended he wasn't there. Finally, Sgt. Clay Wentworth, fed up with the idiot lieutenant, stood, looked him in the eye, raised the bottle, and, taking a long healthy drink, said something that cut to the heart of the subject: "Sir, you don't belong here!" Taking a hard look around him and realizing he was in way over his level, the lieutenant backed out of the tent and left. When Lieutenant Kinane heard about him later, he jumped all over the black lieutenant's ass. The lieutenant never bothered the Lurps again. And the Foul Dudes partied on!

# 10

# Song Be

On 14 January 1968, men of the 1st Brigade 101st Airborne Division started arriving in the Song Be, Binh Long Province. Song Be was strategically located on the Cambodian border, in the middle of a major North Vietnamese Army staging area. It was also one of the main resupply points where the Ho Chi Minh Trail crossed into South Vietnam. The LRRP detachment was one of the first elements of the 1st Brigade to arrive in the Song Be area. The Lurps were promptly put on security and defense of the perimeter surrounding the base camp. The airfield was located just outside of the town of Song Be, up on a plateau. A heavy expanse of bamboo abutted the runway and grew on the plateau. To the east of the runway, about one mile away, Nui Ba Ra rose 2400 feet, overlooking one end of the airfield and the town of Song Be. The 1st Brigade forward base was on the northeast side of the airfield, on the plateau. The engineers bulldozed out areas in the thick bamboo fields to accommodate the various units of the brigade. The earth was red, and red dust soon permeated everything.

Song Be was a wild place. Clay Wentworth says that on the rare occasions when he went into town, he saw the enemy intermixed with the populace, and they were not happy at his presence. The enemy encountered in the Song Be area were NVA regulars, and they were not shy about letting their presence be known. Soon after the brigade moved into the area, Chuck set up a mortar at the end of the runway and shot down a C-130, using a mortar tube as an antiaircraft weapon. As soon as the brigade landed, the enemy started probing actions and sniper activity. The brigade responded by intensifying patrols and setting night ambushes. These patrol assignments were handed to the LRRP detachment. A couple of uneventful patrols were carried out by the Lurps before they hit paydirt.

The brigade staff eventually noted that the NVA were setting ambushes in one area and utilizing certain trails to infiltrate it. The LRRP detachment was to patrol this area during the day and set ambushes during the night. The ambush site was to be picked at the patrol's discretion. A heavy team was put together under the command of S.Sgt. Lester "Superspade" Hite. The patrol members included Clay Wentworth, Tom Dokos, Harvey Bieber, Ralph Duckett, Gene Ackerson, Craig Vega, Dennis Keene, Doc Norton, Steve Peterson, Tyrone Woods, and Peter Rossi. The heavy team exited the perimeter wire, walking off the plateau and patroling toward the base of the solitary mountain that held the target area. During their patrol, they found a suitable ambush site and returned to it that evening.

Tom "Greek" Dokos recalls: "We went out on that mission expecting to get Chuck, that's how much we felt the enemy was moving about. We hadn't been in the area before, but it didn't take long to figure it out from the markings on one of the main trails we found and how well worn it was. We found a good ambush site and set up. We were in a tree line, and in front of us, where we thought the movement would come from, was a small clearing about twenty-five meters long. Short grass grew in the clearing two or three feet high. Beyond the clearing, the vegetation and tree line started again. The trail came out of the tree line and ran through the clearing, through our wooded area, headed toward the brigade perimeter. I felt we had moved into the ambush site too early because we set our claymores out, covering the kill zone, and then sat around waiting, not expecting anyone until later that evening, when it would be getting dark."

Clay Wentworth and Peter Rossi were rear security. The ambush site was on the main trail that ran parallel to the moun-

tain, and their position was twenty-five meters off a back trail
that intersected it at a ninety-degree angle, coming in from the
mountain.

Clay Wentworth set his claymore up on the back trail. It was
his custom when setting out his claymores to set the mine, then
pause and listen for a while before inserting the blasting cap.
Things were quiet. He armed his claymore and returned to his
rear security position with Rossi.

"It was still light, and I figured Chuck was hours from
showing up," Wentworth recalls. "I figured I would have time
for one more cigarette. I sat down and leaned back against my
rucksack, which was against a tree, and I laid my rifle right
beside me. I lit my cigarette with a Zippo lighter my good
friend Marty Dostal had recently given me. Engraved on it was
Snoopy with a pair of jump wings and the words 'Dostal
LRRP.' I held the lighter in my hand about sixteen inches away
from my face and grooved on it for a second. All of a sudden,
here come a couple of green tracers between me and the
lighter—right between my eyes and the lighter! My reaction
was that I rolled over on top of my rifle and jumped up with my
rifle in the middle of this thing. Everything was opening up,
and it was really cool. I looked out toward where the fire was
coming from and saw all these green tracers coming in, about
sixteen inches above the ground. I automatically pulled up my
16 and could see the muzzle flashes. I followed one line of
green tracers and saw the muzzle flash where they started. I
allowed for the length of an AK and let go a burst. I knew I got
the dude, because his tracers were coming in level, and as I was
firing, the tracers started rising, like the guy was hit but he was
still holding the trigger down. As he was falling backward, the
tracers were going in the air. What the hell was the dude
thinking, carrying tracers in his first magazine? But it was all
right by me."

Meanwhile, Dokos was eyeballing movement coming out
of the far tree line into the clearing on the trail.

"I was seeing two of them," Dokos recalls. "One right
behind the other, both carrying AK-47s, and a third one
coming out of the tree line. Then something happened. We

were going to let them get right into the middle of the clearing and fucking make sure we wasted them. The first two were already close, twenty-five or thirty feet away. I don't know if they noticed something and stopped, and then somebody opened up, or what the deal was. But something initiated the opening rounds, and the shit really hit the fan. Everyone who had a clear shot opened up on rock and roll. The first two guys went down—I mean right down quick—and the third guy went down as he was firing. We couldn't see the bodies because they were lying flat in the grass. We waited for a while, and nobody else was in the tree line. The third guy had come out a little behind the other two, and we weren't receiving any fire from him if he was still alive. We weren't expecting large groups because they had been operating in small team cells. So we waited and didn't get any return fire. We watched the bodies, to see if one would rise. On the edge of the clearing and the opposite side of the trail from my position was a lone tree with brush around the base. Duckett went out real quick; he didn't wait very long because he wanted the AK the first guy was carrying. He said he wanted the AK, and he must have knocked that first guy down. He crawls out there with his M-16, and he got pretty close. I wasn't sure because the grass was tall and blocked my view. All of a sudden, the third Chuck is getting up, kneeling. We thought he was dead. But now he's aiming his AK at Duckett and starts firing. It happened so fast, it took all of us by surprise. Duckett is about twenty feet from the lone tree, and starts rolling over and over toward the tree with AK rounds following, peppering the ground and stitching right up the tree as Duckett got behind it. Duckett is a pretty cool customer. He comes up kneeling and leans out to the side of the tree, and now they're both firing at each other at point-blank range! Goddamn! (laughs) You know, it's movie time! They're both blazing away at each other on their knees, and the Charlie lost. He got hit in the head. You could see it happen when the guy's head snapped back. We're all watching with our jaws on the ground. Duckett got his AK, and by this time it's starting to get dark. We didn't want to get the rest of the weapons and the stuff laying out in the clearing in case any more Charlies show up. It was not important. We waited until morning to do that."

All night long, the Foul Dudes were shooting M-79 rounds out toward the trail where the Charlies had come from. The next morning Craig Vega, Clay Wentworth, and a couple of other Lurps went out to check the bodies and gather the weapons. They examined the Charlie who Duckett had done his little dance with. When a Lurp picked up the AK-47 and released the magazine, he found that it was empty, and the AK was on full auto. Jacking the bolt back, he found one round in the chamber. So that dude had died fighting, with just one shot left. One of Duckett's rounds had struck right along the weapon's receiver group, right by the bolt, glanced off and hit the Charlie in the face, killing him. A couple of other rounds had hit the stock. All the Lurps were saying, "Goddamn. One more round and he might have done it!" The Foul Dudes gathered the three enemy weapons and web gear and went back inside brigade perimeter for some rest.

## Going Home

During leave back in the States, after I completed my first tour with the Lurps, I was sitting in the Cosmopolitan Bar in Rockville Centre, Long Island, the hometown of Captain Kangaroo. Earlier we had eaten some very good Italian food, and we stopped by the Cos bar to drink a few beers. It was Allen (Teddy Bear) Gaskell's favorite watering hole, catering to the college crowd, young people, our peers. TB and I were twenty-one years old. I was TB's guest, so he was showing me the town. It was New Year's Eve day, and I was starting to come down with the flu. We had drunk a couple of pitchers of beer with two of his friends and a couple of college girls, one of them a pretty blond with blue eyes and a determination to inhale not only all the beer she could, but also a drink made with gin and other things. Something was brewing in this young lady, I thought, like she wanted to ask me the time of day. I could also feel attitude in her—and in other people in the bar—something akin to when you're approaching trouble, big trouble.

She downed her mixed drink, slammed the glass down, bored into me with her .44-mag eyeballs and spit out, "Well, how many babies did you kill in Vietnam?"

I was midsip and almost swallowed the beer glass. I didn't know the subject of Vietnam had even been discussed in our surroundings, but it didn't take a Rhodes scholar to figure it out: TB and I were deeply tanned and had short hair. Like a good ambush, her attack was deadly and effective. A one-year-tour Lurp, I had to be a one-year-cool Lurp, but that was tough with claymore mouth and napalm eyes raking me. The cute blond college coed was trying to blow my ass away while I was trying to draw on my Foul Dude training to determine the best way to counterattack. I knew I was in her gun sights. Around us ears were stretching and waving in the direction of our booth. Snickers and guffaws could be heard; she hadn't exactly whispered. I drained my glass of beer, stalling for time and going over the options: (A) I could grab the pitcher and pour it over her head to, you know, kind of cool her down; (B) I could grab the pitcher of beer, pour it over her head, and then smash her face with it and fight the whole bar—tempting, but too harsh for such an innocent statement; or (C) like a lightbulb going on, I could employ the most gracious axiom of the Foul Dude's High Saving steps: "Let it live." I set my glass down, emitted a healthy belch of malodorous garlic breath right in her face, stared her right in the eye, and said, "Not fucking near enough, bitch. That's why I'm going back!"

She started to speak but was interrupted by a long-haired college dude who started to tell me I was going to be in big trouble, but his words died away when he looked into my eyes. He saw it, the place you don't want to be, where they keep the vicious animals that might just jump out and bite your hands off, tear your arms off your shoulders, and feed them to you. He unassed my AO, and I headed to the bathroom and punched a few holes in the wall, being lucky not to encounter any wall studs in the process. I was seeing red, felt betrayed, confused by images of what that statement brought out in the bar. They loved what she'd done; some believed we were baby killers. The boys in the bar didn't have enough sand in their shorts to say that, but she had, and that said something for her. I don't believe TB even knew what had gone down because he was somewhere else when it happened. When he got back, he found everyone, as he said, "agitated."

New Year's Eve 1967 was the loneliest time I can recall. By that night, the flu was right at home in me, Teddy Bear was enjoying his friends, and just as midnight struck I left the bar with all the hugs and good wishes for the New Year of 1968. I couldn't stand it; the only person I knew was TB, and he was into good cheer with his friends. I felt good for him, but the incident that day had struck home. I walked for a good hour, just thinking about the past year and what had gone down, who had made it and who hadn't. I couldn't relate to what was going on—everyone's concerns seemed trivial. What really hurt was some of these people believed I was a baby killer, a person to be shunned. I wasn't good enough to be in this here United Fucking States. I had been picking up on the vibes in airport terminals, hearing snide remarks, but my happiness at being back in the world had insulated me from it. I had been warned about it by Pizza Joe and other brothers in the Lurps but had concluded that what they'd experienced had been isolated incidents. This was different; it had come from a totally different element, from a female. A total putdown. How insensitive, naive, spiteful, and callous could a person be? That night it totally hit home, the statement we always said in the Nam: "It don't mean nothing. . . ."

I left Teddy Bear and New York and flew back to Los Angeles to spend the remainder of my extension leave with my folks. We had started out there earlier when TB and I had come home on 12 December. I had just completed a one-year tour with the Long Range Reconnaissance Patrol, 1st Brigade, 101st Airborne Division, and TB had done eighteen months with them. We had extended to go back along with Jaybird Magill and Wolfman Kraft. Lurping was catching, and we felt anybody worth his salt should extend.

We had come home to the happiness of Mom and Dad. My

Mom had been so happy that I was home. She had cooked TB and me a great dinner. As we all sat around the dinner table, Mom was talking about how glad she was that I was out of there. But TB was looking at me like, "You mean you haven't told her you're going back, huh? This will be real fucking interesting, you asshole." Yeah, a regular B-52 arc light.

I dropped the five hundred pounder right at the dinner table, about how "they" were making me serve some extra time, but then, not liking to lie to my folks, I spilled my guts. Even so, I compromised with a little white lie: that I would be going to a real safe area in country with milk and ice cream and a five-day work week with weekends off. The only thing I was honest about was that I would be getting an early out from the army. My mother made herself believe my fairy tale, but I could tell Pop was calling bullshit; he had the good grace to not call me on it. Thank you, Pop.

After I got back from New York, the novelty of being back in the States deteriorated rapidly. I found myself wanting to return. I felt I didn't belong; noises made me nervous; but I didn't bolt back because we had all agreed that we would return together. Jaybird had a wife, and I was kind of hanging around for him to finish his thing. Finally he called me one night and said, "Marty, we gotta get out of this place; we gotta go home."

"What do you mean? You are home," I said.

He said, "You know what I mean. I don't feel right, people are giving me static, and I almost punched out some people at a party my wife's friends threw."

"Oooh, I think I know what you mean," was my reply. We arranged for the four of us to meet at Fort Lewis because that's where we were leaving from to fly back to the Nam. We were going home. . . .

We landed at Bien-hoa Airbase on the morning of 25 January 1968. From there we took off on a C-130 and landed at Phan-rang, rear base for the 1/101, Phan-rang at 1100 hours. Jaybird, Doc Kraft, and I went to collect Marty Dostal, who had opted to spend his R&R leave in Thop Cham, a "suburb" of Phan-rang. He spent it at a bar called the Hole-in-the-Wall with a girl named Moon. The bar was owned by Lurch Cornett, who ended up doing six tours in Nam and whose story reads like an epic novel. Moon ran the bar for Lurch, and Marty enjoyed his leave so much, he didn't know how long he had been there and didn't care; he figured someone would come looking for him when it was time to go back.

We sat around drinking Ba Muoi Ba beer and smoking, catching up on the gossip in a back room adjacent to the bar. All of a sudden Moon came running into the room all excited, telling us to unass the AO and get up on the roof. Oh, Moon—that woman was a saint. We left through the rear of the bar and saw a riot rolling down the alley, a couple of GIs in the forefront battling it out with the mob. There had to be 150 people in that alley, and it sounded as if someone had disturbed a hornet's nest. We *di-di*'d up the stairs to the roof, where Doc Kraft found some bricks and proceeded to nail some of the mob. The rioters swept into the back room, through the bar, and out the front door, totally destroying or stealing everything in the process. Well, Lurch's business venture came to a screeching halt right there, not that he was much of a businessman. I think he was just giving Moon and her relatives a place to live. And the bar added color to our lives. Marty Dostal had no choice but to head to the forward area with us.

We flew out of Phan-rang early next morning to Song Be and the brigade's AO. Because the 1st Brigade was General Westmoreland's fire brigade, we moved often. We arrived at the Lurp area around 1000 hours and went to the big squad tent to find a platoon full of strangers. All of a sudden I heard, "Hey, Marty brother, what's going on? Welcome back." It was Superspade, S.Sgt. Lester Hite, the badass Lurp from St. Louie. We did the power dap all around, and then Superspade said that he was taking a heavy team out on an S&D (search and destroy) and asked if we wanted to go for a "walk in the park." He figured a man gets rusty if he doesn't practice what he preaches. Of course we said yes.

Our old rucks and LBE (load-bearing equipment) had been scavenged, so we had to put new ones together. Anybody who has ever done some serious humping knows how important it is to custom fit LBE to yourself. All the ass-kicking hardware is on it, and ammo and grenades weigh, so if you don't adjust the suspenders and pistol belt to take the weight evenly, your hips and shoulders will be worn to hamburger very quickly.

Top Smith welcomed us back and issued us rock and roll sticks (M-16s), never mentioning one word about our being twelve days AWOL. I didn't get the same rifle I had before I left. I took the new one, quickly cleaned it, and worried about going out without test firing. Some of the other guys helped load or lent us the magazines we needed. Jaybird, TB, Doc Kraft, and I were ready to go in the record time of one hour. While we were getting ready, Superspade had been giving us the lowdown on what we would be doing on this walk in the park. It would be a standard S&D patrol outside the base wire, and when it got dark we would set an ambush at a trail junction. There was an unusual amount of enemy activity close to the base camp, and the Lurps had been pulling these patrols for the previous two weeks, making contact every time they went out. They hadn't been pulling any recon missions. With the '68 Tet holidays fast approaching, Operations and Intelligence felt something was coming down. Time proved them oh so right.

The brigade base camp was situated on a plateau surrounding the airstrip. Song Be, the town, was at the west end of the airstrip. The surrounding area was thick with bamboo growth interspersed with patches of single canopy jungle. On the north side was a small valley about 800 meters wide that nestled onto Ba Ra Mountain, the dominant terrain in the area.

We exited the perimeter wire at the edge of the plateau and slid into the valley. Superspade was walking point, I was walking his slack, and Jaybird was directly behind me. Some of the other guys were Crazy Pete Peterson, Jerry Prouty, Doc Kraft, Doc Norton, Tyrone Woods, Nick Caberra (machine gunner), and Teddy Bear bringing up the rear. Twelve Foul Dudes looking bad, dressed to kill, and on the hunt for Mr. Charles. Man, it felt good to be back in the saddle.

We traversed the valley and cut a high-speed trail at the base

of the hill mass. We didn't want to walk the trail, so we paralleled it heading east, but we got channeled back into the trail by
the bamboo growth and a small stream that ran along the trail.
We bumped the trail again where a rock escarpment projected
from the base of the hill, and the trail made a dogleg around the
cliff and proceeded on following the contour of the hill. Superspade had no choice but to step onto the trail and use it. About
forty meters along the trail, Superspade had rounded the bend
in the dogleg. I was right in it, and Jaybird was five to seven
meters behind me when I heard a distinct *pssst-pssst* and two
words in Vietnamese coming from my right.

I glanced over and about chewed on my heart. Not fifteen
meters away an NVA with dark-green PJs and floppy hat stood
waving me over. Sitting behind him and to his left were two
more. They must have heard Superspade and seen me when I
entered the bend. The jungle growth and the sunlight filtering
through it dappled and lengthened the shadows. That, plus my
small size, faded tigers, and the cammo on my face must have
fooled them. If they had seen Superspade, who is black, or Jaybird, a redhead, that would have done us in. Luck and fate
never failed to amaze me.

My reading of the situation took but a split second. I could
see a small look of doubt flicker on the standing guy's face. My
body language gave the impression that I had acknowledged
them, and I took two more steps forward, which put a clump of
bamboo three or four feet wide between them and me. As I was
doing this, I could tell Superspade was alerted and reacting,
and when I got behind the bamboo, I glanced at Jaybird. He
was holding back, and it was like a well-orchestrated dance,
with everyone in step. No talking, no arm waving; it was as if
the three of us were plugged in on the same wavelength, riding
a 10,000cc adrenaline rush. We knew our shit was weak, and
the only course was the bold line. Heart in mouth, Jaybird and
I came through the opening on the right side of the clump with
Superspade entering on the left.

I will never forget the look on the VCs' faces when we
broke into their view. It was as if time were moving in slow
motion. We all three opened up at about the same time. I shot

the second one who had been sitting down. He was just getting up, AK in hand, when I literally blew him out of his Ho Chi Minh sandals (which I still have at this writing). As this was going down, my eyes widened because behind the two guys sitting there, I suddenly saw three or four more starting to react to the situation. Damn! How many more were there? I lifted my bullet stream into their area. Jaybird hit the guy who was standing then shifted when he saw the movement in the stream bed. Because of the angle of his approach, Superspade saw one of those in the rear sighting in on us with an RPG-7 rocket launcher. Superspade shot him in the arm and shoulder area, which caused him to drop it. As our magazine change came up, Superspade yelled to get the Mike Golf (M-60 machine gun) talking and to set up some rear security. It was a bad magazine change in that we all ran out at the same time. The NVA took up where we left off. It was ugly, trying to change magazines while Charlie's was trying to put a lick on us. But luck was with us because in the excitement of the moment, their fire was high. I got my second magazine in, rolled to the left, and opened up again. All of a sudden, I was empty again. Man, that was fast! I inserted my third magazine and had hit the release on the bolt receiver when I realized I had a ruptured brass stuck in the chamber. Oh shit! The horror of horrors—a jammed rifle in a firefight. It's about the ugliest feeling I have ever experienced. I grabbed a grenade, threw it, and readied another as it went off. I threw the other one in time to see two Chi-Com potato mashers come in. *Boom, boom!* Superspade grunted in pain. I yelled to see if he was hit, and he said, "Not bad." Meanwhile, the rest of the team was strung out on the trail, unable to maneuver because the cliff and trail to their front were a beaten zone from all the bullets coming in, and there was impenetrable bamboo growth to their right flank and rear. TB told me later he had emptied a couple of clips into his rear security zone. We had not heard anything from them because of the noise from the automatic weapons and exploding grenades.

The second there was a lull in the firing, feeling naked, I did a speed crawl back down the trail and saw old Nick Caberra with the MG. I said, "Come on, Nick," and grabbed extra belts as Nick brought the machine gun forward. Having just come up, Nick didn't know where to aim so I started shooting the machine gun, showing Nick where we needed it. Then he took the machine gun back, and I assisted him. Meanwhile, Jaybird and Superspade were going through their ammo at a very high rate. The NVA had been taken totally by surprise by the speed and violence of our attack, and I'm sure their only thought was breaking contact. If they had attacked, they could have rolled the three of us easily, especially with one weapon down. The tracers from the machine gun set the bamboo undergrowth on fire, and before long a fire was raging. It swept through the area where the NVA had fallen back.

We secured the area. Standing there, panting and dripping sweat, coming down off the adrenaline rush, smelling the cordite and burned powder, the nauseating, sweet copper smell of blood, I happened to look at Jaybird's face. He had this expression on his face like, "Wow! Two hours back in, and less than forty-eight from the States, and we're in the middle of it!" I had the same thoughts and feelings. Superspade looked at us, and said, "Welcome back to the Nam!"

As we were policing up the RPG-7 and spare rockets, rucksacks, and other equipment, I looked down in the stream bed and found the Ho Chi Minh sandals stuck in the mud where the previous owner had hastily exited them. A thought of the blue-eyed blond college coed crossed my mind, and I thought, "Honey, your babies are all grown up. You don't have to worry about them. You just have to worry about us because we'll be after their ass every chance we get!"

Air-fucking-borne, honey, it don't mean nothin'. . . .

## Gold Leaf

We policed up the rucksacks and weapons we had taken off the enemy. By then the fire had swept through the large bamboo thicket. After unsuccessfully trying to track the blood trails, we took off, heading back toward the brigade perimeter. We had moved about 200 meters from where we made the contact and we came across a solitary hootch, with two out-buildings for animals. Superspade decided we needed to check it out. It was overlooked by the plateau on which the brigade was situated, and I didn't think the enemy would utilize it as a position, not so close to the brigade perimeter. I thought it was probably occupied by a farmer and his family and therefore pretty harmless.

We approached it tactically and discovered it was occupied by a woman, two young children—a boy and a girl around three and five years in age—and a man—seemingly a typical family of four. I stayed back and took in the scene from a distance. At first I took it for what it represented: a family living in the shadow of an airborne combat brigade and probably unhappy to be in that situation.

But then my sixth sense kicked into gear. The woman and children seemed terrified, trying to act normally, but still really uptight. They were scared of us, but even more, they were scared of the situation. What situation? We hadn't shown any undue attention or hostility toward them. No doubt they had heard the firing and contact just moments before, but their fear seemed to be directed at the man. The woman and the children were clinging to each other but not seeking comfort from the man. He was not a farmer: he looked too intelligent, too clean cut. He smelled of discipline, of military. His bearing was military right down to his haircut and physique. Most farmers, if scared, would be very submissive, bowing, groveling, any-thing to get on our good side, especially if they were worried about their family. The man got close to them but was obvi-ously trying to keep them under control. I felt strongly that the man didn't belong there.

Superspade, Teddy Bear, and I talked it over a little bit, and I told them what I was thinking. They agreed with my suspi-cions, and we decided to conduct a thorough search of the hootch. We searched it completely, and I began to feel that maybe we were reading the situation wrong, but then Jaybird hit paydirt. On one of the outside walls Jaybird discovered a false wall, with a space between the outside face of the wall and the inside. Inside the wall were several bundles covered with cloth. One bundle held four cloth sacks, and in each sack were two bundles of piasters held together by rubber bands, eight bundles total, all in large-denomination notes. The other bundle held the clincher: two binders about eight by ten inches, each an inch and a half thick and quite heavy for their size. The cover was made of cloth, a bright, pretty, deep red, that came around and overlapped, completely encasing the book. We opened the cover, and it was filled with sheets of gold leaf separated by pages of thin paper. Vietnamese writing was stamped on each sheet of gold leaf. Man, it was beautiful, but what in the hell was this dude doing with it in such a rundown shack?

Meanwhile, the man had basically clammed up. We policed the family up, tied the guy's arms behind his back, and blindfolded him. We took off, entering the perimeter wire where we had left it. Tiger Force was in, and they were the ones on perimeter guard where we had exited. We stopped long enough to bullshit with them and, having heard the whole thing, they asked about the contact. I knew one of the fire team leaders; we had served together a lifetime before in Biebrich, Germany, and we caught up on each other. (He later was killed in June 1968 in the Ashau Valley.) Then the Lurp platoon driver came by and picked up the prisoner, Superspade, Jaybird, and me, along with the RPG-7 rocket launcher, spare rockets, and rucksacks to take to S-2/S-3. When we arrived at the TOC, they told Superspade to take the prisoner and materials down to the Military Intelligence detachment for interrogation. I turned in the weapons, and Superspade took off with the prisoner. Because it was getting late in the day, they decided to let us spend the night inside the wire.

We got back to the Lurp area, and I secured myself a bunk and got some equipment together, especially a new M-16. Pfc. Nick Caberra came over and started talking with me. He asked me if I was a Chicano and if I could speak Spanish. I had just met him that morning as I had been scrambling to get ready for the "walk in the park." I said yes to both, and he offered me a shot of whiskey and a drink of a beer, which I accepted, and then he got down to what was on his mind. Nick told me he didn't like anyone taking over his weapon but also that he understood why I did it. It was okay, but not to do it again. He had been carrying the machine gun. I appreciated that Nick understood the reason why I had done it. I valued Pfc. Nick Caberra's opinion because he was forty-two years old and a combat veteran of World War II and the Korean War. He had seen it all and done it. Later on Mark "Wolverine" Thompson told me a story about his time as a cherry engineer attached to A Company, 1/327 Battalion back in June 1966 at Dak-to. The unit had taken quite a few casualties, and Wolverine was on the detail loading the dead into a Chinook. While walking one body up the tail ramp of the helicopter, the head fell out of the poncho the body was wrapped in, and that really affected Wolverine. But the platoon sergeant came up and said, "Mark, it's better him, than you, and if you keep your act together, you won't be one of these!" Wolverine appreciated that. The platoon sergeant was Pfc. Nick Caberra. Twenty-seven years in the army and stripe bare but leading a platoon in combat.

So ended my first day back in Lurps—what a rush! Less than forty-eight hours back from the world.

Early the next morning we all said good-bye to Top Lloyd Smith. I was going to miss him. He had come to the Lurps at Phan-rang in late January, and he had been an unusual platoon sergeant because he always went out in the field. Forty-two years old, a senior NCO, and he could still hump you into the ground. He commanded through respect: he never raised his voice, but when you fucked up he usually pointed it out by just looking at you. He was fair but tough. He had broken me in as a team leader, always going out with me, saying he wanted to make sure I was ready. That was partly true, but he liked the bush. I had a big lump in my throat when I said good-bye. I would have died for the man.

Lieutenant McIsaac had ordered a handmade Randall "Scout" knife, the type many of the Lurps carried. This knife was engraved:

TO LLOYD "STRAIGHT" SMITH, FROM LONG RANGE RECON, 101ST ABN VIETNAM, FORTUNA FAVET FORTIBUS.

In the Delta with a MAT team and unable to present the gift, Lieutenant McIsaac mailed the knife to the LRRP detachment, asking that it be presented to Top from all of us.

Lieutenant McIsaac comments, "When I took command of the Lurps, I was a young second lieutenant who had grown up in the Airborne, and had been an Airborne NCO. I thought I knew my stuff. Then I met Top. He taught me more during my time with the Lurps than I learned throughout my whole military career. Top could get more out of a man with a glance than another person could with a threat or a scream. I never heard Top raise his voice in anger. He was not a classic lifer, but a real Airborne NCO. He was both a leader and a doer. You followed Top not because you feared him, but out of respect. With the knife I wanted to show Top our appreciation and respect from the whole detachment."

To illustrate exactly what the general consensus of the platoon was concerning Top Lloyd Smith, the following extract is drawn from a letter of 28 March 1992 from Boss Weisberger:

I was sitting eating lunch with a friend and fellow vet from the 173rd Airborne. I raised the issue of my attending my first reunion and how I looked forward to seeing some of the Foul Dudes. I mentioned that at age twenty, I was incapable of a number of things. One of which was seeing Top as a human being. He was above that, being older than me, an NCO, my platoon Sgt., an old hard Lurp. He was distant and of course had little or no interest in sitting with us at night, getting ripped, and listening to the Doors on volume-warp twelve. His job was to run the platoon, but more than that, he was there to accomplish the mission without losing us. I looked upon Top with all the respect that I was capable of at that stage of my life. I was, in my own eyes, somewhat immortal, egotistical, and greatly ignorant. Twenty-five years later I think I am a bit more capable of seeing things in perspective.

Throughout history, Top has been there. He probably stood by campfires and walked the lines with the Roman

Legions. He talked to the young troopers about keeping their Pilum and Gladius sharp. He was also across the rivers in Germania getting the young tribesmen ready for their first clash with the "Wall of Steel." He has carried swords and axe, pikes and muskets. He has had bushy beards, handlebar mustaches, been clean shaven with whitewalls. He wore skins and leather armor, metal plate, buckskins, baggy pants, and . . . tiger stripes.

We have had fighting Generals and business manager Generals come and go, but we have ALWAYS had Top. He has been and will be the constant force in the military throughout history. I don't believe any army would function without him. I know that the Brits, the Wehrmacht, the Soviets, and the NVA all relied on Top. Like any young, dumb, and full-of-come trooper, I know that "my Top" was the best of the best. It was not fear that had me obey his orders, it was pride and a very real desire to live up to standards he seemed to embody. Had he merely told me that I had let the platoon (and himself) down, it would have been more painful than a whipping. It follows that the other constant in history are the young troopers that he has led and kept alive.

Lt. Mike Kinnan was our platoon leader, but he was on R&R. Sergeant First Class Boozeman was still in the platoon but was also on R&R. That made Superspade our ranking NCO. He was our acting platoon leader and platoon sergeant. He decided that we all needed to take showers at the shower point. We loaded onto our three-quarter-ton Lurpmobile, still named Rommel's War Wagon, and went down to the shower point, where we found some people getting dressed. What made it unusual is that they were putting on tiger stripes and flower-power cammies. I naturally figured they were Special Forces. One of our guys asked one of them what outfit they were with, and he answered, "We're the Lurps."

Superspade overheard them and walked up to them and asked them, "Lookee here now, who you jokers be?"

They answered, "We're the 101st Lurps."

Superspade answered, "No way, because you jokers got it all wrong. *We're* the 101st Lurps!"

Everybody was copping an attitude, because it seemed as though a "Lurp" stand-off was in the making, and we were ready to kick some ass. After a minute of rapid-fire talk, this other dude pipes up that they'd just left Fort Campbell. Superspade said, "Well, hell, that makes a difference; we can talk."

This NCO, who was an E-7 and wore a black baseball cap, and as I found out later was Sergeant First Class Brue-baker, said, "We're the Division Lurps, Company F, 58th Infantry, Long Range Patrol."

Here was my future, but I didn't know it at the time, and we were ready to go to blows to uphold the sacred honor of the Lurps and our newly acquired platoon leader, Superspade. We headed back to the Lurp area to get ready for our next mission, which was for the morale and welfare of the troops.

The previous night we had been discussing the fact that there was no beer to drink. So Wolverine, Keener, Jaybird, and I, with several others, planned a mission. The execution of this mission was carefully figured out. . . .

While I had been away on my extension leave, the detachment had moved several times after Chu Lai, and now we were perched right on the Cambodian border. The LRRP detachment had always been in a running engagement with the first sergeant ("First Pig") of Headquarters Company, the company to which we were assigned for administrative purposes. But the bureaucrats of Headquarters Company could not stand a bastard outfit like ours so close to the political structure of the brigade. The First Pig was known to us as "Patches" because he was fond of wearing every patch associated with the combat infantry soldier even though he abhorred the idea of combat or anything associated with it. Patches hated the Lurps and made it his mission to make life as unbearable for us as he could. However, he could only do that when we came out of the field. He decided that, to control the Foul Dudes better, he would locate the MP company next to the Lurps in the rear area. Because we operated for Operations and Intelligence and because our missions were classified, our rear area was always enclosed by concertina wire, separating us from the rest of the brigade. Patches felt alienated by that, and it pissed him off. Another source of irritation to him was that on one of the earlier moves of the brigade, most of the headquarters section was in a C-130 crash that killed some very good people. Patches was pissed because he had heard that the Lurps threw a party, celebrating his death. This was presumptuous and premature celebrating on the part of the Lurps.

Burdened with their new mission, the MPs looked at us as the source of all their law-enforcement problems, but it was hard for them to bust us because we were constantly rotating in and out of the field. They were also pretty intimidated by the claymores hanging on the wire directly facing them. If they had looked a little closer, they could have seen that the wire leading out of the claymores back to the charging handles was commo wire without blasting caps inserted in the claymore body. But it was very convincing!

While I was away, an incident had occurred that was "touchy" with the MPs. The MPs lugged a conex-container jail around as the brigade shifted around Nam. Made of steel, it must have been unbearably hot for any unfortunate soul who was stuck in it. Now, it seems that a line doggie *was* incarcerated in it for some reason or other, but some unknown person or persons sympathized with the prisoner and decided to break him out. A series of ventilation slots had been cut in the box's door, and it was padlocked with an impressive-looking lock. Using a small quantity of C-4, the perpetrator(s) blew off the lock. For the man inside, fully enclosed in steel, it must have been like being inside a bell; the prisoner literally had his "bell rung"! This story was related to me by some Lurps who for some reason knew all the juicy details. I wondered if the prisoner had any say on whether he wanted to be busted out. Anyway, the blame was laid on the Lurps.

But back to my story and our dire need of beer.

It was decided that we would have to camouflage our mission and have the blame laid on someone else's shoulders. Jaybird, a former MP, volunteered for a harrowing mission behind enemy lines. He inserted about 0200 hours and low-

crawled under the side of an MP tent to acquire his first helmet liner. Then, figuring his mission was taking too long, he
donned the helmet liner and just boldly walked around, grabbing the required equipment, MP brassards, and other helmet
liners. At one point, an MP asked him a question, but he said
he was just checking the security of the tent and to go back to
sleep.

After getting back from the shower point, Wolverine, who
was to be the mission team leader, got MPC (military payment
certificates) from everyone in the platoon who had any. He
rolled it into a large impressive bundle held together by a
rubber band. The team—Wolverine as teamleader, Keener as
driver, Jaybird, Doc Kraft, and me as security—got into
Rommel's War Wagon. Meanwhile, the rest of the platoon had
been readying the truck, smearing mud on the identification
numbers displayed on the truck's bumpers.

We drove toward the town of Song Be, to a place we
had reconned on the way to the shower point. We drove by
and checked it out once more, then pulled into a side road
to put on our cammo, MP brassards on left shoulders, and
MP helmet liners. Wolverine wore a captain's double silver
bar on his helmet. Planning for a mission is very important;
nothing can be left to chance. This mission had been well
planned.

In a cloud of red dust, we pulled up to a roadside stand. It
was a typical black market operation of the kind that the Vietnamese got to run so well, thanks to pus-gutted REMFs. To the
casual observer, Rommel's War Wagon, with its blue bucket
seats, looked like a typical work detail: an officer and driver in
front and three gofers in the back. With one exception, it *was*
an MP work detail! Following the plan, Keener kept the truck
running while Wolverine got out waving his fat roll of MPC,
declaring his need for American beer. Mamma-san's eyes narrowed with suspicion when we pulled up, but she went ballistic
with greed when she spotted the roll and knew instantly what
we needed. Right down to his New Jersey accent, Wolverine
reminded me of a Jack Nicholson character. A brief negotia-
tion took place before (Captain) Wolverine waved us three

peons off the back of the truck to load the beer, per the plan. When Jaybird and I finished loading the last four cases, we jumped into the truck, and assumed our defensive roles.

As any good Lurp knows, the most vulnerable aspects of a Lurp operation are the team's insertion and extraction. If fate picks a time to shit on you, that will be when. We didn't want to hurt anyone; we were just thirsty. Wolverine asked Keener out of the corner of his mouth, "Are you ready?" When he got an affirmative reply, Wolverine suddenly jumped into the truck, and Keener peeled gravel getting away from there. With this sudden turn of events, Mamma-san let out a wail of despair, and a Popular Forces soldier who had been lounging around the stand came running out and leveled his M-1 carbine at us. Doc Kraft, who was on the side closest to the stand, let off a sustained automatic burst over their heads with his M-16 rifle. Doc recently recalled, "I didn't want to hurt anyone, I just wanted them on their stomachs, so I aimed about five feet over their heads and into the top of the stand." Seeing the top of the stand shredded turned the PF soldier into a crawler real fast.

We took off in a mad dash for a short ways and then slowed down to normal speed. Soon there was an empty field with weeds and jungle growth up next to the road. We threw helmet liners and brassards into the weeds and proceeded to the brigade and Lurp area.

We arrived back to a hero's welcome. We had gotten ice for the beer on the way back from the shower point. We had acquired twelve cases and felt we had struck a blow against the black market. We disposed of the evidence in short order. Oh, what a night!

That night we had received a Patrol Warning Order that three teams would be going out on a search and destroy and then would be pulling ambushes. The next morning we were preparing to go out when a black MP staff sergeant and four troopers carrying M-16s entered the Lurp area. It was a tense moment. The MP NCO had an attitude, and his troopers were clearly scared shitless. He confronted our platoon sergeant and platoon leader, Superspade, and said that someone had entered the MP tent and stolen property that had been used in committing a robbery. He had, he said, hard evidence that the Lurps were involved. With these suspicions came a litany of complaints, real and imagined, that would have occupied the docket of any worthy prosecuting attorney for quite a while.

The whole time our leader, Superspade, was quietly listening. He was a formidable and intimidating person. When he was deep in thought he would fold his arms across his chest, his right hand holding his chin in the crook of his hand, index finger absently stroking a knife scar that ran down his left cheek toward his jaw. He was built like a linebacker. His shirt was off but he was wearing four different strings of beads and a body-count rope. He wore size-thirteen combat boots that had been worn white from beating the bush, and a couple of square bandages covered holes on his back where shrapnel had been dug out the day before.

Superspade's demeanor wasn't deterring the MP NCO, but it sure had his young troopers uptight. Or it might have been the sight of the whole LRRP platoon gathered around, nonchalantly holding their weapons. Superspade let the sergeant go on for a while longer without uttering a word. Finally, when he had heard enough, he held up his hand and cut the sergeant off in midsentence.

"Lookee here, brother," he said, but was rudely cut off by the NCO, who snapped that he wasn't Superspade's brother. Superspade retorted by saying, "Well, then, look here, you pus-nutted, slack-jawed, worthless piece of cop shit, where the fuck is the security in your living quarters? It could have been Chuck that crept into your sorry-ass tent and stole your equipment. You're lucky he didn't cut some throats. As far as the hard evidence, where is it?"

The MP sergeant, his guts running to sand, pointed at all the empty beer cans that were littering the ground.

Superspade kept on his running commentary: "These are empty beer cans, and you're claiming somebody stole some beer. This shit was brought up from Phan-rang two days ago by these men," he said, pointing to me.

"I advise you to get you and your sorry-ass-looking troops

out of my AO. I ain't got time for your chickenshit, jive-ass turkey talk, coming in here breaking bad when we're going out hunting Chuck and when we find him we're going to kill his sorry ass. If you want to join us, saddle up; if not, unass my AO. We got better things to do than listening to your sorry-ass accusations!"

At that point, all of us Foul Dudes would have followed him through the gates of hell. The MP sergeant could only stammer that he *knew* we were guilty and that higher-ups would be hearing of this. It was over. Superspade turned to us, winked, and said, as he kicked some empty beer cans out of the way, "You jokers be ready in twenty minutes to saddle up and exit the wire, and clean up this damn mess."

We exited the wire and split the platoon. Half the men went with Superspade and the other half with Teddy Bear. Jaybird and I were walking the point, and we walked off the plateau using a big trail that ran down into the small valley. We had just gotten down onto the valley floor when, lo and behold, we ran into the Charlie we had taken prisoner the day before. Mr. Moneybags, with his entire fictional family, was out for a stroll. We couldn't believe it! He wasn't Ho Chi Minh, but he might as well have been. Somehow he had been released, and he actually had a smug look on his face as we passed each other on that trail. His "family" still looked scared. We continued east down the valley, passed the burned-out area where we had our little firefight, then button-hooked south toward the brigade perimeter. Toward late evening we moved into an ambush site that covered a trail running up the plateau and brigade perimeter. It was an uneventful night except that just as it was getting dark, a machine gun across the small valley opened up on the perimeter wire, with some of the rounds and green tracers coming into our ambush site.

The next morning we patrolled again through the valley, working west. We heard some firing early that morning, but it was hard to tell exactly where it was. About 1100 hours, off a small trail, I smelled something dead—not rotting yet, but we could hear the flies buzzing. I finally located the body, and damn if it wasn't Mr. Moneybags. Somebody had hosed him down, and he hadn't been dead very long, maybe about four hours. A very dead body and another mystery for us. We let him lie and continued back to the perimeter.

We returned to the platoon area around 1300 hours. It was the eve of Tet, the Year of the Monkey, Vietnam's most treasured holiday, and a cessation of hostilities for the next forty-eight hours was supposed to start at 1800 hours. We figured we would be kicking back for the next day or so. Around 1500 hours, Operations and Intelligence sent an operations order requesting that the Lurps field two heavy teams: one was for an ambush at a junction where three trails ran together, located at the southeast base of the mountain that overlooked our brigade area; another would be going down by the river close to the statue of Mary and led by Sgt. David Sloan. The statue of Mary was about fifteen feet high and had been put there by Catholic nuns who had a mission in the area. Because of the recent enemy activity so close to our brigade area, Operations felt that something was about to happen. Superspade decided he would lead the other team. No team was assigned, but eleven other people volunteered to go with him. I was one of them.

About thirty minutes before sundown we were trucked to the east end of the brigade perimeter. A draw cut back into the plateau where the airfield and the brigade perimeter were situated. The 101st Airborne perimeter wrapped around the draw, and where it bent around and ran east, the ARVN's perimeter began. The ARVN perimeter went east and then cut back south, enveloping the east end of the runway and adjoining the town of Song Be. We were going to use the draw to get down into the valley and across to the ambush site. We had our last cigarette, and just about twilight we stepped out of the wire. We worked down the edge of the draw, just inside the vegetation, for about seventy meters. Then Superspade held us up, and we quietly went into our normal defensive wheel.

We held and listened for about ten minutes. We could see down into the valley and hear the occasional muted voice from the perimeter we had just left. The little valley was ominously quiet. Toward the town of Song Be we occasionally heard a

string of firecrackers or an automatic weapon fired by some
early reveler. The hair on my neck was standing up, and the
reptile in my head kept saying, "Bad shit—bad, bad shit." I
was next to Superspade, and he bent over and whispered in my
ear, "I don't like this at all, Marty, there's some bad shit out
there."

I replied that I could feel it, too. Superspade made a command decision right there. He told me we were going to reverse
movement and go back about thirty meters from the perimeter
and slightly to the left of a bunker that had a commanding view
of the left side of the draw, where a little knob offered plenty of
cover from the downhill side of the draw. We called the bunker
on their radio frequency and told them a couple of people were
coming back to see them. We put the heavy team into position,
and then Superspade and I went back through the wire and
talked to the dudes in that bunker and the next bunker to their
left. Superspade told them exactly where we would be and that
we would be acting as the listening post for those two bunkers.
At the first sign of trouble, we would contact them on the radio
and come back through the wire.

We also discussed artillery and mortar support with the
dudes in the bunker. With those small important details out of
the way, we went back out the wire and rejoined the team. It
was quiet. Once in a while we would glimpse a muted light
briefly out in the small valley.

Tet is celebrated with plenty of firecrackers. Promptly at
2300 hours, we heard firecrackers being lit. As midnight
approached, the Vietnamese really started lighting them off,
with soldiers firing their weapons into the sky. I was lulled
by what looked like a celebration, but suddenly shit really
started flying. Out on the valley floor farther east mortars
coughed as rounds left their tubes. I had never before seen
122mm rockets flying at night, but I saw them that night. The
coordination of the attack was phenomenal. Everything was
being directed at the ARVN's side of the perimeter and the
town of Song Be itself. APC engines raced and quad fifties
boomed. Green, white, and red tracers were soon crisscrossing

the night sky as a horrific firefight was underway. It had all of us saucer-eyed and thanking Superspade silently for his sixth sense and the determination to act on it. If we had done as ordered, we would have been right in the maneuvering area of the attacking enemy force, making us more of a liability than an asset.

We began to hear movement in the center of the draw. We quietly radioed the bunkers about what we had heard and that we were coming in. We were met at the wire by a couple of dudes from the bunkers, and we split our teams between the two bunkers. Soon we had artillery and mortar fire exploding up the length of the draw. At the top end of the draw were a couple of dusters with quad fifties that hosed the length of the draw. Screams sounded out of the draw but not for long; the enemy force that had been trying to infiltrate up the draw was promptly shut down. The rest of the night remained quiet in our sector, but over on the ARVN side and into the town of Song Be, they were in a fight for their lives. Several NVA battalions had launched a major attack on the town and almost succeeded in taking it. Since it was not more than a half mile from our position, we listened to the sounds of the battle all night long.

Sergeant Sloan on his ambush site by the river had spent a quiet night. Just before daylight, he received a call telling him to bring his team back into the wire. The team was met by Rommel's War Wagon and transported to the perimeter that was adjacent to the town of Song Be. Sergeant Sloan's team advanced about 200 meters into the outskirts of Song Be and came upon NVA who were lining up civilians and machine gunning them. Sergeant Sloan's team quickly became embroiled in a firefight with the enemy until Operations and Intelligence had them drop back into the wire because they were afraid the team would be encircled by the enemy and cut off from reinforcement. That morning, Sergeant Sloan's team was airlifted on a C-130 into Tan-son Nhut Airport in Saigon to be held in reserve as a reaction force for airport security.

Unknown to us, the rest of Vietnam was embroiled in a major enemy attack that came to be known as the '68 Tet Offensive. Twenty-two major cities were captured by the enemy across South Vietnam. The security of the U.S. embassy in Saigon was broached, but the intruders were soon recaptured by elements of the 101st Airborne. The city of Hue would be in enemy hands for over three weeks. The enemy paid a heavy price: the Tet Offensive dearly cost the National Liberation Front (Vietcong); it was almost totally annihilated and ceased to be an effective fighting force for the remainder of the war. The U.S. and South Vietnam military won a very decisive victory in Vietnam during the '68 Tet Offensive, but we lost the war back in the United States. It was the start of the long slide downhill and the eventual loss of the Vietnam War for the United States.

Months later, when I was back at P training just about ready to leave for the States, I had a visit from Brother Weems and Superspade. Brother Weems was heading for Special Forces CCC/SOG (Command and Control Central/Special Observation Group) and tried to talk me into going with him. It was a tempting idea, but I knew it was time for me to leave Vietnam because I didn't want to reenlist. We partied together that night, and Superspade and I got to talking about the events leading to Tet. I told Superspade that it amazed me that though Mr. Moneybags had been caught with all that gold and piasters, he had still been turned loose. Superspade chuckled and that sly smile played on his face.

"You see this gold tooth I got made after coming down to Bien-hoa from Song Be?" he asked. "Well, Mr. Moneybags paid for it!"

Superspade had turned in his prisoner and four rolls of piasters, but he did not turn in the gold leaf and four other rolls of piasters. He figured the dude was going to buy his way out, which he did, but he wanted to test him; if he didn't bitch about the missing money, Superspade would know he was NVA. That morning before we found the body, Superspade had a team out. When he was moving back to the wire, he had run into Mr. Moneybags by himself. Superspade said he might have let him live, but Mr. Moneybags was arrogant, as if he had bought Superspade with his silence. Mr. Moneybags knew that Superspade knew that he was the enemy but figured he was safe. It was his final and fatal mistake.

# Epilogue

Five days after the start of the Tet Offensive the 1st Brigade LRRP detachment was notified that it was to be disbanded.

The 1st Brigade, 101st Airborne, was once again becoming part of the 101st Airborne Division; the 1st Brigade's life as an independent maneuver element was coming to an end—and with it the brigade's provisional Long Range Reconnaissance Patrol detachment. That was a shock to all of us, especially those of us who had extended our tours in Vietnam to stay in the Lurps. Some of the Foul Dudes were still on extension leave and wouldn't hear of the change till they got back. That included Lurch Cornett, Tom Dokos, Eddie Cecena, Harvey Bieber, Dirk Sasso, George Peppers, Brother Weems, and a host of others. Of course, by then Lt. Dan McIsaac was already down south with Mobile Advisory Team 16. He later commanded Recon, 2/503, 173rd Airborne in Vietnam. Top Smith had rotated home. On arriving back from leave, the five of them put in 1049s for 5th Special Forces Group. They were all graduates of MACV Recondo school and should have been welcomed with open arms, but Patches, in his cowardly and midget-minded way, sent them all to an infantry line company. That was Patches' way of getting revenge on the last of the Foul Dudes under his thumb. Some of us were given the choice of continuing on with Division Lurps or going to the Security Platoon. Security Platoon was basically an "ash and trash" unit, one whose members did the demeaning jobs like burning shit, KP, and any other detail that was thrown their way. Their ranks were filled with people mostly trying to stay out of the fighting. It was a far cry from being a Lurp. Some of the Foul Dudes were not even given a choice, just assigned by Headquarters Company as they saw fit. A few of the Foul Dudes were assigned to line companies by the revenge-minded First Pig, Patches. I opted for Division Lurps but would never ever again experience the camaraderie and professionalism that was the Long Range Reconnaissance Patrol, 1st Brigade, 101st Airborne Division. It was the end of a brotherhood forged in war, and the end of the Foul Dudes.

Lurch was headed to the division rear area, to teach medical topics to new arrivals while he waited for the Mess Association crooks to clear out so he could go back to Special Forces. He later joined the Phoenix Program and went on to serve five more tours in Vietnam.

Brother Weems was already on his way to MACV–SOG (Military Assistance Command, Vietnam–Special Observation Group) Command and Control Central, the extreme edge of the game, where he would later be wounded by an RPG round hitting his extraction helicopter. Medevacked to the hospital at Camp Zama, Japan, Brother Weems eventually went AWOL from the hospital and returned to running missions for CCC, leaving Vietnam at the end of the war.

Virgil "Puke" Palk welcomed Brother Weems to CCC, doing multiple tours, and would remain in the service. Superspade was recruited by Command Sergeant Major Gergen of the 2/327 to take over the battalion's Hawk Recon Platoon, and would later work for Command Sergeant Major Gergen at the Fort Benning Ranger Department.

Ernie Winston went to Tiger Force and was later killed. Patrick "Mother" Henshaw had gone to II Corp LRRPs and was killed in action on 19 December 1967. Pizza Joe Remiro went to the 3/506 Recon Platoon. John Chadwick never made it to Tiger Force. Instead he was assigned to an infantry line company. He eventually joined the air force and became a pilot on C-130 Hercules aircraft. Larry Beauchamp would come back for two more tours. Bill Scanlan stayed with 1st Brigade

Headquarters but moved back to a commo job doing a couple
of more tours. Dave Sloan went to MACV and then eventually
to the 173rd. He would spend two more years in Vietnam, all
of them with combat outfits.

Larry Forrest, Alfred Smith, Pop Tomlinson, Dave Skau,
Robert Doty, Joe Nash, Ron Bourne, Mike Flynn, James
Fogt, Arthur Doame, Donald Davis, Phillip Henry, Thomas
Camp, Joe Johnson, Norman Lambert, Gerald Lavecchia,
Franklin Lee, Pascual Meza, Paul Miller, Thomas Moore,
Thomas Payne, Ron Pitts, Jerry Roth, Tommy Russell, Melvin
Ruttan, Sam Sealy, Walter Smith, William Sopko, Wilbur
Sumpter, James Tadlock, William Vaughn, Pappy Webb,
Pappy Lynch, Uncle Earl Wheeler, John Dietrich, Jim Bethel,
John Buford, Walter Bachek, and numerous other Lurps were
continuing their military careers back in the States, but most of
them would have subsequent tours in Vietnam.

Jack Waymire was killed in action on his twenty-second
birthday, 9 January 1967, while serving with Special Forces.
His death was written about by S.L.A. Marshall in a book titled
*Ambushes*. In early February 1968, on his second tour with the
101st, M.Sgt. Philip Chassion was killed in action while going
to the aid of one of his men.

The surviving core of the 1st Brigade LRRP detachment
was absorbed into the newly arrived 101st Airborne Division
Long Range Patrol Company. This Division LRP Company
was soon to be designated F Company, 58th Infantry (LRP),
and a year later would be redesignated L Company, 75th
Rangers. With these two units, the story of the 101st Airborne
Lurps, the saga of the *SIX SILENT MEN* continues. . . .

# Appendix A

### Tools of the Trade

Like any good craftsmen, the Lurps had their tools, both "as issued" and modified for the peculiar needs of their mission. Obviously, the enemy did also. Both sides showed exceptional ingenuity in devising improvements over the basic designs of weapons, munitions, and ancillary equipment.

Fought in the latter part of the twentieth century, the Vietnam War utilized methods of killing that ranged from prehistoric mantraps to then-state-of-the-art equipment such as silenced submachine guns, man-portable grenade launchers, and starlight scopes (passive night-vision devices). It is clearly beyond the scope of this book to list all the equipment and munitions used by our teams or the enemy. A wide range of weapons and calibers was dumped into Southeast Asia prior to the Vietnam War and used by the NVA/VC. They were of American, French, Japanese, Chinese, Russian (and Communist-bloc) make. It was possible for an American soldier to be injured or killed by a French 8mm Lebel bolt-action rifle, a German MG34 machine gun, or an M-1 Garand.

The Lurps were allowed considerable latitude in modifying equipment. The M-79 grenade launcher was almost always modified, especially before the XM-148 appeared in Vietnam. They were chopped by cutting the shoulder stock to the pistol grip and removing the sights. The lack of sights was no hindrance to an experienced grenadier. Holsters of canvas and other materials were modified or made to carry the weapon on the LBE belt.

It was common for team members to carry personally owned knives and pistols. For example, two Lurps, "Dirty Ernie" Winston and Pizza Joe Remiro, carried two-inch barreled .38 Special revolvers. George Peppers had a 9mm Browning Hi-Power. Most other Lurps were issued or acquired the military .45 automatic. Most everyone had his own "special knife." Randall knives were top items, as were Gerber daggers, an assortment of Puma and Buck hunting knives, Western and Case bowies, and of course John Chadwick's hatchet. Boss Weisberger carried a Kukri that his father had carried in the China-Burma-India theater in World War II.

The M-16 was the tool of our trade. The same rifle with a ten-inch barrel and telescoping stock was referred to as a CAR-15. Both rifles used a detachable twenty-round magazine (a thirty-round magazine became available later on in the war) and were capable of full- or semiautomatic fire. Any groundpounder viewed his rifle as personally his and carried it with familiarity and confidence. We camouflaged them with tiger-stripe material, tape, or camouflage stick. A cleaning rod was taped to the forearm and upper receiver or inserted into a hole drilled in the forearm. The three-prong flash suppressor caught on twigs or shrubbery and we taped it to prevent that. All slings and their swivels were removed from the rifles.

Instead of the issue M-16 rifle, Lurps often carried different "main guns." Dirty Ernie Winston carried a twelve-gauge shotgun, the barrel cut nearly to the magazine and the stock cut to the pistol grip. He also had cut the stock on a 7.62mm M-14 and attached an M-16 pistol grip, and cut the barrel back to the gas-tube plug. That produced a handful of booming, flaming volcano when fired on full auto! Other weapons carried were the World War II–era M-3A1 .45-caliber Grease Gun, M-1 Garand, and M-1A1 Thompson.

The LRRP detachment also employed a number of British Mark IIS submachine guns, 9mm with integral silencer. It was blowback operated, with a thirty-two-round side-mounted magazine. It was a select fire but was not intended for full auto use.

The following is a basic list of weapons employed by the LRRP detachment:

### M-16/M16A1/CAR-15
Length: 39 inches; Barrel: 20 inches (CAR-15 10 or 11.5 inches); Weight: 6.3 lbs.
Gas operated, select fire, magazine fed, and a cyclic rate of fire of 700 to 900 RPM.
5.56 NATO. Ammunition used was M193 Ball, or M196 tracer (red tipped).

### M-60 General Purpose Machine Gun
Length: 43.75 inches; Barrel: 25.6 inches; Weight: 23.05 pounds.
Gas operated; full auto, disintegrating link belt; cyclic rate of fire was 600 RPM.
7.62 NATO. Ammunition used was M-80 Ball with M-62 Tracer linked every fifth round.

### M-79 Grenade Launcher
Barrel: 14 inches.
Single shot, break-open operation.

### XM-148 Grenade Launcher
Length: 16.5 inches; Barrel: 10 inches; Weight: 3 pounds.
Single Shot, slide-open operation, mounted below M-16 barrel.
Caliber: 40mm. Ammunition used M-38 or M-406 HE rounds. Effective casuality radius 5 meters.
XM-576E1, multiple projectile (shotgun round, 20 pellets).

### Browning Heavy Barrel M-2 Machine Gun
Length: 61.1 inches; Barrel: 45 inches; Weight with tripod: 128 pounds.
Recoil operated, select fire, disintegrating link belt, 450–500 RPM.

Ammunition used was 50 cal. BMG. M2 Ball, M10 Tracer (every fifth round).

## M-72 Series LAW (Light Anti-Tank Weapon)

66mm Heat Rocket; Total weight: 5.2 pounds.

Smooth bore, single shot, discard.

Effective range 200 meters.

## M18A1 Claymore Mine (Antipersonnel)

Weight: 3.5 pounds, 1.5 pounds of C-4 explosive; 700 steel balls; 100 feet of electrical wire with electric blasting cap M4. Two detonating wells to allow dual priming. Initiatior generated by M-57 electrical firing device (clacker). Produces a 3-volt electrical pulse. Carried in the M-7 bandoleer.

## GRENADES:

M26 Fragmentation; AN-M8 Smoke (white), M18 Smoke (red, yellow, violet, green); M34 White Phosphorous; MKII A-1(pineapple grenade, World War II/Korea); AN/M14 TH3 Incendiary. ABC-M25A2 and ABC-M7A2 CS/CN riot-control grenades.

The weapons employed by enemy forces and encountered by the Lurps will be limited in coverage to Russian design as follows:

## AK-47 Assault Rifle (Avtomat Kalashnikova)

Length: 34.25 inches; Barrel: 16.34 inches; Weight: 10.58 pounds, 8.87 pounds for AKM

Gas operated; select fire; 30-round detachable magazine; 600 RPM.

7.62X39mm; Ball type PS; Tracer T45 (tracer was green tipped).

## SKS Carbine (Samozariadnya Karabina Simonava Obrazets)

Length: 40.16 inches; Barrel: 20.47 inches; Weight: 8.8 pounds.

Gas operated, semi-auto. Ten-round nondetachable magazine. Swivel-mounted bayonet attached.

Ammunition same as AK-47.

**RPD Light Machine Gun (Ruchnoi Pulemet Degtyareva)**

Length: 40.8 inches; Barrel: 20.5 inches; Weight: 15.6 pounds.

Gas operated, fully automatic. 100-round metallic link in a detachable drum. 650–750 RPM.

Ammunition same as AK-47.

**Mosin-Nagant Series (bolt-action rifles and carbines; Model 1891 through 1944)**

Length: 40–51.37 inches; Barrel: 20–31.6 inches; Weight: 7.5–11.3 pounds.

Manually operated; 5-round internal box magazine.

Sniper version equipped with either 3.5X PU or 4X PE scope.

Caliber: 7.62X54R. Available in Ball Type L; Tracer Type T (green tipped).

**Torkarev Semiautomatic rifle, SVT38 and SVT40 (Samozariadnya Vintovka Takareva Obrazets)**

Length: 48.1 inches; Barrel: 24.6–25 inches; Weight: 9.24 –10.8 pounds.

Gas operated; 10-round box magazine. Scoped sniper models.

Ammunition used same as Mosin-Nagant.

**Degtyarev DP and DPM light machine gun; RP46 Light machine gun**

Gas operated; fully automatic; using 47-round pan magazine at 650 RPM.

Same ammunition caliber as Mosin-Nagant.

**SG43 SGM Heavy machine guns**

Gas operated; fully automatic; 250-round belt or drum; 600–700 RPM. Same caliber as Mosin-Nagant.

**Degtyarev Heavy machine gun (Model DSh K38 and 38/46)**

Length: 62.5 inches; Barrel: 42.1 inches; Weight: 78.5 pounds.

Gas operated; fully automatic; 50-round metallic link; 540–600 RPM. Wheeled, tripod and vehicle mounted.

Caliber: 12.7X107mm.

**RPG-2/RPG-7 (Rocket-propelled grenade)**

40mm tube with an 85mm diameter head; HEAT round PG-7; Antipersonnel round OG-7. Fin and spin stabilized.

Loaded length: 52.6 inches; Loaded weight: 19 pounds; 4–6 RPM.

Optical sight PGO-7 2.5X magnification.

The Soviet weapons listed above were produced by a number of countries within their sphere of influence. The Chinese and Communist bloc supplied weapons to the North Vietnamese, who had little ability to produce their own.

# Appendix B

### Standing Orders
### Roger's Rangers, 1759

1. Don't forget nothing.
2. Have your musket clean as a whistle, hatchet scoured, sixty rounds powder and ball, and be ready to march at a minute's warning.
3. When you're on the march, act the way you would if you was sneaking up on a deer. See the enemy first.
4. Tell the truth about what you see and what you do. There is an army depending on us for correct information. You can lie all you please when you tell other folks about the Rangers, but don't ever lie to a Ranger or an officer.
5. Don't never take a chance you don't have to.
6. When you're on the march, we march single file, far enough apart so one shot can't go through two men.
7. If we strike swamps, or soft ground, we spread out abreast, so it's hard to track us.
8. When we march, we keep moving till dark, so as to give the enemy the least possible chance at us.
9. When we camp, half the party stays awake while the other half sleeps.
10. If we take prisoners, we keep 'em separate from one another till we have time to examine them so they can't cook up a story between 'em.

11. Don't ever march home the same way. Take a different route so you won't be ambushed.

12. No matter whether we travel in big parties or little ones, each party has to keep a scout twenty yards on each flank and twenty yards in the rear, so the main body can't be surprised and wiped out.

13. Every night you'll be told where to meet if surrounded by a superior force.

14. Don't sit down to eat without posting sentries.

15. Don't sleep beyond dawn. Dawn's when the French and Indians attack.

16. Don't cross a river by a regular ford.

17. If somebody's trailing you, make a circle, come back to your tracks, and ambush the folks that aim to ambush you.

18. Don't stand up when the enemy's coming against you. Kneel down, lie down, hide behind a tree.

19. Let the enemy come till he's almost close enough to touch. Then let him have it and jump out and finish him up with your hatchet.

# Glossary

**AA**  Antiaircraft.

**acid pad**  Helicopter landing pad.

**AFB**  Air Force base.

**air burst**  Explosive device that detonates above ground.

**aerial recon**  Reconning a specific area by helicopter prior to the insertion of a recon patrol.

**airstrike**  Surface attack by fixed-wing fighter/bomber aircraft.

**AIT**  In the U.S. Army, Advanced Individual Training that follows Basic Combat Training.

**AK**  A Soviet-bloc assault rifle, 7.62 cal., also known as the Kalashnikov AK-47.

**A Troop or Alpha Troop**  Letter designation for one of the aerorifle companies of an air cavalry squadron.

**AO**  Area of Operations, specified location established for planned military operations.

**ao dai**  Traditional Vietnamese female dress, split up the sides and worn over pants.

**ARA**  Aerial Rocket Artillery.

**ARC Light**  A B-52 air strike.

**Arty fan**  An area of operations that can be covered by existing artillery support.

**ARVN**  Army of the Republic of (South) Vietnam.

**Arty**  Artillery.

**ATL**  Assistant team leader.

**A Team**  Special Forces operational detachment that normally consists of a single twelve-man team composed of eleven enlisted men and one officer.

**bac si**   Vietnamese for doctor.

**baseball**   Baseball-shaped hand grenade with a 5-meter kill range.

**BC**   Base camp.

**BCT**   In the U.S. Army, Basic Combat Training every trainee must complete upon entering service.

**BDA**   Bomb Damage Assessment.

**beat feet**   Running from danger.

**beehive**   Artillery round filled with hundreds of small metal darts designed to be used against massed infantry.

**berm**   Built-up earthen wall used for defensive purposes.

**Bird Dog**   A small fixed-wing observation plane.

**black box**   Sensor device that detects body heat or movement. They were buried along routes used by the enemy to record their activity in the area.

**black PJs**   A type of local garb of Vietnamese farmers, also worn extensively by Vietcong guerrillas.

**blasting cap**   A small device inserted into an explosive substance that can be triggered to cause the detonation of the main charge.

**blood trail**   Spoor sign left by the passage or removal of enemy wounded or dead.

**Blues**   Another name for the aero-rifle platoons or troops of an air cavalry squadron.

**body bag**   A thick black plastic bag used to transport American and allied dead to Graves Registration points.

**beau coup or boo koo**   French for "many."

**B Troop or Bravo Troop**   Letter designation for one of the aero-rifle companies of an air cavalry squadron.

**break contact**   Disengaging from battle with an enemy unit.

**bring smoke**   Placing intensive fire upon the enemy. Killing the enemy with a vengeance.

**bush**   The jungle.

**buy the farm**   To die.

**C-4**   A very staple, pliable plastique explosive.

**C's**   Combat field rations for American troops.

**C&C**   Command and Control.

**CA**   Combat assault.

**cammies**   Jungle-patterned clothing worn by U.S. troops in the field.

**cammo stick**   Two-colored camouflage applicator.

**CAR-15**   Carbine version of the M-16 rifle.

**Cav**   Cavalry.

**CCN**   Command and Control (North), MACV–SOG.

**Charlie, Charles, Chuck**   G.I. slang for VC/NVA.

**cherry**   New arrival in country.

**Chi-Com**   Chinese Communist.

**chieu hoi**   Government program that encouraged enemy soldiers to come over to the South Vietnam side.

**Chinook**   CH-47 helicopter used for transporting equipment and troops.

**chopper**   G.I. slang for helicopter.

**chopper pad**   Helicopter landing pad.

**CIDG**   Civilian Irregular Defense Group. South Vietnamese or Montagnard civilians trained and armed to defend themselves against enemy attack.

**clacker**   Firing device used to manually detonate a claymore mine.

**CO**   Commanding officer.

**Cobra**   AH-1G attack helicopter.

**cockadau**   G.I. slang for the Vietnamese word meaning "kill."

**Col.**   Abbreviation for the rank of Colonel.

**cold**   An area of operations or a recon zone is "cold" if it is unoccupied by the enemy.

**commo**   Communication by radio or field telephone.

**commo check**   A radio/telephone operator requesting confirmation of his own transmission.

**compromise**   Discovered by the enemy.

**contact**   Engaged by the enemy.

**CP**   Command post.

**Cpt.**   Abbreviation for the rank of Captain.

**CS**   Riot gas.

**daisy chain**   Wiring a number of claymore mines together with det cord to achieve a simultaneous detonation.

**debrief**   The gleaning of information and intelligence after a military operation.

**DEROS**   The date of return from an overseas tour of duty.

**det cord**   Timed burn-fuse used to detonate an explosive charge.

**didi**   Vietnamese for to run or move quickly.

**diddy boppin'**   Moving foolishly, without caution.

**DMZ**   Demilitarized Zone.

**Doc**   A medic or doctor.

**dong lai**   Vietnamese for "don't move."

**double canopy**   Jungle or forest with two layers of overhead vegetation.

**Doughnut Dollies**   Red Cross hostesses.

**drag**   The last man on a long range reconnaissance patrol.

**Dustoff**   Medical evacuation by helicopter.

**DZ**   Drop zone for airborne parachute operation.

**E&E**   Escape and Evasion, on the run to evade pursuit and capture.

**E-1 or E-2**   Military pay grades of Private.

**E-3**   Military pay grade of Private First Class.

**E-4**   Military pay grade of Specialist Fourth Class or Corporal.

**E-5**   Military pay grade of Specialist Fifth Class or Sergeant.

**E-6**   Military pay grade of Specialist Sixth Class or Staff Sergeant.

**E-7**   Military pay grade of Sergeant First Class or Platoon Sergeant.

**E-8**   Military pay grade of Master Sergeant or First Sergeant.

**E-9**   Military pay grade of Sergeant Major.

**ER**   Enlisted Reserve.

**ETS**   Estimated Termination of Service.

**exfill**   Extraction from a mission or operation.

**extension leave**   A 30-day furlough given at the end of a full tour of duty after which the recipient must return for an extended tour of duty.

**FAC**   Forward Air Controller. Air Force spotter plane that coordinated airstrikes and artillery for ground units.

**fast mover**   Jet fighter/bomber.

**fire base**   Forward artillery position usually located on a prominent terrain feature used to support ground units during operations.

**finger**   A secondary ridge running out from a primary ridgeline, a hill, or mountain.

**firefight**   A battle with an enemy force.

**fire mission**   A request for artillery support.

**fix**   The specific coordinates pertaining to a unit's position or to a target.

**flare ship**   Aircraft used to drop illumination flares in support of ground troops in contact at night.

**flash panel**   A fluorescent orange or yellow cloth used to mark a unit's position for supporting or inbound aircraft.

**field** Anywhere outside "friendly" control.

**FO** Forward Observer. A specially trained soldier, usually an officer, attached to an infantry unit for the purpose of coordinating close artillery support.

**FNG** "Fucking New Guy." Slang term for a recent arrival in Vietnam.

**foo gas or phou gas** A jellied gasoline explosive that is buried in a 55-gallon drum along defensive perimeters. When detonated sent out a wall of highly flammable fuel similar to napalm.

**freak or freq** Slang term meaning a radio frequency.

**ghost or ghost time** Taking time off, free time, goofing off.

**grazing fire** Keeping the trajectory of bullets between normal knee to waist height.

**grease** Slang term meaning "to kill."

**Green Beret** A member of the U.S. Army Special Forces.

**groundpounder** Infantryman.

**grunt** Infantryman.

**G-2** Division or larger operations section.

**G-3** Division or larger intelligence section.

**gook** Derogatory slang for VC/NVA.

**gunship** An armed attack helicopter.

**HE** High explosive.

**H&I** Harrassment and Interdiction. Artillery fire upon certain areas of suspected enemy travel or rally points, designed to prevent uncontested use.

**heavy team** In a long range patrol unit, two five- or six-man teams operating together.

**helipad** A hardened helicopter landing pad.

**Ho Chi Minh Trail** An extensive road and trail network running from North Vietnam, down through Laos and Cambodia into South Vietnam, which enabled the North Vietnamese to supply equipment and personnel to their units in South Vietnam.

**hootch** Slang for barracks or living quarters.

**horn** Radio or telephone handset.

**hot** A landing zone or drop zone under enemy fire.

**HQ** Headquarters.

**Huey** The Bell UH helicopter series.

**hug** To close with the enemy in order to prevent his use of supporting fire.

**hump**   Patrolling or moving during a combat operation.

**I Corp**   The northernmost of the four separate military zones in South Vietnam. The other divisions were II, III, and IV Corps.

**infil**   Insertion of a recon team or military unit into a recon zone or area of operation.

**Indian Country**   Territory under enemy control.

**immersion foot**   A skin condition of the feet caused by prolonged exposure to moisture that results in cracking, bleeding, and sloughing of skin.

**incoming**   Receiving enemy indirect fire.

**indigenous**   Native peoples.

**intel**   Information on the enemy gathered by human, electronic, or other means.

**jungle penetrator**   A metal cylinder, lowered by cable from a helicopter, used to extract personnel from inaccessible terrain.

**KIA**   Killed in Action.

**Killer team**   A small Lurp/Ranger team with the mission of seeking out and destroying the enemy.

**LAW**   Light Anti-tank Weapon.

**lay dog**   Slang meaning "to go to cover and remain motionless while listening for the enemy." This is SOP for a recon team immediately after being inserted or infilled.

**LBJ**   Long Bien Jail. The in-country military stockade for U.S. Army personnel convicted of violations of the U.S. Code of Military Justice.

**LDR**   Leader.

**Lifer**   Slang for career soldier.

**LMG**   Light machine gun.

**LOH or Loach**   OH-6A light observation helicopter.

**LP**   Listening post. An outpost established beyond the perimeter wire, manned by one or more personnel with the mission of detecting approaching enemy forces before they can launch an assault.

**LRP**   Long Range Patrol.

**LRRP**   Long Range Reconnaissance Patrol.

**Lt.**   Lieutenant.

**Lt. Col.**   Lieutenant Colonel.

**LZ**   Landing zone. A cleared area large enough to accommodate the landing of one or more helicopters.

**MAAG**   Military Assistance Advisory Group. The senior U.S. military headquarters during the early American involvement in Vietnam.

**MACV**   Military Assistance Command Vietnam. The senior U.S. military headquarters after full American involvement in the war.

**MACV Recondo school**   A three-week school conducted at Nhatrang, South Vietnam by cadre from the 5th Special Forces Group to train U.S. and allied reconnaissance personnel in the art of conducting long-range patrols.

**MACV–SOG**   Studies and Observations Group under command of MACV that ran long-range reconnaissance and other classified missions over the borders of South Vietnam into NVA sanctuaries in Laos and Cambodia.

**mag**   Short for magazine.

**Maguire Rig**   A single rope with loops at the end that could be dropped from a helicopter to extract friendly personnel from inaccessible terrain.

**Main Force**   Full-time Vietcong military units, as opposed to local, part-time guerrilla units.

**Maj.**   Major.

**Marine Force Recon**   U.S. Marine Corps divisional long range reconnaissance units similar in formation and function to U.S. Army LRP/Ranger companies.

**Medevac or Dustoff**   Medical evacuation by helicopter.

**MG**   Machine gun.

**MIA**   Missing in Action.

**Mike Force**   Special Forces mobile strike force used to reinforce or support other Special Forces units or camps under attack.

**Montagnard**   The tribal hill people of Vietnam.

**MOS**   Military Occupation Skill.

**MP**   Military Police.

**MPC**   Military Payment Certificates. Paper money issued U.S. military personnel serving overseas in lieu of local or U.S. currency.

**M-14**   The standard issue 7.62-caliber semiautomatic/automatic rifle used by U.S. military personnel prior to the M-16.

**M-16**   The standard issue 5.56-caliber semiautomatic/automatic rifle that became the mainstay of U.S. ground forces in 1967.

**M-60**   A light 7.62-caliber machine gun that has been the primary infantry automatic weapon of U.S. forces since the Korean War.

**M-79**  An individually operated, single-shot 40mm grenade launcher.

**NCO**  Noncommissioned officer.
**NDP**  Night defensive position.
**net**  Radio network.
**NG**  National Guard.
**no sweat**  With little effort or with no trouble.
**Number One**  The best or highest possible.
**Number Ten**  The worst or lowest possible.
**nuoc mam**  Strong, evil-smelling fish sauce used to add flavor to the standard Vietnamese food staple—rice.
**Nungs**  Vietnamese troops of Chinese extraction hired by U.S. Special Forces to serve as personal bodyguards and to man special strike units and recon teams. Arguably the finest indigenous forces in Vietnam.
**NVA**  North Vietnamese Army.

**OP**  Observation post. An outpost established on a prominent terrain feature for the purpose of visually observing enemy activity.
**op**  Operation.
**op order**  Operations order. A plan for a mission or operation to be conducted against enemy forces, covering all facets of such mission or operation.
**overflight**  An aerial reconnaissance of an intended recon zone of area of operation prior to the mission or operation, for the purpose of selected access and egress points, routes of travel, likely enemy concentrations, water and prominent terrain features.

**P-38**  Standard manual can opener that comes with government-issued C rations.
**P's or piasters**  South Vietnamese monetary system. During the height of the Vietnam war, 100P was equal to about $0.85 U.S.
**P training**  Preparatory training. A one-week course required for each new U.S. Army soldier arriving in South Vietnam, designed to acclimatize new arrivals to weather conditions and give them a basic introduction to the enemy and his tactics.
**pen flare**  A small spring-loaded, cartridge-fed signal flare device that fired a variety of small colored flares used to signal one's position.

**peter pilot**   Military slang for the assistant- or copilot on a helicopter.

**Pfc.**   Private First Class.

**Pink Team**   An aviation combat patrol package comprised of an LOH scout helicopter and a Charlie model Huey gunship or an AH-1G Cobra. The LOH would fly low to draw enemy fire and mark its location for an immediate strike from the gunship circling high overhead.

**pith helmet**   A light tropical helmet worn by some NVA units.

**pork chop**   A bad deal, destined for failure.

**POW**   Prisoner of War.

**PRC-10 or "Prick Ten"**   Standard issue platoon/company radio used early in the Vietnam War.

**PRC-25 or "Prick Twenty-five"**   Standard issue platoon/company radio that replaced the PRC-10.

**PRC-74**   Heavier, longer range radio capable of voice or code communication.

**Project Delta**   Special Forces special unit tasked to conduct long-range patrols in Southeast Asia.

**Project Gamma**   Special Forces special unit tasked to conduct long-range patrols in Southeast Asia.

**Project Sigma**   Special Forces special unit tasked to conduct long-range patrols in Southeast Asia.

**PRU**   Provincial Reconnaissance Units. Mercenary soldiers who performed special military tasks throughout South Vietnam. Known for their effective participation in the Phoenix Program where they used prisoner snatches and assassinations to destroy the VC infrastructure.

**PSP**   Perforated Steel Panels used to build airstrips, landing pads, bridge surfaces, and a number of other functions.

**point**   The pointman or lead soldier in a patrol.

**Puff the Magic Dragon**   AC-47 or AC119 aircraft armed with computer-controlled miniguns that rendered massive support to fixed friendly camps and infantry units under enemy attack.

**pulled**   Extracted or exfilled.

**punji stakes**   Sharpened bamboo stakes, imbedded in the ground at an angle designed to penetrate into the foot or leg of anyone walking into one. Often poisoned with human excrement to cause infection.

**Purple Heart**   A U.S. medal awarded for receiving a wound in combat.

**PX**   Post Exchange.

**radio relay**   A communications team located in a position to relay radio traffic between two points.

**R&R**   Rest and Recreation. A short furlough given U.S. forces while serving in a combat zone.

**Rangers**   Designation for U.S. long range reconnaissance patrollers after 31 January 1969.

**rappel**   Descent from a stationery platform or a hovering helicopter by sliding down a harness-secured rope.

**reaction force**   Special units designed to relieve a small unit in heavy contact.

**redleg**   Military slang for artillery.

**REMF**   Rear Echelon Mother Fucker. Military slang for rear echelon personnel.

**rock and roll**   Slang for firing one's weapon on full automatic.

**Round-Eye**   Slang for a non-Asian female.

**RPD/RPK**   Soviet-bloc light machine gun.

**RPG**   Soviet-bloc front-loaded anti-tank rocket launcher used effectively against U.S. bunkers, armor, and infantry during the Vietnam War.

**rear security**   The last man on a long range reconnaissance patrol.

**RT**   Recon Team.

**RTO**   Radio/telephone operator.

**ruck**   Rucksack or backpack.

**Ruff-Puff or RF**   South Vietnamese regional and popular forces recruited to provide security in hamlets, villages, and within districts throughout South Vietnam. A militia-type force that was usually ineffective.

**saddle up**   Preparing to move out on patrol.

**same-same**   The same as.

**sapper**   VC/NVA soldiers trained to penetrate enemy defense perimeters and to destroy fighting positions, fuel and ammo dumps, and command and communication centers with demolition charges, usually prior to a ground assault by infantry.

**satchel charge**   Explosive charge usually carried in a canvas bag across the chest and activated by a pull cord. The weapon of the sapper.

**Screaming Chickens or Puking Buzzards**   Slang for members of the 101st Airborne Division.

**SEALs** Small U.S. Navy special operations units trained in reconnaissance, ambush, prisoner snatch, and counterguerrilla techniques.

**search & destroy** Offensive military operation designed to seek out and eradicate the enemy.

**SERTS** Screaming Eagle Replacement Training School. Rear area indoctrination course that introduced newly arrived 101st Airborne Division replacements to the rigors of combat in Vietnam.

**SF** U.S. Special Forces or Green Berets.

**Sfc.** Sergeant First Class (E-7).

**Sgt.** Sergeant.

**shake 'n' bake** A graduate of a stateside noncommissioned or commissioned officer's course.

**short timer** Anyone with less than 30 days left in his combat tour.

**short rounds** Artillery rounds that impact short of their target.

**single canopy** Jungle or forest with a single layer of trees.

**sit rep** Situation Report. A radio or telephone transmission, usually to a unit's tactical operations center to provide information on that unit's current status.

**Six** Designated call sign for a commander, such as "Alpha-Six."

**SKS** Communist bloc semiautomatic rifle.

**sky** To run or flee because of enemy contact.

**slack** Slang for the second man in a patrol formation. The point man's backup.

**slick** Slang for a lightly armed Huey helicopter primarily used to transport troops.

**smoke** A canister-shaped grenade that dispenses smoke, used to conceal a unit from the enemy or to mark a unit's location for aircraft. The smoke comes in a variety of colors.

**Snake** Cobra helicopter gunship.

**snatch** To capture a prisoner.

**Sneaky Pete** A member of an elite military unit who operates behind enemy lines.

**snoop and poop** A slang term meaning "to gather intelligence in enemy territory and get out again without being detected."

**socked in** Unable to be resupplied or extracted due to inclement weather.

**SOI** Signal Operations Instructions. The classified code book that contains radio frequencies and call signs.

**Sp4. or Spec Four** Specialist fourth class (E-4).

**Spectre** An AC-130 aircraft gunship armed with miniguns, Vulcans, and sometimes a 105mm howitzer with the mission of providing close ground support for friendly ground troops.

**spider hole**  A camouflaged one-man fighting position frequently used by the VC/NVA.

**Spooky**  AC-47 or AC-119 aircraft armed with Gatling guns and capable of flying support over friendly positions for extended periods. Besides serving as an aerial weapons platform, Spooky was capable of dropping illumination flares.

**spotter round**  An artillery smoke or white phosphorus round that was fired to mark a position.

**S.Sgt.**  Staff Sergeant (E-6).

**staging area**  An area in the rear where final last-minute preparations for an impending operation or mission are conducted.

**stand-down**  A period of rest after completion of a mission or operation in the field.

**star cluster**  An aerial signal device that produces three individual flares. Comes in red, green, or white.

**starlight scope**  A night-vision device that utilizes any outside light source for illumination.

*Stars and Stripes*  U.S. military newspaper.

**stay behind**  A technique involving a small unit dropping out of or remaining behind when its larger parent unit moves out on an operation. A method of inserting a recon team.

**strobe light**  A small device employing a highly visible, bright flashing light used to identify one's position at night. Normally used only in emergency situations.


**TA**  Target Area. Another designation for AO or area of operations.

**TAOR**  Tactical Area of Responsibility. Another designation for a unit's area of operations.

**TAC Air**  Tactical air support.

**tail gunner**  Rear security or the last man in a patrol.

**TDY**  Temporary duty.

**tee tee or ti ti**  Very small.

**ten forty-nine or 1049**  Military Form 1049 used to request a transfer to another unit.

**thumper or thump gun**  Slang terms for the M-79 grenade launcher.

**Tiger Force**  The battalion reconnaissance platoon of the 1/327, 101st Airborne Division.

**tigers or tiger fatigues**   Camouflage pattern of black and green stripes usually worn by reconnaissance teams or elite units.

**time pencil**   A delayed-fuse detonating device attached to an explosive charge or a claymore antipersonnel mine.

**TL**   Team leader.

**TM**   Team.

**TOC**   Tactical Operations Center or command center of a military unit.

**toe popper**   Small-pressure detonated antipersonnel mine intended to maim, not kill.

**Top**   Slang term for a First Sergeant meaning "top" NCO.

**tracker**   Soldiers specializing in trailing or tracking the enemy.

**triple canopy**   Jungle or forest that has three distinct layers of trees.

**troop**   Slang term for a soldier, or a unit in a cavalry squadron equal to an infantry company in size.

**Tri-Border**   The area in Indochina where Laos, Cambodia, and South Vietnam come together.

**tunnel rat**   A small-statured U.S. soldier who is sent into underground enemy tunnel complexes armed only with a flashlight, knife, and a pistol.

**URC10**   A pocket-sized, short-range emergency radio.

**VC**   Vietcong. South Vietnamese communist guerrillas.

**Viet Minh**   Short for Vietnam Doc Lap Dong Minh, or League for the Independence of Vietnam. Organized by communist sympathizers who fought against the Japanese and later the French.

**VNSF**   South Vietnamese Special Forces.

**warning order**   The notification, prior to an op order, given to a recon team to begin preparation for a mission.

**waste**   To kill the enemy by any means available.

**White Mice**   Derogatory slang term for South Vietnamese Army MPs.

**WIA**   Wounded in Action.

**World**   Slang term for the United States of America or "home."

**WP or willie pete**   White phosphorus grenade.

**XF**   Exfil. Extraction from the field, usually by helicopter.

**xin loi/sin loi**   Vietnamese for "sorry" or "too bad."

**XO**   Executive officer.

**x-ray team**   A communication team established at a site between a remote recon patrol and its TOC. Its function is to assist in relaying messages between the two stations.

**Yards**   Short for montagnards.

**zap**   To kill or wound.

*The only day-to-day account of this
elite combat unit in Vietnam*

## Diary of an Airborne Ranger
## A LRRP's Year in the Combat Zone

## by Frank Johnson

When nineteen-year-old Frank Johnson arrived in
Vietnam in 1969, he volunteered for the elite L
Company Rangers of the 101st Airborne Division,
a long range reconnaissance patrol (LRRP) unit.
He kept a secret diary, a practice forbidden by the
military to protect the security of the LRRP operations. Now, more than three decades later, those
hastily written pages offer a rare look at the daily
operations of one of the most courageous units that
waged war in Vietnam. Johnson's account is
unique in the annals of Vietnam literature. It is a
timeless testimony to the heroism of the LRRPs
who dared to risk it all.

Published by Ballantine Books.
Available wherever books are sold.

Reconnaissance deep behind enemy lines
was all in a night's work...

# WAR PAINT
## The 1st Infantry Division's LRP/Ranger
## Company in Fierce Combat in Vietnam

### by Bill Goshen

The eyes and ears of the Big Red One, America's
most famous infantry division, had teeth too—
the Long Range Patrol. Bill Goshen tells it like it
was because he was there, a member of one of
these elite hunter/killer units that spread fear in
the hearts of the VC and NVA.

Published by Ballantine Books.
Available wherever books are sold.